García Márquez

García

SECOND EDITION, REVISED AND EXPANDED

Márquez

the man and his work

Gene H. Bell-Villada

The University of North Carolina Press   Chapel Hill

Designed by Kim Bryant
Set in Dante and Avant Garde
Gothic by Rebecca Evans
Manufactured in the
United States of America

The paper in this book meets
the guidelines for permanence
and durability of the Committee
on Production Guidelines for
Book Longevity of the Council
on Library Resources.

The University of North
Carolina Press has been a
member of the Green Press
Initiative since 2003.

Library of Congress Cataloging-in-Publication Data
Bell-Villada, Gene H., 1941–
García Márquez: the man and his work / Gene H.
Bell-Villada. — 2nd ed., rev. and expanded.
p. cm.
Includes bibliographical references and index.
ISBN 978-0-8078-3351-3 (alk. paper) —
ISBN 978-0-8078-6525-5 (pbk. : alk. paper)
1. García Márquez, Gabriel, 1928– 2. Authors,
Colombian — 20th century — Biography. I. Title.
PQ8180.17.A73Z594 2009
863'.64 — dc22
2009024328

Portions of this work appeared earlier, in somewhat
different form, as "García Márquez and the Novel,"
Latin American Literary Review, Special Issue: Gabriel
García Márquez, 13, no. 25 (January–June 1985): 15–23,
and are reprinted with permission.

cloth   14 13 12 11 10   5 4 3 2 1
paper   14 13 12 11 10   5 4 3 2 1

To

CARMEN VILLADA ROMERO

(in memoriam, 1919–1984)

and

ESTEVAN ROMERO,

for many years of good parenting

Contents

Preface to the Second Edition

García Márquez: The Man and His Work first came out in 1990. In the intervening years, I've been pleasantly surprised at the warm reception it initially drew and then continued to receive, both in and outside of the academy. Besides being awarded a Latin American Studies prize and garnering special journal citations shortly after its appearance, it has also gone through a number of reprintings. In addition, the book still prompts appreciative notes from total strangers—students, teachers, journalists, editors, and general readers—who, from their desks somewhere in the Americas, Eastern Europe, or the Middle East, write to me with their casual queries and observations about the Colombian master. Not a few of those communications, interestingly enough, have come from scientists or medical doctors.

There have been some memorable moments. In one dramatic instance, I was sitting in my office sometime in the early 1990s. The phone rang; I answered; the fellow on the other end identified himself as a heart surgeon in Tennessee who urgently wished to discuss with me *Love in the Time of Cholera*, notably my interpretation of the tragic affair between Florentino Ariza and América Vicuña. Equally moving have been the missives from secondary school teachers (notably Janis Myers in Spencer, Iowa) who have expressed to me their thanks for my book, at times with co-signatures from their students. And the volume was a decisive factor in my being invited to serve as an advisor for Oprah's Book Club during its choice of *One Hundred Years of Solitude* in early 2004.

Since I finished composing the volume in 1988, García Márquez has published three more novels, a one-act play, a new collection of short stories, a book-length work of investigative journalism, and his personal memoirs. The time is thus long overdue for a second edition of my study, now with added, in-depth discussions of the later writings. In the process of working on the new edition, my re-experiencing those recent opuses—savoring their intricate beauties and delving into the complex sources that shaped them—has proved to be a scholar's boon and a constant reader's delight. Moreover, my initial chapters on "Backgrounds" have needed some detailed updating in the light of subsequent developments in García Márquez's life as a public figure, in our very knowledge of the man (as exemplified in masterful biographies by Dasso Saldívar and, more recently, Gerald Martin), and in the larger, ever-changing world itself.

Gabo's later writings aside, there exists yet another, less visible factor that compels me to return to and expand on *García Márquez: The Man and His Work*. With passing time, the Colombian author has achieved an eminence that goes well beyond the usual status of "canonization." As a result, among some younger writers and critics he is perceived as the ultra-Establishment, a long-reigning figure now due for dethronement, or for succession at the very least. The "McOndo" generation in literature has consciously challenged or steered away from the Nobel laureate's artistic vision and political stance; its adherents furthermore resent what they see as a simplistic reduction of Latin American narrative, in international audiences' eyes especially, to folk myths and "magical realism." One hears other writers occasionally being praised at the implied expense of García Márquez; and I've met thirtyish or forty-something scholars who dismiss his latter-day opuses on such grounds as, "Every book he writes is worse than the last."

As I hope to demonstrate in these pages, though, the later García Márquez transcends such intergenerational divisions and rivalries. Some of his post-1990 writings—notably *Of Love and Other Demons* and many of the stories gathered in *Strange Pilgrims*—are among his best. Moreover, notwithstanding the worldwide, legendary stature of *One Hundred Years of Solitude*, García Márquez's total oeuvre resists such easy labels as "magic" or "folklore." Much of his writing prior and subsequent to that amazing book is actually realistic; and in *News of a Kidnapping* he has produced a masterful instance of solidly grounded, objective yet compassionate reportage of the highest order. Similarly, his *Living to Tell the Tale* stands among the outstanding examples of personal memoir in any language. To do justice to that Gabo is my simple aim in this updated study.

My warm thanks go to Sian Hunter, senior editor at the University of North Carolina Press, for first encouraging me to pursue this project; to Tomás Eloy Martínez, fine novelist and director of Latin American Studies at Rutgers University, for furnishing me some useful data on the author; to Isabel Alvarez-Borland of Holy Cross College, Julio Ortega of Brown University, and Willem Klooster of Clark University, for sending me their offprints about the Bolívar novel; to Salvatore Bizzarro of Colorado College, for leading me to Neruda's poem on the Liberator; to Jay Pasachoff, colleague in Astronomy at Williams, for his guidance in tracing eighteenth-century solar eclipses; to Bruce Bagley of the University of Miami, for essential factual and bibliographical tips on the unending Colombian drug conflict; to Clementina Adams of Clemson University, for enlightening me on the geography of her native Barranquilla;

to Greg Dawes of North Carolina State University, for his positive response to this new edition and for his extremely helpful editorial suggestions; to Mercedes Jaramillo, Stella Sánchez, and Linda Senesky, for the gifts of Vallejo's *La virgen de los sicarios*, Restrepo's *Delirio*, and Arana's *Cellophane*, respectively; to Dominique Monti, for clarifying certain aspects of hospital rules in Paris; to Ronald Christ, my loyal yet most demanding and meticulous reader; to Ron Maner, managing editor of the University of North Carolina Press, for undertaking a perceptive, eagle-eyed, learned, and in-depth copyediting of the new manuscript; to Williams College, for its generous leave policy that has allowed me to take on research and travel relating to this volume; to the Interlibrary Loan Services at Williams, for the wondrously efficient access they have provided to dozens of scholarly texts (some of them from quite recondite and obscure journals); to librarians Christine Ménard and Rebecca Ohm, for lending an indispensable helping hand with the arcana of electronic sources; to Zach Randall, Adam Wang, and Jonathan Morgan-Leamon, for helping me with scanning the original volume; and to Audrey, for so much, and more.

Acknowledgments

I wish to extend my sincerest thanks to all who have aided in making this book possible. The earliest ideas I ever entertained about García Márquez were first heeded and encouraged in the 1970s by Enrique Anderson-Imbert and by the late Raimundo Lida, both of Harvard University. At different times over the years, insights and information and other forms of help have been furnished by Ronald Christ of Rutgers University; by the late Gregory Kolovakos of the New York State Council on the Arts; by Eduardo Camacho of Middlebury College in Madrid; by Marjorie Agosín of Wellesley College; by the late Thomas Smiley of Albuquerque, New Mexico; by many a good student in my literary courses at Williams College; and by Professors Antonio Giménez, Norman Petersen, and the late John Stambaugh, colleagues there.

Certain initial portions of the current study were read by Gustavo Mejía of the Vassar-Wesleyan Program in Madrid, and by my wife Audrey Dobek-Bell; their support and corrective details have proved extremely useful. Raymond L. Williams of Washington University, Kathleen Newman of Syracuse University, Randall Hansis of North Adams State College, and Lorraine Roses and Joy Renjilian-Burgy of Wellesley College all kindly offered opportunities to rehearse some of my ideas in open forum. In the days when this project was still in its first stages of research, Nicholas Bromell of *Boston Review* and Chinweizu of *South: The Third World Magazine* allowed me a printed venue for my report on Colombia and my chat with García Márquez. Charles Rossman of the University of Texas, in his capacity as guest editor at *Latin American Literary Review* and at *Contemporary Literature*, prompted me to craft some of my gestating thoughts on García Márquez into essay form. An idea from Audrey Dobek-Bell, followed by the receptivity and work of my friends and colleagues in the Department of Romance Languages—Anson Piper, George Pistorius, and Antonio Giménez—together with concrete support from the Provost's Office at Williams College, allowed me my extended look at the United Fruit Company and its crucial role both in Colombia and in García Márquez.

I am warmly grateful to several individuals in Mexico City—Jorge Aguilar Mora, Josefina Brun, Alva Rojo, Kaia Updike (Williams class of 1984), and the late Luis Vicens—for the essential personal guidance and the specific information I received from them in that town's vast cultural network. Jomí García Ascot, who had been García Márquez's neighbor in 1965–67, was particularly forthcoming with insights into the novelist and his personality. And of course I must express my appreciation to señor García Márquez, his wife Mercedes, and their son Gonzalo for their attentive hospitality on an afternoon in July of 1982.

I am equally indebted to many fine people in Colombia for their aid and friendship. Special mention must be made of the lovely Mejía family in Bogotá—don Eduardo, doña Esther, their daughters Silvia and María and their son-in-law Eduardo Barraza (an old *cuate* from Mexico). In addition, at different moments I was the beneficiary of important knowledge and good company from Germán Castaño, the late Penny Lernoux, Fernando Barberi, señor Germán Vargas and his wife Suzy, and the staff and faculty at the Liceo de Zipaquirá. And I learned a great deal about García Márquez and his national roots from my casual conversations in buses, airplanes, and cafés with strangers, whose unpresumptuous appreciation of their compatriot-novelist will long remain an inspiration to me.

Generous grants from the American Philosophical Society and from Williams College helped cover the sizable costs involved in pursuing research in Mexico, Colombia, and Cambridge, Massachusetts. I must further acknowledge my debt to the Hamilton College Academic Year in Spain and its general director, Jeremy T. Medina, for the infrastructural support furnished me by the program during my tenure as director-in-residence in 1986–87. Finally I must pay my respects to Iris Tillman Hill of the University of North Carolina Press for the interest she expressed in this project as far back as 1983. And additional gratitude is due to Mary Reid at the Press for her thorough, erudite, and sure-handed job of copyediting the manuscript.

To this day I have not forgotten the sheer excitement I felt on first reading *Cien años de soledad* in 1968, and my utter bedazzlement on reaching its concluding paragraph. Since then the idea of writing on the great South American author for his North American devotees has been one small dream of mine, and this book is a modest fulfillment of that dream.

My thanks go out once again to all who have concretely helped in its realization. My hope for now is that the book will prove at least useful, and of course whatever is found wanting in these pages is a responsibility all my own.

G. B-V.

Madrid; Williamstown;

Cambridge, Massachusetts

1986–88

A Note on the Text

All page references to García Márquez's work are given in parentheses within the main text. The Spanish-language edition is cited first, followed by the English translation. By way of example: a passage documented as (*CAS*, 83–84; *OYS*, 34–35) is to be found in *Cien años de soledad*, pp. 83–84, and in *One Hundred Years of Solitude*, pp. 34–35.

There is not at this point any "definitive" edition in Spanish of García Márquez's novels and short stories. Editorial Sudamericana has the authority of having been his first major publisher, but the ongoing economic crisis in Argentina, along with the constant reshuffles in the international book-publishing industry, have made their volumes less than easy to locate. (Still, the Sudamericana edition of *Los funerales de la Mamá Grande* is among the more reliable; hence my using it here.) Spain's Editorial Bruguera in the 1970s and '80s put out handsome, well-bound, uniform series of certain of his works of fiction—but in 1986, Bruguera was officially bankrupt. There are also other editions from elsewhere, with omissions and errata. The only criteria one can apply, then, are such makeshift judgments as immediate availability and physical quality of the editions.

English quotations are from the original U.S. hardback versions, inasmuch as our libraries are most likely to stock them. The sole exception is the Avon paperback edition of *One Hundred Years of Solitude*, which in the United States in the 1970s and '80s became a common enough artifact so as to make it something like the standard reference. The subsequent quality paperback editions by Harper, by contrast, have been subject to changes in pagination.

Abbreviations

SPANISH-LANGUAGE EDITIONS

A   *El amor en los tiempos del cólera*. Barcelona: Bruguera, 1985.

CAS   *Cien años de soledad*. Madrid: Espasa-Calpe, 1983.

CE   *La increíble y triste historia de la cándida Eréndira y de su abuela desalmada*. Barcelona: Barral Editores, 1972.

CM   *Crónica de una muerte anunciada*. Buenos Aires: Editorial Sudamericana, 1981.

CNT   *El coronel no tiene quien le escriba*. Buenos Aires: Editorial Sudamericana, 1970.

DA   *Del amor y otros demonios*. Barcelona: Mondadori, 1994.

DCP   *Doce cuentos peregrinos*. Buenos Aires: Editorial Sudamericana, 1992.

FMG   *Los funerales de la Mamá Grande*. Buenos Aires: Editorial Sudamericana, 1970.

GSL   *El general en su laberinto*. Bogotá: Editorial Oveja Negra, 1989.

H   *La hojarasca*. Buenos Aires: Editorial Sudamericana, 1972.

MH   *La mala hora*. Buenos Aires: Editorial Sudamericana, 1972.

MPT   *Memoria de mis putas tristes*. New York: Vintage Español, Random House, 2004.

NS   *Noticia de un secuestro*. Barcelona: Mondadori, 1996.

O   *Ojos de perro azul*. Barcelona: Plaza y Janés, 1979.

OG   *El olor de la guayaba: Conversaciones con Plinio Apuleio Mendoza*. Barcelona: Bruguera, 1982.

OP, 1   *Obra periodística*. Vol. 1, *Textos costeños*. Edited with an Introduction by Jacques Gilard. Barcelona: Bruguera, 1981.

OP, 2   *Obra periodística*. Vol. 2, *Entre cachacos I*. Edited with an Introduction by Jacques Gilard. Barcelona: Bruguera, 1982.

OP, 3   *Obra periodística*. Vol. 3, *Entre cachacos II*. Edited by Jacques Gilard. Barcelona: Bruguera, 1982.

OP, 4   *Obra periodística*. Vol. 4, *De Europa y América (1955–1960)*. Edited with an Introduction by Jacques Gilard. Barcelona: Bruguera, 1983.

OPa   *El otoño del patriarca*. Buenos Aires: Editorial Sudamericana, 1975.

VC   *Vivir para contarla*. Bogotá: Editorial Norma, 2002.

VPS   *De viaje por los países socialistas*. Cali, Colombia: Ediciones Macondo, 1980.

AP   *The Autumn of the Patriarch.* Translated by Gregory Rabassa.
       New York: Harper & Row, 1976.

CD   *Chronicle of a Death Foretold.* Translated by Gregory Rabassa.
       New York: Alfred A. Knopf, 1982.

CS   *Collected Stories.* Translated by Gregory Rabassa and J. S. Bernstein.
       New York: Harper & Row, 1984.

EH   *In Evil Hour.* Translated by Gregory Rabassa. New York:
       Harper & Row, 1979.

FG   *The Fragrance of Guava. Plinio Apuleio Mendoza in Conversation
       with Gabriel García Márquez.* Translated by Ann Wright. London:
       Verso, 1983.

GL   *The General in His Labyrinth.* Translated by Edith Grossman.
       New York: Alfred A. Knopf, 1990.

L   *Love in the Time of Cholera.* Translated by Edith Grossman.
       New York: Alfred A. Knopf, 1988.

LS   *Leaf Storm and Other Stories.* Translated by Gregory Rabassa.
       New York: Harper & Row, 1972.

LTT   *Living to Tell the Tale.* Translated by Edith Grossman. New York:
       Alfred A. Knopf, 2003.

MMW   *Memories of My Melancholy Whores.* Translated by Edith Grossman.
       New York: Alfred A. Knopf, 2005.

NK   *News of a Kidnapping.* Translated by Edith Grossman. New York:
       Alfred A. Knopf, 1997.

NWC   *No One Writes to the Colonel and Other Stories.* Translated by
       J. S. Bernstein. New York: Harper & Row, 1968.

OL   *Of Love and Other Demons.* Translated by Edith Grossman.
       New York: Penguin Books, 1995.

OYS   *One Hundred Years of Solitude.* Translated by Gregory Rabassa.
       New York: Avon Books, 1979.

SP   *Strange Pilgrims.* Translated by Edith Grossman. New York:
       Alfred A. Knopf, 1993.

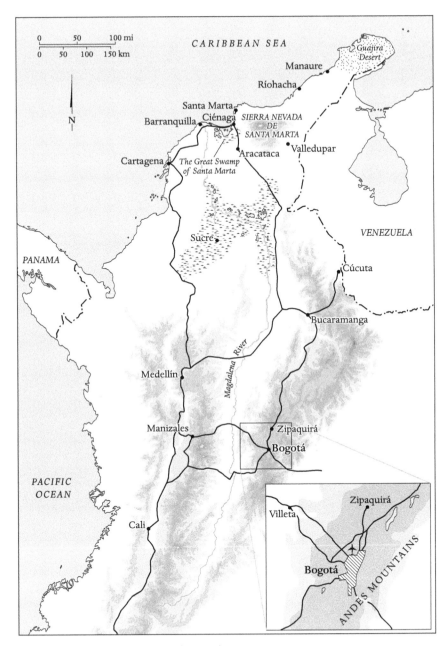

Colombia (Northern, Western, and Central Portions).

García Márquez country is the area northward of and including Sucre.

PART ONE

backgrounds

ONE

The Novel

"The second half of the twentieth century will be remembered as the era of the Latin American novel." Only time will tell whether such a speculation, raised individually by critics Maurice Nadeau and Raymond Sokolov, is actually to be borne out. Still, it cannot be doubted that, beginning with Borges and Carpentier in the 1940s, and Rulfo and Cortázar in the 1950s, the explosion of narrative talent in Hispanic America constitutes a special period in the history of human creativity, a privileged moment when one sees a much-afflicted civilization actively producing and receiving its foundational classics of the literary imagination. And it is not only a question of a few sovereign and "universal" authors' names—admirable though their writings may be—but also, among Latin America's reading publics and intelligentsia alike, a sense that literature truly matters, that its assumptions and art belong to the larger sociopolitical debate and thus contribute in a vital way toward the life of Latin American nations.

To many foreign readers, this panorama of South American creativity has come to be symbolized by the figure of Colombia's Gabriel García Márquez, whose work combines features both of Tolstoy the realist story teller of everyday life and of Dostoevsky the visionary fantasist and satirist. Of course the name García Márquez primarily conjures up his *One Hundred Years of Solitude*, that cultural phenomenon the like of which we see seldom in our times. Here is a great and complex book that, within its covers, includes every possible aspect of human life and, in its art and structure, demonstrates a sophistication and mastery the equal of Melville, Joyce, Proust, Faulkner, or Nabokov at their best. At the same time the book enjoys continued high sales in Colombia, in Latin America, and throughout much of the world. For such a confluence of high art and popular success one needs to go back to the nineteenth century, when entire French families would anxiously await the next installment from Balzac or Hugo, and Yankee audiences would pack the halls in order to see and hear Dickens in the flesh.

It would be impossible to overestimate the impact that García Márquez's chronicle has had on the larger reading public. Some statistics and anecdotes should suffice to convey the extent of its influence. When the Argentine publisher Editorial Sudamericana issued the first edition of *Cien años de soledad* in 1967, initial projections were of gradual sales of ten thousand copies and an annual trickle thereafter. As it happened, the first printing of eight thousand copies sold out in a week, all of them at subway station newsstands in Buenos Aires. Soon the novel was taking the continent by storm, and to this day the pace has not abated, the number of copies sold in the Hispanic world long ago having surpassed the ten million mark.

Cien años de soledad has since been translated into over thirty languages (including pirated versions in Greek and Arabic). Among its fans is Bill Clinton—indeed, it's reportedly his favorite novel. When in the White House, President Clinton lifted a three-decades-old U.S. travel ban on García Márquez, whom the State Department in the 1960s had deemed a dangerous element, placing him on the immigration "blacklist." But they were unable to limit the American sales of his most famous book. There are millions of copies in print of the Avon and HarperCollins paperback editions, and on commuter trains, park benches, or Amtrak cars it is common enough to see a scraggly-bearded sophomore or a chic secretary fully engrossed in their *One Hundred Years of Solitude*.

In Soviet Russia the book sold a fast million copies in that country's foreign literature magazine. A touching instance of the amazement it seems to have caused there is the story—often cited with delight by García Márquez—of the elderly Soviet woman who copied out the entire text of the novel word by word, in order to make sure that she had really read what she had read. On the other hand, the Russian version of *One Hundred Years of Solitude* is the only translation from which García Márquez's original sex scenes have been expurgated, suggesting that it is not only the author's politics that can make a society's custodians nervous.

But it is in Colombia and the rest of Latin America where the impact of the book has been widest and deepest, and where, as a result, the novelist himself enjoys the status of a kind of unofficial hero, is feted in a style more commonly reserved for athletes or movie stars. Of few serious writers today could it be said that most of his compatriots know of him and his writings, but in fact during my travels in Colombia I am constantly struck by the variety of casual strangers—nurses, salesmen, social workers, bankers, industrialists, government bureaucrats—who are joyfully acquainted with *One Hundred Years of Solitude* and with the man's other works too. Readers as well as reporters often allude to García Márquez by his nickname "Gabo" and even the diminutive form "Gabito" (it is as if the *New York Times* were to refer to E. L. Doctorow as "Ed"); news headlines routinely echo phrases from García

Márquez's fiction or see events through his narrative plots and characters; in Barranquilla I have seen businesses bearing names like "Farmacia Macondo" and "Edificio Macondo"; and there has been a modern "Hotel Macondo" in the resort town of Santa Marta.

Tales abound of the effect that *One Hundred Years of Solitude* has had on readers across Latin America. Carlos Fuentes, Mexico's best-known novelist, likes to remark that his own cook reads García Márquez. The Colombian himself has told of an Argentine maid who refused to get back to work until she had finished the last page of the history of Macondo. García Márquez also recalls warmly that visit he made to rural Cuba in the early 1970s, when a group of peasants he was chatting with asked him what he does for a living. And he answered, "I write." To the question, "What do you write?" he replied, "I wrote a book called *Cien años de soledad*," at which point the peasants cried out as one, "Macondo!"

One of the most dramatic instances of the sheer power that García Márquez's book has to seize the Latin American consciousness is this personal recollection by the U.S. novelist and journalist Ron Arias:

> I remember riding a crowded bus one day in Caracas, and two women who looked like secretaries on their lunch break were laughing over certain episodes they'd read in *Cien años de soledad*. I joined in; then it seemed half the bus did. This was in 1969 and it was the year's bestseller. Everyone who had read it was bringing up his or her favorite character, and we were all howling together. The book as a whole had struck a common chord with us all, since historically we had all come from Macondo . . . , we all had a tío [uncle] or two in a revolution, and I'm sure there were people in our lives chasing more than butterflies.[1]

Arias is right in tracing the direct appeal of *One Hundred Years* among Latino audiences to its broad array of Latin character types: the old *tío* sitting on the house doorstep; the revolutionary evoking past campaigns; the unrelenting womanizer; or, in archetypal Úrsula, the steadfast and endlessly toiling mother figure. With hindsight, the fable of Macondo's spectacular success can be further attributed to its lucid and accessible prose style, its attitude of serene wonder, its rapid-fire narrative of action and adventure, its compelling tales of romantic love, its exuberant episodes of bawdy sex, its humorous sequences of popular myth and fantasy, its muralistic intimations of the entirety of a continent's failed past, and, last but not least, its ribald and generous sense of humor. From start to finish in *One Hundred Years of Solitude* there is an underlying tone of irreverence toward officialdom, the perspective being not so much that of a society's victims or *les misérables* as of ordinary townsfolk who find themselves set upon by powerful forces and who, through struggle, play, and eroticism, through work, esoteric studies, love, and just living, somehow resist—even if in the end they are all resoundingly defeated.

By creating a narrative of ordinary Latin folk that is without a hint of insincerity or condescension, and by articulating a kind of history "from below" that is nonetheless joyous and shuns the dual traps of either idealized heroes or piteous victimization, García Márquez has given poetry, magic, and dignity to Latin American daily life and can thus be thought of in all justice as a "people's writer." For all its modernistic sophistication, his novelistic art springs organically from local values and experiences, much as the art of jazz, however many lessons it may assimilate from Bach, Ravel, or Stravinsky, grows "naturally" out of the musical concerns specific to African-American culture. The way in which American jazz buffs will speak affectionately of "Thelonious" or "the Duke" can be likened to the references to "Gabo" one finds readily in Hispanic conversation and media.

This intimate relationship of García Márquez to the people of Latin America became most manifest in the spontaneous outpourings of public sentiment and jubilation with which, on the morning of 21 October 1982, the news of his Nobel Prize was greeted. "GABO NOBEL DE LITERATURA," said a succinct newspaper headline in Colombia, where many a celebration was taking place in the streets.[2] Back in Mexico City, where García Márquez has had a home since 1975, the entire student population of an elementary school arrived in front of his house in El Pedregal and greeted him with a congratulatory chorus.[3] Later in the day, needing a respite from the constantly ringing telephone, the author went out for a drive; on the road strangers honked their car horns and nodded at him respectfully, and when his BMW stalled at a stoplight and he had some trouble getting it to start again, a voice from a nearby vehicle shouted, "Hey, Gabo, the only thing you're good for is getting the Nobel Prize!"[4] To an unprecedented extent, then, García Márquez went beyond his original status as novelist to become a mass phenomenon, a special kind of public figure whose work inspires not only admiration and respect but personal warmth and affection from most all. Seldom in our time does the higher art of literature gain so broad a following.

These human-interest accounts would add up to little more than idle gossip were it not for the special genius and achievement of the man himself. García Márquez's Nobel Prize in literature came in official acknowledgment of many things, among them the author's global readership (notably in the Third World) and also his radical humanitarianism, a key criterion in the Alfred Nobel legacy. At the same time the Swedish Academy's statement bows respectfully to high aesthetic norms and observes that "each new work of [García Márquez] is received by expectant critics as an event of world importance." And in further recognition of his having created an entire human geography, fully inhabited by an array of characters who reappear from book to book in a variety of situations, the Nobel Committee compared the breadth and stature of García Márquez to those of past masters such as Balzac and Faulkner. Moreover, they praised the Colombian's "wild imagination" for having fashioned an art that successfully "combines the fantastic and the realistic."

One normally does not rely on the press releases of prize committees as a starting point for literary reflections, but in this case the Nobel people did raise pertinent issues by evoking the distinctive aspects of García Márquez, the man and the writer—such items as his broad literary canvas, his creative use of fantasy, his political leftism, his immense popularity, and of course his undeniable artistic greatness. In recent years this specific combination has been in short supply, in both advanced capitalist and socialist cultures. Today in the North Atlantic countries there are but a handful of novelists of whom it could be said that they exhibit enduring artistry, produce an oeuvre of totalizing vision, enjoy worldwide readership, participate in progressive causes, and crystallize new ways of applying the fantastical imagination to human experience.

It was not too long ago that North American literary critics like Leslie Fiedler were making pronouncements to the effect that "the Novel is dead." And indeed at the time a relatively barren narrative panorama in the West (Germany excepted), along with the electronic paradise then being sung by media visionary Marshall McLuhan, did seem to suggest that the glory days of prose fiction were over. In retrospect, however, the doomsayers seem to have misconstrued their poor home harvests for a universal drought, inasmuch as it was during that same decade that an entire constellation of Latin American writers were clearly demonstrating the formal and cultural renewability of the novel and its resources. And it was García Márquez who was doing the most to help save the novel from itself, to rescue it from the narrow little impasses and byways in which Euro-American prose fiction writers had taken refuge and set up their shop.

It might be helpful to recall the world situation of the novel in 1967, the year when the long chronicle of Macondo was being typeset and bound by its lucky Argentine publisher. In the United States, prose fiction was in a state of directionless anomie. Norman Mailer, only slowly recovering from the ideological attacks on his brilliant *Barbary Shore* (1951), had proved as yet incapable of replacing the grandeur of his first book, *The Naked and the Dead* (1948). Nabokov, the other United States postwar novelist of record, was sliding into the onanistic, cranky self-indulgences of *Ada*. Meanwhile both WASP and Jewish novelists had fully restored traditional realist narrative, though none seemed able or inclined to enrich that nineteenth-century form with the social knowledge, insights, and vision of the nineteenth-century Europeans. Instead they concentrated on suburban angst and on minutiae of the Self, producing a quasi-claustrophobic art best characterized as "solipsist realism."

Saul Bellow's one attempt at total narrative in *The Adventures of Augie March* had suffered from a pervasively flat, gray lifelessness, and John Updike's portrayal of an entire town, in *Couples*, was to focus on a matter so trivial as sexual spouse-swapping (literally who's sleeping with whom), veiled through the mists of New England religiosity. Clearly, from the heights of Hemingway, Dos Passos, Faulkner, or even Henry Miller's *Tropics*, a lapse had taken place. The richest and most powerful nation on earth was producing novels that were materially thin and formally impoverished. What Arthur Miller deplored about the American theater in the 1950s was perfectly applicable to the fictions of that decade: he complained of a "narrowing field of vision" and an incapacity to distinguish "between a big subject and a small one, a wide and narrow view."[5]

In Soviet aesthetics, and among its defenders and imitators on the Western left, the problem was precisely the reverse—though there was one basic resemblance. What we know as "socialist realism" amounted alike to a restoration of the nineteenth-century genre, revived in this case through a state dictatorship, a rigidified sociocultural code, and a bastardized Marxism reflecting the narrow intellectual boundaries of Stalinism. With its search for a "positive hero," socialist-realist fiction worked from a conception of character portrayal the very opposite of fine-grained subjectivism, a simplified psychology that, paradoxically, was appropriate less for realism than romance. This aesthetic came best argued, of course, via the programmatic critical writings of György Lukács, who, for all his awesome erudition and middle-European *Kultur*, remained ever obstinate in his distaste for modernist experimentation, his negation of narrative "inwardness," and his personal dogmatic preference for fully rounded characters à la Balzac. On the other hand, those "critical realist" efforts whereby Soviet-inspired European and Latin American authors had hoped to denounce social ills resulted only in novels that (as García Márquez himself frequently observes) nobody reads and never overthrew any tyrants. In sum, Soviet-style aesthetics offered neither relief from nor alternatives to the wispy apolitical introspectiveness of U.S. cold war narrative.

In the British Isles and France only Samuel Beckett, the last of the great avant-garde purists, could be said to have broken genuinely new artistic ground in the novel. And it is no mean irony that he achieved this by fiercely paring down his material and experiential range, by rejecting the populous and panoramic Dublin of his compatriot's *Ulysses* for the hermetically sealed jar of his own *The Unnameable*, by reducing fiction to the haunted voice and melodious murmurings of an isolated old man. Granted, there was the absolute perfection and beauty of his form and prose style, as well as an emotional register that masterfully encompassed everything from comic bawdy to pained nostalgia: the word "tragicomedy" describes his slender fictions as aptly as it does the *Waiting for Godot* to which it serves as subtitle. Nevertheless, the Malones and Morans and Mahoods of this Franco-Irish minimalist—with their ramshackle bikes and crutches and their travels through the mud—lead an existence that is as vividly and palpably textured as it is slim, desolate, and scanty. The remnants of reality in *Watt* and *Molloy*, while far more memorable than anything to be found in Updike or Bellow, only helped to underscore the profoundly solipsized nature of the world of Beckett's choosing.

Not a few practicing critics in the 1960s were wondering what kind of up-to-date fiction could be possible in the wake of *The Unnameable* or *Texts for Nothing*. The sense of narrative art run aground in its straits seemed additionally confirmed by postwar literary developments in France, where the spirit of vanguard exploration was being carried on by what became known as the *nouveau roman* movement (after the polemical manifesto by Alain Robbe-Grillet, *For a New Novel*). Working under the double shadow of Joyce and especially Beckett, practitioners such as Nathalie Sarraute, Michel Butor, Claude Simon, and Robbe-Grillet himself considerably expanded the technical arsenal of novel writing and in turn were to exert a decisive influence on budding Latin Americans like Cortázar and Severo Sarduy.

At the same time, the New Novelists expressly set out to narrow still further the human content—the characters and feelings, the simple raw pleasures, and the "soul" as it were—of the novel form, looking upon such drastic circumscription as a progressive advance. Confronted by what they saw as an era of general loss of novelistic authority and of widespread incapacity to believe in literary characterization (*The Age of Suspicion*, as the striking title of Sarraute's book of essays would put it), in response they contrived elusive shadowy beings or highly restricted first-person narrations, together with a purposely flat, cool, colorless prose and a descriptive objectivism aimed at transcending such obsolete notions as "humanism" and "tragedy." Convinced that they had found an alternative both to the withered values of classical bourgeois fiction and to the shrill dictates of leftist *engagé* art, they carved out their working space in a self-conscious technicism, a neat and brittle formalism that, in retrospect, seems terribly academic, quietist, and cold. Of the *nouveau roman* group only Claude Simon evinced some larger historical vision and profundity of feeling, a factor surely instrumental in his being singled out for the 1985 Nobel Prize, though his undeniable depths are, alas, much obscured by his prose style and an excess of preciosity.

By 1967 there were informed Euro-American readers who were aware that, in Latin America, something new in literature was coming into shape. Already the work of the Cuban Carpentier and the Argentine Cortázar had been proving that the divers exquisite corners into which the novel had painted itself were neither final nor necessary. But it was *One Hundred Years of Solitude* that was to make the definitive difference. Breaking from the claustrophobic atmosphere that had permeated French and American writing, García Márquez reopened the doors and windows and took on the life of the streets, giving us a vast panorama in which every grand historical situation—from utopian harmony and dizzy prosperity to flaccid decadence and class war—was fully conjured up. The book came written with utter authority, had the voice of a wise yet involved and caring speaker who—like an African *griot*, or a super-narrator of folk epic and fairy tale, or an ancient biblical scribe—truly knows everything about everyone in a society, from its high notables to its sullen rejects, and moreover sees fit to tell the whole world about them.

Further, instead of those novels with four or five characters typical of Updike or Butor, the Colombian author evoked a total world in which every conceivable human type played some role. Here were enterprising pioneers, heroic revolutionaries, calculating merchants, moralistic clerics, rigid monarchists, ruthless conservatives, fiery syndicalists, shallow opportunists, wild visionaries, sober scholars, old-fashioned prudes, earthy voluptuaries, exotic nomads, sensitive aesthetes, bureaucrats and imperialists, fops and swingers, and more. Here there was maternal warmth, personal hauteur, filial piety, mature friendship, marital stability, lonely isolation, and a moving instance of tragic true love. Here one found bittersweet liaisons without a trace of the maudlin, casual sex without any contrivance or prurience. Here were growth and decay, high seriousness and low comedy, sadness and joy. *One Hundred*

Years of Solitude came as a reminder to the literate that such things as eroticism and humor and love and politics all form part of the larger human story and can once again belong to literature itself.

By having chosen as his narrative focus the chronicle of a family in one town, García Márquez hit upon the aptest medium for such a panoramic exploration of human diversity. Nevertheless, it was clear from the start that *One Hundred Years of Solitude* was not just one of those conventional "family sagas" of the kind regularly cranked out by facile writers and then dizzyingly marketed by American hype. Any reader sensitive to certain twentieth-century issues could see in *One Hundred Years* the politically "progressive" mind that cohabited with a highly sophisticated artistry. Here was a man of the left who had learned and assimilated many a lesson from Kafka, Faulkner, Virginia Woolf, and other Euro-American modernist figures. What is most remarkable about *One Hundred Years* in this regard is that it remains in the leftist camp even as it breaks with Stalinist "rules." Older dogmas of realism were now effectively challenged by a visionary imagination rooted as much in Caribbean folklore as in Western technique, were brushed aside by a verbal magician capable of conjuring up with supreme ease such items as a levitating priest, a rain of yellow flowers, a beautiful young virgin rising up to heaven, and a military massacre which the authorities erase from memory literally overnight.

In the same way, the Lukácsian demand for rounded and fully developed characters was discarded in favor of what are mostly a series of cartoon-like stereotypes, all brilliantly conceived and thoroughly interlinked. Straight linear narrative was replaced by a conception of time that, while developmental and evolutionary enough to be "Marxist" in its general contours, was also structured and articulated as a myriad of subtle flashbacks and foreshadowings. Finally, the intricate web of parallelisms, congruences, and repetitions that typifies *One Hundred Years of Solitude* gave evidence of a meticulous craftsman who takes quite seriously the formal aspects—the "carpentry," as he often has called it—of novel writing. Form-conscious without being formalist, García Márquez had proved once and for all that literary experimentation need not exclude humanitarian concerns nor be escapist or subjectivist, and that established realism is neither the last word nor the sole means available to the progressive imagination and its assumptions and intuitions. As García Márquez likes to remark to interviewers, "Reality is not restricted to the price of tomatoes."

García Márquez of course is most noted for his unforgettable use of magical and fantastical materials, and in due time we shall examine this side of him, his most original, no doubt. Ironically, García Márquez himself is averse to the term "fantasy" and on several occasions has characterized himself as "a realist writer," speaking for his form as well as subject matter. "Reality" for García Márquez consists not only of everyday events and economic hardships but also of such things as popular myths, beliefs, and home remedies—not just "the facts" but what ordinary people say or think about those facts. The daily life of northern Colombia in particular is a world richly textured with folk legend and superstition, and it became one of the objectives of a mature García Márquez to recapture this folk quality in his art and thereby go beyond all "the limitations that rationalists and Stalinists from all eras have attempted to impose" upon a larger and variegated reality (OG, 84; FG, 59–60). The "fantastical" in García Márquez derives in great measure from the lived fabric of Latin American experience.

Among the kinds of "fantasy" that most stand out in García Márquez is his artful exaggeration, his constant but careful doses of narrative gigantism—a rain over Macondo that lasts almost five years, or, in *The Autumn of the Patriarch*, a dictator who lives maybe two centuries. As García Márquez sees it, however, disproportion also forms part of reality in Latin America, with its rivers so wide one often cannot see across them, and its earthquakes and tempests the likes of which are not seen in Europe (OG, 85; FG, 60). "Hurricane" in fact is a word of Caribbean Indian origin, and there have been recorded instances of South American rainstorms that go on for months. (Of Wordsworth, Aldous Huxley once remarked that the poet would have entertained a less beneficent view of "nature" had he grown up in the tropical rain forests.) To convey this disproportionate reality the folk imagination of García Márquez in turn further exaggerates, tells history as a tall tale, giving us a 107-to-232-year-old patriarch who is himself a multiple version of those four-decade autocracies of flesh-and-blood grotesques such as were Juan Vicente Gómez, Rafael Leónidas Trujillo, and the Somoza clan.

Indeed, both *One Hundred Years of Solitude* and *The Autumn of the Patriarch* are carefully constructed around real-life historical materials, and the former title regularly crops up on the assigned-reading lists of many a Latin American history and politics course in U.S. college classes. For *One Hundred Years* is among other things a great novel about politics, dealing as it does with such subjects as civil wars, labor strikes, and military repression, all of it reimagined by a man who, along with Orwell and Sartre, qualifies as one of the twentieth century's great political writers—"political" in the broadest sense of the word. As author, García Márquez shows unusual insight into the deepest and most intimate recesses of power, whether it take the form of the quiet infiltration of Conservatives into Macondo, the harsh revolutionary dictatorship of a hysterical Arcadio, the wily maneuvers and populist rhetoric of an illiterate Caribbean tyrant, the false love and honeyed blandishments of a heartless whore-turned-grandmother, or the momentary sway that a humane Liberal dentist can gain over a local despot-turned-patient. In a continent where people tend to be much preoccupied with the question, "Who's in power?," García Márquez's fiction puts together and brings vividly to life the experiences that make this obsession a concrete everyday reality.

And yet referring solely to the "political" side of García Márquez does not do him full justice. As will later be noted, he is also one of literature's great humorists, a genius of comic ribaldry in the best traditions of Rabelais. In addition, he is one of the master novelists of romantic love, capturing its obsessions, flights, joys, pains, whims, and fancies as few authors can today. And he is among the most powerful writers of human solitude and isolation, of abandonment and loss, of the lonely battle for survival, of desolation and even "alienation." Few solitudes in fiction can compare with that of the illegitimate Aureliano Babilonia, friendless and bereaved, with total knowledge being his scant consolation as Macondo rushes to its end.

While in his earlier, shorter works García Márquez had dealt quite beautifully with each one of these basic human concerns, in his more ambitious books he integrates them into a single long story. Sociopolitical life is made to encompass romantic love and eroticism; erotic life and love are in turn subtly enmeshed with the narrative of politics. In the 1950s, however, as a concession to the needs and guidelines of his orthodox friends in the Communist Party, García Márquez did hew temporarily to a more circumscribed and traditional realism, but with *One Hundred Years* he would put this approach definitively behind him. As he himself notes, what brought on this shift was his "finally realizing that I had a commitment not to the social and political reality of my country but to the entire reality of this world [i.e., Colombia] and the other, without minimizing any single one of its aspects" (*OG, 82; FG, 56*).

By so daring to take on the whole of reality—private and public, local and global, quotidian and fantastical—the Colombian author succeeded in effectively widening once again the experiential horizon of the novel, a form that, in the United States and France since 1955, had been restricting its sights to the insides of middle-class heads or to outside objects like centipedes and venetian blinds, even as it remained decidedly oblivious to most everything else. In our time a common enough complaint in U.S. literary polemics is the claustrophobic world of those many novels of "sex and alienation in suburbia" and of "divorce on the upper East Side,"[6] while American publishing shoptalk makes ever-rigid distinctions between "love novels" and "political fiction," between "action narrative" and the genre of "humor." The genius of García Márquez is that he dispenses with set boundaries and brings all such experiences, and more, into his books.

Aside from his having produced some great works, then, the most significant achievement of García Márquez is his having led the art of fiction back to real life and restored to prose narrative the hurly and burly of reality in all its rich and contradictory manifestations. The author himself is a living summary of all these contradictions. A visionary fantast and master fabulator, he is also the self-described "realist writer" and lyrical historian of his world. A highly self-conscious and sophisticated artist and a master stylist, he seldom comments on purely literary matters and is sublimely bored with aesthetics, criticism, or theory. A great comic novelist with a mischievous and "tropical" sense of humor, he also articulates a profoundly tragic vision and is himself a rather melancholy and intensely private man. A declared foe of Western imperialism, as mentors he claims Euro-American modernists like Faulkner and Woolf. A man of the people, born and raised in some impoverished Caribbean settlements, still fond of salsa music and dance, he is also the globe-trotting cosmopolite, a man of high culture who cites Bach and Bartók among his favorite musicians. A convinced socialist who gives time and money to left-wing causes, he rejects the Soviet cultural model and can write with great eloquence about so bourgeois a subject as romantic love.

This is the García Márquez whose world, life, and art, I hope, will be conveyed within the following pages.

TWO

The Country

In colonial times the area then known as Nueva Granada was to inspire Spanish imaginations as the land of El Dorado, "the Golden One," referring to an inaugural ritual of the Chibcha Indians in the mountains near Bogotá. The actual ceremony consisted of the new tribal chief, covered with gold dust, being borne on a raft along with a cargo of gold objects on sacred Lake Guatavitá, where as an offering he would sink the precious items and immerse himself in the water.[1] Today the image of Colombia is more one of coffee advertisements, emerald stones, drug scandals, and inevitably, political violence. Were it not for García Márquez's writings, "Colombia" in the minds of non-Hispanics would evoke little more than those conquistador fixations and television stereotypes. His verbal inventions are that country's best export, providing as they do a necessary counterimage, an in-depth introduction to a national reality far richer and more manifold than any media imagery will allow.

That reality, taken for granted in García Márquez's work, is large and variegated. In surface area Colombia is almost twice the size of Texas; its population hovers around thirty million. Its geographic spread includes the sparsely settled eastern plains, the high chill of the Andean chain and Bogotá, the coastal heat of the Caribbean provinces, the desert desolation of the Guajira peninsula jutting to the northeast, the lush "eternal spring" of the western Cordillera Central and the Cauca Valley with its cities Medellín and Cali, and the vast, humid Amazon bush dipping four degrees south beyond the equator. Colombia is the one mainland South American country blessed with both Atlantic and Pacific littorals; it shares borders with Venezuela, Ecuador, Peru, and Brazil; and through Panama (formerly Colombian territory) it has a Central American frontier. While from this geographic assortment Garcia Márquez would choose the bright sands of La Guajira and the most rarefied of Andean redoubts as settings for some of his livelier episodes, the bulk of his fiction takes place in imaginary or unidentified towns and villages located on or near the Caribbean shore.

The total cultural reality of Colombia is also belied by a certain standardized ecological and ethnic image. Most foreigners—other Latin Americans included—tend to think of Colombia as Andean and Indian, a notion reflecting the political power of Bogotá, some nine thousand feet above sea level, with its gray mists and soft greens, and its lightly copper-complected inhabitants descended from Chibcha-cum-Iberian admixtures. For all its visual spectacle and central authority, however, Bogotá is just one part of greater Colombia. García Márquez country is actually the Colombian north coast, a region that, in its clime, ethnicity, and architecture, seems directly transplanted from the Antilles.

Caribbean Colombia's tropical heat and ocean breezes, its aromas of raw fish and seafood, and its intense maritime greens and blues are features instantly recognizable to anyone familiar with Cuban or Puerto Rican landscapes. Formal men's wear in García Márquez's world consists of elegant Cuban-style *guayabera* shirts rather than coats and ties. And the spoken language—in contrast with the stuffy, sibilant formality of Bogotá speech—is notable for its spontaneous and informal flavor, its dropping of final and preconsonantal *s*'s, and its Antillean slang words such as *chévere!* ("great!"). The city of Cartagena is a special case in point: its salt-worn façades, elaborate balconies, narrow streets, and colonial stone fortress projecting out into the sea all bring to mind the picture-postcard look of older portions of Havana and San Juan. Music in Colombian coastal towns has a tropical beat, and salsa bands and drumming groups can be seen performing in the open air on summer nights.

The general "atmosphere" of northern Colombia and the ethnic composition of its peoples are of a distinctively African character—not surprisingly, inasmuch as, for three centuries, Cartagena was a major port in Imperial Spain's black slave trade. The number of African slaves imported into Nueva Granada has been estimated at two hundred thousand, most of them from Congo and Angola. As a result there are a fair amount of transplanted African place-names in the Colombian north, such as a brook in the Mahates township called "Angola."[2] There are also cultural artifacts, notably musical instruments, and one well-known researcher recalls having bought a gaily colored wooden mask of a bull from a hawker in Barranquilla, then later encountering in a museum in Dakar, Senegal, an almost identical mask that originated in Guinée-Bissau, where it had had agricultural-ritual uses.[3] Thirty miles to the south of Cartagena lies the legendary settlement of San Basilio de Palenque, founded in 1599 by fiercely independent runaway slaves, the descendants of whom still retain many African ways. With utmost ease the working women balance heavy loads on their heads as they tread long distances. And Palenque Spanish dialect has a sizable Bantu lexicon, for example, the words for "they," "son," "ox," and "testicle." The Bantu noun for "banana," in fact, is "macondo."[4]

The peoples of Caribbean Colombia are known as *costeños*, an adjective meaning "coastals." Region-proud, they like setting themselves off from what they see as those cold, stiff, haughty Bogotá dwellers, whom they call *cachacos*, an untranslatable nickname that, though basically denotative and neutral, in certain contexts can carry all the pejorative weight of a Texas farmer pointing east and referring scornfully to "those Yankees." Regional sentiments of this sort are captured here and there in García Márquez's fiction. In the Spanish original of *One Hundred Years of Solitude*, when self-righteous Fernanda del Carpio launches her four-page harangue and complains of the contempt with which the Buendías have regarded her, she expresses special hurt at her in-laws' having called her a *cachaca* and even having lumped her together with "the *cachacos* sent by the government to shoot down workers" (*CAS*, 359). There is also that moment in *The Autumn of the Patriarch*, gentler in its irony, when the rustic dictator, having no concept of geographical distinctions outside his Caribbean patch of land, is much amused at the fine dancing skills of "these *cachacos* from Europe."

The *costeños* can also take some pride in their historical roots. For obvious reasons of access the Caribbean coast was the first part of the country subject to Spanish "discovery" and colonization. Columbus himself on his fourth voyage explored the area and encountered the central waterway now known as the Magdalena River. Santa Marta, at the foot of the Eastern Sierra Nevada, was founded by Rodrigo de Bastidas in 1525, though abolished by papal decree in 1562 and rebuilt in 1577. The first continuous Spanish settlement in all Colombia, then consisting of a typically modest series of thatched huts, is Cartagena, dating from 1533. (What originally bore the name Santa Fe de Bogotá was not established until 1538, by forces under the man thereafter remembered as conquistador of Nueva Granada, Gonzalo Jiménez de Quesada.) From these ragtag beginnings there followed two centuries of inland penetration and colonization, as in the case of Sebastián de Belalcázar, who, after having had a hand in conquests ranging from Nicaragua to Peru, went on to found the Andean (and earthquake-prone) town of Popayán in 1536, and then pushed on in an extended pursuit of outlets to the sea. The initial collective roamings that precede the founding of Macondo, and Jose Arcadio Buendía's later search for the ocean, both correspond to this early period in Colombia's past.

The Caribbean settlers were also to endure the regular incursions of the rival power of the British, whose pirates often launched surprise raids from their ships. Francis Drake attacked and occupied Cartagena briefly in 1586, and in 1596 he bombarded, sacked, and razed Riohacha, an event with which the second chapter of *One Hundred Years* begins. Later, in 1811, during the period of the struggle for independence, Cartagena would earn the distinction of being the first Colombian city unilaterally to sever ties with Spain, while on the other hand Santa Marta is where a tired and disillusioned Simón Bolívar would breathe his last in 1830. A century after resisting Imperial Spain's gunfire, much of the coastal zone from Santa Marta to Aracataca (birthplace of García Márquez) would become the scene of the bitter United Fruit Company strike of 1928, in which hundreds of workers died at the hands of government troops, a bloody episode later refashioned by the novelist into the suspenseful climax of his Macondo chronicle.

Under the colony, as port of embarkation for precious metals bound for Spain, Cartagena had enjoyed enormous if unequal prosperity. During the nineteenth century, by contrast, it was to stagnate economically, although this, ironically, would help save its architecture. With its circumambient military walls, stately colonial buildings, and charming arcades, old Cartagena is one of the most spectacularly preserved seventeenth-eighteenth century cities in the Americas, a fact that has made possible its use as visual backdrop for such historical films as Gillo Pontecorvo's *Burn!* and Roland Joffe's *The Mission*. Its wealth of past associations and gracious atmosphere were no doubt key factors in García Márquez's decision to set his most traditionalist novel, *Love in the Time of Cholera*, in a coastal city much resembling Cartagena. In addition the town's Colonial past and its association with the slave trade made it just the right choice of location for *Of Love and Other Demons*, a book in which Afro-Hispanic society, custom, and folkways, and the inhumane traffic itself, all play a significant role.

The twentieth century, on the other hand, would see the economic emergence of Barranquilla, some one hundred miles northeast of Cartagena. The town is especially known in the Spanish-speaking world for a humorous 1940s pop song with the catchy chorus, "Se va el caimán, se va el caimán. / Se va para Barranquilla" ("The alligator's going, the alligator's going. / He's off to Barranquilla"). The refrain in turn echoes a local folktale about a man who metamorphosed into the big lizard in order to spy on women bathers.

Barranquilla, customarily looked down upon by Bogotá's *cachacos* as a "city of shopkeepers," actually has the lively cosmopolitanism of a port culture, what with its strategic location on the mouth of the Magdalena River, and its steady influx of new people and ideas from overseas. During García Márquez's apprenticeship there in the early 1950s one could encounter such varied personages as German pilots from the First World War, Jewish refugees from Hitler's Reich, and escaped convicts from French Guiana (*OG*, 60; *FG*, 43). Though not strikingly attractive architecturally, Barranquilla would become an enterprising town, and was the first Colombian urban center to know telephones, electricity, and radio.[5] The Colombian national airline, Avianca, was actually founded in Barranquilla with German capital in 1916, under the name SCADTA. Between 1942 and 1944 there was a small U.S. naval base in operation there. And in the 1950s Barranquilla would boast an unusually fresh and active literary circle that decisively nourished a young and struggling García Márquez. The author pays the city a touching homage in *Memories of My Melancholy Whores*, a novel filled with Barranquilla landmarks and thoroughfares that never once cites the town by name.

Due east from Barranquilla is the small town of Ciénaga (literally "swamp"). It was here in the main square, on 5 December 1928, that an army massacre of striking banana workers and their families took place, an incident made flesh in the climactic scene in *One Hundred Years of Solitude*. Those victims are publicly memorialized today via an imposing monument located near the town's bus depot, a sixty-foot, black-metal sculpture of an Afro-Colombian field worker, machete held high in his right hand.

Some fifty miles south one encounters Aracataca, the author's birthplace and the initial inspiration for his mythic Macondo. Its name, from the two indigenous words *ara* ("clear water") and *cataca* ("Indian chief"), is often shortened in casual conversation to "Cataca." Population has since tripled from its roughly 14,000 souls in 1927. A typically poor and dusty rural settlement made up mostly of modest frame dwellings topped with zinc roofs, it had no paved roads until the 1990s. The path to the cemetery that concludes Gabo's story "Tuesday Siesta" still exists. Today a bright-yellow billboard bearing a portrait of the author at town's entrance announces Aracataca as his original home. The site of Gabito's first house is now a museum that draws a fair share of tourists, domestic as well as foreign.

Another couple of hundred miles further south is remote, isolated Sucre, of difficult access even to seasoned travelers. With its stream that cuts through the town, it serves as modified setting for a number of key stories in *Big Mama's Funeral* and for the novels *No One Writes to the Colonel*, *In Evil Hour*, and *Chronicle of a Death Foretold*, and was specially scrubbed up for Francesco Rosi's unfortunate 1987 film version of Gabo's horrific latter book.

Returning to our eastward trek along Colombia's northern shore, we arrive at Santa Marta. Today a chic coastal resort with a skyline dotted by high-rise hotels, Santa Marta is better known to Colombians as the place where, in 1830, their venerated independence leader Simón Bolívar—resigned to his defeat, yet at least accompanied by loyal allies—breathed his unexpected last. Here, fittingly, is where the riverboat journey in *The General in His Labyrinth* reaches its sad end.

Driving east from Santa Marta one encounters the foothills of Colombia's third, short mountain chain, the Sierra Nevada. The migrant Buendías cross this rugged range by foot on their way to founding Macondo; a wealthy Mr. Daza does the reverse journey by mule train, in order to get his daughter Fermina away from her dreamy suitor in Cartagena and on to the safety of relatives in distant, festive Valledupar. And a full two hundred eastward miles on the coast takes us to the small port city of Riohacha (population 95,000), an old, remote, frontier town that, in García Márquez's work, often looms mysterious and even sinister. Poverty-stricken yet teeming with street life, its chief importance is as gateway to La Guajira, the stark desert world depicted in the author's "Innocent Eréndira."

Until recently the only large-scale productive activity on this barren, Massachusetts-sized peninsula was the extracting and processing of sea salt, today still a major concern. The marginality of the region, however, is precisely what had made possible the cultural survival of its native Wayrúu, known as the Guajiros and numbering approximately one hundred thousand.[6] Indeed, La Guajira is the only extensively "Europeanized" part of Colombia in which the original peoples have continued to live as a society of their own and communicate in their own language, and whose beautiful, smooth-skinned, round-faced women wear traditional dress. Their *mantas*, flowing gowns in deep solid hues and lively prints amid the reddish-brown sands of the desert, are nothing less than striking. The men, by contrast, wear Western garb, and in Riohacha and smaller settlements like Manaure much of the population is clearly of assimilated Guajiro stock.

A traveler in the Guajira wilderness sees taciturn indigenous families housed in the clusters of wooden sheds that dot a desolate landscape. They eke out their living from a few goats, the salt works, the crafts and *mantas* sold in the tourist trade, and the odd jobs they perform as the subproleariat of a frontier economy. The more prosperous among them move about the desert on lone bicycles. The other vehicles plying La Guajira are mostly cargo trucks, not a few of which are transporting contraband. Amid the Guajiros and the array of mixed-blood Hispanics one encounters the occasional European on assignment or adventure. In 1988, for instance, I met a couple of young English petroleum engineers who were on contract from Texaco to look into the prospects for exploratory drilling off the Guajira shore. Meanwhile, beginning in the early 1990s, U.S. mining companies have moved in and set up open-pit, extraction operations in the Guajira area, where the coal is of unusually high quality and "clean." So massive an undertaking has resulted in disruption of the indigenous people's lives, forced transfer of the populations of entire villages, and repression and assassination of numerous labor union activists.[7]

"Innocent Eréndira" deftly evokes this universe, complete with goats, smugglers, a photographer on a bike, a pious Dutch settler, Indian villages, and many Guajiro secondary characters—for example, the wise and sharp-tongued mother of young Ulises, and the nameless servants and errand boys used and abused by Eréndira's heartless grandmother.

From his most youthful literary days García Márquez was a man intensely conscious of his *costeño* roots, often praising them at the expense of the Bogotá style of life. In a subtle dig at his Andean rivals the twenty-two year-old journalist reflected, "There are cities with ships and cities without ships. That is the only acceptable distinction, the only truly essential difference" (*OP*, 1:207). The *costeño* readers of that column knew exactly what was meant, and the young columnist would write many more such pieces in defense of "the Atlantic coast, that great carrier of Antillean folklore" (*OP*, 3:958). He would glorify the yearly carnival at Barranquilla—a legendary collective ritual with which he later climaxed the tenth chapter of *One Hundred Years* as "the time when we are granted the right to go out of our minds" (*OP*, 1:158). He would praise the African roots of Caribbean music, often singling out for attention the *vallenato* songs (so called because they originate in Valledupar), which consist either of love tunes or Iberian-style *romances* (narrative ballads) sung to the accompaniment of percussion and accordion, and hence serve as a kind of model for *One Hundred Years* and *Love in the Time of Cholera*. And in the second newspaper column he ever published, at age twenty, he lauds that folk accordion as "a proletarian instrument" (*OP*, 1:79), repeating the compliment from time to time in his later articles about the folklore of the coast.

Among the favorite composers of the mature García Márquez would be the Hungarian Bela Bartók. The claimed affinity is not accidental. Like a youthful Bartók, who traveled the villages of his native land to compile and record its folk melodies, the young Colombian would play the role of un-academic anthropologist and roam about the coastal region, observing its folkways and bringing these experiences into his journalism and, later, his art. One of his recurrent devices in his early days as reporter was the "you are there" travel piece in which he tells of a purported train or bus trip and furnishes sketches of ethnic passengers sharing space with him. In one of his earliest sketches he evokes a black woman seated across from him on a bus, her features highlighted by a large red-and-yellow kerchief and two large round earrings. From the roadside there drift in the sounds of *gaitas*, the long folk flute of Colombia. At a bus stop their group is joined by some Guajiro Indians headed down from Santa Marta to sell their traditional aphrodisiacs and herbal medicines . . . (*OP*, 1:96–98, 585–90).

The African presence in his Caribbean-coastal world is a cultural reality frequently taken note of by the young García Márquez in his 1950s columns, where he would reflect on the black people of San Basilio de Palenque or comment in passing on the songs that Negro workers improvise when they are out in the fields cutting sugarcane (*OP*, 1:750). Later in life García Márquez would become dramatically aware of his own African roots. On a journalistic assignment to recently liberated Angola, where he had gone to gather material for some political articles, he also arrived at the realization that "I'm a *mestizo* [mixed-blood]. . . . In Angola I found that in many of the traditional African art forms there are aesthetic manifestations very much like the ones we have in the entire Caribbean area. Because I'm Caribbean, recognizing this fact made me see into myself and realize I'm a *mestizo* and at the same time made me start observing more clearly the historical conditions of our countries."[8]

Long before his personal discovery, however, García Márquez the cub reporter was drawing fruitfully from the legends and rituals of the Colombian coastal region. In some early articles that have since become minor classics, he conjured up the African atmosphere of La Sierpe, where people pray for the quality of their rice crops and observe Good Friday not with solemn abstinence but by stuffing themselves publicly with food. He also tells of La Marquesita, "the Little Marquise," a fabled Spanish woman who could revive a dying man simply by knowing his physical description and his residence. And there is the tall tale of a "Green Mama" who lived two hundred years and owned so many heads of cattle it took them nine days just to file past; on her land there was buried treasure, and when a local character went in search of its riches he found himself surrounded by strange animals, "winged quadrupeds with the heads of birds, and curlews of metallic and resplendent plumage" (*OP*, 1:867; *OP*, 2:117). Other coastal legends tell of a white crocodile, of a family that could walk on water, of Jesusito, a carved statuette of a black man with powers to cure the blind and crippled and to stave off wild beasts, or of Pacha Pérez, a famed professional mourner who, at age 185, was transformed by a devil into a snake (*OP*, 2:136, 146, 151).

One can immediately sense here the folk origins of many an episode and character in García Márquez's best fiction—the decrepit angel in "A Very Old Man with Enormous Wings" who performs a series of mistaken miracles, or the fabled if unconfirmed healing powers of the tyrannical Patriarch, or the recurrent anecdote of the young girl changed into a scorpion (or spider) for having disobeyed her parents. There is also Francisco el Hombre, the two-century-old vagabond in *One Hundred Years* who travels around Macondo and other nearby towns, composing and singing songs that bring news and personal messages, an almost medieval *jongleur* sort of figure whom the novelist actually lifted from coastal folklore.

García Márquez's own black characters typically reflect local distinctions, mobility, and styles—such as Mr. Carmichael, the loyal servant and housekeeper to a self-centered, childish widow of Montiel; the bucktoothed "monumental Negro," lawyer to the forlorn colonel to whom no one writes; the prostitute Nigromanta, who initiates Aureliano Babilonia in sex and, for a fee, lends an ear to his unrequited laments about Amaranta Úrsula; and the general array of mulatto extras and mistresses in *Chronicle of a Death Foretold* and especially *Love in the Time of Cholera*, with its sensual yet efficient business administrator Leona Cassiani. His cast of African characters and evocation of their ways expands significantly in *Of Love and Other Demons*, where the slave quarters function as a kind of humane alternative to the harsher world of white colonialism, and where African religious beliefs and deities' names are assigned pivotal moments in the plot. More important than the presence of any individual character, however, is the loving and masterful way in which García Márquez recreates an entire world of oral legend and tradition—oral residue being perhaps the least studied or understood aspect of all prose fiction from Cervantes to the present.

García Márquez's informal explorations into the folklore and demography of the Colombian Atlantic coast constitute a pioneering effort toward understanding a world that, to this day, is still relatively unknown—for a number of reasons. Among them is the vestigial legacy of white chauvinism and Bogotá snobbery, forces that slight a region precisely because of its African element. There is also the methodological problem posed by a mixed culture: observing African ways and customs will obviously present fewer difficulties in Africa itself than in an overseas outpost where Hispanic, Indian, and black have long intermingled. And there are the assorted physical dangers—the sociopolitical violence, and more recently the crime and banditry spawned by unemployment and the drug traffic. But as a privileged "insider" within coastal culture, García Márquez was able to actively experience and then artistically recapture what is, in his words, a richly textured "reality that was living inside people's consciousness."[9]

While few foreigners may be aware of Colombia's internal cultural nuances, its recurring cycles of political violence are touched upon frequently enough by the world press and even depicted somewhat frivolously in Hollywood entertainments like *Romancing the Stone*. García Márquez himself came of age as a writer during Colombia's era of *la Violencia*, the bloody and informal civil war that would persist from 1946 to 1965, affect half the land surface of the country, and take up to two hundred thousand lives, mostly in rural areas. It is one of the most confusing conflicts in human history, easily rivaling such terrible instances of Hobbes's "war of all against all" as were Lebanon during the 1970s, Yugoslavia in the 1990s, and Iraq in the 2000s.

The origins of *la Violencia* go back to the nineteenth century, when a youthful nation-state that went through three name changes, and lost its Venezuelan and Ecuadorian territories, would also know some seventy local uprisings and eight civil conflicts, culminating in the "Thousand Days' War" of 1899–1902, which claimed at least one hundred thousand lives and in which García Márquez's grandfather was a colonel in the Liberal ranks. Actually, during the decades following independence from Spain in the 1820s, most of the new Latin American republics would be bled by intermittent warfare between feudal-minded Hispanophile Conservatives on one side and Liberals modeled after Anglo-French principles on the other. In Nueva Granada and what was finally named "Colombia," however, the interparty clashes were especially harsh, with casualties typically reaching the five- and six-figure range.

At first there did exist clear ideological distinctions: early on Colombian Conservatives favored centralized government, a powerful church, and limited suffrage, whereas their Liberal challengers advocated greater federalism, broader tolerance and secularization, and expansion of individual rights. In time Conservatives would steal away Liberal rhetoric, the Liberals themselves would compromise here and there, and in the long run there came to be little generally to differentiate the respective ideas, demographic bases and practical goals of the two leading parties. In the twentieth century they would evolve as multiclass organizations with both militant and moderate wings, and with affiliation more a matter of family loyalties than ideology.[10] The Liberals have comprised everything from secular-minded industrialists who simply hate priests and landowners who need armed protection against Conservative troops, to inspired revolutionaries like Jorge Eliecer Gaitán and committed *guerrilleros* of every stripe.[11] The Conservatives have had their quasi-Fascist elements, but also prominent politicians whose conceptions of civil society scarcely differ from those of any New England centrist.

Colombia in this regard is something of an anomaly in Latin America. The leading nations on the continent are known for having large mass-based populist parties: the APRA in Peru, the Peronists in Argentina, certain sectors of the PRI in Mexico, and the leftist coalition that held electoral power in Chile from 1970 to 1973. Colombia's two hegemonic parties on the other hand show ideological continuities rather than contrasts, their duumvirate presenting a spectrum not unlike that of the political options in the United States. The situation inevitably invites jokes: for example, in Colombia "the Liberals drink in public and pray in private, while Conservatives pray in public and drink in private";[12] or as somebody remarks in *One Hundred Years*, Conservatives attend church at eleven and Liberals at five.

The history of *la Violencia* is a daunting one; what follows herewith is the briefest possible synopsis. In the 1946 elections the Liberals found themselves split between Gabriel Turbay's moderates and Gaitán's dissident leftists. The presidency therefore went to Conservative Mariano Ospina Pérez. From 1946 to 1948 armed clashes flared up between adherents of the two parties in nine provinces. The fighting was often aided and abetted by Liberal army and police officers who sabotaged security operations.

Such conflicts may well have remained sporadic or under political control had it not been for the terrible events of 9 April 1948. At 1:05 P.M., on a crowded street in downtown Bogotá, the fiery, humane, erudite Liberal leader Gaitán was shot dead at close range by a lone gunman, apparently a Conservative fanatic who claimed to be driven by "powerful forces." A vengeful mob soon kicked the assassin to death and dragged his body through the streets. Moreover, for the rest of the day the center of Bogotá became the stage for a spontaneous orgy of violence by Liberal rioters, who proceeded to sack most government buildings (including the Capitol), trash many churches, set fire to the Conservative daily *El Siglo*, overturn cars and trolleys, and joyously loot and share in the stocks of liquor stores. The army spent hours simply paralyzed; the Liberal *pueblo* ("the people") had made the streets their own and were even being joined by Liberal police. By late evening Bogotá's main district looked like London after a V-2 attack. The dead may have reached as high as twenty-five hundred. The Conservative government and the U.S. ambassador both blamed Communists.[13]

El bogotazo (roughly "the Bogotá coup") is the term by which this carnival of fire and destruction would be known abroad. Colombians call it simply *el nueve de abril*, a date carrying for them the same weight as do 22 June 1941 for Russians or 7 December for North Americans. A drastic shift in Colombia's ongoing conflicts had been signaled, and in a few provincial cities the *bogotazo* actually sparked brief takeovers by "revolutionary juntas."[14] Tragically, however, political emotions now took their ugliest possible turn. Virulent hatred quickly became a normal component of rural interparty strife. Assassinations and armed clashes were to be routinely climaxed by decapitations and castrations, drawings and quarterings, with pregnant women and whole families hacked to pieces. Some reactionary gunmen referred to as *pájaros* ("birds")—extreme, pathological cases—achieved wide notoriety; for example, Teófilo Rojas "Chispas" ("Sparks") was renowned for committing two assassinations per day on average.[15]

For almost a decade the government sectors would show a confusing mixture of brutality and impotence. A crucial year was 1949: President Ospina had Liberal departmental governors ousted; Conservatives in Congress took to blowing whistles to drown out opposition party speakers; and in September, Conservative House members actually drew revolvers and shot at Liberals, murdering the man who currently had the floor. Liberals talked of impeaching Ospina; he responded by dissolving Congress and other local bodies, and imposing a state of siege. (The latter was not in fact lifted until thirty years hence.) In the presidential elections that November, Laureano Gómez, a Conservative, was elected by 1,140,620 votes to 14 (there was no Liberal candidate).[16]

Gómez was the acknowledged leader of the Conservatives' extreme right wing, with General Franco's Spain as their model, and reactionary nostalgic *Hispanidad* their ideology. Accordingly, upon his accession to power in 1950 Gómez unleashed against the Liberals a war of repression comparable to that of any military dictatorship. (At the same time he provided generous concessions to foreign oil firms, and contributed thousands of troops to the war in Korea—the only Latin American chief of state to have done so.)[17] Insurgents were dealt with as bandits, a policy that further exacerbated hatreds. The opposition—mostly Liberal, though with some scattered Communist focal points—resisted just as ruthlessly, killing Conservatives and torching their villages with equal fervor. While lacking sufficient strength to overthrow the central government, they possessed enough of a broad base to dig in as a counterforce of their own. Over 90 percent of the eastern plains, for instance, was in rebel hands, and in other zones the police could make merely transitory shows of force. There were areas in which "all manifestations of the public administration disappeared," notes researcher Paul Oquist, who quite aptly describes *la Violencia* as a "partial collapse of the state" in Colombia.[18]

Aside from the terrible toll in loss of life and of loved ones, the most heartrending tragedy in rural Colombia was the large scale of socioeconomic dislocation. Quite simply, "land-grabbing" of a nonideological sort became a common practice during *la Violencia*. Anyone who had the guns and the power could and would steal away other people's property. The big land-owners' armed bands on retainer helped them swell their lands yet further, and in areas where the state still had authority, the police and military frequently connived in the takeovers. The number of farms thus seized has been placed at 393,648 by Paul Oquist.[19] In the process two million peasants were forced to abandon their individual plots of land and the assorted rural dangers, fleeing to the relative peace but rootless poverty of the larger cities.[20]

The armed conflict was largely plebeian in character—peasants or lower-middle-class elements who had spontaneously become fighters and leaders. The elites of the two parties, by contrast, mostly avoided the battlefield. In time, however, the bloodletting came to be too much both for the ruling circles and the broader *pueblo*, and the coup d'état by General Gustavo Rojas Pinilla on 13 June 1953 was jubilantly welcomed by all political sectors excepting the Communists and the Gómez faction of the Conservatives.[21]

The general's four-year regime presents a similarly contradictory picture. He retained in his administration many civilian notables from both parties, in order that neither side would feel it had lost. He negotiated with guerrilla groups and offered amnesty to all who would lay down their arms. Eventually he also sought populist credentials by pushing for higher taxes on the wealthy, initiating social projects for workers, launching a new labor organization that had *Peronista* links, and campaigning for a "Third Force," a people-army coalition with that of General Perón as its model. At the same time, though there was a dramatic lull in the fighting during the first stages of the Rojas presidency, when spontaneous economic and vendetta violence flared up once again he would order renewed combat against Liberal guerrillas, massacre protesting students, censor domestic news, and shut down key Liberal newspapers.[22]

With the relatively bloodless overthrow of General Rojas on 10 May 1957, there began the period of the so-called National Front (1958–74) during which the elites of the two chief parties decided to set aside their differences and stress Colombian unity. In practice this meant a political consortium whereby, every four years, a Liberal and a Conservative would alternate regularly in the presidency, and power also would be shared equally in the cabinet, with half the ministries going to Liberals and the other half to Conservatives, regardless of which party happened to be occupying the presidential seat. All other groups were formally excluded from the *Frente*. In the meantime the interparty aspects of *La Violencia* would peter out, though strife would persist into the early 1960s in the form of psychopathic banditry, much of it by teenaged boys whose entire families had been murdered in the war.[23]

In retrospect *la Violencia* can be seen as a frustrated social revolution, a progressive upheaval gone awry, a groundswell of a movement that, with the loss of its charismatic leader Gaitán, became directionless and at the same time remained incapable of locating an ideological space outside of the traditional Liberal party framework.[24] The result was the eventual degeneration of its energies and sights, first to the immediate concerns of clinging onto local power, then to revenge on Conservative neighbors, and in the end to apolitical banditry. Meanwhile many of the fundamental conditions that ultimately gave rise to *la Violencia* — poverty, unemployment, and dissatisfaction with the status quo, to name just a few — persist today. With the 1980s there emerged a new phase of violence, a complex struggle involving the half-dozen guerrilla groups (nationalist as much as Marxist), the right-wing paramilitary squads, the enormously rich *narcotraficantes* and their private troops, and the national army and police themselves, who routinely make their presence felt and their automatic weapons visible on the city streets and rural highways. The government, though formally a liberal democracy, can show fast and furious repression, as in the 1979 arrest orders for a thousand individuals, many of them prominent artists and intellectuals.

Though the war chapters in García Márquez's greatest novel are clearly set in the nineteenth century, the events as depicted are inevitably colored by the more recent experience of *la Violencia*. One sees high-handedness from the Conservatives, factionalism among Liberals, eventual dilution of party principles, and confused and inconclusive fighting. Such episodes constitute a classic literary instance of past history imaginatively recreated through the eyes of the present. In some of García Márquez's shorter works, moreover, the times of *la Violencia* and of the Gómez and Rojas Pinilla dictatorships serve as basis and as the very source of the action: for example, the private confrontation between rebel dentist and military mayor in "One of These Days"; the security forces who have murdered the nameless and forgotten colonel's only son; the uncensored foreign news read and commented on by his doctor; the thuggish José Montiel, who has gotten rich by forcibly seizing others' lands, with government help; the mounting chaos of *In Evil Hour*; and the deliriously high-flown rhetoric of the National Front, marvelously parodied in "Big Mama's Funeral." Not accidentally, two of García Márquez's most ambitious full-length novels are each built around one of those "archetypally" Latin American collective experiences — political violence (*One Hundred Years*) and barracks dictatorship (*The Autumn of the Patriarch*).

The Catholic church also holds a special place in Colombian history. As in the rest of what would become the Spanish Empire, the clergy played a key role in helping to capture the new lands and establish the new society, pacifying and making converts of the Indians and — in what were religious, civic, and "political" enterprises — having churches built. Friars accompanied the imperially designated magistrates: Franciscans came to Santa Fe de Bogotá with the first Spanish judges. And they took the lead in education: in 1563 the first chair of grammar in Nueva Granada was followed by the Dominicans, who shortly thereafter established one in philosophy as well.[25]

Still, historically speaking, even by Ibero-American standards the church in Colombia has been unusually retrograde and obscurantist. Some lively controversy was stirred up in the Colegio del Rosario in 1762 when a learned scientist, José Celestino Mutis, taught the revolutionary hypothesis that the earth actually revolves around the sun.[26] Since independence the church has continued to hold great sway with its Conservative allies. The Colombian Constitution of 1886 begins with the words, "In the name of God, supreme source of all authority." More recently, at the height of *la Violencia*, priests denied sacraments to Liberals; a bishop threatened with excommunication anyone who dared cast a Liberal ballot; and in 1949 the National Bishops' Conference prohibited voting for any Liberal candidate who might "wish to implant civil marriage, divorce, and coeducation."[27]

Given his Liberal family ties and leftist commitments, it is not surprising that, in his writings prior to *The Autumn of the Patriarch*, García Márquez has virtually no character portraits sympathetic to priests, the sole exception being the newly arrived, courageous cleric known as the "Pup" in the early *Leaf Storm*. Otherwise, churchmen in his fiction are either lovable old fools ("One Day after Saturday") or weak, hypocritical moralists ("The Tuesday Siesta"); or they are timid, apologetic, and ineffectual in the face of government terror, preoccupied far more with the moral quality of the movies being seen by their parishioners than with the blood being shed by local political feuds (*In Evil Hour*). Or they are narrow-minded, destructive, and overtly tyrannical, as are both Bishop Toribio and Abbess Josefa in *Of Love and Other Demons*. In the worst of cases, the clergy in García Márquez are enemy agents, notably Father Nicanor Reyna in *One Hundred Years of Solitude*, who is the spiritual advance guard for the encroaching Conservatives, and whose levitation miracles are performed chiefly to gather money for a church building (a structure hitherto not deemed necessary by the Macondians).

In the Colombia of the 1960s, however, there occurred certain church-related shifts that would ultimately have some effect on García Márquez's representations of religiosity. There was the legendary "guerrilla priest" Camilo Torres (a former classmate of the young novelist-to-be), who, having arrived at the view that a true Christian is a militant revolutionary, lived and died for that principle by joining up with a rebel organization, only to be killed shortly thereafter in battle with the Colombian army in 1966. And it was in the Colombian city of Medellín in 1968, at the Second Latin American Bishops' Conference, that the higher churchmen would declare their much-publicized "preferential option for the poor." This momentous statement is now retrospectively seen as the birth of what would later be called "Liberation Theology," the movement within certain segments of the Catholic church whose proponents call for a clergy committed to the just struggles of the poor, and who, in varying degrees, accept Marxian analyses of society.

It is not accidental that, in the wake of these newer currents, García Márquez too would eventually present a more complex picture of the church. Though in "A Very Old Man with Enormous Wings" he still pokes good fun at priestly narrowness and Vatican hairsplitting, in "Innocent Eréndira," by contrast, the oppressed heroine finds a short-lived solace and refuge in a convent, where she actually makes the touching, poignant statement (indeed, the only time she ever expresses such a feeling), "I'm happy." Similarly, in the fourth chapter of *The Autumn of the Patriarch* there is Monsignor Aldous from Ethiopia, "a real stud of a priest" who talks like a man of the people, plays ball on the beach, loves the local music, gets drunk with *vallenato* singers, and has the courage to get into a fistfight with one of them when the wiseacre dares to insult God. Moreover, the heroic and ethical Monsignor Aldous — perhaps the one truly positive character in García Márquez's panoramic novel of sordid Caribbean intrigue — successfully resists the dictator's maniacal effort to have his mother Bendición Alvarado canonized into sainthood. Unlike in his earlier fiction, then, García Márquez in these works can tell of some of the more estimable roles the Catholic church has played in Spanish America — as occasional haven and sanctuary for the downtrodden, or as focus of resistance against many a wily demagogue who, when in need of mass support against easy targets, will whip up a persecution campaign against the clergy.

Several decisive episodes in García Márquez's fiction have to do with U.S. power and imperialism: the comic and horrific banana company sequences in *One Hundred Years of Solitude*, the manipulative do-gooder Mr. Herbert in "The Sea of Lost Time," the occupation by U.S. Marines in "Blacamán the Good," and the extravaganza of *The Autumn of the Patriarch*, endless in its supply of high-pressure U.S. ambassadors plus its fantastical climax, the efficient removal of the Caribbean Sea by Yankee engineers.

Both historical and literary imagination are at work here. Actually, though its national soil has never been occupied by American troops, Colombia in the last century has twice felt the heavy hand of U.S. power. What is now the Republic of Panama was formerly Colombia's northernmost province. The canal talks at the turn of the twentieth century were to cause heated debate in the Colombian Senate, where there was highly vocal opposition to the American demand that a ten-mile strip alongside the canal be transferred and deeded to the United States. In the end the U.S. government under Theodore Roosevelt helped foment in Panama a separatist political movement more fully responsive to the American demands. U.S. warships then made a show of force in the area, blocking access to any expeditionary troops that could have been sent by Bogotá (who in the end offered no resistance). Colombia hence shares with Mexico the distinction of being the other Latin American republic to have seen its territory sizably diminished by U.S. power. Perhaps the Panama Canal, that miracle of American know-how and product of U.S. empire, is also the ultimate inspiration behind that miraculous García Márquez episode of American know-how: buying, divvying up, and carrying off an entire sea.

The other direct, large-scale visitation by U.S. power in Colombia occurred in the coastal north, when, starting in 1900, the banana plantations of the almost proverbial United Fruit Company would grow and expand to become a virtual state-within-a-state. Besides possessing the best lands, the Boston-based firm came to have its own railroads, irrigation canals, and telegraph systems as well. The company's harsh labor policies finally led to the 1928 general strike by thirty-two thousand field workers, which in turn drew massive occupation and bloody repression by the Colombian military (who, evidence suggests, were in the pay of United Fruit).[28] Estimated casualties for the reprisals would range from a low hundred to several thousand, but at any rate the entire episode caused a major crisis both in the coastal area and in the central government. All of this is of course immediately recognizable as the culminating series of events in *One Hundred Years of Solitude*, to be examined in further detail in chapter 6.

Although the literature of Latin America was to start attracting world notice only in the 1950s, from earlier dates there had been worthy authors laboring on the continent, particularly poets. The turn-of-the-century *modernistas*—Latin America's equivalent to Parnassianism, Symbolism, and Art for Art's Sake—would spread their reforms through all of the republics and on to old Spain, thoroughly rejuvenating and transforming a Spanish verse that, since 1700, had stagnated in false pomp and bloated rhetoric. In addition, such populous countries as Mexico and Argentina could point to an existent if uneven roster of novelists of social conflict and short story writers of metaphysical fantasy, whose ambitious, crafted narratives laid the groundwork for future masters like Rulfo and Borges. And there were the cases of isolated individual genius, such as the Brazilian comic novelist Machado de Assis (1839–1903), or the incomparable Peruvian poet César Vallejo (1892–1938), who only recently has begun to receive the kind of attention and understanding he deserves. For continental ferment in narrative and a truly world-historical level of novelistic production, however, Latin America would have to wait until its grand moment in the second half of the twentieth century.

In this already rough and disparate panorama, Colombia before García Márquez was notable for its literary marginality. The country could lay claim to a handful of lasting works of prose and verse, flashes of genius scattered through four centuries of colony and republic, but no continuous or sustained traditions of high creativity. In a nation where the Bogotá elites touted their capital as "the Athens of South America" and took particular pride in their city's spoken Spanish being thought of as the best outside of Spain, there inevitably prevailed a solemn, curatorial attitude toward language and an immoderate regard for proper and correct writing. Official Colombian oratory, appropriately enough, is a phenomenon that still outdoes its original Castilian models in rhetorical formality and grandiloquence, in stylized purity and strict avoidance of colloquial registers.

Colombia in fact used to be renowned for its academicians and philologists, notably Rufino José Cuervo (1844–1911), who achieved fame with his work on grammars and dictionaries, and whose name is co-memorialized in Bogotá's prestigious scholarly center, the Instituto Caro y Cuervo. In addition, the Academia Colombiana de la Lengua, founded in 1871, was the first of its kind and today remains the most highly regarded in the hemisphere. From its magisterial neoclassical mansion in downtown Bogotá, with its well-appointed library facilities, triumphalist artworks, imposing semicircular auditorium, and leather-upholstered chairs, it wields an influence second only to that of its corresponding royal counterpart in Madrid, determining which words, phrases, and structures are acceptable among the Colombian literate. Several presidents of Colombia, it is worth noting, have also been published (if largely conventional) poets and/or have served as presidents of the academy.[29]

Any repute that "pre-Gabo" Colombian letters did enjoy outside Colombia stemmed primarily from three separate texts: a proto-*modernista* poem, a prose romance, and a naturalist novel.

José Asunción Silva (1865–96), a highly gifted but ill-fated lyrist, had the misfortune to lose most of his poetic manuscripts in an Atlantic shipwreck, and eventually died by his own hand at age thirty-one. Silva is still remembered throughout the Hispanic world for his third "Nocturno," a luscious, dreamy, nostalgic, fifty-three-line evocation of youthful love cut tragically short by death, and later revived by the spectral shadows of a moonlit night. With lines of verse ranging in length from four syllables to twenty-two, it is a tour de force of experimental prosody, and its subtle puns and rigorous bipartite structure add up to one of those rare instances of technically brilliant, miraculously inspired lyric art. Its verbal music and resounding cadences make the "Nocturno" a favorite at young Hispanics' poetry recitals, and its echoing refrains have become common enough currency for many a Spanish-language writer casually to cite and crib from them, much as English writers will unattributedly quote celebrated lines out of Tennyson or T. S. Eliot.

Perhaps the most renowned author in all of late-nineteenth-century Latin America was a Colombian, Jorge Isaacs (1837–95), whose one novel, *María* (1867), tells of the chaste, selfless, impassioned love between a sensitive, upper-class young man named Efraín and his cousin, the mysteriously beautiful yet purehearted María of the title, who when orphaned had moved in with Efraín's large family and their hacienda near Cali and who in the end dies of an unspecified disease—presumably epilepsy—before reaching her twentieth year. The doomed romance languidly unfolds in the Cauca Valley toward the Pacific, and the rural setting—with its herons and eagles and villages under the tropical sun—is evoked by Isaacs (or rather by Efraín, the narrator) with exceptional warmth, skill, and accuracy.[30]

Isaacs was to see *María* gain an enormous following, though he himself earned little from its hemisphere-wide success. In Mexico alone there were fourteen editions of the book, and for a while many Hispanic newborns would be baptized "Efraín" or "María," much as, in the wake of Erich Segal's *Love Story*, there was a surge of American baby girls being named "Jennifer." Enjoying good sales to this day, *María* is typically scorned by adult Latin

Americans who in their teens would read it weepingly and now look back with embarrassment at their flow of adolescent tears. But it is a much better work than is commonly granted, in its style and artistry comparable to Bernardin de St. Pierre's *Paul et Virginie* and Chateaubriand's *Atala*, after both of which *María* was modeled.[31] And with its colloquial dialogue that still remains fresh, its deep and expertly conveyed love of nature, and its two interpolated slave narratives that subtly replicate the main story line, *María* deserves recognition for the thoughtful and sophisticated novelistic performance it actually is. The Isaacs house and immediate grounds today serve as a handsome museum and park an hour's drive outside Cali.

When the ants, vegetation, and wind engulf the last of the Buendías, García Márquez may well be purposely parodying the ending of *La vorágine* (1924; *The Vortex*), the only novel by poet and activist José Eustasio Rivera (1889–1928). The book—which ends with the succinct words "They've been swallowed up by the jungle!"—tells of the multiple adventures of protagonist Arturo Cova and his upper-class mistress Alicia, who flee Bogotá and head for Colombia's eastern plains and then the rain forests, where they will experience all manner of frontier violence and economic intrigue. In addition, *The Vortex* is an exposé of the slave-labor conditions then prevailing on the immense rubber plantations in the wilderness, the horrors of which the author himself had attested to as a government official. Rivera's narrative shows great exuberance and vitality, with large doses of thick description and fast action. He marshals his vast lexical resources in portraying a world virtually dominated by mosquitoes, crocodiles, electric eels, piranhas, and the like, as well as such standard inanimate dangers as river rapids and whirlpools. Truly multiethnic in its cast of characters, *The Vortex* fits in sketches of frontier whites, blacks, Indians, mixed-bloods, and their local ways. There is also, in the imposing Turkish-Arab madam and adventuress Zoraida Ayram, a vivid precursor to innocent Eréndira's unforgettable and heartless grandmother.

To our eyes today, however, *The Vortex* seems like a relic, the work of a man trying too hard to come up with the definitive book about South American violence and nature. Despite the surface realism, the novel is so overstuffed with barn burnings, cattle rustlings, and fistfights in which the hero *always* wins, that in the end the book is unconvincing. Dozens of characters come and go, presented with little sense of narrative system or shape, and the unrelenting white-hot prose lacks serenity. Before Rivera, numerous other Latin American writers had attempted to transcribe and capture their overwhelming reality via the medium of Zolaesque naturalism. "That thing called *The Vortex*," as García Márquez once referred to it in a literary essay (*OP*, 1:268), stands out as the most ambitious and thus most nobly failed instance of what in retrospect was a largely failed trend.

Two other Colombian literati worth notice are Tomás Carrasquilla and Germán Arciniegas. The first (1858–1940), now remembered as the author of several novels set in the Antioquia area, is an accomplished regionalist who, with his sharp eye for social detail and well-tuned ear for everyday language, was able to recapture the texture of his traditionalist milieu and populate it with a variety of colorful male and especially female types, furnishing memorable portraits of them and their folk customs, all with a delicacy, grace, and a gentle irony distinctively his own. A true literary artist and the creator of a rich oral style that never succumbs to excess, Carrasquilla neatly exemplifies the sort of valuable writer whose strengths are local without necessarily being universal. The field of essay and literate popular history, in a now-lost nineteenth-century vein, is represented by Arciniegas (1900–1999), who in his thirties and forties published some skillfully told, almost novelistically rendered accounts of the Conquest and other grand Latin American themes. Several of his works were translated into English, but, as he achieved an international following, Arciniegas seems to have written increasingly with his foreign readership in mind and in the process lost his touch, an unfortunate Latin American pattern that had in the Mexican poet Octavio Paz one of its more recent intellectual avatars.

The above are Colombia's officially "canonized" authors, those who, before the publication of García Marquez's best-known book, were deemed worthy of rereading, reprinting, and in-depth study. Further observations are in order concerning two other narrative artists of earlier date who, while still published and sufficiently reputable at home, have yet to receive outside of Colombia the attention that is their due.

The son of a conquistador, Juan Rodríguez Freile (1566–1640) lived most of his long life in Bogotá and, at age seventy, finished writing his unclassifiable opus, the *Conquista y redescubrimiento del nuevo reino de Granada . . .* (the original full title takes up an entire page).[32] The manuscript languished for two centuries thereafter, only seeing print in 1884 under the short title *El carnero de Bogotá*. Today among Hispanic readers it is alluded to simply as *El carnero*—literally "The Ram" or "The Sheepskin," reasons for the adopted name remaining conjectural.

In what is ostensibly a historical chronicle, the robust, good-humored Rodríguez Freile simply uses that received format as a springboard for all sorts of fanciful divagations, including Boccaccio-like tales of sexual intrigue, quasi-ethnographic accounts of picturesque Indian customs, and fantastical anecdotes about golden alligators, for example, or about an Afro-Hispanic sorceress who peers into a bowl of water and spies on her mistress's philandering husband (who is off in distant Hispaniola). Rodríguez Freile time and again picks up on his meager historical narrative only to abandon the thread yet once more, and the entire text comes off as a lengthy and elaborate spoof. Spontaneous and rough, and less than polished in its prose, *El carnero* sometimes suggests modern cartoon films, what with its endless procession of head bashings and practical jokes. There is also a fair amount of ironic digression à la Laurence Sterne ("Will the reader be so kind as to wait for a moment . . ."), and even a Shandyesque interruption of an anecdote-in-progress via two full lines of sets of three dots (... ... ...), the author solemnly explaining that a page is missing from the original.[33]

Throughout *El carnero* Rodríguez Freile shows what is almost a novelist's feel for the immediate homely details of urban daily life. While he often will indulge idly in the conventional moralizing of his time, the righteous reflections usually seem tongue-in-cheek, though the occasional harsh attack on those who hunger for power does suggest some personal conviction. Much as with García Márquez, our wise seventeenth-century chronicler is simply fascinated by the irrational force and compulsions of erotic passion and the utter sway it can gain over people's lives. In the political realm one notes an episode that looks to be a textual source for the plot of García Márquez's *In Evil Hour*, its culminating scene included: Rodríguez Freile tells the story of some libelous sheets that mysteriously crop up around Bogotá early one morning in 1578. A frenetic manhunt ensues and, on grounds of handwriting similarities, a youth is accused and tortured, then eventually released on orders of a judge who declares the boy innocent. (The outcome in García Márquez's early novel is somewhat less happy.) In the narrative desert that was Imperial Spain's America, where works of fiction were explicitly banned from importation, Rodríguez Freile stands out as an individual voice and a true original. Not accidentally, García Márquez read *El carnero* in high school, and there are obvious affinities of outlook and spirit between the humorous colonial chronicler and the modern journalist, humorist, and novelist.

Knowing that such judgments can be risky, I will venture to say that the best single "pre-Gabo" novel in Colombia is *Cuatro años a bordo de mí mismo: Diario de los cinco sentidos* (1934; Four Years on Board with Myself: A Diary of the Five Senses), written at the tender age of twenty-five by Eduardo Zalamea Borda (1907–63), who would later become one of his country's most eminent newspaper columnists and editors. Something of an "underground classic" today, *Cuatro años* is a uniquely inspired and compellingly comical tale of travel, suspense, romantic adventure, and personal discovery, narrated by an unnamed protagonist who hails from Bogotá and as of the start is a mere seventeen years old. With typically adolescent zest he recounts his maritime journey to, and then his protracted roamings about, the Guajira desert and his human encounters there amid the prickly pears, huge mounds of salt, plays of color and light, and "eternally blue sky." Early on in the novel there is a beautiful description of Cartagena, and in the course of the narrative we read lively accounts of the Indians' way of life, which is eloquently and unsentimentally praised. Afro-Hispanics also play a major role in the wandering youth's experiences, Zalamea capturing their distinctive speech-rhythms and phonetics without a hint of facile condescension or local color.

The bulk of *Cuatro años*, however, consists of the young hero's quasi-picaresque "memoir" of odd-jobbing and just living amongst a succession of frontier roustabouts, Zalamea Borda deftly grasping and delineating their divers group chemistries, sex rivalries, and clique "politics." In addition, the narrator, who is unabashedly girl-crazy, frequently rhapsodizes about individual women and is not averse to brandishing three exclamation points ("¡¡¡Oh. . . !!!") when transcribing those effusions. And yet, save for these unrestrained outpourings on the part of a delightfully dreamy youth, the book itself is notable for its controlled, understated, low-key prose, which is of a consistently high quality and is also perfectly suited to both narrator and what is narrated.

Cuatro años a bordo de mí mismo somewhat suggests Mark Twain's own frontier memoir *Roughing It*, and is perhaps more organic in conception than the North American classic. It also looks ahead to Alejo Carpentier's *The Lost Steps*, though without the Cuban writer's portentousness and solemnity. As far back as April 1950, a judicious twenty-two-year-old García Márquez would deem *Cuatro años* a fine work of fiction and one of the few Colombian novels deserving of translation into other languages (*OP*, 1:268). And in his own memoirs he describes it as "a novel that opened unsuspected horizons for our generation" (*VC*, 135; *LTT*, 109). Today still fresh and a sheer joy to read, *Cuatro años* is indeed a remarkable book, one of those flashes of inspiration that dot literary history and remain marginal to the "canon" of respectable texts.

When everything is said it must be admitted that the overall picture of Colombian letters before 1960 is a fairly bleak and desolate one. As García Márquez himself, still developing as a journeyman writer, would observe in April of that year, the field of the novel in Colombia's century and a half of independence has little more to show than a scatter of titles by single-book authors. Referring to J. M. Vargas Vila (1860–1933), who did pour out some twenty-seven works of commercially successful fiction, García Márquez pointedly remarks that "only the bad Colombian novelists have written more than one novel" (*OP*, 3:789). At the very time of García Márquez's harsh pronouncements, however, what with the sense of urgency awakened by *la Violencia*, the lively intellectual ferment on the Colombian north coast, the revolutionary process unleashed in Cuba, and the inspiring example of what Faulkner had achieved in Mississippi, there was a shared feeling that serious efforts had to be undertaken to improve the literary situation in Colombia itself. Within García Márquez's milieu in particular there appears to have been present the unstated intuition that *the* novel of Caribbean Colombia was waiting to be written.

By pure chance there appeared in 1962 a couple of novels chronicling the final phases of grand old families in a Caribbean-coastal small town. *Respirando el verano* (The Breath of Summer) by Héctor Rojas Herazo recounts the rapid moral and physical decay of such a clan following the death of their ninety-some-year-old matriarch Celia. The book makes use of Faulknerian oscillation with time, and toward the end features a fine interior monologue by Celia herself, who retells the entire story from her perspective. There are also some sharp character sketches and vivid evocations of daytime heat upon the shore, though in the end *Respirando el verano* feels less than complete and remains at the level of a potential work of art.

Much the same could be said of *La casa grande* (The Big House) by Álvaro Cepeda Samudio, a close friend of García Márquez and the basis for the character "Álvaro" in *One Hundred Years*, chapter 18. The eponymous big house and its resident family, torn by hate and not without their incestuous rituals, are approaching their last days; and the 1928 banana strike and massacre, which happens to be among the key episodes in Cepeda's novel, brings further rifts within the ranks. Once again the hand of Faulkner is in evidence, as in a chapter made up entirely of long sentences of reminiscences, or an episode in which some innocent young soldiers cross paths with gaudily attired street whores and never so much as realize it, in obvious imitation of the comical scene depicting two proper country boys in a New Orleans brothel in *Sanctuary*.

Despite their limitations, these and other novels by coastal authors constitute a substantial forward development in the seriousness and craft (again, the "carpentry," as García Márquez likes to call it) of fiction writing in Colombia. Only three years hence, in Mexico City, García Márquez was to be seized by inspiration and would seal himself off in his room to labor full-time on a manuscript that, while dealing with the very same subjects as had Rojas Herazo and Cepeda, would become the great novel of Colombia and—as it happened—of Latin America.

To fashion works that would elevate Colombian literary standards was a goal, moreover, toward which García Márquez had consciously been striving. Halfway into his thirty-second year, and with the youthful *Leaf Storm* now behind him, the budding novelist would pass judgment on the literatures of *la Violencia* and of Colombia and (with no arrogance or bumptiousness on his part) find it all sadly wanting. In "Two or Three Things about the Novel of 'la Violencia,'" a polemical piece that stirred up some debate when it appeared in 1959, García Márquez notes that the readers of those several dozen such novels "seem to agree that all of them are bad." Owing to Colombia's peculiar lacks, every novelist "had to start from scratch, and you can't get a literary tradition started in twenty-four hours." As García Márquez sees it, the first mistake was the attempt to describe all the physical carnage—"the decapitations, castrations and rapes"—rather than capture the general atmosphere of terror occasioned by *la Violencia* and its crimes (*OP*, 3:765). His counter-model is *The Plague* by Camus, who was well aware that the horror is experienced not by the corpses but by the survivors—and not only by the pursued but by the pursuers, by the poorly paid Colombian cop who also lived in fear. "No human drama can be unilateral" (*OP*, 3:767). Later, in his greatest works, in spite of his own sympathies García Márquez would be artistically fair both to Liberals and Conservatives, victims and executioners, oppressed and oppressor.

In April 1960 García Márquez raised the polemical ante with an article provocatively entitled "Colombian Literature: A Fraud to Our Nation." The piece appears to have been occasioned by the First Colombian Book Festival of June 1959. The three hundred thousand volumes that, as a result of the festival, had sold briskly in the ensuing week, did confirm the existence of a Colombian reading public that was ample enough. What was missing, remarks García Márquez, was a sufficiently large roster of qualified Colombian authors (*OP*, 3:787). Uncharacteristically raising his voice, García Márquez informs the self-satisfied cultural elites that there are in Colombia no imaginative writers, living or dead, who merit world stature. Noting the ever-prevailing panorama of desolation and mediocrity, he cites as an instance a short-story contest sponsored by *El Tiempo* in which out of more than three hundred entries only the three prizewinners showed any talent or skill whatsoever. In his complex but clear diagnosis García Márquez deplores the lack of "an authentic sense of what is national" among Colombian writers (a lack which, with his personal researches into the nation's history and coastal folklore, he himself had been attempting to remedy). And again he regrets the absence of true craftsmanship, a commitment to which, admittedly, can pose "physical and mental difficulties," and moreover requires both "courage" and—as he puts it—"a certain muscular enthusiasm" (*OP*, 3:790–91). Without these and other such preconditions, Colombian literature will remain—in García Márquez's unsparing final phrase—"a fraud to our nation."

These polemical essays give a taste of what García Márquez saw as his personal calling at the time, his fierce determination to *do* something about Colombian letters, to raise the level of artistic performance and craft, to both widen and sharpen local literary vision, and in that way to help give Colombian experiences their universality. As we know, he eventually succeeded in his mission, and both Colombia and the world community of readers are now all the richer for it.

When reading even his grandest of works, however, his foreign admirers should bear in mind that, for all the lessons he learned from European and American authors, and for all the subsequent and miraculous "universal" adulation, García Márquez is very much a product of Colombian—specifically northern Colombian—life, that his intuitions and world view grow out of the multiethnic demography of that region, and that the social divisions, ideological struggles, and geographic differences within Colombia are a constant underlying presence in his oeuvre. Just as a budding Faulkner was to follow Sherwood Anderson's advice and understand that "my own little postage stamp of soil was worth writing about and I would never live long enough to exhaust it," a youthful García Márquez would discover his Caribbean-coastal patch of land and reinvent with words his little slice of tropical terrain. He is every bit as much a Colombian author as Joyce was Irish or Tolstoy Russian. While (as we shall see in a later chapter) the works of Virginia Woolf, Kafka, and Faulkner would guide and teach the young writer, the experience of Colombia had previously shaped the young man's mind and soul.

THREE

The Writer's Life

The story of García Márquez's life is one of steady growth of a number of vocations, all of them interrelated. First, obviously, there is that of writer, both of fiction and journalism (the two of course being narrative crafts), and more broadly his role as lyrical historian of his region and of Hispanic America. Closely linked with his mission as writer are his principles as man of the left. Though he never was a full-time militant, from his twentieth year García Márquez's art and actions were the work of an independent socialist who, in the wake of *One Hundred Years of Solitude*, would use his literary fame and marshal his writing skills publicly to support progressive causes. In addition, being true to his extended family origins, García Márquez would flower most freely as a stable family man and father. Last but not least, he was to remain loyally attached to his oldest friends, those predating his sudden success and wealth. Till late in life, García Márquez would set aside his afternoon hours as time to be spent with family and friends (as well as with any casual strangers who may have gained access to him).

He was born in the sad and unpaved town of Aracataca on 6 March 1927 (not 1928, as generally thought), the eldest child of Luisa Santiaga Márquez and Gabriel Eligio García.[1] His first eight years, however, would be spent with his maternal grandparents, Tranquilina Iguarán and Colonel Nicolás Márquez. The two latter had strongly opposed his parents' marriage, partly because Mr. García was poor, illegitimate and a newcomer to Aracataca but most of all because he belonged to the Conservative camp, against which Nicolás had fought fiercely in the Thousand Days' War. They tried their best to block the courtship, sending Luisa off to stay with a variety of relatives and even managing to have Gabriel Eligio transferred to Riohacha, on the Guajira. But Gabriel Eligio, very much in love with the Colonel's daughter and determined to woo her, would regularly send her loving messages by wire (he was a telegraph operator). His perseverance did finally break through the Márquez family barriers; Luisa Santiaga's parents resigned themselves to the situation, and in June 1926 the lovebirds were wedded in Santa Marta Cathedral. Gabriel Eligio nonetheless resented his in-laws and refused to live in Aracataca, "that charnel-house for the poor." The young couple thus set up house in distant Riohacha. Later, in a conciliatory gesture, Luisa would be sent to her parents' in order to give birth to baby Gabriel in Aracataca.

The boy's formative experiences were those of the classic extended family household in which an endless array of cousins, nephews, grandchildren and other distant kin (the Colonel's illegitimate children included) are constantly dropping in for a visit. Two sets of memories in particular would stay with him—the adult women, and his grandfather, the soldier. The women ran the house and took good care of little Gabito, encouraging his curiosity and his story-telling bent. Being somewhat superstitious, they were given to saying or doing certain things he would later memorialize. His grandmother Tranquilina, who went blind in old age, used to tell all manner of amazing stories with a straight face, and would talk about people without distinguishing between the quick and the dead. His aunt Francisca wove her own shroud; when he asked why, she replied, "Because I'm going to die, little boy" (*OG*, 11; *FG*, 12). Once the job was done she lay down and breathed her last. Besides these actions—now familiar to the novelist's readers—select names were to survive in his books. There was an aunt Petra, and Cotes was the second surname of his mother Luisa. "Iguarán," grandmother Tranquilina's maiden name, was to be retained as that of the materfamilias Úrsula Buendía.

Colonel Márquez was an old-fashioned, small-town gentleman who liked fine lotions, carried a pocket watch with a thick gold chain, and always wore a vest and tie. In his youth, in Riohacha, he had shot a man who had been pestering him, and then left for Aracataca when the counterthreats became impossible. (He often would say, in retrospect, "You can't believe how a dead man weighs you down.") During his combat years he reportedly sired a dozen illegitimate children, but his leadership was also to make Aracataca into a Liberal bulwark, and as an old man he was given to reminiscing about the horrors and glories of war. In 1929, as town treasurer, he provided eye-witness testimony at some celebrated Colombian congressional hearings on the recent banana workers' strike and military massacre. An excellent parental surrogate, he taught the boy the use of the dictionary, led him hither and yon about town, and took him for a visit to the Bolívar house in Santa Marta. Whenever the circus came to Aracataca the Colonel used to take little Gabo along, and at the United Fruit Company stores he would open up the frozen fish boxes and let the boy ponder the miracle of ice. To the end of his days the man would wait fruitlessly for a government pension that was due him, and following his death his widow Tranquilina was to wait even more.

The old Colonel died when the boy was only in his eighth year, but he would always be remembered by García Márquez as "the person I've gotten along with best and had the best communication ever" (*OG*, 18; *FG*, 18). The memories of the man clearly served as the inspiration behind many of García Márquez's key personages and narrative events, although, according to the novelist himself, the nameless Colonel in *Leaf Storm* is the only one of his characters who actually bears a close resemblance to Colonel Márquez, being all but "a detailed copy of his image" (*OG*, 19; *FG*, 19).

Members of the family used to recall with some disdain the heady days of the "banana fever," the 1910s, when the United Fruit Company (UFCO) expanded into Aracataca, bringing in hordes of migrant workers and a delirious, "gold rush" sort of atmosphere. Though falling world prices and the massive strike had brought UFCO into cyclical decline by 1928, the other-worldliness of the separate Yankee compound would remain vividly imprinted on García Márquez's mind—the wire fences; the ever-neat green lawns; the swimming pools with outdoor tables and umbrellas; the tall, blond, ruddy-faced men in their explorer outfits; their wives decked out in muslin dresses; and their adolescent daughters, playing tennis or going for casual drives in their convertibles around Aracataca (*OG*, 14; *FG*, 14). Such memories of great-power colonialism would mingle with those of family life and eventually become integrated into a mature García Márquez's literary art. Some five miles north of Aracataca there was a banana plantation by the name of "Macondo." The vast farm, now parceled out among local owners, continues to operate today, and in 1988 there still stood a general store bearing a rusted sign saying "Acueducto de Macondo." The living conditions of the workers did not appear to have greatly improved over the intervening sixty years.

Though García Márquez eventually would bloom as one of the most locally rooted of authors, his biography before the 1960s is characterized by a surprising amount of dislocation and instability. After first attending Aracataca's Montessori School (a place he would remember fondly and appreciatively), in 1936 he was finally sent to live with his parents, whom he had met just recently. They were living in Sucre, the river port whose configuration would later serve as model for the nameless town in *No One Writes to the Colonel* and *Chronicle of a Death Foretold*. Following the death of grandfather Nicolás the boy was dispatched for elementary school as a boarder at the Colegio San José, in Barranquilla. By age ten he was writing humorous verse, a practice that would continue with his transfer to the Colegio de Jesuitas in that same city. Throughout his school days "Gabito" would be noted as a slim, taciturn, and introverted boy, averse to sports, "so serious he was known as 'the Old Man.'"[2] Although in future columns and interviews the great writer was to assume a vigorously anti-academic stance, in his school years Gabito was actually an excellent pupil who received top grades. His teachers were very much impressed and saw in his youthful poems a budding literary genius.

A scholarship award in 1943 found the boy headed as a boarding student to the Liceo Nacional de Zipaquirá, a high school for the gifted located in a small town some thirty miles outside Bogotá. Today a mere hour's jet flight from the coast, at that time the complicated journey from Barranquilla required a week's travel—first by steamer up the Magdalena River (a trajectory the novelist would recount in moving detail more than four decades hence in *Love in the Time of Cholera*), and then by train further up into the Andes. Bogotá itself has since evolved into just another bright cosmopolis with the usual chic brand names and transnational boutiques, but to the thirteen-year-old from the tropical lowlands it was very much a shock, with its gray clouds and drizzle, its ever-present chill (temperatures at night can drop to the forties Fahrenheit), its hidebound religiosity (church bells chimed for rosary at sundown), its emotional reserve, its men in formal black, and its streets with not a woman in sight (*OG*, 54–56; *FG*, 40–41).

Little Gabito reportedly wept on first seeing this strange *cachaco* universe. Zipaquirá, in fact, would prove to be even chillier and grayer. The town's architecture and setting, however, were attractive: the main square, dominated by its massive early-eighteenth-century cathedral and surrounded by multistory buildings graced with continuous wooden dark-hued balconies, looks like a medieval plaza from old Castile transplanted piece-by-piece onto the Andean savannah. These beauties meant little to the lonely youth, and two and a half decades later, when writing *One Hundred Years of Solitude*, García Márquez would make the stuffy Fernanda del Carpio and her snobbish parents the deluded chief denizens of a somber, viceregal town clearly modeled after Zipaquirá. Meanwhile Gabo sought immediate solace for his adolescent solitude in the bold, vigorous fantasy worlds of Alexandre Dumas and Jules Verne.

The boy did well in his humanities subjects, somewhat less so in the sciences. There were also some advantages. The Liceo was of good academic quality; and Gabito's science and mathematics teachers were men of the left who, during recess, would introduce the bright youngster to Marxist thought and social and economic history. For their daily entertainment fellow students would read novels out loud at the barracks-like dormitory; Gabito often suggested titles. It was in this fashion that he first became acquainted with *The Three Musketeers*, *Notre Dame de Paris*, and *The Magic Mountain*, the latter eliciting lively adolescents' debates as to whether or not Hans Castorp and Claudia Chauchat bed down together.[3] The first two of these books, it bears noting, are historical romances that typically combine established fact and imagined fiction—much as García Márquez would eventually do in his greatest writings.

Meanwhile all these losses and displacements—the death of foster parents, the more problematical relationship to his immediate kin, and the uprootings from places known at a tender age—were giving Gabito an early taste of that adult experience of profound, inexplicable solitude. Aracataca consequently had assumed in his mind the status of a boyhood paradise and lost Eden. A return trip at age sixteen into that very past, however, was to prove crucial to his growth and development. Because grandmother Tranquilina Iguarán de Márquez had recently died, his mother Luisa Santiaga and himself were returning briefly to Aracataca for the prosaic business of selling off the family home. To his surprise, the adolescent boy finds not the idyllic world that has loomed large and mythic in his memory, but an unbearably hot, dusty village, its impoverished wooden shacks as silent and desolate as a ghost town (it is the siesta hour). The strange intensity of the visit is further heightened when his mother happens upon a woman friend from years past, seated quietly in her little shop; the two women embrace and weep speechless in front of the amazed boy for (as he would later recall it) a good half hour[4] (*OG*, 15–16; *FG*, 14–15). Soon thereafter Gabito knows that he has to be a novelist; he starts work on a long narrative entitled *La casa* (The House), writing several hundred pages until finally completing and abandoning it in 1953.

Graduating from the Liceo in 1946 and returning to the family fold in Sucre, the young man bowed to parental pressure and in 1947 once again went up to Bogotá, this time to enroll as a law student at the Universidad Nacional. (In Latin America, as in Europe, law is an undergraduate course of study.) One of his professors there was Alfonso López Michelsen, who from 1974 to 1978 would serve as president of Colombia. Among his classmates was Camilo Torres, the future "guerrilla priest," and the two students became close friends. Still, young Gabo felt sadly and thoroughly bored with his law studies, and he performed indifferently. Floating about in a state of chronic personal depression, he led a life confined in the main to the lecture halls, the boarding house, and the nearby cafés, where, book in hand, he would show up unshaven and badly dressed. On weekends he would board a tramway, ride back and forth between terminals, and bury himself in volumes of verse by the Spanish classical authors or by the "Piedra y Cielo" ("Stone and Sky") poets, an important Colombian avant-garde group from the 1930s. Occasionally he and a stranger might strike up a conversation and discuss a poem or two[5] (*OG*, 57; *FG*, 41).

It was during his freshman year in law school that García Márquez wrote and published—almost on a kind of dare—his first still-tentative short story. What happened was that Eduardo Zalamea Borda, then the literary editor and reigning critic at *El Espectador* (and author of *Cuatro años a bordo de mí mismo*, examined in our previous chapter), had run an essay in which he dismissed the younger generation of Colombian writers as lacking in talent. In spontaneous response to Zalamea's challenge García Márquez produced "The Third Resignation," a somewhat morbid account of a young boy presumed dead in his coffin for eighteen years, yet whose mind remains alive with sensations, memory, and imagination. The nineteen-year-old novice writer submitted the story; to his astonishment it appeared the next Sunday in *El Espectador's* literary supplement, with an introductory note by señor Zalamea Borda hailing "the new genius of Colombian letters." García Márquez often recalls the serious burden of responsibility he then felt, an almost painful need to be worthy of Zalamea's generous praise and not let the man down.[6] In the next half-decade he wrote and published in *El Espectador* another ten short fictions, most of them equally introspective, no doubt autobiographical in their fantastical close-ups of angst and isolation.

The assassination of Gaitán on 9 April 1948 and the *bogotazo* (see chapter 2) were permanently to alter the aimless, lonely drift of Gabo the late-adolescent and outsider. The hitherto self-absorbed student of law now witnessed an explosion of large-scale collective lawlessness, with who knows how many frenzied thousands caught up in mass rioting and pillaging throughout the city. García Márquez's own circumscribed world suffered the direct effects when the government building next to the boardinghouse where he'd been staying caught fire, the smoke seeping into the *pensión*. In the chaotic flight that followed, the young writer's books and manuscripts were mostly left behind. With the Universidad Nacional shut down indefinitely, moreover, Gabo's law studies were now forcibly—perhaps mercifully—interrupted. He sought and obtained transfer to the Universidad de Cartagena, continuing as a so-so student, gradually abandoning the classrooms, and in the end never receiving his bachelor's degree.

The move north was nevertheless the first step in Gabo's return to his Caribbean roots and rediscovery of that culture. His being newly present in the region is also what chanced to lead him to his lifetime occupation as journalist. The appearance of his short story in *El Espectador* had earned him some recognition among coastal literati, and during a casual street encounter with the Afro-Colombian novelist Manuel Zapata Olivella the latter invited him to do some writing for the recently founded Cartagena newspaper *El Universal*.[7] Soon thereafter the twenty-year-old apprentice had a five-hundred-word daily column of his own, in which his sprightly imagination could range freely over most any topic of his choosing. (Among the subjects he dealt with in his first month as columnist: the accordion, the helicopter, the length of women's skirts, astrology, twins, parrots, Joe Louis, and the daily comic strip *Bringing up Father*.) He had gotten off to an auspicious start, for the personal column is a genre of which he would produce thousands of specimens over the years and excel in masterfully throughout his life as a writer.

Around that time García Márquez also befriended the young writers and artists of what eventually came to be known as the "Barranquilla group"—now as much a byword in Colombia as "the Black Mountain Poets" or "the Russian Five" are elsewhere. The spiritual father of the group was Ramón Vinyes, an aged and erudite Catalonian book dealer and prolific writer of unpublished plays and fiction (all in Catalan). Being up on the latest European and U.S. literary trends, he enthusiastically initiated his youthful acolytes—including Gabo, who took the bus trip from Cartagena anytime he could—into many of the leading modernist authors. Later García Márquez would memorialize Vinyes as the wise Catalonian book dealer of Macondo, who passes on Sanskrit primers and other esoteric tomes to the ever-studious Aureliano Babilonia.[8]

Suddenly in early 1949 the Cartagena newspaperman's budding apprenticeship was interrupted when he contracted pneumonia. Bedridden for several months at his parents' place in Sucre, Gabo wrote his Barranquilla friends asking them for some reading matter. They willingly obliged by dispatching three cartons filled with Spanish translations of Faulkner, Hemingway, Joyce, Virginia Woolf, and more.[9]

At the start of 1950 García Márquez moved to Barranquilla, where the largest coastal newspaper, *El Heraldo*, had hired him as a staffer to liven up their pages with a daily column of the sort he had been doing for *El Universal*. The articles began appearing in January 1950, in a narrow column format under the heading "La Jirafa" ("The Giraffe," the nickname he'd given to one of his dance-hall partners), and were morbidly signed "Septimus," after the shell-shocked outsider in Virginia Woolf's *Mrs. Dalloway*. García Márquez used to write his columns during the afternoons, at the offices of *El Heraldo*. After closing time he'd stay behind, working on his novel *Leaf Storm*. Later on in the evening there were the all-night book-talk and boozing sessions at the Happy Bar (spelled "Bar Japi") with his friends Alfonso Fuenmayor, Álvaro

Cepeda, and Germán Vargas, the young literary Turks of the "Barranquilla group."

El Rascacielos—"The Skyscraper"—was the name of the four-story building located on Calle del Crimen ("Crime Street" [sic]) where García Márquez took lodging in Barranquilla. The bottom floors housed some law offices; the upper ones, a brothel. Gabo had an arrangement to sleep on the top floors after returning from his literary carousals, in whatever boudoir he could find vacant at dawn. On mornings when he was short of money for his bed and shelter, he would leave his manuscript to *Leaf Storm* as security with the gatekeeper. Occasionally, from an adjoining bedroom he might overhear some local politico and one of the "staff" girls engaged in lively talk about the man's many leadership achievements (and otherwise not much action). The whores treated Gabo as a family friend, generously sharing their lunches with him. The grateful novelist would later put much tender and positive feeling into his prostitute characters. One woman in The Skyscraper, an Afro-Hispanic named Eufemia, would reappear in the last chapters of Macondo as the voluptuous Nigromanta, who duly deflowers a bookish and unworldly Aureliano Babilonia. The town bordello also functions as a kind of safe haven in *Chronicle of a Death Foretold*[10] (OG, 62–63; FG, 43–44).

Young Gabo's professional ties with *El Heraldo* were to last three full years, through the whole of 1952. From a human and social point of view they constitute the happiest period in García Márquez's life. He had made some intellectually compatible, lifelong friends, and would later pay them the homage of assigning their first names to the only four pals a reclusive Aureliano Babilonia is lucky enough to have. He was brimming with ideas and high spirits and alive with writerly energy, and from ages twenty-two to twenty-five he had his own signed newspaper column in which (within the limits of existing government censorship) he could write pretty much as he pleased. In those years he also was to complete the writing of *Leaf Storm*, for which during the remainder of his life he would retain a great deal of affection. And, though still financially unsettled, he did not yet find himself faced with the multitudinous pressures and temptations that artistic mastery and worldwide fame would one day bring in their wake.

If 1948–52 are García Márquez's bright happy days of apprenticeship, 1953–67 are the *Wanderjähre*, the rougher times as journeyman writer and reporter. In December 1952 Gabo left his job (though keeping his friendly ties) with *El Heraldo*, the day-to-day writing having become too routine for his still-growing talents. The following year, 1953, he spent doing a brief stint (along with his brother Luis Enrique) as a salesman of encyclopedias and technical books in the Guajira region. The novelist was later to recall that elusive period as one of meager encyclopedia sales but much reading of Virginia Woolf, and the episode itself is gracefully evoked in a distinctive paragraph two-thirds of the way through "Innocent Eréndira," where sibling Luis is replaced by fellow writer Álvaro Cepeda. In the course of that curious little adventure Gabo encountered and conversed with a fellow whose grandfather was the man who long ago had been murdered by Colonel Márquez; he also hung around for a week with Rafael Escalona, the most renowned singer-songwriter of *vallenato* music. Later that year Gabo would temporarily hold a high editorial post at *El Nacional*, another daily in Barranquilla. There is little sign of major writing activity by García Márquez during those fluid twelve months, evidently a time of transition.

In February 1954 García Márquez moved to Bogotá and began work as a staff reporter for *El Espectador*, the more liberal of the two large national dailies, with almost a century of life to it. The job brought both greater prestige and more restrictions. Much of the writing was on an assignment basis—brief and inconsequential fillers (the editors indicating the allotted space with their thumb and forefinger) or lengthy features on subjects not of great concern to García Márquez, such as a profile series on a famous bicycle racer of the moment.[11] He did produce some memorable reports on, say, the Dead Letter Office and on frontier settlements in the Chocó region near Panama (*OP*, 2:295–323 and 355–60). But, whereas his coastal essays are mostly first-rate, a surprising amount of the Bogotá production is workmanlike and even mediocre.

There were some gains, however. Among García Márquez's multiple tasks was doing movie reviews, and he quickly read up on the existing film bibliography.[12] In the process he would soon become the first-ever regular film critic in Colombia, though not a particularly remarkable or original one. While he did immediately recognize the historic import of Truffaut's *The 400 Blows*, he also predicted imminent failure for the new widescreen medium. On the other hand, his independent judgments sometimes aroused the wrath of movie-theater managers, who would put in angry telephone calls in order to register their displeasure over a particular García Márquez review.[13]

García Márquez's almost innocent ability to scandalize certain people became notably manifest in the aftermath of his talks with a sailor named Luis Alejandro Velasco, the sole survivor out of a group of eight castaways from a Colombian navy destroyer that, en route from Mobile, Alabama, had hit unusually rough waters. Velasco was to spend ten days aboard a raft, rowing south, and to García Márquez he now recounted such memorable highlights as the passing airplanes that had ignored him, the captured seagull that he had attempted to devour, the recurrent threats and terror from encircling sharks (one of which actually ate up an oar), the eerie nocturnal sounds of sea fauna, and his own final swim to safety when at last glimpsing the Colombian north shore (*OP*, 3:566–652).

Velasco himself was, García Márquez notes, a "born storyteller," and his tale was intrinsically exciting. Its serialization in *El Espectador* caused something of a sensation, not least because it became evident that the ship's journey had been characterized by shady dealings—overweight contraband, and life rafts unequipped with food or water. (In the wake of Gabo's fame, the account appeared in book form in 1970, under the title *Relato de un náufrago* [*The Story of a Shipwrecked Sailor*].) Already *El Espectador* had been experiencing various sorts of direct harassment from the Rojas Pinilla dictatorship, and the Velasco stories now elicited threats of real government reprisals. With a view to getting García Márquez temporarily out of trouble, the editors sent him to Geneva to cover the "Big Four" conference, and thence to Rome in case Pope Pius XII were to die from one of his notoriously prolonged hiccup spells. When this latter scoop did not materialize García Márquez enrolled for a few weeks at that city's Centro Sperimentale di Cinema, but found the curriculum too academic and theoretical for his needs. He also did some traveling in Poland and Hungary. Little did he suspect that he would be staying in Europe for more than two years, through December 1957.

By mid-1955 García Márquez was arguably the most renowned newspaperman in Colombia, and his time served overseas—it has been said—would mercifully rescue him from the trap of local journalistic fame.[14] As European correspondent for *El Espectador* he would now earn a decent three hundred dollars a month and perform creditably at his new and more difficult set of tasks. Working pretty much alone, and lacking that vast organizational apparatus of the U.S. news agencies, he mostly cribbed from other reports and added his own uniquely personal, humorous, "tropical" touches thereto.[15] His creative side would become especially evident in a lengthy series of articles dealing with two major scandals and trials—one on some French government leaks, another on a sordid and labyrinthine Italian murder case—in which he applied his best techniques of novelistic suspense, suddenly breaking off the series just as the respective solutions were at hand (*OP*, 4:174–236 and 305–98).

García Márquez moved to Paris in January 1956, there finding out to his chagrin that *El Espectador* had been shut down by Rojas Pinilla. A successor daily under the name *El Independiente* was to be launched in February, with

Gabo still on the payroll—only to suffer the same fate exactly two months later. At this point García Márquez decided to pocket the money that *El Espectador* had sent him for return fare, and stay on in Paris to write full-time instead. In a hotel garret on Rue de Cujas (a typical Latin Quarter street) he started work on what would be *In Evil Hour*. However, a subplot took on a life of its own to become *No One Writes to the Colonel*, completed after eleven drafts in January 1957.

That bittersweet novella of day-to-day hunger was based in part on the author's experiences of the moment. Waiting in vain for the reopening of *El Espectador*, and having only meager success in rounding up free-lance assignments, García Márquez survived for a protracted spell on returned bottle deposits and on the good graces of his landlady, who let him accumulate several months' back rent. During these months García Márquez lost so much weight that, commenting on a photo of his which he had sent home, his mother remarked, "Poor Gabito. He looks like a skeleton."[16] It was also the initial stages of the French war in Algeria, and the Parisian police, mistaking the scruffy Colombian for a suspicious Arab, would sometimes harass him on the streets.[17] (*OG*, 96; *FG*, 65). He also seems to have worked briefly for the Algerian National Liberation Front and even spent an unspecified time in jail. The details, however, remain obscure.

Meanwhile, in August 1956 Plinio Apuleyo Mendoza,[18] an old friend from law school days in Bogotá, had landed an editorial post at *Élite*, a slick illustrated weekly in Caracas belonging to the Capriles chain (the Hearsts of Venezuela). It was thanks to Mendoza that, through March 1957, Gabo could do some free-lancing for that magazine, though most of the dozen or so hastily written pieces from those months are impersonal and indistinctive, having been targeted for an unfamiliar audience.[19] Later, in the summer of 1957 he and Mendoza (who had just resigned his job at *Élite*) would travel together in East Germany, Czechoslovakia, and the Soviet Union. In the wake of that journey García Márquez wrote some subtly balanced accounts of daily life in the "East-Bloc" countries; it was only as an end result of the Khrushchev "thaw," however, that he was finally able to find a home for them two years hence in *Cromos*, a Bogotá glossy.

November found García Márquez in London hoping to work on his English, but after a month of crafting short stories and shivering in a hotel room he received in the mail a plane ticket to Caracas and a note from Mendoza informing him that *Momento*, yet another slick magazine where he had just been appointed executive editor, was asking García Márquez to join their writing staff. The poverty-stricken novelist actually hesitated before accepting the surprise invitation. Gabo's difficult and uncertain trial years on the Old Continent, with their many ups and downs, and the manuscript of one beautifully succinct novella to show for his troubles, were now apparently over.

It was Christmas Eve when he arrived in Caracas, and with Plinio Mendoza's help he soon found a *pensión* room in San Bernardino, a peaceful residential district located near the center of town. García Márquez's Venezuelan phase could not have been better timed. The hated dictatorship of General Marcos Pérez Jiménez was teetering in what would turn out to be its final weeks, and the country was rife with aborted uprisings, clandestine leaflets, and speeches by courageous clerics, as well as frequent night curfews, news blackouts on radio and television, outrages by the security forces, and *pronunciamientos* by General Pérez Jiménez himself. At one point the offices of *Momento* were actually raided by military police who arrested everybody in sight, García Márquez being spared only because he chanced to be out at the time of the lightning sweep.

Following a series of barracks revolts the dictator finally gave up and, on 21 January, fled for the United States, his suitcases typically stuffed with millions of U.S. dollars. García Márquez now witnessed that mixture of mass jubilation and official caution that characterizes the end of tyrannical regimes, an experience to be captured by him almost twenty years hence in *The Autumn of the Patriarch*. During the subsequent euphoria of the democratic transition he published a few retrospective articles about certain memorable struggles against the dictatorship, such as the thousands of antigovernment leaflets that, at a clash between some women demonstrators and a truncheon-wielding policeman, rained down on them suddenly from the tower of the metropolitan cathedral (*OP*, 3:555–64).

In March the Colombian wanderer made an unexpected visit to Barranquilla and married his lifelong sweetheart Mercedes Barcha, a striking beauty of Egyptian origin whom he'd first proposed to when she was age thirteen. Because of her exotic appearance, his friends used to call her "the sacred crocodile," the nickname by which he would dedicate the volume *Big Mama's Funeral* to her. His well-earned measure of stability, however, was quickly shattered two months later by a crisis within the ranks of *Momento*. On 13 May, in what would become a notorious episode, Venezuelan students stoned and spat upon U.S. Vice-President Richard Nixon; in response the editor-in-chief of the magazine composed an editorial condemning the action, and supporting the United States as "a friendly nation with which we are naturally linked." Taking advantage of a brief absence on the part of their boss,

Mendoza and García Márquez affixed the man's initials and ran it as an individual's opinion piece rather than as the magazine's official position. A dispute ensued; the two friends resigned, and García Márquez eventually took a managing-editing job at a gossipy scandal sheet called *Venezuela Gráfica*, a straitjacket that allowed for little free writing time.[20]

Within just months, right-wing dictatorships had tumbled in both Colombia and Venezuela. The ignominious flight of Cuban tyrant Fulgencio Batista on 1 January 1959 and the triumph of Fidel Castro's guerrillas would awaken still greater expectations in a García Márquez caught up in the daily grind and elaborate deceptions of the sensationalist press. Soon thereafter García Márquez was one of several journalists invited by the revolutionary government to witness Castro's "Operation Truth," a media campaign aimed at countering the anti-leftist bias of the U.S. news agencies. At the trial of Batista henchman Jesús Sosa Blanco, García Márquez heard a catalog of bloody horrors that would further arouse in him the desire to write a novel about Latin dictatorship.

Among the ideas being vaguely entertained by García Márquez at the time was that of returning to Barranquilla and starting a film school there. The Cuban government, however, had decided to launch its own news agency, Prensa Latina, under the direction of an Argentine expatriate named Jorge Massetti. At the behest of Plinio Mendoza, the novelist and his pregnant wife left for Bogotá in May, where the two old friends had the job of mounting a Colombian branch of Prensa Latina. They built from ground zero, organizing shifts, watching teletypes, and sending two daily reports to Havana. Meanwhile, baby Rodrigo was born on 24 August and later baptized by none other than Camilo Torres. In retrospect, 1959 was a very revolutionary year for García Márquez.

Jorge Massetti stopped by in Bogotá in 1960 and observed that Prensa Latina needed able writers at other posts. Later that year García Márquez spent six months in Havana, and in early 1961 he started work as one of two staffers at the agency's New York City branch office. Occasional threatening phone calls came from émigré right-wing Cubans who would remind the author of his wife and child; he kept an iron rod by his desk (*OG*, 99; *FG*, 70). On one occasion, during the drive back to his Queens apartment he actually saw a car moving alongside his—with a gun pointed directly at him. Among his major assignments as a U.S. correspondent was to cover President Kennedy's 13 March press conference on the newly founded Alliance for Progress. In mid-year, however, there arose in Cuba the "Sectarianism" crisis whereby the pre-Castro, old Stalinist party types had attempted to maneuver themselves into power, elbowing out Massetti along the way. In a gesture of solidarity with Massetti, García Márquez resigned from his Prensa Latina job.

Finding himself once again unemployed, he, Mercedes, and Rodrigo now embarked on a long Greyhound bus trip that included the American South, García Márquez always having wanted to see from up close the hot, backward, dusty towns only recently immortalized by Faulkner. The family would get a direct taste of Faulkner's world when on several instances, being perceived as Mexicans, they were turned down for hotel rooms. Mexico, ironically, was their destination. With $100 in his pocket and another $120 sent by Plinio Mendoza to the Colombian consulate in New Orleans, Gabo's journey would take him to Mexico City, where he hoped to write film scripts.

Unable at first to secure work in movies, he applied for a job as editor-in-chief of two fluffy periodicals, *Sucesos* (Events) and *La Familia*, recently bought up by Gustavo Alatriste, a well-known media entrepreneur (and producer, among other things, of some of Luis Buñuel's best Mexican films). García Márquez likes to recall how at that time the soles of his own shoes were loose and floppy, and for the job interview, scheduled at a bar, he arrived in advance so as to sit with his legs covered up (*OG*, 100; FG, 70). He did get the position, and for two years he handled everything from layout to warmed-over fillers (the periodicals' chief fare).

In the fall of 1963 García Márquez resigned his job at the glossies to begin work at the Mexico City branch of J. Walter Thompson, where he lasted a few months before moving on to the Stanton, Pritchard, and Wood advertising agency, itself a branch of McCann-Erickson. At about this time he finally began fulfilling his dream of writing film scripts. For the next two years he would write over a dozen of them (some in collaboration with a talented young novelist named Carlos Fuentes), mostly potboiler melodramas filled with duels and shoot-outs and unrequited love.[21]

García Márquez would later look back at most of this work in the moving-pictures medium as unsalvageable. "Landing" after more than a half-decade of uprootedness and floating, García Márquez now began with Mexico City a close relationship almost as constant as that with his native Colombia. Behind him there was some solid if unrecognized literary achievement. During his time with *El Espectador* in Bogotá he had started work on the stories that would make up *Big Mama's Funeral*, crafting them with utmost care over the next five years in Europe and Venezuela, little suspecting that those bittersweet miniatures would one day become anthology and classroom favorites. And in a Paris garret he had conceived and then spent a year giving verbal life to the trim and tragicomical *No One Writes to the Colonel*. First appearing in Colombian newspapers and small journals, neither of these compact narratives would see book form until 1962. Back in Paris he had also begun the troublesome novel that would bear the title *In Evil Hour*. Ironically, it was this flawed work that, still in manuscript, won the 1962 Esso Prize in Colombia, then failing to achieve anything like acceptable print format until 1966. The prize money did help pay the maternity-ward bill for second son Gonzalo, born on 16 April 1962.

Following completion of *In Evil Hour*, García Márquez drifted into a serious case of writer's block. Barring a found manuscript that will prove things otherwise, one can safely state that from 1961 through 1964 García Márquez was unable to come up with a single new, strictly "literary" piece. Biographer Saldívar has given us the day-to-day details and probable causes—financial pressures, demands from his job as well as film work, and personal dissatisfaction with the formal features of his writing thus far—of the author's creative slump, and future scholars will surely flesh out this history.[22] Whatever the reasons, García Márquez must have meant it when around this time he used to say to his friend, the Colombian poet and business executive Álvaro Mutis, "I'll never write again."[23]

What finally drew García Márquez out of his slumbers is one of the most dramatic instances ever reported of the sheer power of inspiration. As García Márquez recalls it, he and the family were riding in their white Opel along the Mexico City–Acapulco highway, when all of a sudden he found he could imagine every last word of the book he had been trying to get out of him since 1942. "It was so ripe in me that I could have dictated the first chapter, word by word, to a typist."[24] He did a fast U-turn and asked Mercedes to handle the family finances for the next six months while he wrote this novel. And back in his room ("the Cave of the Mafia," as it came to be called) write he did, obsessively, eight hours a day, the book taking on a life of its own as the months rushed by, the author looking glum on the afternoon when he had had to kill off Colonel Buendía, and meanwhile Mercedes secretly pawning the television set, the radio, a wall clock, and an eggbeater, and all manner of late payments in rent and credit from the butcher, and emergency loans and emotional support coming from various friends, including a Catalan couple next door to whom the book, entitled *Cien años de soledad*, was finally dedicated.[25]

Eighteen months and a ten thousand dollar debt later there were thirteen hundred pages of typescript, plus a variety of working diagrams and sketches which the author promptly destroyed.[26] Earlier in the year Editorial Sudamericana in Argentina had chanced to write García Márquez about the possibility of reprinting his former work, and they agreed to look at his novel-in-progress instead. As he and Mercedes were readying the manuscript for the mails she worried to herself (she would later confess), "And what if, after all this, it's a bad novel?" (OG, 107; FG, 75). Further misadventures took place: as the couple were walking toward the post office the box holding the typescript fell open and some pages started blowing all over the street. And arriving at the stamp window they lacked the money for the full postage, and so mailed out only half the novel, García Márquez rounding up the balance for the second half later in the day.

Having expected good reviews but modest sales—the lot of his previous books—García Márquez was caught off guard by the lightning success. In the initial few months of bestsellerdom and limelight he found himself hotly pursued by reporters seeking interviews, by a publisher offering him a house on Majorca in exchange for his next novel (supposedly to be composed there), by women sending photos of themselves in exchange for his personal mail, and more. Over the next two years the fame would spread worldwide, with major prizes for the book in France and Italy and good sales in the United States.

Soon finding it impossible to work under such conditions, in October 1967 García Márquez and his family packed off to Barcelona with a view to living incognito, putting an end to the phone calls, and writing in peace. A roving García Márquez had once shunned Franco's Spain out of loyalty to exiled Republican friends, but in the late 1960s Barcelona was becoming a center of cultural and political opposition to the regime, and there was also a fair share of expatriate Latin American writers, among them the Peruvian Vargas Llosa, who rapidly became a friend and advocate of the now-celebrated Colombian (until their personal and ideological rift in 1975). In addition, García Márquez wished to observe a right-wing tyranny in its waning days, as part of his research for a novel about Latin dictatorship.

The original plan was to spend maybe a year on the book; it grew into a seven-year project. He also found the puritanical austerity of Franco's Spain very much at variance with the flamboyant excess, the amoral eroticism, and tropical informality that had always characterized those Caribbean tyrannies of which he was now creating a historical-geographical composite. Halfway through the long writing process García Márquez and his family took off on a full year's leave, exploring the Caribbean country by country, so that in his mind the novelist might "bring back the fragrance of guava." They returned to Barcelona; his imaginary despot's life crept to its terminal lonesome gasps; and in 1975 (coincidentally the year in which Generalissimo Franco was to die) the long-awaited *The Autumn of the Patriarch* appeared and quickly sold a half-million copies, though its dense and difficult prose would put off many hopeful readers, who had been expecting a return trip to Macondo. With the other book he had always wanted to write now written, García Márquez purchased a house in Pedregal San Angel, a suburb of Mexico City, where, with his wife and visiting sons, he would continue to spend most of his writing year.

In the interim García Márquez had begun using his global fame as an instrument of support for various left-wing causes, or for "quiet diplomacy" between warring parties. When in 1972 he received the prestigious Rómulo Gallegos Prize in Venezuela, at the ceremony he publicly donated the entire sum to the parliamentary Movimiento al Socialismo (MAS), and his $10,000 Neustadt Prize (1972) he gave away to the Committee in Solidarity with Political Prisoners. García Márquez was active in the Bertrand Russell Tribunal hearings on South American dictatorships, and he participated in various ways in the campaign of President Omar Torrijos of Panama to have the legendary canal and the adjoining areas placed under Panamanian sovereignty.

With his pen and contacts García Márquez aided the Sandinista guerrillas in the struggle against the fifty-year-old Somoza tyranny, and between their victory in 1979 and their defeat at the polls in 1990 he made every possible effort to defend them against the vicious U.S. media-cum-military onslaught that followed. On occasion he used his influence with Fidel Castro to help secure the release of a Cuban political prisoner, and at different moments has served as an intermediary between the Colombian government and certain guerrilla factions.

Early in 1981, amid a great deal of international fanfare, the seemingly simple, deceptively brief novel *Chronicle of a Death Foretold* appeared, its two million copies issued in simultaneous editions by Colombian, Spanish, Argentine, and Mexican publishing houses. At the time García Márquez was in his native land and was considering settling down there once again. On 26 March, however, he returned to Mexico, where he requested political asylum (a fairly traditional Latin American procedure). Back in Bogotá the Liberal government of Julio César Turbay Ayala ridiculed the move and dismissed it as mere publicity-mongering for García Márquez's new book. In the novelist's defense it should be said that Colombia, with its permanent state of siege still in effect, had been rife with rumors of plans for large-scale repression and of lists of a thousand leftist intellectuals marked for arrest, among them García Márquez. In addition, certain M-19 guerrillas had "confessed" that García

Márquez was one of their prime sources of funding, and his outspoken views and his Cuban ties would not have been of help should an extreme situation have arisen. Surely the example of the Pinochet coup, which had destroyed Chilean democracy and led to the detention, torture, and death of many left-wing artists—including Pablo Neruda (whose house was invaded and ransacked by army troops, and who was made to lie face-down at gunpoint for some days, only to die of cancer a week later)—must not have been far from García Márquez's mind.

Even after world sales of *One Hundred Years of Solitude* had freed him from financial want, García Márquez never was to abandon his journalistic calling. Now, however, he could allow himself the luxury of "advocacy" journalism. Whether reporting on the final struggles of President Allende in Chile, the liberation of Angola from Portuguese rule, the situation in postwar Vietnam, the actions of the Sandinistas in Nicaragua, or the literary intellect of French socialist François Mitterrand, García Márquez would bring narrative insight, eloquent prose, and Caribbean wit to matters close to him, and moreover could state his position without fear of being blackballed or sacked. One of the principal venues for these articles was *Alternativa*, a magazine he helped found and fund in Bogotá in 1974. Starting out as a biweekly, it shifted to weekly format within a year, and despite such pressures as a mysterious bomb that damaged its offices in 1975, and constant shortages of cash, it enjoyed more or less continuous publication until it was forced to fold in 1980. An inability to reach sufficiently sizable circulation, combined with a decision not to include advertising, finally rendered the project economically unviable.[27]

In 1980 García Márquez initiated a ritual of repairing to his house in Cuernavaca on Saturdays and composing a weekly column. Syndicated in a couple of dozen Hispanic newspapers and magazines, the pieces dealt with subjects ranging from Bach's cello suites to the "disappearances" of writers under the murderous and stupid Argentine military regime. These little essays were to provide some of the liveliest, wisest, most distinctly personal magazine reading in Spanish for three consecutive years. In addition, by 1982 he had started preliminary work on what he was describing as a love story; an unexpected second windfall, however, was once again radically to change his life and temporarily cut into his creative routines.

In the decade following publication of *One Hundred Years of Solitude*, García Márquez had been the recipient of a long list of international honors, including an honorary doctorate at Columbia University in 1971 (where he refused to wear a necktie) and a medal of the French Legion of Honor from French socialist François Mitterrand, whose 1981 presidential inauguration García Márquez attended (along with Carlos Fuentes, Augusto Roa Bastos and Julio Cortázar). The 1982 Nobel Prize, however, seemed to have come out of the blue. Until then it had been more or less assumed that, for the next round of Latin Americans, the literary Nobel would "naturally" go to Octavio Paz, the avant-garde poet, oracular essayist, and neoconservative elder cultural statesman of Mexico. At age fifty-four, García Márquez now found himself the youngest such laureate since Albert Camus.

He rose to the occasion. When García Márquez and several dozen friends departed Bogotá for Sweden they were bade farewell by President Belisario Betancur himself, who jubilantly declared, "All of Colombia will be keeping Gabo company!" In addition, the entourage included sixty performers from six different Colombian dance and music ensembles who would bring a full week of tropical festivities to the chiaroscuros of Stockholm in the fall.[28] For the ceremonies García Márquez wore not a European coat and tie but the traditional white linen *liqui-liqui* suit of the continental Caribbean.[29] And for the Nobel Lecture he overcame his timidity about public speaking and delivered a stirring evocation of the special beauties and political tragedies of Latin America.[30] There were those who expressed displeasure at the manifestly ideological flavor of the speech, but in all it was the most festive such ceremony in nearly a century. As the coordinator of the events remarked to some friends of García Márquez, "Never in all my years with the Nobel organization have I seen the Swedes in so vibrant a mood."[31]

The originally stated aim of García Márquez was to utilize the prize money to help launch a new newspaper in Colombia, under the name *El Otro* (The Other One).[32] However, what with financial difficulties and the obstacles posed merely by the existence of the established press, his worthy project never came to fruition. The will and popularity of a great novelist are not in themselves enough to sustain so ambitious a project as a mass circulation daily.

The aftermath of the Nobel made for months of added obligations, and García Márquez was unable to resume the writing of his novel-in-progress until late in 1983. Taking a sabbatical from his weekly columns from February to September 1984, he rented an apartment in Cartagena—where his parents were now living—and worked on the book eight hours a day, absorbing the old city environment in the afternoons the better to depict it in his narrative. Within a year he returned to his house in Mexico City and there became a convert to the computer, marveling at the speed with which the word processor allowed him to compose the remainder of the novel. In 1985, wearing the three floppy disks around his neck, he flew to Barcelona and delivered the "manuscript" to Carmen Balcells, his literary agent. Printers were soon put on rush order—the job was done in two weeks—and the binders were instructed to produce a physical volume that would endure rather than disintegrate on first reading. And on 5 December 1985 a million copies of *Love in the Time of Cholera* were officially issued in the four most populous Spanish-speaking countries.[33] At a formal gathering in Bogotá, former president Alfonso López Michelsen presented the Colombian edition of the novel with an eloquent and learned speech tracing the book's artistic kinships with Proust.

From the mid-1980s on, García Márquez's life pattern is one of continued growth as a man of words and imagination, a verbal master branching out into ever-new narrative topics and materials. The background to his subsequent works we shall leave for later chapters, for now simply mentioning that he went on to compose *The General in His Labyrinth* (1989), a novel about the final months of liberator Simón Bolívar; *Doce cuentos peregrinos* (1992; *Strange Pilgrims*), a dozen short stories that capture the divers experiences of Latin Americans visiting or stationed in old Europe; *Of Love and Other Demons* (1994), a spare, luminously beautiful historical fiction set in Cartagena circa 1780 and focused on such sensitive issues as slavery, Afro-Hispanic culture, Catholic church politics, the colonial elite, and an improbably pure yet intense romantic bond; and *Memories of My Melancholy Whores* (2004), a quasi-novella about a cultured, yet emotionally crippled, nonagenarian scribbler's latter-day awakening to the joys and possibilities of true love.

In addition, faced with his country's unending cycle of narco-violence, García Márquez produced *News of a Kidnapping* (1996), a book-length work of investigative journalism dealing with a select group of ten high-profile victims of Colombia's brutal and nightmarish drug wars. And in the wake of his own near-fatal illness (see below), the grand old man gave to his devoted fans an intimate account of his childhood, adolescence, and literary apprenticeship in *Vivir para contarla* (2002; *Living to Tell the Tale*), Gabo's only in-depth memoir to date.

During his post-Nobel years the author moved temporarily into serious creative work for theater and cinema. In the mid-1980s he did the scripts for a set of six films entitled *Amores difíciles* (rendered into English as *Dangerous Loves*), produced under the auspices of Spanish National Television. Five veteran Latin American cinéastes and one Spaniard were assigned the respective jobs of directing each movie. The cycle, issued in 1989, screened largely at art houses and museums. Some of the films—notably *Milagro en Roma* (which

later in turn provided the basis for García Márquez's short story "La santa")—
soon became classics in their own right. Another, *The Summer of Miss Forbes*
(also a subsequent story by that name), featured in the chief role the renowned German actress Hannah Schygulla. The title of the series especially
fits the film *Yo soy la que buscas* (*I'm the One You're Looking For*), a disquieting
account of a rape victim who obsessively seeks out the perpetrator and, in
the process, falls in love with him.

In 1987 Gabo penned his only known play, *Diatriba de amor contra un hombre sentado* (*A Diatribe of Love against a Seated Man*—still not translated). The
format is unusual: the work in its entirety consists of a passionate, hour-long
soliloquy declaimed by Graciela, a Caribbean housewife (country not specified), in which she raves at her mute, newspaper-reading spouse (actually a
mannequin) and reminisces about different moments in their quarter century
of marriage. Come the end, she applies a match and sets fire to her distracted
husband's newspaper. The piece, written for Argentine actress Graciela Duf-
fau, had an initial premier in Havana in 1988 and its world début later in
Buenos Aires, in 1994. While resembling such experiments in monologue as
Strindberg's *The Stronger* and Cocteau's *La voix humaine*, the piece differs from
those European works in its author's signature trait of irreverent and outrageous humor, studded as it is with one-line jokes.

Meanwhile, when in his sixties, Gabo's role as a public figure took on
more of a professional and less "political" cast. Ever being sought out for
the support of worthy causes, García Márquez's concrete actions and deci-
sions would carry greater weight, coming as they did from a Nobel laureate.
Hence, in 1986, with Argentine filmmaker Fernando Birri, he helped found,
near Havana, the Escuela Internacional de Cine y Televisión. Castro's Cuba,
of course, could boast a remarkably advanced, high-quality movie industry,
and the school benefited from access to that technical infrastructure and its
trained personnel. The center has garnered considerable world prestige,
drawing visits from such noted figures as U.S. filmmakers Stephen Spielberg
and Francis Ford Coppola.

In addition, among García Márquez's self-appointed missions as a cultural
figure is the task of better nurturing Latin American journalists, in particular
at the Fundación para un Nuevo Periodismo ("Periodismo" = Journalism).
Co-founded by Gabo in 1993, the foundation is supported in part by UNESCO
and by the Inter-American Development Bank. In yet another instance of
his print-media ventures, Gabo in 1999 used his own money to purchase the
Colombian edition of the prestigious Spanish newsweekly *Cambio* (Change),
for which he then went on to contribute some on-site, nuts-and-bolts report-

ing. The author's broader role in such journalistic enterprises, however, is advisory; his strengths and interests have never been of the administrative sort, and it goes without saying that any everyday office and personnel chores would steer him away from his commitments as a writer.

Since his sudden wealth and fame in 1967, García Márquez has taken residence in a number of world capitals, with homes in Barcelona, Paris, and Mexico City. In the early 1990s, though, he commissioned an entire sandstone-colored house with a large terrace, to be designed and built for himself and his family, from the ground up, in Cartagena. It was the definitive return to his *costeño* roots as he moved into, and once again made himself part of, that city's daily life, going for afternoon strolls and chatting with ordinary folk who approached him out on the street.

Old age and its bodily infirmities gave García Márquez a serious jolt in 1999, when he was diagnosed with lymphatic cancer. Fortunately, high-end treatments in both Bogotá and Los Angeles (where, thanks to President Bill Clinton's having lifted the travel ban on him, the novelist could now go with relative ease) saved the author's life, and he has since been in remission. Having faced the abyss, he felt spurred by the experience to plunge into the writing of his volume of memoirs, *Living to Tell the Tale*.

The following year, however, Gabo's illness generated yet another, slightly bizarre literary offshoot. A purported farewell to this Earth, in which the author invoked the Almighty and talked of being a rag doll, began to appear under García Márquez's byline, in several languages, all over the Internet. Entitled "The Puppet," it listed the things Gabo would supposedly do had he more time remaining. (A typical instance: "I would enjoy a good chocolate ice cream.")

Only after millions worldwide had read the swooning adieu did García Márquez repudiate the valedictory as an utter hoax, as something so "cursi" ("corny," "pretentious") he could never have produced it. Subsequent investigations revealed what had actually happened: The piece, it seems, was originally penned by a Mexican ventriloquist, a "speech" to be pronounced at public performances by his faithful puppet. A Peruvian journalist then got hold of the text, affixed to it the novelist's name, and went on to disseminate the lament accordingly. Such are the unforeseen hazards of fame in this age of instant, personalized global telecommunications.

In the meantime the accolades for García Márquez and his achievements continued to accumulate. An absolute high point was on 6 March 2007, when an international celebration was held at Aracataca on occasion of the author's eightieth birthday. In his later decades he also enjoyed an unusually close friendship with Cuba's Fidel Castro. Gabito's old age, however, has been darkened by ongoing memory loss, a painful process briefly evoked in Gerald Martin's monumental biography of the novelist.[34]

His international stature notwithstanding, García Márquez, as we've seen, is a man strongly attached to the land of his youth. And indeed his fiction since *The Autumn of the Patriarch* would become even more local in its preoccupations and focus. Remaining steadfastly loyal to those individuals who gave him emotional and financial sustenance when he most needed them, by the same token he has resisted the shallow allure and temptations of media fame and glitter. The only true friends García Márquez actually claims are those predating *One Hundred Years of Solitude*, and it is they and his closely knit family who shield him from the many solicitors and fortune-seekers that regularly descend upon him at public functions or come knocking at his door. Though a sweet and sociable man who fundamentally takes pleasure in being with other people, were he to attend to even half the requests and invitations that come his way (be they genuine or opportunistic) he would find himself with no time left for his top priorities: writing, family, and friends.

FOUR

The Man & His Politics

Garcia Marquez's mornings have been traditionally reserved exclusively for writing. Awake at six o'clock, he sips a cup of coffee and reads the newspaper in bed. He then puts on his writing gear (blue one-piece coveralls with a front zipper), and if in Mexico City he heads for the specially made bungalow he has in his backyard. There, amid heating to offset the mountain chill, and the background strains of one of his several thousand classical recordings, he works until one or two o'clock, after which he has lunch with family and other intimates, to whom he might dedicate the rest of the day. Anyone wishing to see the man must go through an obstacle course consisting of old friends, the housekeeper, his sons, and his wife and meet with the successive approval of each.

Owing to his hands-on experience in journalism, García Márquez is of all the great living authors the one who is closest to everyday reality. No doubt the trade taught him to write clearly, in a prose style accessible to the general reader. When asked about the influence of the journalist on the novelist, however, García Márquez tends to dwell not so much on clear prose as on the practice of writing regularly with discipline, and also on the custom of including those little details that help make a stretch of prose convincing—much as he did in *One Hundred Years* with Father Nicanor Reyna's cup of hot chocolate or with Mauricio Babilonia's yellow butterflies.

To an unusual degree, García Márquez is the poet of plebeian and street life. It is the world that he claims to know best and to deliberately have cultivated, and in truth few novelists can match the understanding, eloquence, and dignity he brings to his depictions of smugglers, street performers, prostitutes, cockfight gatherings, and other extra-official "people's" subjects (not to mention workers' strikes and political uprisings). By the same token García Márquez has all his life written with passion and commitment about popular culture—indeed its vindication has long been a kind of personal mission with him. In his twenties he wrote articles in praise of comic strips and suggested that they may constitute a legitimate literary genre (this some decades before "graphic novels" became an accepted term). Along similar lines he has often eulogized such Afro-Hispanic musical forms as the guaracha, the mambo, and the bolero. All these pop-cultural phenomena he recurrently celebrates at the expense of the frock-coat and top-hat set, the solemn academicians and stuffy priests who look down upon African-based music, the upper-class ladies who on occasion even condemn it as the work of Satan himself.

Reading the journalism of the young García Márquez one encounters a twenty-year-old whose attitudes, temperament, and worldview are fully formed and not terribly different from those of the man in his sixties and seventies. His youthful columns already convey his own distinctive sense of humor, the irreverence and dreamy charm that sees a funny side to the most hallowed of social customs (official banquets, beauty contests) or that seeks out the many colorful oddities to be noted in this world, such as a Texan named Robertson who keeps a dromedary in his chicken coop, or a Chinese man whom the young reporter claims to have seen sitting under a mango tree reading the Bible, or a little boy who has written Santa Claus asking for three hundred tricycles (*OP*, 1:474, 736, and 497). On the other hand, refreshingly absent from García Márquez's early articles is the facile male chauvinism that was typical of the Caribbean humor of that time; not accidentally, much of García Márquez's fiction would both satirize machismo and give special prominence to women.

Coming from a nation that is the most solemn in Latin America, one where Bogotá academicians and grammarians have traditionally cast a long shadow over culture, García Márquez early on would define himself as antiacademic, antiestablishment, and antisolemn. Closely bound up with his cultural stance is his thoughtful and subtle political leftism. In the same way that his writing career initially took shape in conscious opposition to the Colombian literary status quo, García Márquez's socialist and anti-imperialist views are in principled opposition to the global status quo dominated by the United States (what Henry Luce of Time-Life celebrated as "the American Century").

Already in his youthful columns García Márquez used to get in his digs at Western anticommunist obsessions—the nationalistic right-wing products of Hollywood hacks, or the subliminal ideology of many an innocent-looking American comic strip. Of course it was the time of *la Violencia* in Colombia, when official censorship was further compounded by the more complex dynamic of self-censorship, and as with most writers a typical García Márquez ruse was to ridicule right-wing forces in *other* countries. Or he would cloak his politics in human-interest accounts, notably the three eloquent reports published in December 1954 on Colombia's Korean War veterans, where he tells of the misery and poverty of many of the returnees, the ways in which they were misled and defrauded as to benefits, the public image that exists of their being mentally deranged, and the story of the war hero who pawned off his medals (*OP*, 2:402–16). The articles are models of scrupulous, factual presentation conveying a sharp political message.

García Márquez's leftism and his whimsical humor are both a lively force in his journalism, though completely integrated within his literary style and worldview, much as they later evolve as part of his novelistic practice. There were also commitments of an activist kind. Beginning with his *El Heraldo* days in Barranquilla, García Márquez had some sort of temporary affiliation with the Communist party of Colombia, paying monthly dues and even having "regular personal encounters" with its chief, who in Bogotá would chance to live a few blocks down the street from the author.[1] During the late 1950s García Márquez actually was to bend his narrative technique to adjust to party demands for greater "realism" in the arts, and his leftist commitments become all the more clear in his work as a Prensa Latina staffer from 1960 to mid-1961.

The exact nature of García Márquez's youthful party ties has remained obscure, and of course it would be impolite of any interviewer to ask. Nevertheless, García Márquez has always been an independent leftist, a Marxist of his own kind, one who maintains a typically Latin American respect for Soviet achievements, while rejecting the defects and privately spurning the Muscovite model itself. (In this regard his stance is not unique but in fact typical for Latin American intellectuals, most of whom lean decidedly left.) This attitude comes through in his late 1950s articles on Communist Eastern Europe, fresh, humane, and astute in their observations.[2] As all journalists ritually do, he remarks on the false glitter of West Berlin and its essential function as an "immense agency for capitalist propaganda," while at the same time he notes the unforgettably sad ambience of East Germany (*VPS*, 25 and 42). García Márquez's sense of history enters into play, however, when he reflects that East Germany's dour leaders have slavishly followed Soviet experiences without taking their local realities into account, and further reminds readers that the better German Communists had been eliminated by the ancien régime of Hitler, the survivors in turn having been eliminated by the current ruling group (*VPS*, 47.)

Coming as he does from one of the most wretched and oppressed regions on earth, García Márquez cannot resist recalling that in all of Eastern Europe and the USSR he saw just one beggar (*VPS*, 89). Similarly he states, "With the same good faith with which we believe the unfavorable things, one must also believe that there is neither hunger nor unemployment in the Soviet Union" (*VPS*, 176). He is nonetheless struck by the extent to which an industrial superpower is still very much a rustic nation vaguely suggestive to him of the rural villages of his own native land. Grown adults come in their pajamas to meet the train and wave it goodbye, and the new high rises in Moscow, with their pastry-architecture styles, are "the same little houses of Ukrainian small towns expanded to heroic dimensions" (*VPS*, 133). He sees the tragic side to the best and worst of that vast country: "There is nothing in the Soviet Union that was not the work of Stalin" (*VPS*, 156). And most Kremlinologists would have agreed that, as García Márquez notes, the astounding advances of the Soviets in heavy industry have also been paid for in decades of ungainly garments and bad shoes.

There are some notable foreshadowings of García Márquez's fictional material in his East European reports, striking instances of the novelist being influenced and inspired over time by the journalist. He dwells on the conservative, "convent-like" atmosphere of the Polish city of Krakow, a "Catholic bulwark" (*VPS*, 104); later, in *One Hundred Years of Solitude*, the hapless daughter of stuffy, conservative, self-righteous Fernanda del Carpio will eventually end up in a convent in Krakow. And just as the Buendías in their tropical isolation will discover ice and invent sherbet on their own, the Soviets, an awed García Márquez observes, really do reinvent modern appliances such as the refrigerator (VPS, 175). At the time of García Márquez's travels it is the relatively benign, more hopeful era of Khrushchev, and he remarks on how many Soviet citizens had taken to doubting the existence of Stalin, who used to address the crowds twice a year from the balcony (*VPS*, 155); the patriarch of García Márquez's novel will similarly evolve into a remote and shadowy figure whose existence becomes doubtful, and he will put in an appearance on the palace balcony exactly once in his life.

In the end García Márquez's reportorial view of Eastern Europe is not so much Marxist or leftist as that of a knowledgeable and sensitive Latin American. Unlike observers from the liberal, industrialized West, who then routinely compared Soviet-bloc societies to a far more fortunate United States, García Márquez instead sees in the other Europe the economic progress and the absence of mass poverty, as well as the cultural residues from a recent feudal and rural past. Having experienced, and even taken his lumps from, "Free World" Latin American dictatorships, he naturally would not be given to pious and utopian laments about the absence of constitutional liberties in an Eastern Europe never known for such benign traditions. The articles show his best qualities as a writer; they are good *journalism* above all, left-wing though neither partisan nor celebratory, genuinely objective rather than loftily churlish, facile, or denunciatory. By contrast with most American news dispatches from east of the Elbe, one is never aware of an official and relentless imbalance or a narrow ideological agenda in García Márquez's East European reports.

Well into his eighth and ninth decades García Márquez would remain consistent in his independent-leftist stance. Criticized by orthodox Communists and neoconservatives both, he has remained above the fray, refusing to get involved in vicious polemics or to respond to dishonest attacks. While some prominent Latin American authors have made lucrative careers as courtiers and defenders of American globalism, García Márquez has adhered to the riskier path of noting what is positive and defensible about revolutionary movements in the Third World. Of course, being an imaginative enough person he is not so naive as to deny the existence of repression and even torture in Cuba, and is fully aware of the darker side of the Soviet Union. As one who has worked for the mass media off and on since 1948, however, he also knows that, were he to voice any public criticism of the Cuban Revolution, the news headlines next morning would read, "GARCÍA MÁRQUEZ ATTACKS CASTRO'S CUBA." It is hence understandable why, during the sordid episode involving Heberto Padilla in 1971 (when, on orders from some bureaucratic rivals, the excellent and feisty Cuban poet was arrested for a month and made to "confess" to vague misconduct), García Márquez at first did express his concern over the matter, but later refused to sign the famous open letter to Fidel Castro in which sixty internationally renowned cultural figures from three continents vigorously condemned the action as reminiscent of the worst of Stalinism.

In the same way, García Márquez's view of the United States is both Latin American and his own. While liberal-minded West Europeans who survived Hitler's Reich have reason to think of American power as a liberating force, the Colombian's first experience of Americans was the combination of banana colonialists in Aracataca and the stories he heard about the 1928 workers' strike and army massacre. That memory of American control was to stay with him and eventually be mythified in the second half of his greatest book. In addition, as a man whom the U.S. immigration authorities maintained on their "subversives list" and denied a visa for thirty years, in his own life he has known the sheer silliness of American anticommunist manias and the strict limits of America's fabled openness to all opinions. Nevertheless, like most educated Latin Americans he respects what is positive about United States civilization—its authors, its civilian technology, its best journalism (he reads *Newsweek* as well as *The Nation*), and its better universities. His elder son Rodrigo even attended Harvard College, graduating in 1982 with an A.B. degree in history, and later went to Los Angeles to work in film.

When all is said it should be clear that García Márquez at heart is not an ideologue, in the sense that ideas for their own sake have little attraction for him. Rather he is a writer and an unorthodox radical for whom ideas are simply part of his everyday life, practice, and activity as an artisan of prose. He would be the first to recognize that slavish adherence to any purist "line" leads neither to good art nor to a good society. After all, in his own best fiction he deliberately set out to transcend and do away with the narrow limits and tired schemes of social-protest literature. To García Márquez, imagination and intuition matter more than do set formulas or complex thought, and reality itself is of greater import, is far more miraculous than any human mind's conceptualizations thereof. And while his leftism is principled, consistent, and evident enough, it has none of the notorious rigidity or inflexibility of old Stalinist theory and praxis. Finally, to those who begrudge him his accidental riches ("How can he, a leftist, have all those houses?"), it bears re-emphasizing that, since 1967, García Márquez has donated frequently and generously to progressive causes, and utilized his wealth and influence to help raise journalistic and cultural standards in the Spanish-speaking world, in his native land especially. Moreover, there are worse things in life than affluence gained from the writing of great books!

García Márquez's friends have remarked that he is at heart a melancholy man who conceals his deepest self even from his most intimate associates. During his childhood, as we noted, "Gabito" was an introverted boy who shied away from groups and sports. His kind of writing—with its outrageous humor and endless irony that grow from a solid and well-rooted commonsense folk wisdom and political radicalism—seems to have emerged as a means of reaching out and becoming part of his community, and obviously he has achieved that worthy aim. Today, for all his international success, García Márquez impresses one as a sane and serenely balanced, even "normal" sort of person. His mustachioed visage recalls that of many an ordinary Latin American in Caracas or Camagüey, and it is easy to imagine him in his morning overalls swapping jokes at the corner café with the jukebox repairman or the bartender. His very name is common enough; Hispanics named Gabriel García probably number in the thousands, and for the combination "García Márquez" there are twenty-eight listings in the Madrid telephone book alone, twenty-six in the Mexico City one.

As a writer, García Márquez belongs to world literature. As a man, he has managed to remain sufficiently close to his world to be thought of as something of a Latin American Everyman.

FIVE

The Readings

For all his ordinariness, his plebeian perspective, and his insistence that he is still basically one of the eleven offspring of the telegraph operator of Aracataca, García Márquez is a man of wide erudition, literary and otherwise. It is also true that he makes little display of his book learning, owing in part to his healthy suspicion of any pomp or solemnity surrounding literature. A novel for García Márquez is a practical concern, something that the writer writes and readers then read and perhaps enjoy. He has consistently manifested a benign indifference to the process whereby great works of human wit or passion are academicized, monumentalized, and finally devitalized in the form of "masterpieces." As a result he stands out as perhaps the one great Latin American author of fiction who—his occasional polemics and appreciation pieces aside—has written virtually no literary criticism. What literary reflections have issued from his pen are neither analytical nor theoretical but anecdotal or evaluative, practical comments closely bound up with his task of seeking out the traditions most suitable to his aims as a writer.

This critical silence also grows out of García Márquez's original situation as an apprentice writer who, from the first, simply lacked a past "canon" of reliable national works from which to learn about the novelist's trade. While a beginning European or even a United States or Argentine novelist has some heritage of proven texts to pick and choose from, a fledgling Colombian prose writer at mid-twentieth-century was faced with a minimal list of home titles and had to build an inner library without much guidance from past masters or current exegetes.

On the other hand, for an inspired young scribbler such a lack can be a blessing in disguise. Starting out with next to nothing, the writer is less likely to feel weighed down or intimidated by the accumulated works of the past (the unfortunate situation in French and U.S. letters today). Indeed, when not mediated and domesticated by the official cultural authorities, the process of reading and discovering the European "classics" can develop into a vital experience and intellectual adventure. In addition, one becomes highly self-motivated as a budding literary practitioner, dependent in great measure on one's personal resources and writing projects. Significantly, García

Márquez was to build his literary foundations either on his own or through his Caribbean-Colombian friends, who were every bit as committed as he was to flouting the hegemonic culture and academicism of Bogotá.

Not that García Márquez is in any way averse to the need for a solid and thorough literary background. As he said to a Cuban reporter in 1979, "There's a tendency to underestimate literary culture, to believe in spontaneity and invention. Actually literature is a science one has to learn, and there are 10,000 years standing behind every short story that gets written. And to know literature you need modesty and humility. All the modesty that gets in the way of writing is needed in order to study all of literature, to know what the hell was being done 10,000 years ago, where we stand in the history of mankind. . . . Ultimately you learn literature not in the university but from reading and rereading other writers."[1]

As one might expect, García Márquez here is speaking in part for himself. Speaking to a Colombian left-wing magazine, *El Manifiesto*, he notes that after discovering Kafka, "I set out just like that, at eight o'clock next morning, to find out what the hell had been done in the novel from the Bible on up to what was being written at the time. For the next six years I dropped out of studying, I dropped everything."[2] And he read mostly novels. The strategy of taking on the entire history of "the novel" would ultimately bear him fruit; in 1971 he was to admit to a Spanish reporter, "I felt so happy when I was writing *One Hundred Years of Solitude*. In my dreams I was inventing literature."[3] This astonishing admission confirms many a reader's intuitions; among the critical commonplaces about the story of Macondo is that, in its more than three hundred pages, it sums up, assimilates, and integrates a multiplicity of literary traditions stretching as far back as the Bible.

In secondary school García Márquez had given himself an education in the poetical classics of the Spanish Golden Age. Beginning in 1947 his reading fare would extend to the literatures of Mediterranean antiquity and Europe, the U.S., and Latin America, from which over time he would pick as his mentors whatever authors best happened to fit his own writing needs and temperament. While he became well acquainted with the novels of, say, Balzac and Dreiser, they would not exert any particularly noticeable influence on the development of his art. And while he also did dutifully read books like Rivera's *The Vortex* or a renowned Latin American like the Guatemalan Miguel Ángel Asturias, he seems to have studied them chiefly as a means of learning which mistakes to avoid and what *not* to do in literature.

In addition to his slow but steady self-grounding in the established literary repertory, before the actual task of composing his major novels García

Márquez would consult on an ad hoc basis literally hundreds of informational books (biographies of dictators, for example). What we will be examining in this chapter, however, are those literary narratives that were to play a decisive role in molding and directing García Márquez's novelistic vision and practice, works that either deal with the kinds of subject matter that specifically interested him, or that spoke to the very depths of his worldview and thereby furnished him a model for articulating it, a means of giving it a verbal shape. The growth of any writer, after all, consists of seeking and finding answers to the basic questions, "What to write about?" and "How to write about it?" In the self-education of the novelist García Márquez, these chosen precursors would serve him as his "school."

Franz Kafka was the very first author to have sparked something definitive in the crucible of García Márquez's imagination. With minor variants, this is how the Colombian likes to tell the interviewers about his discovery. Either in his seventeenth or nineteenth year, on the recommendation of a Bogotá friend named Jorge Álvaro Espinosa, he picked up a copy of *The Metamorphosis*. He read that disquieting first paragraph, about a Gregor Samsa who wakes up to find himself transformed into a man-sized insect and deals with it as a mere inconvenience, concerning himself rather with the mundane task of trying to get ready for work.

Young Gabo was dazzled; the effects on him were both immediate and lasting. García Márquez recalls, "When I read that I said to myself, 'Holy shit! Nobody'd ever told me you could do this! So it *can* be done! Shit! That's how my grandma used to tell stories, the wildest things with a completely natural tone of voice."[4] A remote Czech-Jewish writer, with his flat unregional Prague German, translated into a flat if lucid Spanish prose, had crystallized a reality much in the manner of grandmother Tranquilina Iguarán, inserting bizarre events into an ordinary setting and relating those anomalies as if they were just another aspect of everyday life.

Moreover, the adolescent writer-to-be now suddenly "understood that there existed other possibilities in literature besides the rational and academic ones I'd learned about in secondary school. And I found my true path as a writer."[5] In our time of course Franz Kafka has entered the available cultural vocabulary and become a standard reference—"Kafkaesque" is now a common enough English adjective. In 1945, however, the Czech author had been dead just over twenty years; *The Metamorphosis* wasn't much older than that, and a sensitive young South American mind in search of new literary models would understandably have been struck by the sheer newness of Kafka's narrative world.

In the wake of his discovery the Colombian novice was to read as much Kafka as he could (no doubt in Borges's translations). In a column from 1950, for instance, he alludes in passing to that bittersweet little parable "The Hunger Artist" (*OP*, 1:76). At this point in his life, however, García Márquez was less than well served by Kafka's mesmerizing influence; tales such as "The Burrow" or "Investigations of a Dog" seem to have impressed the dejected young man more by their morbid portrayals of loneliness and isolation than by their deeper strands of irony, humor, and satire. It is no doubt under their lopsided spell that Gabo wrote those strangely dark stories—"Eyes of a Blue Dog," "Eva Is Inside Her Cat"—depicting individuals trapped within their graves or bodies or heads. García Márquez was clearly trying to imitate Kafka's "subjective" atmosphere without having taken note of his more "objective" settings—his urban middle-class interiors, or the physical and precisely rendered, almost palpable world of his animal fables.

Following his move back to Caribbean country García Márquez would rediscover his roots and concentrate on being a more local and realistic author. The lessons he had first learned from Kafka come to full fruition only when he at last forges a single vision that blends realist narrative with strange, bizarre, magical, uncanny, or otherwise unreal events, first in his luminous if transitional short story "The Sea of Lost Time" (1961) and finally in what became the classic instance of magic-cum-realism, *One Hundred Years of Solitude*. While Colombian-coastal folklore taught García Márquez about the importance of popular myths and his grandmother provided an almost audible narrative voice, the enigmatic and prophetic short stories of a German-Jewish insurance-law functionary from Prague inspired him with a literary approach that ultimately made possible the miracles and monsters now commonly associated with Macondo.

The next major influence on García Márquez comes from the Greek tragedians, whom he discovered at age nineteen in Cartagena. As he tells it, a drinking mate there (later a customs lawyer) by the name of Gustavo Ibarra said to him at one point, "All those things you're reading are well and good, but they lack a base. You need a foundation."[6] The fellow knew his ancients by heart, and for years he loaned young Gabo his copies of the Greco-Roman classics, even quizzing him informally from time to time.

From reading Sophocles in particular García Márquez was to glean certain essential insights and devices that would stay with him throughout his life as a writer. There are some telling early allusions. *Leaf Storm* bears a long epigraph from the *Antigone* and, not accidentally, depicts a situation identical to that of the great Athenian play: a protagonist defiantly chooses to bury a man who had been harshly repudiated by the larger community. In a lighter vein, García Márquez's first mature and typically humorous story, "One Day after Saturday," has its quirky ninety-four-year-old priest Father Antonio Isabel, who in his youth had read Sophocles in the original and now refers to the classical authors as "the little ancients of old" ("los ancianitos de entonces").

García Márquez has praised *Oedipus Rex* on numerous counts, singling it out above all as the work that taught him the most about power, a phenomenon that would obsess him and which he would masterfully dissect in *The Autumn of the Patriarch*.[7] While in our time Freud's discoveries have conditioned us to read Sophocles's play along perhaps unduly psychological lines, García Márquez's observation serves as a reminder that, starting with the very title, the hero Oedipus is designated *Tyrannus*, "King," and that the ensuing drama goes on to depict the unique responsibilities and dilemmas of a man who had murdered and married his way to the throne. The famous lament about blight and pollution with which *Oedipus Rex* begins is an eloquent anticipatory reflection on that most hallowed of ethical-political commonplaces: unpunished crimes and arbitrary acts in the highest ranks of a nation are a disease that will spread throughout the social body.

That power conversely blinds its holders to reality is another basic truth we see unfold in *Oedipus Rex*. As the seer Tiresias remarks to Oedipus, "You have your eyes but see not where you are, in sin"; and the more pragmatic Creon admonishes him, "If you think obstinacy without wisdom / a valuable possession, you are wrong."[8] The intimate tragic portraits of Colonel Buendía and of the nameless patriarch both show men who fail to see their own sins and for whom "obstinacy without wisdom" becomes a way of life.

García Márquez also likes humorously describing *Oedipus Rex* as history's first detective novel and moreover the only such work in which the sleuth in the end finds out he was the criminal. In a wry observation in October 1952 the young author notes that Sophocles broke the rules of detective fiction long before the latter genre even existed—a significant concern for a twenty-four-year-old rebel who at the time was intent on breaking literary rules, particularly those then dominant in Colombia (*OP*, 1:843). Years later, in *Chronicle of a Death Foretold*, García Márquez would produce a kind of detective narrative that breaks some bedrock rules: from early on we know the identity of the two murderers, while never finding out whether their hapless victim was truly guilty of having dishonored their sister Ángela. In addition, there is in *Oedipus* that legendary sense of a destiny intractable, of events preordained—precisely what we sense throughout and realize in the last pages of *One Hundred Years*, as well as in the casual street encounters that punctuate the tense plot of *Chronicle*. (Not surprisingly, Jean Cocteau's own remake of *Oedipus Rex* bears the title *The Infernal Machine*.)

The horrific climax of *Oedipus Rex*—the hero's violent self-blinding and his mother Jocasta's suicide by hanging—takes place offstage. In similar fashion *Antigone* ends just as the heroine is being led away to execution. These typical procedures of Greek tragedy García Márquez would put to good effect in some of his best works, in which decisive events are made to occur "outside the text." In his very subtle short story "Artificial Roses" the quiet, delicate protagonist Mina is jilted—though we do not actually witness it firsthand, finding out about it mostly indirectly, through her attitude and actions. The texts of "Tuesday Siesta" and *Leaf Storm* abruptly break off at the long-awaited moment when, respectively, the strong-minded woman and the unnamed colonel will confront hostile populations. *Love in the Time of Cholera* comes to its end just when the relationship between Florentino and Fermina, after a fifty-year wait, is being consummated. Even *The Autumn of the Patriarch*, its reports of literally thousands of deaths notwithstanding, depicts only one actual murder at the hands of the dictator. Similarly, *Memories of My Melancholy Whores* lets its readers speculate as to the future of the "romance" between the bachelor nonagenarian and his silent, slumbering, adolescent partner. (By contrast, in *Chronicle* we read so much about Santiago Nasar's "foretold" death that García Márquez is virtually obligated to give readers a detailed account of the event in the novel's final pages.)

But there is in Greek tragedy a yet deeper structure as exemplified in the *Antigone*. In that Sophocles work the heroine openly defies the kingly authority of her uncle, Creon, who had decreed that the body of Antigone's brother Polyneices must lie unburied, in symbolic punishment for the latter's having borne arms against his native land. Antigone in turn takes it upon herself to bury Polyneices, citing as justification her duties as sister and the higher laws of the gods. One sees here an irresolvable conflict: the laws of a community versus the legitimate rights of family and of the dead. Commenting on the respective positions of Creon and Antigone, the play's chorus expresses the evenhanded judgment, "Both sides have spoken well."[9] These words succinctly sum up the underlying worldview of tragic genre (as elucidated by Hegel and A. C. Bradley)—a ritualized clash between equally valid though mutually irreconcilable opposites, between, for example, ambition and loyalty (*Macbeth*), love and friendship (*Othello*), or passion and duty (*Antony and Cleopatra*).[10] The miracle of tragedy is that we can feel pity for the perpetrators of horrendous deeds, for victimizer and victims both, for Othello as well as Desdemona.

The pattern can be seen throughout García Márquez's work. In *One Hundred Years of Solitude* alone we may note José Arcadio Buendía's contradictory aptitudes for both political leadership and pure science, Amaranta's pronounced "vocation for incest" versus the socially necessary prohibitions, or the final couple's foredoomed conflict between their blissful passion and their mundane but essential housekeeping chores. And there is in *No One Writes to the Colonel* the stubborn opposition between physical hunger and family honor (as symbolized by the fighting cock), in "Artificial Roses" the struggle between young Mina's broken heart and her grandmother's tough solicitousness, and in "Tuesday Siesta" the tension between criminal laws and a mother's affections. In *Chronicle of a Death Foretold* there is the possible innocence of Santiago Nasar confronted with the Vicario clan's need for a sacrificial vendetta, while in *Love in the Time of Cholera* there is a battle of five decades between conjugal affection and romantic ardor. It is no mean paradox that one of literature's great humorists also articulates a profoundly tragic sensibility.

Almost as important in shaping García Márquez's vision and craft was the Bible. As a good South American leftist he may have little truck with organized religions, but the author knows his Scriptures and assimilates them to his purposes. When I asked him in 1982 about his relationship to the Bible, he reminisced on having read it in high school for "all the good stories" found between its covers. On several other occasions he extols it as "un libro cojonudo donde pasan cosas fantásticas" (roughly, "a hell of a book where amazing things happen" [*OG*, 70; *FG*, 49]). His youthful journalism shows extensive familiarity with the Bible. As early as June 1948, in a humorous article on twins, he has a full paragraph on Rebekah's having birthed both hairy Esau and smooth Jacob (*OP*, 1:93). Awed by the Bible's myriad characters and fantastical tales, in April 1950 he marvels at Balaam, "whose own donkey gave him phonetics and speech lessons," or Joshua, who, "not satisfied with having stopped the sun . . . had enough strength to blow a trumpet that would bring down the walls of Jericho" (*OP*, 1:203). And in July 1952, invoking these instances along with Sodom and Gomorrah plus the inevitable Samson, García Márquez celebrates the biblical use of exaggeration—a device that would evolve as one of his own trademarks (*OP*, 1:795).

Having come of age at a time of almost apocalyptic violence, García Márquez has always been drawn to material suggestive of the Apocalypse of the book of Revelation. Faced by the ominous plague of dead birds in a sultry Macondo, his Father Antonio Isabel in "One Day after Saturday" tries to remember "if there was a rain of dead birds in the Apocalypse." The most obvious apocalyptic moment in García Márquez of course is the concluding paragraph in *One Hundred Years*, where Macondo is blown away by what is actually portended elsewhere as a "biblical hurricane." And just as in Revelations the dead are to be judged after the Book of Life is opened, Macondo is swept to destruction at the very moment that Melquíades's "book" is deciphered.

The apocalypse of García Márquez nevertheless intentionally differs from the vision revealed to John. The physical destruction in the Bible, contemplated long before the opening of the Book of Life, leads not only to the end of the world but also to "a new heaven and new earth" (Rev. 21:1). By contrast, the end of Macondo comes *after* the unlocking of the secrets of the parchments, and what follows is no new heaven but rather the end of those races who "did not have a second opportunity on earth." Even the means of destruction differ. In Revelation one finds thunder, lightning, earthquakes, hail, and fire mixed with blood, locusts, and a burning mountain thrown into the sea — while the air is absolutely still, the four angels having held it back, "that no wind might blow on earth" (Rev. 7:1). What destroys Macondo is precisely what is missing from the biblical Apocalypse. "Hurricane," appropriately, is a word of Caribbean Indian origin.

Many a critic has taken note of the "biblical" aspect of *One Hundred Years of Solitude*, a book about the genesis, exodus, growth, corruption, and final destruction of a people.[11] Macondo at first is like a Garden of Eden where death is unknown, and where, things lacking names, the villagers must unwittingly emulate Adam, who "gave names to all cattle and to the birds of the air, and to every beast of the field" (Gen. 2:20). Also like Adam, the eventual fall of José Arcadio Buendía results from his excessive desire for knowledge.

Though the exodus from Riohacha chronologically precedes the founding of Macondo, in the novel it takes place in chapter 2, the same position of the book of Exodus. And just as the Jews fled Egypt and spent years in the wilderness before reaching the promised land, José Arcadio Buendía (who combines features of Adam, Abraham, Jacob, and Moses) and his followers flee Riohacha and wander for two years in the South American wilderness before settling on "the land that no one had promised them." Jacob dreamt of a ladder and God said that the land on which he dreams shall be his (Gen. 28:10); José Arcadio Buendía dreams of a city made of walls and mirrors and decides to found Macondo. Recalling the plagues that shake Egypt, Macondo is subsequently smitten by epidemics of insomnia and amnesia, and later by the rain of dead birds. The Buendías' long genealogy inevitably suggests those scriptural "begats," and just as there are various important cases of incest in the Bible, the founding couple of Macondo are cousins and their elder son marries their adopted daughter. Joshua lived to be 110, Job to 140, and Adam to 930; Úrsula and Pilar Ternera survive well into their hundreds.

At various points in the Bible the Jews will turn wayward, forsaking and sinning against their God, and in punishment He will visit a variety of political and natural disasters on them. In Macondo the Buendías stray from their historical roots and struggles, becoming dissolute, corrupt, and soft, the easy prey of Yankee entrepreneurs or ravenous ants. The five-year rainstorm inevitably brings to mind the biblical Flood, though rather than cleanse Macondo and allow its people to start anew, the rains are the beginning of the end — there is no Noah among the Buendías. Other, more casual, biblical parallels in *One Hundred Years* are the sibling conflict between Amaranta and Rebeca (suggestive of Cain and Abel); Rebeca toting in a bag the bones of her first parents (Moses took with him those of Joseph); and baby Aureliano Babilonia, the foundling in a basket, who (unlike infant Moses in the bulrushes, the future deliverer of his Jewish brethren) will unlock the truths leading to Macondo's tragicomic, apocalyptic end. Throughout *One Hundred Years of Solitude* the Bible is both artfully echoed and respectfully parodied.

What there is of the Bible in *The Autumn of the Patriarch*, by contrast, is the purest parody. While the dictator-protagonist is more childlike and boyish than "patriarchal," this unimpressive man, whose name may or may not be "Zacarías" (i.e., Zechariah, one of the lesser prophets), is frequently likened by his compatriots to God. The tyrant's namelessness as well as his referring to himself with the words "I am what I am" are suggestive of the terrible and remote Hebrew deity.[12] The adjective "messianic" is more than once applied to him, and he is Christ-like in his reported powers of healing the sick, his relationship with the palace lepers, and his earnest call for the children to come to him. In the crowds there are actually signs celebrating "the Magnificent who arose from the dead on the third day" (*OPa*, 37; *AP*, 34).

In the light of the full reading we find out that those attributed qualities are largely false, and the same is all the more so of other biblical traces in *Patriarch*. Leticia Nazareno, the only woman who will succeed in trapping the dictator into marriage, has a surname signifying "of Nazareth," like Jesus, but the erstwhile nun will prove to be even more amoral and grasping than her murderous husband. Similarly, the only one of the hundreds of sons recognized by the mighty patriarch and known to us by name is his little boy Emanuel, a name meaning "God with us," given by Isaiah to the future Messiah and frequently applied to Jesus Christ, though this child in military regalia is a travesty of the messianic, and is torn to pieces by dogs before he reaches puberty. In the more degraded world of *The Autumn of the Patriarch*, the Bible and whatever higher notions it represents are less of a narrative model than a sourcebook for some cruel and bitter jokes.

If from Sophocles and the Bible the apprentice Colombian learned some of the most venerated, mythic, and lofty ways of writing, from the comical, lowlife, late-medieval universe of François Rabelais in *The Histories of Gargantua and Pantagruel* he learned ways of giving verbal shape to the more plebeian side of our humanity, to irreverence, ribaldry, and burlesque. There is a friendly nod at the Frenchman in the last chapter of *One Hundred Years*, where Gabriel, one of the four friends of Aureliano Babilonia, wins a trip to Paris and departs with "two changes of clothing, a pair of shoes, and the complete works of Rabelais" (*CAS*, 435; *OYS*, 371).

Already in his early columns García Márquez is alluding admiringly to the great French satirist. In February 1950 he conjures up the wondrous spectacle of guests gorging themselves at banquets, and compares them to "the most noble example of Pantagruel" (*OP*, 1:176). He repeats the comparison in numerous like passages, and in his great book he will create an inspired "noble example" of his own in the character Aureliano Segundo, one of the most memorable specimens ever imagined of joyful bibulousness and gluttony. Similarly attracted to Rabelais's legendary hyperbole, García Márquez reflects on "Ted Evans, the tallest man in the world," who is traveling aboard the ship *Queen Mary* on his way to joining the ranks of an American circus, and the author naturally refers to Mr. Evans as "a flesh-and-blood version of Gargantua and Pantagruel" (*OP*, 1:717).

Rabelais's most renowned literary trait is of course this gigantism, as revealed in the subsequent adjective "Gargantuan." His hero Gargantua typically has a mare as big as six elephants, and for a lance he uses a tree. Rabelais's hyperboles often stand out for their arithmetical precision; Gargantua spent eleven months inside his mother's womb; feeding him will require 17,913 cows; and when he urinates on the city of Paris he drowns 260,418 people, "not including women and children."[13] From this numerical exactitude García Márquez was to pick up more than a few lessons. For his classic instance of precise exaggeration there is the cloudburst of "four years, eleven months, and two days" that will wreck Macondo. Or there is in chapter 5 the hilarious description of the return of José Arcadio, who had circumnavigated the globe sixty-five times, whose *entire* body is covered with tattoos, who consumes sixteen raw eggs, and who Indian-wrestles five men at once. And in "Innocent Eréndira" there is the wicked grandmother's collection of clocks, so many that it takes the oppressed young heroine six hours merely to wind them.

Gargantua's twenty-four-yard codpiece, decorated by his governess with garlands, ribbons, and flowers, is just one instance of Rabelais's constant joking with turds, urine, and penises, the ribald side of his art whence comes the word "Rabelaisian." Out of many equivalent passages in García Márquez we may cite the last chapter in *One Hundred Years*, where Amaranta Úrsula paints clown's eyes and Turk's mustaches on Aureliano's "portentous creature," bedecking it with bow ties and tinfoil hats. Some of the Colombian's tenderest, most delicate and humane shorter fictions—"Artificial Roses," "Baltazar's Prodigious Afternoon," *No One Writes to the Colonel*—have as their high point an obscenity, usually one denoting defecation, and Big Mama's final act is a resounding burp. *The Autumn of the Patriarch* is a long Rabelaisian orgy, with its rustic barracks dictator who spouts profanities by the dozen and its crucial episodes having to do with bowels, testicles, and behinds. Still, the ribaldry of Rabelais and García Márquez is not the vulgarity and prurience one might find today in fraternity gatherings or locker rooms. Rather their bodily references celebrate life in all its manifestations and take joy in what are normally considered the least noble aspects, the animal side of human existence. In spite of the comparatively degraded reality he deals with, few authors are as life-affirming as is García Márquez.

Equally important in Rabelais is his satire on specific political and religious figures, his vigorous mockery of lawyers, officials, and church hierarchs, conveyed with fantastical long lists and exuberant displays of erudition. At the same time Rabelais's wildest episodes have to do with real-life places and people: describing actual statues, naming fifty hamlets from Pertou, or, for Pantagruel's itinerary, combining ancient Celtic routes to the utopian land of death with details of Jacques Cartier's New World explorations.[14] García Márquez's satirical portraits of oligarchs, entrepreneurs, corrupt soldiers, bureaucrats, U.S. imperialists, and the clergy likewise constitute a major element in his art. So gentle a story as "A Very Old Man with Enormous Wings" has a hilarious spoof of scholastic hairsplitting both from the village priest and the high clerics in Rome. While doctors and dentists tend to be positive figures in García Márquez, he generally enjoys ridiculing lawyers, notably the sextet in top hats and frock coats who periodically show up in Macondo, ever for hire to twist truth for the authorities' ends. "Big Mama's Funeral" is pure satire in a Rabelaisian vein, with its plebeian perspective, its feverish prose, its breathtaking catalogs of beauty queens, street vendors, and political clichés, and its humorous sketches of church, army, oligarchy, and state.

The protagonist of *The Autumn of the Patriarch* is an exaggerated composite of a number of Latin dictators, and the absurd actions of Yankee characters in García Márquez's work will be recognizable to anyone familiar with the continuing history of the United States in the Caribbean.

Nevertheless, the satire in García Márquez is not of an angry or malignant kind. Though in 1951 he did publish an ironic essay praising cannibalism as a useful alternative to war (*OP*, 1:577), his mockery stops short of the distilled bile or savage indignation we associate with Swift. His anti-solemnity and his fundamental loyalty to the folk cultures of street and public square are rather the expressions of his larger belief in the possibility of a better world. As the great Soviet scholar Mikhail Bakhtin observed about Rabelais, García Márquez's fiction helps deflate official truths and reinterpret them from the point of view of people's laughter.[15] The Colombian who began his career as a daily humorist, chuckling at one funny topic per five-hundred-word column, was eventually to grow into a major artist of laughter who aims his prose, wit, and vision at all the spurious values dominant in Latin America and elsewhere. It's no surprise that a restless twenty-year-old satirist would find in a wise and earthy Rabelais a kindred spirit and comic teacher.

To discuss the presence of Faulkner in García Márquez is to enter a much vaster world of regional likenesses, personal affinities, and bonds linking master and disciple. In fact the Faulknerian influence on Latin American writers—on García Márquez but also on a good number of others—has been the subject of entire monographs.[16] In the years since achieving fame, García Márquez often attempted to underestimate Faulkner's formative role and claim that he discovered the Mississippian only after having begun the writing of *Leaf Storm*—an understandable reaction to those reviewers who had in turn been overstating his Faulknerian side, and even dismissing his work as mere imitation Faulkner.

The collected early journalism of García Márquez, however, does help confirm just how deep was the mark that the North American had left on the trans-Caribbean novice. By July 1949 García Márquez was discussing Faulkner with his friend Ramiro de la Espriella (*OP*, 1:135), and from a July 1950 review of the film version of *Intruder in the Dust*, it is obvious that by then he was well acquainted with *As I Lay Dying* (*OP*, 1:380). The most casual reference to Faulkner in young Gabo's daily columns is a paean of praise to "the old man," as the faithful admirers in Barranquilla liked calling him. Faulkner, we read, is "the most extraordinary and vital creative artist in the modern world," is "the greatest figure in world literature," and is "one of the most interesting [novelists] of all time" (*OP*, 1:363, 490). In April 1950 Gabo makes a passionate plea for the writing of Colombian novels that would be "happily influenced by Joyce, Faulkner, and Virginia Woolf" (*OP*, 1:269); and in February 1951, serenely dispatching the protest novels of the Peruvian Ciro Alegría and all the "scholiasts of Marxism," with their attacks on "decadent modernism," he frankly states that "my favorite authors for the moment are Faulkner, Kafka, and Virginia Woolf, and my fondest hope is to write as they do" (*OP*, 1:581). So immersed was a twenty-two-year-old Gabo in Faulkner's work that at some point he actually raised doubts, wondered out loud to his friends whether "in the end it'll turn out that Faulkner is just some damned master of rhetoric who's got us all caught up in his web of words."[17]

At any rate García Márquez soon set out to write in *Leaf Storm* a novel of shifting narrative viewpoints centered round a coffin, too obviously modeled in its plot and format after the Faulkner of *As I Lay Dying*. However, as the young man starts finding his own voice in the mid-1950s he will slowly assimilate Faulkner's lessons, not just imitating the Mississippian's subjects and devices but adapting his vision and artistry to northern Colombian realities and personal needs. It is not accidental that, having found in Faulkner a way of depicting those oppressed, poverty-stricken subtropical settlements, with their fabled heat and dust, a mature García Márquez would like claiming Faulkner as a fellow "Caribbean" author who shapes and reinvents an American world not unlike the one he himself first knew in Aracataca.

It is precisely this world that García Márquez tries putting together in *Leaf Storm*, and to which he will then give contours and palpability in the scorching mid-afternoon hush of "One Day after Saturday" or "Tuesday Siesta," or in the early-morning chill and dampness of "Artificial Roses" and "One of These Days." Both in Macondo and the nameless "town" he will fashion communities as self-contained as is Faulkner's Yoknapatawpha County, complete with recurring personages and legends plus old ghosts all his own. As his equivalents to the crude but money-skilled Flem Snopes and his kin, who succeed in edging aside the tired old Sartoris and genteel Compson clans, García Márquez will create the colorfully devious, wily shopkeeper Don Sabas in *No One Writes to the Colonel* and *In Evil Hour*, and the more gangsterish Montiel of the two seriocomical short stories. Similarly, the mythicized references to Colonel Buendía that crop up in each of Gabo's early volumes are evocative of a remote and heroic history scarcely lingering on in the town's more brutish present of corruption, militarism, and greed.

That history comes to full fruition in *One Hundred Years of Solitude*, a novel combining the best of *Sartoris*, *The Sound and the Fury*, and *Absalom, Absalom!*

all in one. Being family chronicles (or portions thereof), these three books show an expected wealth of personality types, something at which García Márquez too would always excel. *Absalom, Absalom!*, Faulkner's greatest novel, is almost a prototype for García Márquez's own masterwork, inasmuch as it tells of the collective wanderings of Sutpen and his retinue prior to the founding of his estate; the subsequent rise and fall of his fortunes; the ruined house that, with three surviving family members, will be consumed by fire a century hence; and such little details as Sutpen's silent arrival from the Civil War (a harbinger of José Arcadio's single-word return from his travels), Rosa's sudden departure one day (much in the manner of Santa Sofía de la Piedad), the incestuous element in Charles Bon and Judith (the bane of the Buendías' history), and the French architect and Haitian slaves, foreigners with a role roughly analogous to that of the occasional Italian or West Indian who shows up in Macondo.[18] The women serve as the backbone of Faulkner's families in decline—Jenny in *Sartoris*, Dilsey in *The Sound and the Fury*, Clytie in *Absalom, Absalom!*—much as they do in *One Hundred Years* and all of García Márquez's narrative world.

Equally important as Faulkner's "subjects" are the celebrated novelistic "forms" he fashioned in his greatest books. The most fundamental of course is his representation of time, the chronology that moves constantly back and forth over decades, in combination with the shifts from character to character, all of whom recount their portions of the story only as they understand it. In an earlier novel like *Sartoris* Faulkner still worked within a traditional, sequential, third-person format and even relied on so "classic" a background convention as portraying the emergence of electricity, motorcars, and airplanes. The narrative innovations he creates soon thereafter are not mere techniques or devices but the instrument of his maturing personal vision. Seeing society not as nineteenth-century realists did, as a constant linear and evolutionary development then known as *"progress,"* Faulkner instead chronicles a South where local progress is nonexistent, time is stationary, and past and present coexist with rather than succeed each other. Given that the preferred milieu of his imagination is the noble and heroic antebellum ruling class who live the long aftermath of defeat and are being displaced by upstart Snopeses, it is not surprising that as author Faulkner would depict his present as a mere shadow of the past. Similarly, in a decayed world where old notables have lost all legitimacy, while the new rich are unattractive human specimens, no one is allowed to discourse with more authority than anyone else.

This unified form and vision is among the most profound and enduring of the lessons that García Márquez learned from Faulkner. Also writing about an area that has known centuries of poverty and oppression, where Iberian conquistadors and their elite descendants have the authority of invaders essentially, and where even the worthier struggles of the just have been compromised or vanquished, his own representations of local realities would have been less than adequately served by linear, developmental narrative procedures. Consequently, through most of his novels García Márquez utilizes and then further transforms Faulknerian perspectivism. Though on first inspection *One Hundred Years* seems chronologically ordered, within its larger bounds time undergoes all manner of shifts, these often seamlessly executed. The very opening sentence evokes three different time levels, and is not picked up on or explained until the concluding page of the first chapter; chapter 2 in turn starts out by displacing us four generations into the past; and in the end we find out that all the episodes in the book have been prerecorded as coexisting in one instant. The unfolding pattern of repeated names, with its implications of stasis, is a grand structure with origins traceable to the two John Sartorises and two Quentins in Faulkner.

The Faulknerian legacy of form attains unprecedented heights in *The Autumn of the Patriarch*, with its continuous present at the opening of each chapter and its collage of many pasts assembled within the main text, these latter coming alive via the multitude of voices ranging from the tyrant himself and his associates to the humblest slum dweller or the fresh young schoolgirl, all of them numbering somewhere in the low hundreds at least. Even so brief a book as *Chronicle of a Death Foretold* has (1) its suspenseful account of a serenely unknowing Santiago Nasar's final, fatal stroll through town, alternating with (2) the chain of rumor that fails to reach him, (3) the earlier romantic happenings that have led tragically to a homicidal situation, and (4) the two decades' hindsight that are furnished by the minor character García Márquez, a youthful resident then and a sober investigative reporter now. Similarly, both *Love in the Time of Cholera* and *Of Love and Other Demons* start out in an emotionally charged present that is slowly elucidated via a series of extended flashbacks covering some five decades.

Like Faulkner studying Mississippi history on his own since seventh grade, the apprentice García Márquez would read widely in the lore and history of Caribbean Colombia and the Antilles. Like the character Quentin Compson and Faulkner himself, of García Márquez it could well be said that "his very body was an empty hall echoing with sonorous" names and legends of people now lost. And just as Faulkner would remark wistfully of Colonel Faulkner's once-heroic world, "There's nothing left of the old place, the house is gone and the plantation boundaries, nothing left of his work but a statue,"[19] in the same way the memory of Colonel Buendía recedes to become nothing more than the name of a dusty, tree-lined street. And yet, though they write of tropical paradises decayed and lost, both the Mississippian and the Colombian will dignify and bring beauty to what on the surface seem lives of degradation, will mythify an entire physical and human landscape, giving it a shape and a density in the process, even an aura of magic and mystery.

While a youthful Gabo would find in Faulkner a vast horizon that fully integrates geography, history, climate, family life, and narrative experiment, Virginia Woolf would furnish him a model of pure and committed artistry, a general approach to novel writing, and an entire repertory of prose techniques, formal patterns, and specific sorts of scenes. "The great Virginia," he called her in passing in 1950, one of his many casual allusions to those European and U.S. literary figures then being discovered by a young and eager García Márquez (*OP*, 1:269). This stated affinity for Woolf may at first seem surprising, however, given the Englishwoman's fabled preciosity, her somewhat narrow range of feeling, her upper-middle-class snobbery, and her personal distaste for any hint of plebeianism, let alone ribaldry, in the arts. And yet in various ways her hand can be detected in the larger conception and the concrete details of García Márquez's narrative work.

First there is Woolf's incessant creation and variation. Her fecundity as a writer notwithstanding, with each major book she comes up with a new form; no two novels from her mature phase are alike. In keeping with this creative approach there is the overarching importance she assigns to the total composition of a narrative, her subordinating all action and character to a larger formal pattern, be it the single broad sweep of *Mrs. Dalloway*, the tripartite arrangement of *To the Lighthouse*, the mosaiclike fragmentation of *Jacob's room*, or the grand conception, almost operatic, of *The Waves*. Likewise each of García Márquez's novels is a new literary venture begun virtually from scratch; while many of his admirers would have wanted another *One Hundred Years*, in his fiction he makes every effort to avoid repeating himself. And in his most famous book as well as in *The Autumn of the Patriarch* and *Chronicle of a Death Foretold* the meticulously crafted, tapestrylike design takes full precedence over the countless intrigues and bloody deeds.

Both in minor details and in certain of his major scenes García Márquez took some creative cues from Mrs. Woolf. There is in *To the Lighthouse* the silent and loyal Mr. Carmichael, a poet who lingers about the margins of the Ramsay household; perhaps not accidentally, the widow Montiel's loyal house servant is a West Indian regularly referred to as *señor* Carmichael. *Orlando* in particular, read by Gabo in Borges's translation, was to contribute in no small measure to the form and content of *One Hundred Years of Solitude*. Woolf's little divertissement covers a three-hundred-year period lived by the eponymous hero/heroine, whose personality, with sex change and all, persists over the three centuries. Just as Orlando's "biography" is something of a literary history of England, so the Buendía "chronicle" is a fantasticated history of Colombia. Early on in Woolf's book there occurs the "Great Frost," reported as a historical event and given special vividness through magical touches, such as a woman who turns to powder and is blown away in a puff, or "a whole herd of swine frozen immovable upon the road."[20] The winter catastrophe is then followed by a great thaw and a flood, suggestive of the insomnia and amnesia plagues and five-year rains visited upon Macondo.

At one point Orlando—like elder son José Arcadio—flees and spends time with the gypsies; and across the years she will view the dizzying series of technological changes (factories, hot running water, radios, airplanes) with an incredulity not unlike that of the disoriented Macondians. Throughout these massive transformations there endures an oak tree with a symbolic value roughly that of the almond trees of Macondo. In the final pages of the book we see Orlando seeking her true self and, like Aureliano Babilonia, living the ecstasy of an all-encompassing subjective wisdom. At the same time *Orlando* is a bit of a private spoof, as is made manifest in the author's preface, where she lists all of her friends in acknowledgment. Similarly, of *One Hundred Years* García Márquez often says that it is a book utterly lacking in any seriousness. In its final chapters he brings in as characters his three best friends, his Catalan mentor, his wife Mercedes, plus himself, and at various moments in the course of the narrative he will allude indirectly to novels by his fellow Latin Americans Fuentes, Carpentier, and Cortázar.

One of the most striking moments in *The Autumn of the Patriarch* is that scene in which the nameless tyrant sits on the terrace of his house and takes in "the whole universe of the Antilles from Barbados to Veracruz," including "the perfumed volcano of Martinique," the Dutch tulips in Curaçao, the "blue dogs" of Haiti, and the "automobiles going the wrong way" in Trinidad (*OPa*, 39–40; *AP*, 55–56). It is not coincidental that early on in *Orlando* the hero climbs a hill "so high indeed that nineteen English counties could be seen beneath, and on clear days thirty," a vista that includes "the English Channel," "forts on the coast," and "the spires of London."[21] In a comparable passage in *Jacob's Room*, young Jacob Flanders is reported as standing on the Acropolis, whence we are made to visualize a geography that at first covers the Sea of Marmara to "the uplands of Albania and Turkey," and soon sweeps across "great towns—Paris—Constantinople—London."[22] These episodes come, respectively, near the beginning and toward the end of Woolf's two novels, a fact that suggests their strategic importance within her formal and geographic vision. By the same token, García Márquez's Caribbean panorama occurs immediately before the episode that concludes chapter 1, that fantastical reenactment of the first arrival of European navigator Columbus with his three ships.

Actually Virginia Woolf's grand architectonics and her closely textured prose both play so decisive a role in the making of *The Autumn of the Patriarch* that a special section is devoted to her influence on that book in chapter 9 of this study. For now we must simply observe that in everything she did she was the high literary artist, ever refining life with broad verbal contours and stylistic craft, and her perfectionist example proved as central in the "education" of García Márquez as were Rabelais in the development of his plebeian side or Faulkner in establishing his regionalism.

Three books by very different authors—Albert Camus's *The Plague,* Daniel Defoe's *Journal of the Plague Year,* and Curzio Malaparte's *The Skin*—all helped an apprentice Gabo focus his interests in specific ways. The first two books, obviously, tell of an epidemic and its horrors; the third (with an opening chapter entitled "The Plague") recounts the deteriorating, infrahuman ambience in the city of Naples toward the end of World War II. They have in common their portrait of collective catastrophe—in García Márquez a constant and recurring situation, from the "leaf storm" of the invading banana company on through the shock waves and public trauma caused by the family vendetta in *Chronicle of a Death Foretold.* Such an obsession, besides originating in García Márquez's own visionary streak, grows out of the years in which he was coming of age—a time when undeclared war in Colombia became a way of life, civilized norms were largely swept aside, and national political discussion inclined toward catastrophic and apocalyptic themes.

The three European books thus spoke authoritatively to a fledgling Colombian compelled on his part to write about the "plague" of *la Violencia,* inasmuch as they too dealt with a broad social cataclysm and its climate of fear, uncertainty, and mass death, and particularly its capacity to bring out the most dramatic extremes of solidarity and selfishness among human beings. Except for *The Plague* they belong to the genre of "witness," factual testimonials so artful in their rendering that they exist in a conceptual limbo somewhere between straight reportage and imagined fiction, and the first paragraph of Camus's novel actually starts out, "The unusual events described in this *chronicle* . . ." (emphasis added).

García Márquez was well acquainted with *The Plague* by April 1951, when in a series of whimsical reflections on rats he made passing reference to Camus's opening chapter (*OP*, 1:740). Later, in the polemic he launched in 1959 about the many bad books dealing with *la Violencia* (see the final pages of my chapter 3), he praised the French author for his biological, medical, and historical knowledge of the phenomenon of plagues, for his "almost casually" inserting the information as documentary base for the novel, and for concentrating less on bodily sufferings and deaths than on the spiritual ups and downs of his people's inner souls. In the end, García Márquez notes, "as an example for the horrific novel not yet written in Colombia, none may be better than the gentle novel by Camus, a brief episode of the human race in which not even the germs of the plague are definitely bad, nor its victims necessarily good" (*OP*, 3:766–67).

Camus sets his serene narrative in the ordinary town of Oran, in colonial French Algeria, and further heightens the concreteness with such statistics as the "6,321 rats collected and burnt in a single day, 25 April,"[23] the high figure made credible by its precision and chronology. As the epidemic seizes hold of the population and the town is fully quarantined, we see the varying reactions of individuals, the weakening of willpower, the decay of commerce and death of tourism, the priest and his sermonizing, the desert winds that compound the general gloom, and several necessary episodes of humor — all of which would provide Gabo with some hints toward his portrayal of Macondians caught in the grip of war or rainstorm. Nevertheless, Camus always "holds back," and this combined physical exactitude and artful understatement were to furnish García Márquez a model for sketching in the barest essentials of large-scale disaster, as he does in *No One Writes to the Colonel*, the *Big Mama's Funeral* stories, and *Of Love and Other Demons*.

Such a lesson in control has a yet deeper strand. Camus's book was written during the early 1940s, at the height of the Nazi occupation of France, and the "plague" in Oran is clearly meant as an allegory for the military troops and their atrocities, though neither Germans, soldiers, nor torturers receive mention in the course of the narrative. In the same way, the nineteenth-century civil war chapters in *One Hundred Years of Solitude* are read by Colombians as indirectly alluding to *la Violencia* of the 1950s, even though Macondo will have ceased to exist by that date. Likewise, the encroaching Americans who become the dominant force in Macondo are never referred to by the narrator as Americans, and words like "exploitation" or "repression" are studiously avoided.

Camus was well acquainted with Defoe's *Journal of the Plague Year*, and indeed cites his English predecessor in the epigraph to his own novel. The circumstances surrounding the publication of the *Journal* are as fascinating as the volume itself. Defoe was a mere five years old when the Great Plague racked London in 1665. Later, basing himself on the stories he had since picked up from relatives, neighbors, coffeehouse clients, and books dating from that era, he wrote his version of the catastrophe, as retold and postsigned by a certain H. F., who at one point defines himself as a saddler by trade.

The hoax worked. Published in 1722, the "journal" enjoyed an enormous success, owing not least to its "you are there" quality—its particularized geography (with names of London streets and areas still standing today), its statistical charts, and its wealth of itemized detail, with references to, for example, the killing of "forty thousand dogs and five times as many cats," or that time in August "when it was reported that 3,000 people died in one night."[24] Defoe's narrative tells powerfully of the loneliness of people dying either in the streets or abandoned in their quarantined homes. In addition, reflecting the fact that Defoe belonged to the antimonarchist and antiaristocratic Puritan sect of Dissenters, throughout his book there is a sense of frivolous, selfish Restoration London now being punished for its luxurious sins, of "some dreadful calamity and judgment coming upon the city,"[25] a sentiment almost grotesquely seconded by the preachers who go about prophesying the imminent destruction of London.

Though García Márquez's early journalism makes no references to the *Journal of the Plague Year*, in subsequent interviews the novelist would confess to an obsessive interest in that one Defoe work. He has even humorously stated that the volume which character Gabriel takes with him to Paris at the end of *One Hundred Years of Solitude* is not "the complete works of Rabelais" but Defoe's fabled *Journal*. In any case García Márquez fully assimilates the literary example of Defoe when he reports with great precision the calamities that culminate his major narratives, sets up a distinct geography with place-names immediately recognizable to northern Colombian readers, and in *One Hundred Years*, floats the implication that, even as Macondo becomes prosperous and frivolous and forgets its egalitarian and heroic past, it lays itself open to domination and destruction by outsiders—and, moreover, that solitude and lack of true solidarity are among the reasons for its eventual ruin.

Malaparte's *The Skin* enjoyed at one time a certain vogue in Latin America, and García Márquez dedicated an entire column in May 1951 to the book, singling it out for its lyricism, humor, narrative technique, and attitude toward life (*OP* 1:645–66). Owing to its prolixity *The Skin* is somewhat dated today, but one can see what it was about the book that attracted García Márquez at the time. Set in Naples—Italy's Third World or, if you will, its Mississippi—the memoir portrays a society in total crisis at the end of the war, with both the old aristocracy and the urban poor floundering about in a dazed, infrahuman decadence. An apocalyptic tone is set by Malaparte's initial account of a scarcely visible black wind that hovers over Europe, and by his later chapter dealing with the 1944 eruption of Mount Vesuvius. Through the journalist-narrator's eyes we also see the arriving Americans, who come across as innocent, well-meaning ignoramuses, and the sequence was surely noted by a García Márquez seeking ways of depicting Yankees objectively, without ideological or emotional interference. Malaparte's final reports of young Fascists being summarily executed by Communist partisans must have struck a young Gabo who, though by then a convinced leftist, would always show sensitivity to the tragedy of positive forces and liberators turning abusive and arbitrary once they reach power—the unfortunate if temporary case with Colonel Buendía and other Liberals in *One Hundred Years of Solitude*.

But the Malaparte episode that elicits the most commentary from Gabo is a chapter in which the body of a little girl (who may or may not be a mermaid or, possibly, even a fish) is served, amid the lettuce, at an officers' banquet at the Allied headquarters.[26] This scene, though purposely somewhat dreamlike and vague, inevitably draws our attention as a primary source for that terrible episode in *The Autumn of the Patriarch*, in which the roasted body of General Rodrigo de Aguilar, bedecked in uniform and medals, is very definitely served, amid cauliflower and bay leaves, at a banquet for the president's personal guard.

The one major Latin American writer who has exerted a proven influence on García Márquez is Juan Rulfo, from Mexico. This according to Gabo's biographer Dasso Saldívar: In 1961, as the newly arrived Colombian was just feeling his way through the thickets of cultural life in Mexico City, he asked his friend and expatriate countryman Álvaro Mutis for literary suggestions. Mutis gave him Rulfo's novel *Pedro Páramo* and the story collection *The Burning Plain*, noting, "Read this stuff, and don't fuck around, so you'll learn something about how to write."[27] That same night a restless Gabo went on to devour *Pedro Páramo*—twice—and plunged into the short stories the next day.

Before Saldívar's biography appeared in 1997, other critics had remarked on certain deep affinities between the two authors; the connection is now documented. In retrospect the link is a logical one, and on numerous fronts. First, there is the narrative geography. In both of his spare yet dense volumes,

Rulfo succeeds in evoking the parched feel and desolate atmosphere of his native, rural Jalisco sans resorting to folk dialect, local color, or descriptive overload—these the bane of much previous Latin American fiction. Moreover in depicting the rise of local crooks and despots and the fact of political corruption, he prudently steers clear of the trap of angry pamphleteering and denunciation, and even utilizes humor to good effect, as in the case of the story "Anacleto Morones" or the ending to "The Burning Plain." And he achieves all this via a prose instrument that is minimal yet beautiful, with no overwritten flights of rhetoric.

In Rulfo's narratives, moreover, the formal art carries as much weight as does the explosive subject matter—perhaps even more. Rulfo, it bears mention, was one of Mexico's first disciples of Faulkner, and the lessons he learned are clearly evident in *Pedro Páramo*, a novel recounted not in linear fashion but through mosaic-like fragments, the passage of time being flattened out into an eternal present via dozens of flashbacks and "flashforwards" stretching over decades. In addition, rather than a single, univocal point of view, the sad saga of Pedro and his town Comala is relayed from the constantly shifting perspectives—Pedro's own included—of various less-than-reliable narrators. As a result, the villainous protagonist is portrayed such that the reader can see him in-the-round and in-depth—can even, in some measure, pity him. The same structural technique is also utilized, on a smaller scale, in Rulfo's now-renowned stories "No Dogs Bark," "The Man," and "Luvina."

Perhaps most important of all, Rulfo in his novel makes wide, fruitful use of what, for lack of a better word, we would now dub "magical realism." The village of Comala is peopled almost entirely by ghosts, wraiths, phantoms, revenants, their presence treated not as strange but as perfectly banal, an everyday situation in which the quick and the dead coexist and converse, and in which the chief narrator, a Juan Preciado now laid in earth, actually chats regularly with the corpse next to his grave, a local woman by the name of Dorotea.

All of Rulfo's signature features as narrative artist are traits easily attributable to a mature Gabo. As a direct heir to Faulkner, Rulfo demonstrated to the younger, still-budding writer that the Mississippian's advances could be brought to bear upon a Latin American setting. The content of Rulfo's two brief tomes, along with his experimental form, his integration of the unreal with the ordinary, and his lapidary style, are all characteristics that would serve the apprentice García Márquez as models from which he might learn. One could venture to say that, without Rulfo's example, *One Hundred Years of Solitude* and *The Autumn of the Patriarch* might not have existed.

Though there are other readings that García Márquez on occasion has claimed as special favorites and even as influences on his art—novels by Conrad, or Thomas Mann, or Graham Greene, for instance—the works examined in this chapter are clearly those that have been the most crucial in guiding and shaping his sensibility, vision, and craft. As mentioned earlier, García Márquez, for all his broad literary culture, is not one to make a fetish out of books, whether old titles or new. He even likes to boast about discarding a volume once he has read it, and in fact his personal library is much less extensive than his collection of music recordings. And yet, in spite of his avowed distaste for highfalutin book-talk or fancy aesthetic schemes, as a writer in the 1940s and 1950s García Márquez started out as a disciple of what for the sake of shorthand we call "the classics." It is with these established, "canonized" works that he first served his apprenticeship, then struggling over the years to develop as journeyman and finally as master in his own right. The Bible, Sophocles, Rabelais, Kafka, Faulkner, Rulfo, et al.—their proven texts are among the many that have helped make our narrative tradition the record of experience, wisdom, and beauty that it is; and with *One Hundred Years of Solitude*, *The Autumn of the Patriarch*, his love novels, and some equally great if shorter works, García Márquez in turn expands, reshapes, and gives a new setting and new life to that tradition.

What his books tell, and how and why, will be the subject of the second half of this study.

The History of Macondo

To approach *One Hundred Years of Solitude* is not just to read a novel but to stumble onto a vast cultural territory and glimpse a dizzying array of people and patterns, horizons and meanings. Its chronology actually spans from the beginnings of European settlement in America to the dislocations of recent times—later sixteenth century to approximately mid-twentieth. Its characters and their actions represent an awesome range of personality types and happenings. Its world comprises the commonplace and everyday along with the extraordinary and the impossible. Its literary heritage includes ancient scripture, exploratory and family chronicle, Rabelaisian spoofery, and colonial romance. And its appeal is to all ideologies: leftists like its dealing with social struggles and its portrait of imperialism; conservatives are heartened by the corruption and/or failure of those struggles and with the sustaining role of the family; nihilists and quietists find their pessimism reconfirmed; and apolitical hedonists find solace in all the sex and swashbuckling. This is a book that in a very real sense has "something for everyone."[1]

Though the wealth of incident in *One Hundred Years* makes summarizing it all but impossible, here are the bare bones of the plot: The Buendías and followers journey south and found Macondo. Patriarch José Arcadio Buendía starts out enterprising but a mania for science drives him mad; wife Úrsula will provide the practical backbone for the clan. Gypsies regularly visit Macondo, bringing new gadgets; Melquíades, their wisest, writes some strange manuscripts before his death, Macondo's first. The Buendías' two sons, José Arcadio and Aureliano, engender respectively the illegitimate Arcadio and Aureliano José with a free-spirited Pilar Ternera; José Arcadio, afeared, runs off with the gypsies. Dance teacher Pietro Crespi courts the adopted Rebeca, and Buendía daughter Amaranta reacts with a poisonous sibling rivalry. At some point a priest founds a church, and Conservative magistrate Apolinar Moscote settles quietly in town to impose central authority, but an uprising led by the founding Buendía at first curbs Moscote. Liberal agitation and Conservative fraud spark a war in which Aureliano will become a famous colonel and Arcadio, briefly, a local despot. With the wars come the deaths of both illegitimate Buendías, Liberal sellout, an inglorious peace, and an embittered Aureliano. Around this time son José Arcadio, home from his travels, marries sister Rebeca; Pietro Crespi now turns to Amaranta, whose rejection drives him to suicide. José Arcadio soon dies mysteriously, as will the mad founder under a chestnut tree. Before his being executed, Arcadio and his common-law wife Santa Sofía de la Piedad will have the Segundo twins (whose identities are switched) and also engender Remedios the Beauty (apparently retarded). End of part one.

Aureliano Segundo, dissolute, will drink, eat, squander, and fornicate full-time with his mistress Petra Cotes, but also enter into misalliance with the beautiful, rich, stuffy Fernanda del Carpio. Their union begets José Arcadio, sent to seminary in Rome to become pope; Renata Remedios, "Meme," fun-loving and girlish, whose affair with auto mechanic Mauricio Babilonia will engender bastard son Aureliano; and Amaranta Úrsula, sent for her schooling to Brussels. Meanwhile, Remedios the Beauty drives many men to love-madness and death until the bright afternoon when she rises bodily to heaven. At some point Colonel Buendía's seventeen bastard sons show up with their mothers; one of them will bring a train, which brings in a foreign banana company, which in turn brings exploitation, corruption, and the murder of the seventeen sons. (The colonel himself dies soon of natural causes.) A workers' strike ensues; José Arcadio Segundo becomes a labor leader, and will be the sole surviving witness of an army massacre of three thousand demonstrators (a slaughter denied by officialdom and everyone else); a five-year rainstorm brings ruin to Macondo. Thereafter Úrsula, the twins, and Fernanda all die severally; Santa Sofía, exhausted, packs off. The bastard Aureliano grows up a bookish recluse, poring over Melquíades's manuscripts; a languid, hedonistic José Arcadio returns from his nonexistent "studies," turns the old house into a den of high pleasure, and is killed by young delinquents. The arrival of Amarant Úrsula with husband Gastón will result in a passionate aunt-nephew incest with Aureliano, the affair facilitated by Gastón's business travels. Her baby is born with the tail of a pig; she dies soon; Aureliano suddenly understands the manuscripts, which contain the entire history of Macondo up through the winds of its destruction and his own death, both to occur the moment he finishes deciphering. The End!

The almost bewilderingly high rate of incident in *One Hundred Years* is paralleled by its enormous cast of characters, many of which share names—four José Arcadios, three Aurelianos, an Arcadio, an Aureliano José, the seventeen bastard Aurelianos from the colonel's seventeen different women, and three females named Remedios. All this can be extremely confusing to first-time readers, who are at a loss as to which José Arcadio or Aureliano is it that does what with whom. These assorted name-groups nonetheless present a clearcut system of personality types that is to remain consistent throughout the narrative. ✕

The pattern is established in chapter 1, where we read of José Arcadio with his square head, thick hair, bodily strength, and lack of imagination, and of Aureliano with his eyes open at birth, taciturn temperament, and occasional flashes of clairvoyance. From the start these juxtaposed descriptions set off the physical and sensualist type, José Arcadio, from the sober, rational, slightly cold yet inspired thinking type, Aureliano. The differences will endure; in the course of Buendía history the extroverted José Arcadios will exist in the immediate realm of the senses and for the satisfaction thereof, indeed will live for sex and become its prisoners; more, owing to a lack either of "imagination" or of any need to exercise their minds, they will steer clear of long-range projects requiring thought or planning. The introverted Aurelianos by contrast are born thinkers who drift naturally into their roles as leaders, craftsmen, entrepreneurs, or scholars, and for whom the erotic and affective will remain largely subordinate to their broader schemes. In chapter 10 Úrsula herself notes that "While the Aurelianos were withdrawn but with lucid minds, the José Arcadios were impulsive and enterprising, but were marked with a tragic sign" (*CAS*, 228; *OYS*, 174). And their ways of death are as telling as their paths of life: whereas the José Arcadios all die suffering as victims of murder or disease (their "tragic sign"), all three Aurelianos die with their eyes open and their mental powers fully intact. ·what about the 17 Aurelianos...

There are exceptions to the pattern. José Arcadio Buendía, as originator of the line, will manifest both tendencies, though not necessarily in equilibrium; Arcadio and Aureliano José, as their variant names suggest, are freaks that stand outside the workings of the system; and while the twins do actually conform to the binary-opposition model, José Arcadio Segundo is the Aureliano of the pair and vice-versa, the result of their mischievous exchange of identifying shirts and bracelets as little boys.

For the women characters there is a similar if less elaborate formal architecture. The elegant cosmopolite Amaranta Úrsula inherits the boundless energy and initiative of her two namesakes, of Úrsula in particular. In describing Amaranta Úrsula's return in chapter 19, the text compares her directly to the great mother-figure and even employs the same adjectives ("active," "small") that had been applied to Úrsula in chapter 1. There is also a less visible line with the women named Remedios, all three of whom remain immature and either die young or disappear from the scene before they are able fully to develop. Girlish Meme, incidentally, is the only character in the entire book who bears a nickname, the symbol of her arrested youth. In addition there is Rebeca, who shows infantile characteristics such as prolonged thumb-sucking, and the initial syllable in her own name suggests her belonging in part to the Remedios camp.

Outside of the Buendía household are Pilar Ternera and Petra Cotes, both of whose first names evoke the firmness of stone.[2] Less than reputable individuals, with questionable occupations (fortune-telling; raffles), their free sexuality is also disruptive to a Buendía propriety solemnly embodied in Úrsula (and, parodically so, in Fernanda). They are the reigning erotic figures in the narrative. Pilar deflowers both José Arcadio and Aureliano, and will serve as matchmaker to *all* other Buendías who seek union with the opposite sex. (As Pilar remarks, "I'm happy knowing that people are happy in bed" [*CAS*, 201; *OYS*, 148].) The exceptions to Pilar Ternera's sexual "school" are the Segundo twins, who in turn are initiated by Petra Cotes, a latter-day avatar of Pilar. The two females present a pattern concretely representing our erotic side, and it is not accidental that the last of the original Macondians to die just before the final whirlwind is Pilar, who outlives her enemy Úrsula, and whose last act was to advise Aureliano to go and seduce his aunt. Her burial at the start of the chapter is capped with the terse reflection, "It was the end."[3]

When questioned publicly on one occasion about all these names-in-repetition, García Márquez quipped, "Is there anybody here who wasn't named after his dad?"[4] In real life, of course, families, prominent ones in particular, do tend to repeat certain names ("John Paul Doe IV"), continuities obviously being implied. The author of a family chronicle is hence under some obligation to represent these repetitions, and more, to depict "family resemblances" (or their obverse side, "family differences") at work. Mann's *Buddenbrooks*, to pick an earlier classic of the genre, has a "Johann" among each of its four generations. The genius of García Márquez is his having exaggerated so typical a household practice to a point of absurd consistency and comic newness.

Given so many repetitions, the temptation is to see in the one hundred years of Macondo a century without change. It is essential, however, to take note of the differing circumstances that attend those seeming recurrences. While Colonel Aureliano Buendía has done battle against the national Conservatives, his grandnephew (and secret namesake) José Arcadio Segundo is to agitate against a multinational firm that represents a later, imperial phase in the story of Macondo and the world. Similarly, Amaranta Úrsula may carry on her great matriarchal ancestor's name and traditions, but she is at the same time a thoroughly modern young cosmopolite, Europeanized, emancipated, something of a swinger, as is her brother José Arcadio, both of them growing up as products of their family's latter-day preeminence.

Repetition versus change of course is what human history is about, and Macondo fans will tend toward the former or the latter according to their own respective ideological preferences. One key moment that dramatically illustrates García Márquez's subtle interweaving of the two is the opening sentence in chapter 10 (roughly the halfway mark in the book): "Years later on his deathbed Aureliano Segundo would remember the rainy afternoon in June when he went into the bedroom to meet his first son" (*CAS*, 228; *OYS*, 174). Its linguistic shape closely replicates that of the famous opening lines of the novel itself: "Many years later, as he faced the firing squad, Colonel Aureliano Buendía was to remember that distant afternoon when his father took him to discover ice" (*CAS*, 59; *OYS*, 11).

The later sentence distinctly echoes the syntax, verb tenses, and lexicon of the first: the adverbial clause of time ("Years later") and then of place, the subject "Aureliano," the predicate "remember" in a quasi-conditional form ("había de recordar" in both originals), and the closure with an infinitive clause (again, "conocer" in both) followed by direct object. The actual *content* of the chapter 10 sentence, by stark contrast, gives us not the heroic Colonel Aureliano Buendía defiantly facing a firing squad (which he will miraculously survive) but the dissolute Aureliano *Segundo* (literally "the Second") on his deathbed, perishing of a throat ailment; what he remembers, moreover, is not the original wonders of ice but the sight of his firstborn José Arcadio, "languid and weepy," who will himself grow up dissipated and irresponsible, possibly pederastic. like pedophilia, but more like grooming?

At this point certain caveats and distinctions are in order concerning the way time is represented in *One Hundred Years of Solitude*. First, and most obvious, the effect of García Márquez's decision not to number his chapters is to make readers think of the book as a single entity whose twenty unmarked subdivisions exist not as discrete segments but interlinked members within a unitary whole: one text. This larger design is further stressed by the book's immediately visible format of lengthy, fluid, event-filled paragraphs interspersed with minimal (if carefully chosen) dialogue. From sentence to paragraph, and from episode to chapter to the full text of García Márquez's seamless narrative, things never stop happening, and time ceases only after the final line. The long-term changes and passing time in Macondo can be more or less periodized into a quartet of "stages" that cluster into chapters as follows: utopian innocence/social harmony (1–5), military heroism/struggle for auιomy (6–9), economic prosperity/spiritual decline (10–15), and final decadence/physical destruction (16–20).

On the other hand, it should be borne in mind that *One Hundred Years of Solitude*, while basically chronological and "linear" enough in its broad outlines, also shows abundant zigzags in time, both flashbacks of matters past and long leaps toward events future — as seen in the structure of the very first two chapters (discussed above, chapter 5). Those mortal scenes of the firing squad and deathbed with which the two key sentences from chapters 1 and 10 start out are not actually to occur until — in each case — over a hundred pages hence. In a similar instance, the youthful amour between Meme Buendía and Mauricio Babilonia is already in full swing before we are informed, later on in the same chapter, about the origins of the affair. Time in the novel is as subject to large-scale narrative shifts as it was in Faulkner's now-classic works; García Márquez's temporal dislocations, by contrast, are unobtrusive, and call as little attention to themselves as do his own more celebrated violations of laws physical and spatial.

One Hundred Years of Solitude is unique even among Latin American novels for the degree to which it successfully integrates private and public concerns. The former comprise such things as family life, sexual desire, and romantic love; the latter include the series of migrations, rebellions, wars, ceremonies, strikes, and repressions. Women figure more prominently in the first than in the second.

For all its fantastical exaggerations, and its natural or political catastrophes (those stereotypical Latin experiences), the narrative center of *One Hundred Years* is its faithful and convincing account of the domestic routines and vicissitudes of the Buendía clan. We read of such expected matters as daily housekeeping, marital tensions, the raising of offspring, children at play, and sibling differences, all scrupulously reported by a wise, omniscient narrator. When Úrsula refuses to move from Macondo and peremptorily reminds her husband to tend to his two sons, when Aureliano Segundo marries a woman whom no one else in the family fold likes, when the same Aureliano Segundo is thrown into a quandary over his teenaged daughter's incommunicativeness, or when the elderly kinfolk withdraw into their silent selves, we see some typically intimate household dramas, familiar and familial both. In addition, at different points García Márquez will take note of the current source of Buendía income, be it Úrsula's candies, José Arcadio's landgrabs, Petra's raffles, or the last José Arcadio's pawned heirlooms and hidden treasure. Even in a "magical" Macondo, the everyday meals come from somewhere.

Romantic love and sexual desire provide the means for close ties outside of the family, and of this there is an abundance. It is nothing short of astounding how wide a range of erotic experience (in the largest sense of the word) is to be found in *One Hundred Years*: for instance, conjugal love (José Arcadio Buendía/Úrsula), adolescent crushes (Aureliano/Remedios Moscote), casual affairs (Pilar Ternera/José Arcadio, later Aureliano), traditional, proper, gracious courtship (Pietro Crespi/Rebeca, later Amaranta), marriage by accident (Arcadio/Santa Sofía de la Piedad), ménage à trois (Aureliano Segundo/Fernanda del Carpio/Petra Cotes), misalliance (Aureliano/Remedios, Aureliano Segundo/Fernanda), torrid adolescent passion (Meme/Mauricio Babilonia), possible pederasty (José Arcadio the seminarian/the four boys), modern "emancipated" marriage (Amaranta Úrsula/Gastón), and impassioned true love leading to *Liebestod* (Aureliano Babilonia/Amaranta Úrsula).

There are of course the inevitable brothels, one of them Pilar's establishment, frequented by some men. And there are the assorted erotic (or anti-erotic) types: José Arcadio the impetuous stud; Rebeca the insatiable wife; Remedios the Beauty, a femme most fatale; Fernanda the haughty and beautiful prude; Petra the eternal mistress; and Amaranta the anguished virgin and the tease, destructive and sad, whose name, ironically, contains the Spanish verb *amar*, but who is herself incapable of love, wanting only those men whom she cannot have while summarily rejecting those whom she can.

One erotic complex persisting like a leitmotif throughout Buendía history is the instinctive impulse toward incest and the corresponding prohibition. The original couple are in fact first cousins (though cousin marriages do admittedly occupy "a special place in the rules of kinship").[5] Thereafter most of the males in the book will either actively seek sexual union with consanguineous females—mothers or aunts—or at the least desire them. Images of Úrsula flash into José Arcadio's mind when he first sleeps with Pilar Ternera; and José Arcadio the seminarian will have his great-grandaunt Amaranta on his mind even when his lifeless body floats in the pool. The earlier José Arcadio actually goes so far as to marry his (albeit adoptive) sister Rebeca.

Of course there is also the concern about babies being born with pig's tails, and it is only because of women's fears of this disquieting eventuality that ordinary incest prohibitions are obeyed by anyone at all. Though Amaranta does lead on Aureliano José for years with her teasing games, she will in time put an abrupt and brutal end to their charade. The single exception to the pattern is Amaranta Úrsula, whose ardent and loving incestuous amour with Aureliano takes place only when the general decay in Macondo has gone so far as to make all social rules irrelevant. By making the dialectic of incest attraction/repression so crucial a force in the Buendías' existence, their Colombian creator succeeds in touching upon the very foundations of human society, for, as anthropologist A. L. Kroeber noted, the incest taboo is "the only universal institution." Or in Lévi-Strauss's words, incest prohibitions are "on the threshold of culture, in culture, and in one sense . . . [are] culture itself."[6]

It is the women of Macondo, moreover, who restrain the larger-scale antisocial impulses of the men and who furnish them basic stability, continuity, and essential order. As Luis Harss long ago remarked:

> In García Márquez men are flighty creatures, governed by whim, fanciful dreamers given to impossible delusions, capable of moments of haughty grandeur, but basically weak and unstable. Women, on the other hand, are solid, sensible, unvarying and down to earth, paragons of order and stability. They seem to be more at home in the world, more deeply rooted in their nature, closer to the center of gravity, therefore better equipped to face up to circumstances. García Márquez puts it another way: "My women are masculine."[7]

Hence while José Arcadio Buendía is vainly pursuing his scientific and technological will-o'-the-wisps, it becomes Úrsula's lot to expand the family home and to bring in income by launching and supervising the animal-candies business; and for all her visionary husband's grand attempts at exploration, it is she who brings back with her from her travels the retinue of new and more "modern" settlers who possess the latest gadgetry and receive regular mail service. In the same way, Aureliano Segundo's monumental dissipation would be impossible without the divers enterprises of his mistress Petra; and once Santa Sofía de la Piedad, the last of the old reliable Buendía women, simply leaves, the house falls rapidly into disrepair. Amaranta Úrsula on her return from Belgium brings temporary renovations and renewed vigor, but the ensuing affair with her nephew leads the two down the path of total irresponsibility, and they all but yield the old mansion to the vegetation and the ants.

Amid Macondo's populous cast about the only personage who comes across as more than two-dimensional, who demonstrates more than simply a few comical traits and performs a multiplicity of legitimate, necessary roles, whose actions go beyond a kind of caricaturesque extremism and whose emotions show a textured depth and empathetic, complex qualities, indeed the only character in García Márquez's book who is treated without a smiling irony, happens to be the greatest of all the women in *One Hundred Years of Solitude*. In the eloquent words of Cuban novelist Reinaldo Arenas (written some years before he turned against the Colombian), Úrsula Iguarán de Buendía is "the bride filled with prejudices on her wedding night; she is the loving mother, concerned, at times intolerable, at times heroic; she is the inconsolable widow who weeps under the almond trees in the afternoons . . . ; she is the centenarian who conceals her blindness so as to avoid pity; she is the almost delirious and withered great-grandmother who knows that preparing a dessert in the kitchen is one of the indispensable rituals for maintaining the equilibrium of the home."[8]

Above all Úrsula is the classic figure of the mother, for Latin Americans especially but for others as well. A woman with no use for gratuitous amusements and who "at no moment in her life had been heard to sing" (CAS, 66; OYS, 18), she is redeemed from joyless drudgery by her moral strength and her sheer energy, activism, and "unbreakable nerves." An unarrogant matriarch who wields considerable authority, it is she who restrains the hotheaded martinet Arcadio, beats him to submission when he is about to shoot Don Apolinar Moscote, and annuls his stupid decrees; she who, when Colonel Buendía is in jail, pushes her way through the prison guards in order to visit her son and sneak him a pistol (but also, being a mother, reminds him to take good care of his sores); she who (in a brief scene of tragic, solemn grandeur) saves Gerineldo Márquez from arbitrary execution at the hands of her same power-intoxicated son the colonel; and she who, in her old age, keeps Melquíades's room in livable condition when a fugitive José Arcadio Segundo ends up hiding there for his remaining days. While many of the more forceful and positive figures in García Márquez's writings are female, amid them Úrsula Buendía stands out as an instance of the potential for simple human greatness.

The public sphere in One Hundred Years of Solitude includes the social movements, the government actions, the technological changes (railroads, movies, telephones), and the ecological developments, and also those organized rituals such as wakes and group mourning, festive orgies and carnival, all of which affect Macondo life at every possible level and give the book its outer boundaries and broad shape. For this purpose García Márquez builds his narrative around the larger blocks of Colombian (and by extension Latin American) history: the early process of Spanish colonization and inland settlement, the bloody wars of the nineteenth century, the repeated instances of illusory prosperity based on a single product, and the hegemonic power of the U.S. economy in our time.

During each of these historical sections García Márquez evokes appropriate sorts of period detail. In the opening chapters we read about the spear of José Arcadio Buendía that, years ago, had been used for hunting jaguars, or the suit of armor and the landlocked galleon inexplicably discovered in the jungle wilderness, or the "three colonial coins" with which José Arcadio Buendía pays Melquíades for a magnifying glass. The raid by British imperialist Francis Drake on Riohacha really did happen, in 1596; here it functions as prime mover in the chain of events starting with the southward flight of Úrsula's great-great-grandmother. Her indulgent spouse is described as "an Aragonese merchant," in other words a Spanish colonist, who will succeed in settling quietly among some peaceful indigenes—the most benevolent of possible fates for either party (and not the only such instance in history). On the other hand, the fact that the Guajiro Indians, Visitación and Cataure, come of princely stock but now serve the Buendías is an example, however benign, of the submission of the native peoples to the Hispanics. (The plague of insomnia / amnesia, brought by Rebeca from the Guajiros, can be seen as symbolic of the Indians' loss both of bodily peace and spiritual history.) The subsequent roamings of the Buendías and the founder's quest for the sea represent typical early Spanish explorers' enterprises.

With the episodes concerning magistrate Don Apolinar Moscote and the ensuing civil wars, García Márquez telescopes two epochs: the bloody struggles for independence from the Spanish Crown (1810–25), and the endless strife between Liberals and Conservatives that characterized the entire nineteenth century in virtually all of the newly founded Latin American republics. Don Apolinar typifies the centralist tradition of old Spain; he is the only important character in *One Hundred Years* with the honorific "Don"; and his very style is that of the straitlaced Spanish bureaucrat. His title, in the original *"corregidor"*—literally "co-ruler" or "co-reigner"—signifies "a magistrate who exercised royal jurisdiction in his community or district" of the Spanish Empire.[9] His sealed, certified rule is opposed by the organically based authority of the founder Buendía, who informs the stolid official that "in this town we do not give orders with pieces of paper" (*CAS*, 111; *OYS*, 61). (Owing to a false etymology, the word *corregidor* looks like "corrector" in Spanish, which prompts José Arcadio Buendía's untranslatable pun, "no necesitamos ningún corregidor porque aquí no hay nada que corregir" [*CAS*, 111].) We also find out in chapter 4 that the meddlesome priest Father Nicanor Reyna had actually been brought to Macondo by Don Apolinar, the two thus reenacting the notorious Spanish alliance between church and state.

At the same time there is on Don Apolinar's office wall "a shield of the republic," and he issues a decree to have all houses painted blue—the official color of the Conservative party of Colombia. His being the appointee of a remote and shadowy government reflects the fact that, until 1987, town mayors in Colombia were not elected locally but assigned by Bogotá.

The chaotic warfare of chapters 5–9 is, by admission of the author, based concretely on Colombia's nineteenth-century conflicts. The character of Colonel Buendía is closely modeled after General Rafael Uribe Uribe, a legendary figure of Liberal politics and of the Thousand Days' War under whose command the novelist's grandfather Márquez fought. Like Aureliano Buendía, Uribe Uribe was born on a rainy day, won no military victories throughout his long career, spearheaded revolts even when the official party line was antiwar, sparked rebellions on the Atlantic coast when hostilities had all but ceased, was repudiated as "irresponsible" by the Liberal directorate, traveled to Central America in search of support from Liberal governments there, served more than one jail sentence, was publicly paraded on the city streets during one of his arrests, enjoyed good personal relations with a Conservative general, and officially capitulated at the Treaty of Neerlandia (named for a banana plantation then owned by a Dutchman).[10]

The Liberal forces in Macondo fail miserably as a result of dwindling support from Liberal landowners, opportunistic proposals from the six lawyers in frock coats (who essentially call for scrapping and selling out the Liberal platform), and the sheer exhaustion brought about by war. Similarly, throughout the history of Latin America, liberalism has few real success stories to offer for like reasons of opportunism as well as the lack of a broad enough economic base or of deeply rooted liberal traditions. The brief spells of arbitrary power enjoyed by young zealot Arcadio and by the *caudillo* Aureliano are suggestive of, say, the long illiberal tyranny of the Somoza clan, who nonetheless were of the Liberal party of Nicaragua. Subsequent to the publication of *One Hundred Years of Solitude* we witnessed the spectacle of bloody military juntas in Argentina and Chile promoting *economic* liberalism while savagely suppressing the more attractive social and cultural aspects of the liberal ideal.

The economic and political takeover of Macondo by the banana firm, the strike by field workers, and the military repression and massacre are all closely based on actual events and specific details of the 1900–1928 period. From modest Colombian holdings the United Fruit Company of Boston would soon grow into a virtual state-within-a-state in a zone stretching from coastal Santa Marta down to Aracataca. As in Macondo, the firm had its separate American-style residential compounds, company stores for foodstuffs, and its own irrigation system and water policy. Hiring its field hands only through subcontractors (so as to avoid Colombian labor legislation), its consistent claim was that United Fruit had no employees on its payroll. Similarly, the six lawyers in *One Hundred Years* argue that "the banana company did not have, never had had, and never would have any workers in its service," and the court establishes "in solemn decrees that the workers did not exist" (*CAS*, 339; *OYS*, 280).[11]

Both in history and in García Márquez's novel the basic demands of the workers were/are for decent health facilities, hygienic dwelling places, one day off in seven, and payment in cash rather than paper scrip valid only in the company's stores. During the agitation for these demands, company executive Thomas Bradshaw was to absent himself in order not to negotiate with labor leaders; García Márquez's Jack Brown pursues this same tactic.[12] And when the thirty-two thousand workers walked out en masse on 7 October 1928, the Conservative government in Bogotá promptly responded with military occupation of the entire area and assignment of strikebreaking troops to cut and ship banana bunches. This sequence is closely retained by García Márquez, as is the state of siege that was officially declared by the government on 5 December.

That evening a few hundred workers and their families were to gather for a demonstration in the central plaza at Ciénaga (a town located some fifty miles north of Aracataca), and an army detachment was then sent there by General Carlos Cortés Vargas—the name of the author of Decree no. 4 in *One Hundred Years of Solitude*. The state of siege announcement was read to the tense crowd, who were given five minutes to disperse, and another minute extra (as happens in Macondo). Gunfire broke out; from a nearby hotel someone heard cries of "¡AY MI MADRE!" (a common Spanish exclamation, roughly equivalent to "Oh my God!"); the phrase is reproduced in García Márquez and rendered as "Aaaagh, Mother" in Rabassa's translation. Witnesses would later report having seen the bodies thrown into trucks which then headed toward the sea—the basis for the novelist's two-hundred-car train piled high with workers' corpses. Following the slaughter the authorities arrested hundreds of labor leaders (a railroad foreman recalled having been on a train filled to the brim with detained workers); in *One Hundred Years*, save for a lucky José Arcadio Segundo, the leaders are wiped out.

Concerning casualties for the entire strike, General Cortés Vargas would cite a figure of 40 dead and 100 wounded. By contrast a prominent union leader, Alberto Castrillón, would calculate the dead at Ciénaga alone at 400; for the larger strike he estimated a total of 1,500 dead and 3,000 wounded-García Márquez thus took for his climactic scene the highest of all reported casualty figures.[13] The human damage was minimized by the Conservative press, the government, and the company's supporters; in Macondo it is simply exorcised out of existence. (On my own visit to Aracataca in 1982, I actually met a retired United Fruit timekeeper who passionately assured me that the massacre had never taken place—"it's all just a story," he said.)[14] The five-year rain in the book is initiated by the company in order to evade negotiations; in their respective Indochina wars, the French and later the Americans regularly seeded clouds in order to cause rainstorms for military ends (the former instance being the subject of a 1954 article by García Márquez—*OP*, 3:873–74).

While the decay of Macondo in chapters 16–20 owes more to Faulkner than to "history," the matter of Aureliano Babilonia is most notable for its autobiographical elements. García Márquez likes to recall how, when he was taking on the writing of the final chapters of his novel, he felt so sure of what he was doing that he decided to really enjoy himself and bring his own favorite people into Macondo. Hence the wise Catalonian who gives old books to Aureliano and leaves behind a roomful of manuscripts on his departure is the now-legendary Ramon Vinyes, the erudite Catalan bookseller who introduced young Gabo to the European moderns and left dozens of unpublished works in Catalan at his death. Aureliano Babilonia's four pals have the first names of Gabo's three drinking buddies in Barranquilla ("Gabriel" being the fourth), his best friends for life. At the pharmacy in Macondo there lives "Mercedes, Gabriel's stealthy girl friend"—a loving reference to the novelist's wife, in her youth a pharmacist. "Gabriel" travels to Paris and relives Gabo's hard times there. (In addition, Julio Cortázar's part-Parisian novel *Hopscotch* is alluded to in Gabriel's sad hotel room where one day the baby "Rocamadour was to die.") Amaranta Úrsula wants two children christened Rodrigo and Gonzalo—the names of Gabo's own sons. This most public of novels is thus also well supplied with private jokes. (The reference to German pilots with whom Gastón is competing in chapter 20 is an oblique allusion to the Avianca airline, first started by German entrepreneurs.)

The public and private spheres in García Márquez's book are by no means separate but rather mingle with and interpenetrate one another. Acts that are seemingly private have social consequences—particularly in the case of marriage, whereby families make a mutual "exchange" of members. Young Aureliano nurtures an adolescent love of Remedios Moscote, who it so happens is a daughter of the Buendías' ideological foe, and the ensuing marriage will in fact help Conservative officialdom solidify its hold on the town. In the same way, the love-at-first-sight that seizes Aureliano Segundo for Fernanda del Carpio is emotion directed at a prime specimen of those very reactionaries against whom Colonel Buendía had once fought, a carnival queen whose "royal guard" in Moorish robes is suspected of having gunned down forty townspeople.

Public developments, conversely, can influence private life in *One Hundred Years*. The banana firm is a case in point. The hapless stranger who, from ogling Remedios the Beauty in the shower, slips and cracks his skull, is one of the many out-of-towners who have converged upon Macondo in search of company largesse. In the same way, it is through Meme's adolescent friendship with some American corporate "brats" that she meets her lover-to-be Mauricio Babilonia, himself a mechanic's apprentice for the banana company. Nevertheless, García Márquez's narrator doesn't insist upon these links — in contrast with the flawed United Fruit trilogy of Guatemalan novelist Miguel Ángel Asturias, where everything from sex to baseball occurs in the shadow of Tropical Banana Inc. While the arrival of the nameless fruit company in Macondo sets the stage for a variety of escapades, erotic and otherwise, these in turn have artistic self-sufficiency and a narrative density and vitality all their own.

In addition to the more conflictual aspects of Macondo public life already discussed, there are the organized rituals — such as the different wakes and public mourning for Melquíades, Pietro Crespi, and Amaranta. And there is the mass merriment of the carnival at the end of chapter 10, evocative of the renowned yearly carnival at Barranquilla, with the crowning of its queen-elect and its conga lines of dancers in bright, colorful costumes — roles here instanced respectively by Remedios the Beauty (whose family name will tragically politicize the event) and by a carefree Aureliano Segundo fulfilling his lifelong dream of dressing up in tiger's garb.[15]

Behind García Márquez's scrupulousness in rendering the history and folklore of his region is a larger fidelity to reality itself. He never lets even the humblest of particulars escape him, be it the clothes a character is wearing on his or her first appearance in the book or the contents of a meal someone might be eating (often fried bananas, a typical Caribbean snack). Because he is telling the story of a family, he does not neglect to mention how each successive brood of children is raised, and by whom. This utter care in the use of detail is beautifully exemplified in an unusually frank recollection made by the author in an early interview, held in the first heat of the book's best-sellerdom. The author talked of his consulting books on alchemy, navigation, poisons, disease, cookery, home medicines, and Colombia's civil wars, as well as "the 24 volumes of the *Encyclopedia Britannica*," and also having to find out "how you can tell the sex of a shrimp, how a man is executed by firing squad, and how you determine quality in bananas. I had to drop a character because I wasn't able to find anybody who could translate seven Papiamento phrases for me; I had to look up a great deal about Sanskrit; I had to figure out the weight of 7,214 doubloons so as to be certain that they could be carried by four kids. . . ."[16] Needless to say, once he became the subject of hundreds more such interviews, García Márquez would be much less forthcoming about the secrets of his trade.

The political objectivity of the novelist is also worth mention. Though García Márquez may personally sympathize with his Liberals, he shuns any depiction of them as virtuous and of their adversaries as merely villainous. While his Conservatives are mostly dishonest and practice electoral fraud (as indeed they have done in history), the Liberals in turn are initially egged on by agitator-terrorist Alirio Noguera, a fraudulent doctor and professional adventurer who is possessed by a mystique of violence and sees assassination as his patriotic duty. Later, during the armed conflict, the Liberal side has as its local leader a resentful, immature, and impulsive Arcadio, the lonely bastard Buendía and "the cruelest ruler that Macondo had ever known," who loves strutting about in his uniform and whose eleven months in power are characterized by interminable decrees, gratuitous executions, and a general ambience of fear. Don Apolinar Moscote is thus not completely off the mark with his off-the-cuff, I-told-you-so sarcasm, "This is the Liberal Paradise."

On the other hand, in General Raquel Moncada, who serves as mayor of Macondo at war's end, we have the genuinely good Conservative, an antimilitarist military man who wears civilian garb, disarms the police, gives aid to Liberals who have lost relatives in the war, and sets up a humane regime in the town. Tragically, in the name of "the Revolution," Moncada is executed by order of Colonel Buendía himself, who most disturbingly embodies the process of political corruption: an intelligent man, idealistic in his youth, later a *caudillo* celebrated by the masses, and eventually driven to harsh and arbitrary rule by "the intoxication of power," who burns down Moncada's widow's house when she dares to defy him, has rival General Teófilo Vargas murdered and then liquidates a young officer precisely for having suggested such an action, and indeed attains such absolute sway that his orders are obeyed even before they are issued! By avoiding any simplistic, Manichaean vision of ideological conflict, García Márquez gives narrative shape to a profound and tragic truth: namely, that retrograde forces can have decent and fair-minded individuals in their ranks, while worthy causes can fall into the hands of infantile zealots, self-seeking opportunists, or hardened cynics.

Of course *One Hundred Years of Solitude* is best known not for its scrupulous realism (a trait in some ways homely, "unglamorous") but for its imaginative flights of fantasy, its unreal sorts of actions such as a levitating priest, a young woman who rises to heaven, and an apparently conscious trickle of blood. It is not that material of this kind is new in literature — like events are commonly depicted in folk myth, classical epic, medieval romance, fairy tale, gothic novel, and science fiction. What is special about García Márquez's book is its perfect integration of these unusual incidents into the everyday life represented in a text largely realistic. Among critics as well as readers there is well-nigh universal agreement that the fantastical element in *One Hundred Years* is neither obtrusive nor gratuitous but rather succeeds in enriching, supporting, and enhancing the narrative and its array of themes.

The fantasy matter in García Márquez's novel forms a broad and diverse spectrum ranging from the literally extraordinary though nonetheless possible, to the farthest extremes of the physically fabulous and unlikely. As an example of the former, the remotely possible, when Colonel Aureliano Buendía shoots himself in the chest, the bullet comes out through his back without having injured a single vital organ. This has been known to occur; when a despondent young Joseph Conrad attempted suicide in Marseilles, it is precisely (and fortunately for literature) what happened. In another instance, Úrsula secretly figures out the exact trajectory of the sun and the configuration of shadows it will cast within the house, day by day, in the course of the year. In fact many an earlier, "primitive" civilization, without technology, has achieved that level of knowledge of astronomy and given it concrete application in its architecture. Similarly, the account of the thousands of dead birds that fall to the ground in the wake of Úrsula's own death is an incident that has been specifically recorded in South America: in 1925 the north-south El Niño current in the eastern Pacific "caused the death of millions of birds, which were hurled upon the shores of Ecuador and Colombia."[17]

The next level of unreality is the systematic use of hyperbole, exaggerated entities represented with a precision that gives them a distinct, palpable, and cogent profile. García Márquez himself has remarked on more than one occasion that if you say you have seen a pink elephant, you will not be believed, but say that you saw seventeen pink elephants flying about that afternoon, and your story gains in verisimilitude. The exaggeration in *One Hundred Years of Solitude*, accordingly, is almost always numerically specific: Colonel Buendía's thirty-two defeated uprisings; Fernanda's minutely crisscrossed calendar of sex (with its exactly forty-two available days); the ten, fourteen, and then twenty men required to overpower the founder in his climactic fit of madness; the rainstorm that lasts four years, eleven months, and two days; and the overnight erasure from public memory of the massacre of banana workers (a telescoping of the lengthy process whereby all societies cover up their darker pasts).

Flying carpets and human levitation, in contrast, are events truly magical, and their author's conjuring craft deserves a closely detailed look. As has often been noted, what makes these unrealities convincing and credible is the entire narrative and physical scaffold that surrounds them. In the classic instance, Father Nicanor Reyna gulps down a cup of hot chocolate each time he is about to rise from the ground. The impression created thereby is that the humble beverage has something to do with the priest's powers (though of course it could be merely ritualistic). The fact that Father Reyna performs this feat with a view to raising money for a church—suggestive of a street-juggling act or perhaps of those eclipses used by Western explorers to impress the natives—serves to demystify its significance somewhat. Father Reyna's divine miracle is moreover put into question by the soberly scientific explanation proffered by a mad but still knowledgeable José Arcadio Buendía. (Their exchange in Latin is as follows. The founder: "This is very simple. This man here has entered the fourth state of matter." The priest: "No, this fact proves beyond doubt the existence of God.")

In like fashion the dead bodies of the love-victims of Remedios the Beauty emanate a sweet, secret perfume, the suggestion being that her mortal effects on the men have obscure biochemical origins. (Norman Mailer in his book on Marilyn Monroe observes that one of the blonde actress's attractions was her distinct fragrance, and dress-shop clerks would remark, "She has a *smell!*") García Márquez's beautiful young innocent is also his literal version of the old femme fatale stereotype, who in this case brings about the *immediate* death of her loving admirers, sans the usual intervening rituals of courtship. Her rise to heaven is in turn a parody of the Catholic folk-legend (and official church dogma since 1950) of the Assumption of the Virgin Mary, the colorful image of which adorns millions of Hispanic homes. (Assumption Day—15 August—is a national holiday in many a Hispanic country, and the capital of Paraguay is Asunción.) Remedios the Beauty waves good-bye as her body rises, her other hand clutching Fernanda's sheets (which the women of the family had been in the process of folding), all of it lending solidity and humor to the event, while Fernanda's petty rage over the loss of her precious old linen distracts from the unreality but also makes it funny. The latter sort of flimflam can be seen in the episode of the flying carpet in chapter 3, presented as merely incidental to the sexual encounter transpiring, back on the ground, between José Arcadio and the gypsy girl; and José Arcadio Buendía's telling the ghost of Prudencio Aguilar to "go to hell" is to treat the phantom more as a common nuisance than as a supernatural terror.

The wilder incidents in *One Hundred Years of Solitude* make perfect sense for their respective characters and situations. The subject matter is often death, an event so typically charged with ultimate emotions and concerns that it calls out for meaningful legend (whether religious or literary) from the imagination. The trickle of blood that travels across town from José Arcadio to his mother Úrsula has obvious Oedipal and umbilical implications (the Spanish word in the original is "thread"); its well-grounded trajectory is described in geometric, almost pedantic detail—and is then rerun in reverse for Úrsula! The rain of yellow flowers at the founder's death represents all of Nature in mourning for a great man ("the king," as the Indian Cataure calls him), a theme common enough in world myths, while the perils of pretension are dissipated by the final mention of the rakes and shovels needed to clear the thick carpet of flowers from the street. Fernanda del Carpio's beautiful non-decomposing corpse perfectly befits a woman for whom appearances and propriety are what have most mattered. The utter finality and shock of human death provide the basis for these eschatological fables and little apocalypses from García Márquez's pen.

In another vein Mauricio Babilonia's swarm of yellow butterflies can be seen as representing a soft, "poetic" side to his sensuality, making the apprentice auto mechanic more than just an aggressive stud, and thus more plausibly attractive to a girlish Meme Buendía. The invisibility of José Arcadio Segundo before the government troops, and the physical rise of the parchments beyond the reach of rampant teenagers, both take place in Melquíades's room, a consecrated space where the gypsy's ghost puts in an occasional appearance, where the secrets of Macondo are to be found, and where everything is therefore possible. The expected wonder of all such happenings is nonetheless displaced as the townspeople routinely accept these extravagant unrealities while reserving their incredulity and awe for technological artifacts like moving pictures or false teeth. The magnets on the very first page of the text are presented by Melquíades himself as an "eighth wonder" and the Macondians are correspondingly amazed, something they will never be in the face of truly fantastical events.

In conversation García Márquez likes to bring up the humble and everyday origins of these episodes, such as the electrician who after every repair job would inadvertently leave behind him (as grandmother Márquez always noted) a white butterfly fluttering about the house. For the story of the rise of Remedios the Beauty the novelist took his remembered cue from a real-life account: apparently there was a young lady in Aracataca who ran off with a traveling salesman; her parents, in order to preempt gossip and deny the disgrace, claimed last having seen her ascending toward heaven, and even commented that "If the Virgin Mary could do it, so can our daughter."[18] The masterful stroke of including Fernanda's linen came to the author reportedly by chance; finding himself stumped, unable to make Remedios the Beauty's comical assumption sufficiently credible, he noticed a maid next door hanging up some wash—whence there arrived the inspiration for the sheets, and the narrative problem was solved.[19]

MAJOR DIFFERENCE

What in the end holds together the many strands in *One Hundred Years of Solitude* is the narrative's consistent unity of voice, a voice unflaggingly sustained throughout the novel. Whether the subject be love or phantoms, orgies or uprisings, the narrator conveys it all with the same serene attitude of imperturbability. García Márquez was retrospectively to credit his story-telling grandmother with having furnished him precisely the style and "sound" he needed, and indeed the descriptive and narrative prose in the book, while neither colloquial nor cutely "folksy," is nonetheless oral in its fluid rhythms, its relatively straightforward syntax and simple lexicon, and its dignified and traditionalist (though unacademic) flavor.

It is a special, distinctively wise voice—omniscient about the townspeople yet still *of* rather than *above* the townspeople. In a fundamental example, the narrator will see both the encroaching Conservatives and the aggressive Americans the way the ordinary villagers see them—as oddly exotic but also as remotely powerful. The only *inside* glimpse we are allowed of the Moscotes or of the Yankees will come via the tender adolescent eyes first of Aureliano (through his love of Remedios) and then of Meme (through her friendship with the manager Mr. Brown's daughter, the stereotypical *gringa* Patricia). "Americans" and "Yankees," it should be remarked, are words notably absent from these chapters, and the strange language the foreigners speak remains largely nameless. Again, company abuses are narrated with a tone of voice indistinguishable from that with which we are told of, say, Aureliano Segundo's dissipation or Meme's frivolity. Despite the importance of the gringos' role in their few chapters, *One Hundred Years* is a book not "about" Yankee imperialism (as is in fact the case with Miguel Ángel Asturias's banana trilogy or César Vallejo's *El tungsteno*)—but about Macondo. The seasoned narrator of García Márquez's text knows that the banana-company exploitation (another absent word), strike, and massacre are key moments and factors, though still only moments, and not the sole factors, in Macondo history.

Just as *One Hundred Years of Solitude* gathers into its prose a vast range of human experiences, it similarly brings between its covers an impressive array of literary genres. Earlier we examined the determining presence of high biblical and tragical elements in this and other García Márquez works. Equally worth a passing glance is his fruitful use of stock conventions from the other end of the generic scale—the popular melodrama. The assassination of Aureliano José in a crowded theater, the violent suicide-for-love of Pietro Crespi, and the obsessive house-by-house search of Aureliano Segundo for the beautiful "princess" he saw once at a carnival—these are shocking or exciting episodes that, from the pen of a less talented and mature artist, could very well have lapsed into cliché sensationalism or pure corn.

Being a family chronicle, *One Hundred Years of Solitude* puts into play a set of patterns known to us from such classics of the genre as Galsworthy's *Forsyte Saga*, Mann's *Buddenbrooks*, and Giuseppe di Lampedusa's *The Leopard*. The Englishman's multivolume work has forty characters, many of whom show similarities of temperament and bear the same name (e.g., Young and Old Jolyon). Particularly worth mention are the founding act of building a country house (seen as a first step toward civilizing the wilderness), the episodes of near-incest, the emergence of artists among the fold just when the Forsyte family is in decline, and the sense of inevitable destruction brooding over the novel's final pages.

Mann in turn dramatizes the differences between sensual and sober character types, the cultural split between north and south Germany, the material progress that accompanies family decline, the consequences of the death of matriarch Elisabeth, the growing physical decay of the ancestral home, and the final loner Hanno, whose musical talents also mark the terminal stages of the old clan. The Sicilian patriarch in Lampedusa's novel actually has an astronomical observatory of his own, and the book tells of such expected matters as sexual rivalries among siblings, shifts brought by marriages with members of contending political forces, and dwindling family fortunes. Of the three works (randomly selected from a host of others) García Márquez may well have read only the German's, but the conventions of the family-chronicle form inevitably emerge out of the subject matter itself.

The larger tale told by *One Hundred Years of Solitude* is quite consciously built around the usages of two interrelated literary traditions: the colonial romance and the chronicle of exploration. The history of Macondo, let us recall, contains such staples of the adventure novel as attacks by pirates, treks through the wilderness, circumnavigations of the globe, buried treasure (discovered by children), and death by killer ants—all typical of the swashbuckling genre. Perhaps the most renowned of colonial romances is Edgar Rice Burroughs's original *Tarzan of the Apes*, today the basis of an occasional action film but at one time the reading fare of millions of young boys. Among its current fans is García Márquez, who often cites the book admiringly.

Burroughs's fast-paced narrative tells of the establishment of a European outpost settlement somewhere in "barbarous" Africa and also shows the development of technology (there are motorcars in the last scene) from that remote vantage point. Meanwhile the eponymous hero, orphaned as a baby by shipwrecked whites, will grow up among apes and lead his primate companions to another area inland; eventually he will discover the importance of writing and become immersed in his studies, and will feel the call of sexuality without quite understanding what it is. Among the details a younger García Márquez might especially have noted are some conversations about an ancient Spanish galleon, an episode involving buried treasure on the beach, and the arrival of a cultured French adventurer named D'Arnot (a kind of harbinger of the erudite and enterprising Gastón, with his palm-oil investments in the Belgian Congo).

Another of García Márquez's favorite references is *Head Hunters of the Amazon: Seven Years of Exploration and Adventure* (1923), by F. W. Up de Graff, a New Yorker who ended up in the Southern American bush almost on a personal whim. His vivid memoir skillfully evokes the sordid ambience of the whites' settlements, with their new rubber wealth, and the boom-town atmosphere in Iquitos, Peru, with its proliferation of get-rich-quick schemes. While understandably shocked at the head-shrinking customs of local Indian tribes, Up de Graff feels some admiration for their ancestral ways, particularly for their remarkably effective folk-medicine techniques. But he is most awed by the natural wonders of the Amazon forest: the "fire-flies as big as June-bugs"; a hill where "the slightest noise" makes "rain . . . come down in sheets" (we are reminded of the yellow plain crossed by Aureliano Segundo, "where the echo repeated one's thoughts"); the spectacle of a fifty-foot anaconda "covered with flies, butterflies, and insects"; and the variety of ants that at times move through the jungle in army columns, destroying everything in their path.

The Renaissance chronicles of exploration came into existence from the moment that *homo Europeus* set out on his path of world conquest and control. The first such narrations are Christopher Columbus's diaries of his four voyages, wherein he describes a wondrous Caribbean world (thought of by him as Asian) in terms of the earthly paradise itself, and recalls such things as a lizard as big as a calf, an ape with the face of a man, and notably, certain reports of Western Cuban peoples who are born with tails![20] His story of an eighty-eight-day sea tempest, however, does seem plausible for the tropics.

On the other hand, Amerigo Vespucci's letters and questionable accounts of his travels stand out as the reason for the very existence of our geographic name "America," inasmuch as it was he who first posited the idea that those lands were not Asia, but "a new world" with "numerous tribes and peoples [and] kinds of wild animals unknown in our country." Among the marvels Vespucci notes are the nonexistence of private property, the free sexual life, and the absence either of jealousy or matrimony among the New World indigenes, who moreover "live for 150 years."[21] Far less known than Vespucci's works is a fascinating book that is among García Márquez's pet references, the *First Journey around the Globe* by Antonio Pigafetta, who traveled with the Magellan expedition and who tells of a wide range of botanical, zoological, and human wonders, such as Brazilians who have 140-year life spans.[22]

Starting as it does at "the creation," at the very dawn of the European presence in these Americas, *One Hundred Years of Solitude* takes this legacy of colonial-exploratory writing and retells it with a difference, stands it on its head. First, the tale is narrated not by distant, literate Europeans but by an engaged voice from within the Macondo "tribe" itself, while the peoples who arrive periodically with their gadgetry to do barter with the Macondians are not the usual blond navigators but some nonwhite gypsies of Asian origin. And whereas Úrsula's and Pilar Ternera's 130- and 140-year life spans are reported simply as local fact, the successive European technologies are shown to be as wondrous to the provincial townsfolk as they might have appeared to the original Native Americans. García Márquez thus skillfully reimagines his New World history, casting the descendants of Spanish settlers in the role of indigenes being encroached upon by royal bureaucrats, proselytizing priests, and Yankee capitalists, all of whom wish to absorb a peaceable Macondo into their vast global schemes.

Hence, though centered on a limited geography — a small town in the Colombian north country — *One Hundred Years of Solitude* tells a story unmistakably continental in its implications. More, going beyond the Hispanic orbit, the book could be read as an instance of yet another legendary tradition, "the great American novel" in the widest possible sense. The spaces evoked have that fabled New World vastness, and one might indeed assimilate Macondo's life course to certain corresponding phases in Anglo-American history — the initial utopian-egalitarian settlements in Massachusetts; the wars, first against a remote Crown and then against Southern conservatives in 1861–65; the rise of giant corporations and their technology both miraculous and destructive; and the hedonism, aimlessness, and confusion of our time.

And we can go still further and—despite García Márquez's own disavowal of such a reading—see his book as a metaphor for the rise and decline of all human civilizations, which from modest and rugged beginnings do grow, ripen, and become wealthy and wise, but also lose sight of their original roots and better traditions, eventually reaching a state of decadence and anomie. The world readership of *One Hundred Years of Solitude* strongly suggests the potential for such global, trans-Macondian applications to the Colombian writer's locally based narrative.

There is yet another aspect of García Márquez's novel that must not go unexamined: the fact that it is one of the funniest books ever written. More than once the author himself has said that *One Hundred Years* is a work "completely lacking in seriousness," and when asked what the novel is "about" he sometimes likes to reply that it is a story of a family that does not want their kids being born with pig's tails. Behind these flippant remarks stands the Colombian's desire to take Macondo away from the academic theorists, to remove all presumptuous obstacles between the book's basic funniness and the common readers whose needs are not purely mental. Chuckles and guffaws may well be more legitimate responses to García Márquez's great novel than are the best and brightest of critical schemes.

The varieties of humor in *One Hundred Years* are simply astonishing. There is the comic incongruity of José Arcadio Buendía's researches, the sadly spurned truth of his declaration that "The earth is round like an orange," and the sheer madness of his desire to daguerreotype God. There is some jesting with names—for example, "Apolinar Moscote," classical Greek followed by a surname suggesting "horsefly,'" or more subtly, the parodic echo in "Fernanda del Carpio" of Bernardo del Carpio, the second greatest medieval Spanish hero after the Cid. There is comic-strip farce in the seismic return of José Arcadio, his one-word greeting, his enormous and thoroughly tattooed physique, his Indian arm-wrestles with five men at the bar, and his whores who pay *him* for bodily pleasure. (In typical cartoon fashion, the episode is consigned to oblivion once it is over.) On the other hand, there are deeper historical and character implications in the endless fun and fornication of Aureliano Segundo, one of literature's great comical sybarites (who is nonetheless bested by the elephantine yet delicate Camila Sagastume, with her "spiritual" theory of eating).

There is also a marvelous political satire of Yankee technology and its more grotesque gigantisms in the elaborate hardware applied by Mr. Herbert to a harmless banana. There is the occasional spoof of florid Spanish rhetoric in the letter from Rebeca's first parents and in Fernanda's four-page harangue, the latter a verbal onrush worthy of Molly Bloom (had the Irishwoman been a snob and a shrew). The loftiness of the pretensions of Fernanda's ancient family—with their golden emblazoned chamberpots—becomes that much funnier when it encounters Amaranta's sharp tongue and pig-Latin reminders of real shit in a postmedieval world. And of course there are the countless ribald scenes involving urination, evacuation, and sex, each one unique and with no trace of locker-room sexism or vulgarity.

And finally what brings together these multiple strands is the formal mastery of it all, the total organization to which García Márquez subjects so awesome a stock of materials. This formal solidity is to be found not only in the novel's macrostructure but, more importantly, in the simplest of details. Though García Márquez likes to hint self-deprecatingly at some forty-two inconsistencies in the book, *One Hundred Years* is a narrative in which most every little fact means something and possesses some future role and function. The treasure buried by Úrsula will fortuitously sustain José Arcadio the seminarian in his debauches; the seventy-two chamberpots purchased for Meme's week-long party will serve José Arcadio Segundo's necessities during his long confinement in Melquíades's room; and the English encyclopedia casually bought from a traveling salesman by Aureliano Segundo is the textual link, the "Rosetta Stone" leading to Aureliano's ultimate deciphering of Melquíades's manuscripts. Meme will die silent in Krakow, a medieval city that, however remote, is still within the Catholic orbit (key concerns of her mother); and Melquíades's having written his Buendía history in classical Sanskrit befits a man whose language and brethren originate somewhere in medieval India.

The concluding chapter to *One Hundred Years* gives us, successively, passionate love, desolate bereavement, and absolute wisdom, followed by a "total" and multiply reinforced ending—the end of the manuscripts, of the Buendías, of Macondo, and of Aureliano himself, who reads about himself reading about the end in a text where he is reading about himself reading about the end . . . and so on into infinity. The last of the breed dies in a solitude that is the bane of all Buendías and is the name of the book; and though García Márquez claims to have come up with the sonorous title only upon completion of the novel, it does convey the lack of solidarity which, as he often points out, underlies the Buendías' disintegration (*OG*, 109; *FG*, 75). (At the same time one should note that García Márquez came of age in an era when ideas of existential loneliness were common currency among the educated.) On the face of it, to produce the novel took him eighteen months of full-time work—but also a twenty-year apprenticeship of wide reading, false starts, and preliminary shorter versions. The origins of the book, the circumstances of its writing, the status it rapidly assumed as "underground" world classic, and the infinite riches of its art will long remain among the more inspiring legends in human culture.

SEVEN

The Master of Short Forms

Had García Márquez never put any of his novels to paper, his shorter fiction would have still gained him some niche in literary history. Already in 1967 the Uruguayan writer Mario Benedetti was to observe that "some of the stories gathered in *Big Mama's Funeral* can be considered among the most perfect instances of the genre ever written in Latin America."[1] We might venture yet further and say that those pieces, along with the novella *No One Writes to the Colonel* and many of the stories collected in *Innocent Eréndira* and *Strange Pilgrims*, put García Márquez in the company of such acknowledged masters of short fiction as Chekhov, Mann, Joyce, Cheever, Alice Munro, or Grace Paley.

The author cites Hemingway as the chief influence on his own story writing. The admission is borne out by the pieces themselves, with their spare, minimal prose that captures life's little disturbances and moments of solitude, evokes major emotion in a snatch of dialogue or in the slightest of gestures. García Márquez remarked in 1950 that "the North Americans . . . are writing today's best short stories" (*OP*, 1:324), and Hemingway in this regard served him as much as mentor as did Faulkner and Woolf for his longer works. Particularly influential was Hemingway's "iceberg" theory of the short story — often cited by García Márquez — whereby the author makes visible only one-seventh of what is to be communicated, the other six-sevenths lying implicitly beneath the narrative's surface.

The stories offer pleasures of a sort different from those we know from *One Hundred Years of Solitude*. They are miracles not of mythic sweep but of understatement, conjuring up as they do the subtle, small-scale, mostly interpersonal upsets and triumphs of common village folk — the sleepy priests, pool-hall souses, provincial wheeler-dealers, troubled but stouthearted women, and the abandoned, the mismatched, or the bereaved. In later pieces, García Márquez will emerge with his visionary side full-grown and include fantastical materials — a wizened angel or a ghost ship. But there is a key element never absent from the Colombian author's stories, be they "magical" or realistic: the climate of his world. Every one of these short pieces has at least a reference either to the intense daytime heat or the tropical rain and its effects on characters' lives (their slowness in mid-afternoon, their ill health in rainy season).[2] The consummate craft of the narratives should also be noted: García Márquez typically spends weeks or even months on a single short story, feeling pleased when completing just two lines in a day.

The slim volume *Los funerales de la Mamá Grande* (*Big Mama's Funeral*) stands quietly as the budding Colombian's first work of genius. The miracle is that we have the stories at all. When García Márquez finished work on its eight pieces in 1959 he made little effort at seeking publication and mostly consigned them to his suitcase. (These were his wandering years.) He did submit "Tuesday Siesta" to a story contest in Caracas, where it rated not so much as an honorable mention.[3] When his friend Álvaro Mutis happened to be spending time in a Mexico City prison, Gabo got a note from the jailbird asking for "something to read." He sent the stories to Mutis, who in turn would loan them to the young Mexican writer Elena Poniatowska, she then absent-mindedly misplacing the manuscript. She happened upon the stories again a year later and returned them to Mutis, who succeeded in placing the collection with the University of Veracruz Press in 1962. García Márquez received a one thousand peso advance, approximately one hundred U.S. dollars at that time. The volume was issued in two thousand copies, sales being slow until the changes wrought by *One Hundred Years*.[4] Today the stories are classics in their own right.

Though García Márquez made "Macondo" synonymous with his territory, the only three of his short stories set in that fabled land are "Tuesday Siesta," "One Day after Saturday," and "Big Mama's Funeral." The others in this volume unfold in a settlement known simply as "el pueblo," "the town," the setting as well for *No One Writes to the Colonel* and *In Evil Hour*. The two municipalities are distinct. "The town" finds itself in a "lull" from political violence and has its own recurring cast of characters—the corrupt mayor, the rebel dentist, Mina and Trinidad, the Montiels—who occasionally allude to Macondo as a slightly remote place.[5] "The town" also has running through it a river large enough to serve as port, and is modeled after Sucre, where the boy Gabo lived in 1936 following the death of his grandfather. Macondo by contrast has the surrounding banana fields and a hotel outside the railroad station, but only vague, distant memories of plantation violence and no central waterway, based as it is on Aracataca, with its marginal stream alongside the village cemetery.

"Tuesday Siesta," which opens the volume, is García Márquez's favorite short piece. It was inspired by the boyhood memory of a woman and a little girl he had seen carrying an umbrella in the afternoon sun (a common enough sight in Aracataca), and someone remarking to him, "She's the mother of that thief" (*OG*, 35; *FG*, 26). In the story she is an outsider who has come determined to argue with the priest and, ultimately, face all of Macondo in order to visit the grave of her only male offspring, recently slain in the act of trying to rob the widow Rebeca.

García Márquez's sure hand is already in evidence in this initial story. The "Tuesday" of the title places the action during an ordinary weekday; "Siesta" evokes the suffocating heat and spectral silence. The authority of the woman is immediately established in her erect posture on the train and in her four initial utterances, all of them motherly commands. At the priest's house she will insist on seeing him and then state her business outright: "The keys to the cemetery." When reiterating her son's name, she adds his second surname and thus indirectly asserts her own identity. (The hint throughout is that there may be no father.) To the aging cleric's sanctimonious query about putting her hapless son "on the right track" the woman counters, "He was a very good man" and compares her boy's thieving to the greater evils of his boxing, while the little daughter interjects her one forceful comment about his battered teeth. The two females thus present a common front against the tired, drowsy priest, who is able to respond only with a formula to the effect that "God moves in mysterious ways" (rendered by J. S. Bernstein as "God's will is inscrutable").

By the end of the story all of Macondo has found out who this woman is, but neither their hostility nor the hot sun can daunt her. "We're all right this way" is her parting remark. Though the narrative breaks off at the very moment when she and her daughter step out onto the street, the author has masterfully set things up so that we know that the two will hold their own against the unfriendly stares and, with quiet dignity, succeed in their mission and even catch their return train thereafter. The nameless mother in "Tuesday Siesta" is one of García Márquez's most memorable figures of womanly strength, and the story's plot shows at work the simple power of parental solidarity and moral authority.

"Artificial Roses" has unusual art and subtlety, even for García Márquez. On the surface it tells of young Mina's not being able to attend mass owing to some wet sleeves, but the real core is the subsequent standoff with her blind grandmother over her secret amour. (The ostensible bone of contention between them is the damp pair of detachable sleeves, which Mina was to put on just before entering church, so as to comply with priestly rules that bar admission to women with bare arms.) The story is notable for two master strokes. First, the reason for the conflict takes place "offstage"; when Mina steps out she will briefly see her boyfriend; he abandons her on the spot and she dashes home. We find this out in the terse, minimal dialogue with her friend Trinidad:

> "What's the matter?" [Trinidad] said.
> Mina leaned toward her.
> "He went away," she said. [i.e. He's gone.]
> Trinidad dropped the scissors on her lap.
> "No."
> "He went away," Mina repeated.
> . . . .
> "And now?"
> Mina replied in a steady voice. "Now nothing."
> (*FMG*, 120–21; *CS*, 180–81)

The remainder of the story tells of Mina's rage at being jilted, an anger she will cruelly take out on her grandmother.

The second beauty of this story is that the reader learns most everything via Mina's grandmother who, though blind, knows that Mina at bedtime turns on the flashlight, writes until dawn, and breathes heavily, that Mina has just broken her morning routines and gone to the toilet twice (the second time, we saw, to discard his letters), and that young, innocent Mina's truculent obscenity is her first ever (a reflex expression of her fury). In all, it is a classic portrait of tender but prickly adolescence confronted by aged wisdom and solidarity (the grandmother stands up for Mina when the latter's more shadowy mother makes inquiries). Mina's name, presumably a nickname for "Tranquilina" (both of which belonged to Gabo's own grandma, Colonel Márquez's wife), further suggests slightness and delicacy. The presence of four women and no visible men in a narrative in which a male sparks the crisis is a special touch (indeed, the subject pronoun "*él*"—"he"—never once appears in the story), and the artificial roses with which Mina earns her living symbolize aptly the illusoriness of her love.

Few novels can capture as economically the tensions of political conflict as do the four pages of "One of These Days," with the yearning for revenge already hinted at in the title's set phrase (often stated with a closed fist). The atmosphere of violence is soon established when the eleven-year-old son of the town dentist casually relays to him the death threat from the mayor—the comic, innocent irony is self-evident—and is further heightened when the dentist checks his own revolver in the drawer. The ragged appearance of the mayor's right cheek, however, quickly reverses the roles: he desperately needs the dentist's expertise. Now our good dentist literally has the upper hand, and will give orders to his hapless patient and also extract political vengeance by skipping the anesthetic (the medical reasons he cites are wickedly spurious). The moment of truth comes with the climactic cold pain suffered by the mayor—brought on by a little flick of the dentist's wrist even as he laconically claims retribution for the mayor's victims. (The Spanish original follows the phrase "twenty dead men" with the direct address "Lieutenant," thus revealing that the town is living under barracks dictatorship.)

In the end, however, the mayor reestablishes his rule with a casual (if respectful) military salute and his concluding quip about his shady finances. This latter reference contrasts sharply with the drab austerity of the dentist's office, a poverty registered midway through the story by the roving eye of the mayor-as-patient. The dentist of course could have assassinated the martinet at this point, though the action would be dishonorable and out of character, and he has had his small victory instead. But it's all a brief respite—no sooner is the mayor on his feet than things are reverting to the status quo ante.

In conceiving this story García Márquez was probably influenced by a strikingly similar episode in the next-to-last chapter of Graham Greene's *The Power and the Glory*. In that climactic scene, a British dentist living in small-town Mexico during the early 1930s replaces a tooth filling for the local police chief, a repulsive and gangsterish brute of a fellow. The dentist is referred to throughout as *Mister* (not "Doctor") Tench, presumably because he lacks a diploma. And like his Colombian counterpart he can only afford a drill that is pedal-operated. The well-heeled patient of course suffers in his seat even as the Brit adds to the whole performance with pointed political chatter. The resemblance between Gabo's now-classic story, and Greene's heightened moment in his most renowned novel, are far too close to be coincidental.[6]

"Baltasar's Prodigious Afternoon" movingly and comically depicts the clash between a naive artist and the ways of the world. Its modest thirty-year-old carpenter (the combined age and occupation are significant) has the pride of a craftsman, but no notion either of the beauty of his handiwork or of the extent of his genius. While his wife Úrsula sees merely the large size of the birdcage he has made, and many villagers care only about its sales value, a cultured Dr. Giraldo and maybe Mrs. Montiel do sense its aesthetic worth and high artistry. Being a man of his word, however, Baltasar declines the opportunity to sell the work to the appreciative doctor, and later just gives it away to the boy Montiel simply because he had promised it to him. All this is in deliberate contrast with the sordid ambience of the Montiel household and its boorish tightwad of a tyrant, "obese and hairy" like a beast, who struts about in his underwear, brutalizes his child, calls Baltasar's cage a "trinket," and both starts and finishes his character role with voluminous shouting (his final word, "Carajo!," is a vulgarism). The son himself, when he cannot have his way, weeps frantically and tearlessly, having learned a few lessons in control from his imperious father.

The generosity of Baltasar ultimately carries the day: he refuses to tell the disappointing truth to the jubilant villagers (his perceived victory over Montiel being perceived as theirs too) and moreover he treats for beers and music the whole night. (Never having consumed alcohol before, he now experiences his coming-out party.) Though he ends up drunk in the gutter, minus his wristwatch and shoes, he has had his moment of glory, complete with cheering crowds and women's kisses.

"Montiel's Widow" is a kind of sequel to "Baltasar": the tyrant, having disregarded doctor's orders, has died of a fit of rage. The story tells two tales, foregrounding that of the widow—a naive, superstitious, self-pitying innocent who remains blissfully unaware of her man's criminality. Being completely subservient to and even disdained by him, she herself has no identity—her name is never revealed. Because of her proper upbringing and her lack of contact with reality, she cannot handle Montiel's empire, which quickly goes to ruin. Only the loyal Mr. Carmichael keeps her afloat; the one thing the widow seems capable of is biting her nails, an appropriately childish and self-indulgent act. To add to the ironies, her children are settled in Europe as beneficiaries of Montiel's gangsterism, and they piously scorn the violence in their native homeland. (The obscene postscript in the daughter's letter has presumably been added on the sly by a prankster in Paris.) The widow's concluding vision of Big Mama is a fantastical, symbolic, oneiric representation of her own impending death.

The story also tells, retrospectively, of Montiel's rise to power and of the townspeople's ongoing reaction to him. Originally a barefoot bumpkin, he gained his wealth and influence as informer for the "brutish" military mayor (the dental patient from "One of These Days," no doubt). Understandably, Montiel's early demise goes unmourned by the villagers and his boorish taste is made manifest in the "mausoleum adorned with electric-light bulbs and imitation-marble archangels." These pages show the sheer genius of García Márquez at work. What could have been a fairly ordinary tale about a banal manipulator who comes into his own during *la Violencia* here takes on a formal and emotional richness by being recounted as a postmortem flashback from the perspective of his ever-loving wife (in many ways just another of his victims). "Montiel's Widow," it bears mention, contains in microcosm what will be the plot and structure of *The Autumn of the Patriarch*: the death of a mediocre oaf and local despot who achieved power by collaborating with military occupiers. As is the case with the best of García Márquez, the story is funny in a bittersweet way.

The two lengthiest narratives in *Big Mama's Funeral* are also the weakest. "One Day after Saturday," however, was García Márquez's first mature story, with physical geography, personal voice, and smiling irony all now sharp and clear in their contours. It deservedly won in 1955 a prize granted by the Bogotá Association of Writers and Artists.[7] Set in Macondo some years after the banana-company massacre, it conjoins three different plots: the plague of dead birds that upsets the widow Rebeca, the swift mental deterioration of the ninety-four-year-old Father Antonio Isabel, and the hapless country boy who finds himself stranded in Macondo and, worse, has gone and left his mother's phony retirement papers on the disappearing train. The three characters are touchingly comical and sad, trapped as they are within their obsessions and limits, and unsettled by their encounters with reality's fantastical little surprises.

Their several lives converge in the climactic scene in church, with a dizzy Father Antonio pronouncing his daft Sunday sermon on the Wandering Jew, a disquieted Rebeca scurrying up the aisle with her arms outstretched and her bitter face turned upward, and a presumably bewildered youth seated in the rear, he and Rebeca both strangers to each other yet taken note of by the priest in his transports. The cryptic ending, however, redeems Father Antonio as he destines the collection plate contents for the wayward young man, who most needs the support and solidarity. The cleric thus performs a useful if eccentric deed on this "day after Saturday," when one of yesterday's mishaps is alleviated if not resolved. Knowing García Márquez's subsequent work, one can assume that in the wake of Father Antonio's act of charity the villagers' lives will revert to their humdrum ways, their gossip enriched by remembrances of this extreme episode.

The central plot of "There Are No Thieves in This Town" is too slight for the story's twenty-six pages, though the repercussions are broad enough. Dámaso's impulsive burglarizing of the only three billiard balls from Don Roque's pool hall seriously dampens the townsmen's leisure time and moreover brings about the cruel and undeserved punishment of the scapegoated Negro. But Dámaso's equally impulsive attempt at sneaking back the three balls after hours is, as Don Roque tells him, the act of "a fool," and the ultimate irony is that he will now be wrongly blamed for the theft of the two hundred pesos too.

The best thing about the story is its portrayal of the twenty-year-old Dámaso and his relations with others. A classic pretty-boy type who spends three laborious hours trimming his mustache and combing his hair, he is the sort of fellow whose appeal to women—whether the youthful whores or his maternal, practical, thirty-seven-year-old wife Ana—is precisely his being a handsome, useless, loutish dreamer lucky enough to live off his movie-star good looks. (There is no mention of him working.) The nameless tart at the dance hall actually pays for his dinner and treats him to free sex. Meanwhile a pregnant Ana has the run of the household money.

Dámaso moreover is an astoundingly primitive macho figure whose very first act on arriving home from the burglary is to grab Ana by her chemise and lift her bodily, and whose final act before departing for the pool hall is to thwack her on the ear. At home he likes playing the boxer; at the dance hall he picks a fight with a traveling salesman (because he objects to the man's teeth), declines the girl's offer of food ("we men don't eat"), and refuses to pay for the check with a dismissive "I don't like queers." In addition, the story evokes the dictatorship, ever briefly, in the prostitute's allusion to the mayor's having ransacked Gloria's room and extorted twenty pesos in reprisal for her defense of the black man's innocence (FMG, 46; CS, 125). As the title might suggest, "There Are No Thieves in This Town" is unusually encompassing and conveys the spirit of street life, of crowds gathered in public places. The length of the story, however, is a flaw.

Both in its panoramic range and its high-pitched prose the story "Big Mama's Funeral" presents a complete break with others in the collection, its form as well as content looking forward to the author's two greatest novels. The piece is told in the highly oral style of a public storyteller or carnival barker, who leans on his "stool against the front door," intent on preempting "the historians." The high pomp of the opening lines ("absolute sovereign," "died in the odor of sanctity") is already being deflated in the very third word of the story ("incrédulos," translated by J. S. Bernstein as "the world's un-believers"). Similarly, the ending of the Spanish version echoes the closing phrase ("por los siglos de los siglos," "world without end," rendered by Bernstein as "forever and forever") of the venerable "Glory be to the Father," itself also spoofed in advance with the narrator's allusion to the sanitation workers "who will come sweep up the garbage from the funeral."

The content of "Big Mama's Funeral" comprises the unnamed republic's highest reaches of political power—all branches of government, broad sectors of the economy, wise doctors of laws, the Metropolitan Cathedral—and crowns it all with a state visit by the pope, who "honored with his Supreme

Dignity the greatest funeral in the world." Throughout the piece this display of authority is self-parodied with such less lofty matters as the matriarch's dying burp, "the historic blahblahblah" that unfolds even as her corpse rots in the 104° heat; or the heirs' rapid ritual of carving up her wealth among themselves. The basic plot is one that García Márquez would repeatedly make the most of: the death of a powerful personage and its consequences for society. Big Mama's own riches originated in a royal decree from the founding of the colony, and under her fabulous rule have grown to encompass holdings that take her three hours to enumerate—the five townships, 352 tenant farms, and a vast array of connections including paramilitary forces (her gun-toting nephew Nicanor), the church (Father Antonio), the health system (the antiquated family doctor and his monopoly), and even the public festivals that happen to have coincided with her birthday.

All this, however, is only a starting point. It is García Márquez's imagination that now soars and takes common political muckraking to inspired heights of vision, grandeur, and wit. Big Mama's power, we are told, takes in "the waters, running and still" as well as the "roads, telegraph poles, leap years, and heat waves" (FMG, 189; CS, 186). From there it is only a further step to the climactic and wonderfully funny paragraph itemizing her "invisible estate" via those thirty-nine set phrases and clichés—for example, "the colors of the flag," "the free but responsible press," "the Communist threat"—that typify the Colombian elite and Latin American oligarchies (FMC, 137; CS, 192). That catalog, moreover, is but one of many—some short, some long—that help give the narrative its grandiose, mock-heroic, tongue-in-cheek quality. (It is as if Whitman had been a satirist.) The story's second paragraph already unfurls a brief geographic-cum-populist registry, but the fun with lists truly begins with the inventory of foods sold at Big Mama's birthday celebrations, rises to a feverish pitch with the roll call of occupations (a touching tribute to the trades of the humbler folk all over small-town Colombia), and reaches a level of explosive farce in the hilarious parody of beauty queens "of all things that have been or ever will be." (Even today, it should be noted, the Colombian daily press regularly carries reports of beauty contests.)

On one level "Big Mama's Funeral" expectedly depicts the economics of power and its shadier practices—for example, the old matriarch's secretly arming her supporters while publicly assisting her victims, or the dead electors who miraculously cast their votes. But it also skillfully captures and satirizes what is often missed even in the best analyses or narratives of politics: namely, the organized appearance and show of power, the visual panoply along with the orchestrated language, the "words, words, words" of power. Once the "heroine" has died, the story passes in review a full battery of ways in which secular and spiritual power visibly and audibly manifest themselves—the solemn gatherings of dignitaries and of worshipful crowds, but also the telling little details such as those busts of Greek thinkers, or, in a more comic-strip vein, those drum rolls onomatopoeically rendered ("ratatat"). Politics in "Big Mama's Funeral" is as much a matter of visual spectacle as it is that of lethal guns or physical property.

When García Márquez was writing "Big Mama's Funeral," no pope had ever so much as set foot in a Latin American country, and the president of Colombia was tall and thin. In order to avoid accusations of excess topicality, García Márquez purposely portrayed his fictional president as bald and chubby. The author's prophetic side, however, once again became manifest when, for the first pontifical visit to Latin America, Pope Paul VI chose Colombia in 1968. The visit inevitably brought out all possible public fanfare—and the president at the time was in fact bald and chubby.

The novella *No One Writes to the Colonel* originated in Paris as an episode within García Márquez's flawed full-length novel *In Evil Hour*. The materials took on a life of their own and became this little masterpiece, the author's first mature and achieved longer work, as subtly understated as any of the best realistic stories in *Big Mama's Funeral*, and as seriocomical. At the same time the length allows for a larger and fuller town portrait, and a more exhaustive treatment of the narrative's three interlinking subjects: fighting cock, military dictatorship, and the old couple's solitude and hunger.

Some of the chief topics are established from the start. The report of scarce coffee in the opening line informs us of the couple's impecunious state. The soon-to-arrive rains of winter will exacerbate the wife's asthma and the colonel's constipation (the latter ailment to be vividly rendered). The initial full event in the story is a funeral for the town trumpeter, which prompts painful reminiscences of their own dead son from the two, as well as the colonel's sober observation that it is the first death from natural causes in years (a hint at obscure violence, and concretely at *la Violencia* for Colombian readers). These themes will consistently dominate the novella's fifty-some pages.

The story first of all provides a masterful, bittersweet portrait of the hungry and lonely couple, he seventy-five, she presumably in the same range. Their son, murdered by the military nine months earlier, had been their sole support—hence her wistful remark, "We are the orphans of our son" (*CNT*, 21; *NWC*, 11). With the colonel's copartisans all either exiled or dead (some violently), the very title conveys both his isolation—the original actually signifies "The Colonel Has Nobody to Write Him"—and his empty pockets. Of course the item of mail most awaited by the colonel is the fabled notice of a government pension, five decades overdue and now quite urgent. On four different Fridays we see him heading down with the highest of expectations to the river port or the post office, only to have his hopes dashed by a terse "Nothing for the colonel." His only consolations are the friendly camaraderie and loans of newspapers from the wise, kindhearted doctor (who also furnishes him medical treatments "on credit").

The figure of the colonel is among García Márquez's most memorable and touching exemplars of human innocence: an ex-soldier yet gentle, timid, wide-eyed, dreamy; unable to counter the wiles of the trickster Don Sabas yet himself blessed with reservoirs of self-irony and belief that are all but wondrous; peaceable, yet ultimately stubborn enough to say "'no" to the sale of the rooster, and then end up pronouncing the most unforgettable final line in all prose fiction. (That closing noun is particularly ironic, given his earlier-expressed aversion to obscenity, as well as his excretory incapacities.) His wife, similarly, is another for Gabo's gallery of shrewd, strong-willed, loyal women; it is she who consistently manages to round up food and at one point elicits from him the jovial hyperbole, "This is the miracle of the loaves and fishes" (CNT, 34). She cuts his hair, suggests ways of securing money, and indeed rather treats the colonel like a child.[8] Only in the bitter quarrel between them in the last pages will the colonel take a firm stand and rebel. Notwithstanding this tense and electrified finale, No One Writes to the Colonel gives us one of the fullest and most loving (if unsentimentalized) portraits of conjugal life in modern literature since Joyce and Beckett.

Directly related to the couple's economic straits and marital discord is the sinister military dictatorship, about whose existence we learn piecemeal, in bits and fragments: the nightly eleven o'clock curfew, the casual talk about censored press and absent elections, the routine church bannings of movies, the hints about the governmental origins of Don Sabas's ill-gotten wealth, the clandestine leaflets that are now and then slipped to the protagonist, and the lightning police raid on the pool hall, with its mute, climactic confrontation between the colonel and the very man who had shot the old couple's son. As in One Hundred Years, the public and the private are openly integrated and fused.

The decisive touch of genius in Colonel, however, is the fighting cock, a dominant presence from the second page on through the last, and a living symbol for most everything that is positive in the story. The bird represents the couple's much-loved and departed son (to whom it belonged), the young people in town (who like just staring at it, and feed it), the colonel's hopes for income from the cockfights in January, and last but not least the ordinary people who congregate in the cockpit (and who, not just incidentally, oppose the military). At one point some youths "kidnap" the bird for a trial fight, and the colonel will chance by and see his rooster in the pit, expertly rebuffing its adversary's every blow. The audience naturally goes wild with cheers and applause both for the rooster (a good one) and its owner, claiming the two for "the whole town" but secretly giving vent to collective solidarity. Hence, though a bone of contention at home, the rooster remains to the colonel his source of personal worth as well as his chief affective link with the community. The figure of the bird thus helps unite the many narrative strands; without it the story would have been just another tender and smiling-sad portrait (if first-rate) of a small town's dignified poor.

At the end of that crucial episode at the cockpit, the bird is duly returned to the colonel. The escapade occurs, significantly, in the last of the novella's seven unnumbered "chapters," where the drift of the narrative makes a radical turn toward the better, even the joyous and luminous.[9] The weather at the start of the section is beautiful and clear. The colonel for the first time shrugs off his "hardened" wife's nagging complaints and he simply bypasses the post office. The newly arrived circus brings a festive atmosphere, prompting his memories of happier days with family and comrades. Now the colonel feels "no regrets," sleeps a "remorseless sleep," and firmly decides that "nothing about the rooster deserved resentment." All of this prepares us for the extensive final scene in which he shoos off the gawking kids, gently announces to his wife that "the rooster's not for sale," and resists every one of her nightlong importunities and worries (however legitimate they may be). Next morning, Sunday, he arrives at that fresh, bright moment of eschatological revelation and scatological eloquence with which the novel disyllabically ends.

With its gray weather, physical discomfort, and economic deprivation, *Colonel* could have been a heavy and oppressive piece, redeemed only by its closing chapter. What further saves it is its sudden surges of humor, many of them from the protagonist himself, who for example confronts the rooster and declares sententiously, "Life is tough, pal," and later warns the staring children, "Stop looking at that animal. Roosters wear out if you look at them so much." In reply to someone's remark about his thinness he self-deprecatingly likens himself to a clarinet. He takes some small joy in noting that his wife's momentary posture reminds him of the fellow on the Quaker Oats label. And he lyrically celebrates life as "the best thing that's ever been invented." (In Spanish the jokes have a proverbial sort of rhythm and flavor, and are thus funnier.) There is also the comical portrait of Don Sabas's eccentric and neurotic wife, with her dreams of the dead, or the truly magical account of thunder that "entered the bedroom and went rolling under the bed, like a heap of stones." These humorous flashes regularly offset the potential bitterness of García Márquez's spare novella of solitude and empty stomachs. Where Knut Hamsun's *Hunger* has its intensely brooding, subjective, "Nordic" anguish, García Márquez's shorter book has its more benevolent, multigenerational, collective, "tropical" levity.

In later years García Márquez would gently repudiate this phase in his evolution as a writer. He came to see the stories, with their "immoderate zeal for visualization," as excessively influenced by the cinema, and in *Colonel* in particular, he said, "I can see the camera. At that time . . . I was working like a filmmaker" (*OG*, 45; *FG*, 33), and was therefore taking into consideration such filmic concerns as the frame, the minutiae of pacing in dialogue and action, and the exact number of steps a character might happen to walk.[10] Back in 1956, of course, García Márquez had served his brief spell as a film student in Rome; not accidentally, these shorter works—what with their subject matter of humble folk in small towns, and their uncondescendingly objective approach mingled with an ironic affectiveness—happily suggest some fruitful lessons learned by the journeyman Colombian from the early neorealist films of de Sica and Fellini. Of all of García Márquez's work, his first neorealist short pieces are the most purely visual, a tendency he would eventually abandon in *One Hundred Years of Solitude*, where visualization for its own sake is minimal and the narrative-structural patterning holds full sway over the verbally descriptive.

Still, these tales are classics of their kind, and if a ripe and full-bodied history of Macondo is a more properly "literary" way of doing fiction, the stories' quiet understatement and their insight into character earn them their secure place in literature. Gabo the young realist is as much the wise artist as is García Márquez the master fabulator.

The story that shows García Márquez on the verge of disclosing the magic of Macondo is "The Sea of Lost Time," written in 1961, printed the next year in the magazine of the National University of Mexico (followed thereafter by the author's three-year writer's block), and first gathered in 1972 in the Spanish volume *Innocent Eréndira*. The setting is an arid and impoverished seaside hamlet on the edge of the Guajira desert, and the plot is threefold: the fragrance of roses that wafts in from the ocean and pervades everything, the arrival of tall and ruddy-faced Mr. Herbert with his philanthropic schemes, and the long swim to ocean's bottom and discovery of a live sunken city as well as a "sea of the dead" with its corpses perfectly intact. The action is experienced largely through protagonist Tobías, a happy innocent along the lines of carpenter Baltasar or the rooster-colonel.

With its insertion of fabulous materials into a commonplace reality, "The Sea of Lost Time" constitutes a breakthrough for its author. First, the daily life of the coastal village is lovingly captured, with its somewhat soured, mostly elderly inhabitants (who also find their consolation in each other), its open-air games of checkers, and the sad brothel with its gramophone and sad, nostalgic, shellac records. The broad intrusions of fantasy owe their success to a minor-magical texture already present at all levels of the narrative. The story has a smiling quality, filled as it is with jokes, dozens of them, ranging from comical exchanges and one-liners in the dialogue to small events, such as the brief, cartoonlike account of a dark raincloud that first hangs over the sea but forthwith "descended, floated for a while on the surface, and then sank into the water" (CE, 31; CS, 217). Mr. Herbert himself is a fantastical entity whose public routine brings out people's extraordinary sides, notably Patricio's forty-eight bird calls. And there are the sudden incidences of pure magic—Clotilde has to "brush the smell [of roses] away like a cobweb in order to get up" (CE, 29; CS, 216), or, because Mr. Herbert asleep uses up the air in Jacob's room, "things had lost their weight and were beginning to float about" (CE, 40; CS, 225). This is as funny a story as García Márquez ever wrote, and the fanciful humor together with the mysterious smell of roses further prepares us for the astounding vision with which the piece ends.

In retrospect the story is, in content at least, a preliminary sketch for *One Hundred Years of Solitude*. There is the unnamed priest who, soliciting money for a church, actually rises physically off the ground, though the event is not made much of. Old Jacob's wife Petra, anticipating her death, prepares her husband's widower outfit—a harbinger of Amaranta's sewing of her own death shroud. The scene in which Tobías visits the unfortunate young prostitute (herself an early version of innocent Eréndira) has descriptions of sweat-soaked sheets and murky air to be retained verbatim when Aureliano visits the same whore in Macondo. Mr. Herbert, here a do-gooder who ends up appropriating Don Jacob's modest house, is a tamer precursor of the shady tinkerer by the same name, who applies the full battery of Yankee technology to a Macondo plantain and serves as advance guard for the fruit company. The conjugal life of a practical Clotilde and a dreamer Tobías who happens to be right anticipates that of Macondo's first couple, while their frolicsome sexuality gives a foretaste of the joyous eroticism to be unleashed throughout those *One Hundred Years*. The ending of the story is as apocalyptic as Macondo's, though watery rather than windy, and not so much biblical as Dantean in overtones, the sea of the dead having "so many of them that Tobías thought that he'd never seen so many people on earth" (*CE*, 43; *CS*, 227), like the city in Eliot's *Waste Land*.

Still, "The Sea of Lost Time" is more striking and novel a story than it is thoroughly successful. There are three plots in search of a suitable central image or character, the figures of Tobías and his wife not sufficing to unify all of the divers strands. In addition, the gentle though conventional narrative style fails to do justice to the bold and unsettling subject matter (as Vargas Llosa first noted).[11] The long, spacious paragraphs of the later García Márquez would eventually emerge as the medium far more appropriate to his complex, panoramic, magical vision. One sees here notable strides in García Márquez's developing imaginative gifts without a corresponding advance as yet in verbal craft and conception.

The other short stories in the Spanish (not the English) collection *Innocent Eréndira* all have fantastical materials in common, the author thus further reapplying the lessons he had assimilated and mastered in *One Hundred Years*. At the same time the narratives have moved north, away from the nameless port and the ancestral Macondo, both of which were inland settlements. The towns now have marine locations on the edge of the Guajira desert. The landscape is correspondingly barren. No bananas grow here—even flowers are a rare and precious commodity.

The new settings express García Márquez's aim at the time of becoming more broadly a writer of "the Caribbean," its geography already being reimagined by him in his novel (then in progress) about a dictator, with an unnamed republic that combines Venezuelan and Colombian features, and a horizon that ranges from the colonial Guianas to the Gulf of Mexico. Moreover, three of the stories are evidently stylistic exercises, practice studies for *The Autumn of the Patriarch*, having as they do the winding syntax and the mid-sentence shifts in pronoun-subjects so intimidating to first-time readers of that book.

"The Last Voyage of the Ghost Ship" in fact consists of a single long sentence, as will be the case with the final chapter of *Patriarch*, though its youthful protagonist and occasional narrator here lives the solitude not of power but of abandonment and alienation. He is fatherless at the outset; his mother soon dies in a freak accident; he survives on the fish he pilfers from docked trawlers, and is despised by the townsfolk, who ostracize him and beat him up. From the start, however, he is determined to prove that his nocturnal sightings of a wandering transatlantic cruiser are not a mere phantasm of his mind. ("Now they're going to see who I am," the story opens—a defiant phrase that appears fourfold.) And though the boy too had initially "thought it was a dream," at the end, from a rowboat, he guides the ocean liner on a halter, and an omniscient narrator tells in dramatic detail of the "living ship" that crashes right onto the shore and lights up the town as the villagers stand and stare in disbelief.

The "aluminum" hulk itself is precisely described, with some freight ("fighting bulls"), an ill passenger, and captain and pilot alluded to in passing, its physical dimensions ("twenty times taller than the steeple and some ninety-seven times longer than the village") ingeniously spelled out, and its 90,500 champagne glasses, now reported as destroyed. The ship even has a name, *Halácsillag*, Hungarian for "Star of Death," García Márquez purposely having chosen a word from a language of a landlocked nation.[12] In all, the story is a suspenseful, luminous account of a lonely truth being vindicated by its lone and ardent knower, who acts to bring and impose that truth, with smashing success, onto those who had once dismissed and scorned him.

The setting already looks forward to *The Autumn of the Patriarch*, with pan-Caribbean allusions to Hindu shops, Dutch Negroes, and Guyanese smugglers, fearsome memories of pirate William Dampier (to be evoked on the very first page of the later novel), and suggestions of Cartagena in the references to distant colonial fortifications and an old slave port across the bay. "The Last Voyage of the Ghost Ship" also has recognizable flashes of its author's humor, such as the brief history of a "murderous" rocking chair so old it can no longer give rest. The piece itself seems inspired by a short narrative of Hemingway's, "After the Storm," set along the Florida Keys and written in long, sinuous sentences untypical for the U.S. author. Hemingway's pugnacious and resentful narrator happens upon a sunken ocean liner, "the biggest I ever saw in my life," where he glimpses "a woman inside with her hair floating about." The story has further magical intimations—"There was a million birds above and all around"—without reaching the subjective heights of García Márquez's six-page sketch.[13]

"Blacamán the Good, Vendor of Miracles" is the first mature García Márquez story narrated exclusively in the first person. It likewise anticipates *The Autumn of the Patriarch*, not only in its dense prose and its chief setting (a fictional yet plausible port city called Santa María del Darién) but also in the key role played by U.S. Marines, who are present at the start and later reinvade, "under the pretext of exterminating yellow fever" (an evident play on our Panamanian adventure). The story's first few pages are a masterful portrait of the roving con artist, Blacamán the Bad, from his colorful outfit of white suspenders and jingle bells to his street-hawker routine and actual sales of "suppositories that turned smugglers transparent." He has been at large since the days of the Imperial viceroys whom he used to embalm (thus being roughly as old as the patriarch), and now singles out the youthful "idiot-faced" narrator—a doppelgänger figure to be self-styled Blacamán the Good—and takes him on as an assistant. We follow the pair on their comical picaresque adventures along the coast, with a brief wink at Chaplin's *Gold Rush* when, in the ruins of a colonial mission in the Guajira, the twosome dine on boiled leggings.[14]

The story is by and large convincing until the moment when the pliant narrator, during a brutal torture session at the hands of his master, accidentally revives a dead rabbit and gains the power to rebel. He breaks off on his own and soon becomes enormously rich in the guise of Blacamán the Good, miracle-healer cum resuscitator and all-purpose wheeler-dealer. Years later he reencounters Blacamán the Bad in lesser straits, who dies of poison in a final performance—only to be kept sealed in an armored tomb and periodically brought back to horrific life there by his vengeful, erstwhile aide. But alas, the narrative in these last pages turns static and loses in cogency. The transition to Blacamán the Good's new life is abrupt and without explanation, and the narrator's recounting of his own daily latter-day successes lacks any tension, coming as it does not from a situation of ongoing conflict but of secure power. "Blacamán" is probably the most promising yet in the end the least effective of García Márquez's later fictions.

In "The Handsomest Drowned Man in the World," the only entity with a name is the eponymous cadaver, whom the villagers choose to call "Esteban." (The Catholic church's first martyr, we may recall, was St. Stephen.) When his tall, strong, broad-shouldered, lifeless body is washed ashore near a seafaring hamlet of "twenty-odd houses," the irruption from another, remote, unknown world excites the romantic, myth-producing imaginations of the sad and isolated townsfolk. He strikes them as proud, "the most virile and best-built man they had ever seen," and from thence they infer for him the power to stop the winds and call fish from the sea. The women in particular fantasize about him, alive and polite as a fellow villager in their lives, and inasmuch as it is they who prepare his corpse for sea burial, they grow particularly attached to their ideas and images of him. The males by contrast get to feeling jealous and look forward to his being returned at last to the deep.

If the women's collective role in this story shows mythmaking's more specifically erotic side, in the ritual ocean burial the affective bonds are extended and "all the inhabitants of the village became kinsmen." Hints at Odysseus's adventure of the sirens help place the incident of Esteban within a larger ancestral continuum of seafaring fable. Through these intimations of a greater and more beautiful cosmos the villagers are reminded of "the desolation of their streets" and (by extension) of their lives. And so we probably can trust the omniscient narrator's prediction that the inhabitants, in response, will thence beautify and make fertile their hamlet, and give it some fame as "Esteban's village."

The shifting points of view in the story correspond to the general cycle of mystery, discovery, knowledge, and finally, emergence of a legend. The floating mass is first sighted by some children, who initially think it a boat or a whale; on realizing what it is as it beaches, they play with the corpse, innocently and insensitively, in the sand. Next, the adult men take charge and transport the cadaver to the village, noting mainly such prosaic, factual matters as its enormous weight and thick muck carapace. Their women then will tend to and dress the body, generating along the way its erotic mythification and its given name. The "splendid" funeral in the drowned man's honor is a rite that completes the process, and thereafter the Esteban myth will spread beyond local soil and shore.

In some of his best long narratives García Márquez forges a kind of fantastical history; here we see him experimenting in turn with a fantastical anthropology, as it were, a "folklore science-fiction" that speculates on the humbler origins and organizational powers of a commonly created and shared popular myth.[15] García Márquez the socialist well knows that the imagination and its dreams are as crucial a force in political life as is economic fact.

"A Very Old Man with Enormous Wings" is subtitled "A Tale for Children," but what fairy-tale characteristics it has are affectionately parodied throughout. On one hand, there is unmistakable magic in the arrival of the winged humanoid, the apparent angel who seems to have crash-landed in the courtyard of Pelayo and Elisenda, a modest rural couple living in a coastal village. On the other hand, everything about the visitor completely contradicts our standard, mythified, Western image of God's angels. Rather than stereotypically young, heroic-looking, and blond, with sumptuous garments and wings all in white, García Márquez's mysterious stranger is dressed in rags is nearly bald and toothless, and has soiled "buzzard wings" strewn with parasites. His being temporarily lodged in the chicken coop further detracts from the dignity we normally expect of other-worldly creatures.

At the same time the official emissaries of the Catholic faith show their comic limitations. Father Gonzaga may bear the name of a legendary Jesuit saint and hero, and indeed he is a robust former woodcutter, but his expectation that the angel should know Latin as "the language of God" demonstrates his innocence of scriptural Hebrew and Greek. Meanwhile, in perfect medieval fashion, the learned argufiers in Rome debate endlessly as to whether the man in question possesses a navel or speaks Aramaic (the language Jesus probably spoke), and they even ask how many times—that old Scholastic chestnut—the stranded angel could fit on the head of a pin! (The simplest solution, of course, would be for the churchmen to betake themselves to the Caribbean village and use the evidence of their eyes and ears; but their Scholastic doctrine has yet to catch up with the empirical method.) Still, it cannot be denied that the visitor has the divine capacity to perform miracles, however skewed they be—such as giving a blind man three new teeth or having sunflowers sprout on a leper's sores. Perhaps they are practical jokes he plays on the gawking townspeople.

For the ordinary folk in this story—their notions as well as their ailments—come across as equally comical: the rustic who thinks the angel should be "mayor of the world," or the invalid woman who counts her heartbeats, or the Portuguese man disturbed by the noises of the stars. García Márquez's humor with his fictive villagers, it should be noted, is mostly gentle and good-natured. The only dark moment comes toward the end, when Pelayo and Elisenda, having gotten rich from exhibiting "their" angel, now build a mansion, and she wears satin shoes and fine silks. In the meantime the very source of their wealth is shooed around and out of the house by Elisenda with her broom, to be finally consigned to the shed. His wings are healing, however, and one spring day he flies off just as Elisenda is peeling onions (the same effect of Fernanda's sheets in *One Hundred Years*), and the onetime moneymaker-turned-nuisance recedes as "a dot on the horizon of the sea" before he disappears for good. Without demonstrating the aggressive satire of Luis Buñuel in movies such as *Simon of the Desert* or *The Milky Way*, García Márquez shares in the great Spanish film director's laughing sensibility.

The name of the story "Death Constant beyond Love" is a bittersweet pun on the title of what may be the most famous single sonnet in Spanish, namely, Francisco de Quevedo's "Love Constant beyond Death," with its closing conceit, often casually quoted, about the lover's dust that will remain forever in love ("polvo seré, mas polvo enamorado"). García Márquez's prose narrative, by contrast, tells of the grim reality of love cut off by anticipated death. No doubt, Senator Onésimo Sánchez is cynical and corrupt to the core, and the illusory props of his electoral campaign neatly symbolize the empty ritualism of his speeches and slogans. And yet one cannot but feel touched by his desire for simple companionship with the young, smooth-skinned, Afro-French beauty Laura Farina during his last few months alive (even if at the expense of his family and reputation). To add to the ironies, he gains "the woman of his life" only by finally giving in to a long-standing request from Laura's criminal father for a phony residence card. Love thus flowers thanks to a secret and sordid deal.

While the art of "Death Constant" recalls that of García Márquez's earlier realist pieces, its politics are not those of military dictatorship but of the quadrennial electoral rite, not of guns or repression but of the circus and spectacle, not of rifle-butts and fear but of the horse-trading, hucksterism, and sheer inertia of the patronage machine. At the same time, from the first line to the last the narrative is one of love and politics, sex and power—the two grand themes of *The Autumn of the Patriarch*. The senator's cultured cosmopolitanism and mostly happy family life, it should be noted, do set him apart from the animal crudity and vulgar greed of the nameless Caribbean despot, but both in the end inspire in us an understanding pity.

In interviews during the 1980s, García Márquez had sometimes talked idly about a projected memoir on the subject of Latin Americans living in Europe. How much of those overseas reminiscences he actually wrote is anyone's guess. What the author eventually did come up with on that score is yet another gathering of short fictions, *Doce cuentos peregrinos* (1992; *Strange Pilgrims*, 1993).

The dozen pieces, inevitably of varying length and quality, all deal with Latin Americans who either reside in or are in some sort of transit on the Old Continent while never fully belonging to it (hence "pilgrims"). The book nonetheless retains certain features and feelings of memoir. Most of the stories include at some point a brief, passing, first-person intervention by an unidentified, participating narrator who once knew and conversed with one or more key characters.[16] In addition, the two pieces "The Ghosts of August" and "Tramontana" are told directly from the personal viewpoint of a man much resembling García Márquez, in the company of his wife and children. Even when, in other stories, the adult reminiscer is not Gabo, he often still has two sons.

As an ensemble, then, the book has the atmosphere of a memoir that brings together a mature person's remembrances of interesting individuals whom, in the course of the years, he has met, perhaps befriended, and then never seen again.

The volume features a first for García Márquez: a seven-page prologue explaining, as the title says, "Why Twelve, Why Stories, Why Pilgrims." Never once previously had the Colombian author traced, within the covers of a book itself, either the source or the process of creating and crafting its contents. His account of those textual "peregrinations" is fascinating, if too complex and convoluted to be summarized here. Yet the prologue is in some ways a preliminary narrative in itself (story number zero, as it were), in which the mystery and randomness of the creative process is conveyed via a set of personal anecdotes—the dream he once dreamt about his own funeral, the peripatetic notebook with sixty-four potential topics that unfortunately got mislaid, the various phases that the twelve final stories went through in their refashioning from journalistic pieces and/or film scripts, and the many, many rewrites.

Furthermore, the deep divide between personal memories and the changes in real life is suggested when he tells of revisiting "Barcelona, Geneva, Paris, and Rome" in order to verify the accuracy of his recollections—and there finding out that, after some twenty years, his lingering remembrances had little to do with a newer Europe. He thus hints at the universal paradox of our remembering things past that are no more, and that nonetheless live on within our memory.

What matters most for our purposes, though, is that García Márquez forthrightly announces the subject matter of his twelve pieces as "the strange things that happen to Latin Americans in Europe" (*DCP*, 14; *SP*, viii)—a loaded topic, as the phrase goes. While Europe weighs heavily on the minds of literate Latins, few on the Old Continent give much thought to the human legacy of the less-than-fortunate republics south of Texas. Moreover, for many Latin Americans the relationship is one fraught with ambivalence. Historically, Europeans in South America have mostly been invaders or settlers who have tended to think of Europe as "civilized," Latin America as somehow "barbaric." Some Latin Americans have accepted and lived this long-standing dichotomy. Others have rejected it on principle. And yet, regardless of their stance, most Latins with any natural curiosity have embarked on a transatlantic "pilgrimage" as a means of broadening their experience and culture. It may be just coincidence that *Doce cuentos peregrinos* appeared in 1992, the year of the Columbus quincentennial.

The word "peregrinos" in the original book title is ambiguous and highly suggestive. On the most obvious level it is an adjective that can denote both the pilgrim characters in the stories and the erratic, pilgrim-like history of the stories' crafting. On the other hand, "peregrinos" could be remotely construed as a noun modifier that refers to the Latin American "pilgrims" themselves.

As expected, several of the Latins depicted here are Colombians. But we also encounter a Puerto Rican wife ("Bon Voyage, Mr. President"), a chanteuse and a magician, both from Mexico ("I Only Came to Use the Phone"), a real Venezuelan novelist ("The Ghosts of August"), a Brazilian sex worker ("María dos Prazeres"), and a boatload of Italo-Argentines debarking at Naples ("Seventeen Poisoned Englishmen"). Other characters hail from unidentified Caribbean lands—the eponymous "Mr. President" and his adopted friend, the young boys in "Mrs. Forbes's Summer of Happiness" and in "Light Is Like Water"—or from anywhere on the continent (the nameless Sleeping Beauty).

In keeping with a "you-are-there" realism, the geography of the different European localities—neighborhood and street names, architectural landmarks, climate traits—is spelled out in some detail. By the same token, snatches of dialogue or references in the relevant languages (French, Catalan, Italian, German) crop up from time to time. Fittingly, nearly all of the stories include some passing allusion to Europe's high-culture artifacts—classical music, operatic arias, canonical authors, and the like. The two stories that diverge from this pattern bring in comparable high masters from Latin America instead. "I Sell My Dreams" sets up a four-page episode featuring none other than the great Chilean bard Pablo Neruda. And "I Only Came to Use the Phone" slips in a reference to Brazilian troubadour Vinicius de Moraes, as perhaps befits a story about an erstwhile pop singer involved with international pop culture.

Three of the pilgrim stories—"Seventeen Poisoned Englishmen," "Tramontana," and "Miss Forbes's Happy Summer"—portray, directly if subtly, the clash of cultures, and moreover turn on its head the long-standing dichotomy of "civilized" Europe vs. "barbaric" America. Perhaps not accidentally, the three pieces are grouped together in sequence.

"Seventeen Poisoned Englishmen" hinges on a clever plot twist. Señora Prudencia Linero, a widow from Colombia, arrives in Naples and comes within a hair of checking in at a third-floor hotel, in a multistory edifice where several such establishments are housed. As she stands in the old-fashioned elevator cage, the physical look of the place attracts her, but she is suddenly repelled by the sight of seventeen English male tourists in sandals and shorts, all dozing in the lobby. Though it is the only place in the building equipped with a restaurant (which she, not knowing Italian, might need), she rides on up to a fifth-floor hotel, whose female owner knows Spanish. Toward the end of the story the señora returns from an outside eatery and now witnesses the corpses of those seventeen Brits being taken out on stretchers: they've been poisoned by oysters served in their hotel dining room. Señora Linero, quite shaken (we infer) at having evaded death on a mere whim, barricades herself in her room and prays.

Aside from its concatenation of colorful events, "Seventeen Poisoned Englishmen" is a touching account of an innocent abroad. The protagonist, from the provincial port of Riohacha, has never set foot outside her desert town, having dedicated herself to her family and her husband, recently deceased. Like many a Catholic innocent, her one overseas dream is to meet the pope and perhaps even be confessed by the pontiff (again, a "pilgrimage," if not touted as such). At first the August heat of the port of Naples reminds her of home, but being an alien voyager quickly catches up with and weighs on her.

The transient nature of personal relations on board ship leaves Señora Linero bewildered. The sight of a dead man in a tuxedo floating on the harbor waters and the indifference of everyone to the spectacle further disconcert her. War ruins (it seems to be the late 1940s) and the fortuitous absence of any welcomers on shore both add to her distraught mood. What shocks her about the sleeping Brits is their bare, pink knees (at that time, adults in short pants were inconceivable in Latin America). Equally shocking are the "almost naked tourists" in the restaurant as well as the couples who dare to kiss in public. The strange fact of a waitress who is blonde inspires pity in doña Prudencia (to a naive Caribbean, all blondes must be upper-class). Already she dislikes Italy, and the festive afternoon atmosphere, the Vespa motor scooters piloted by shirtless men, and the red-light district (where a well-dressed john pursues her) further add to her traveler's discontent. The multiple poisoning at the end is, of course, the final straw. (The Yugoslav priest whom she meets at the restaurant provides a sounding board for her illusions along with a means for dialogue.)

At the same time one could see "Seventeen Poisoned Englishmen" as a narrative not of an "innocent abroad" but of a traveler's rapid disillusion with the prestigious Old Continent. The reminders of World War II, the collective coldness before a gentleman's floating corpse, and the air of frenetic frivolity may indeed prove distressing to a modest, small-town, bereaved elderly lady, who is invariably referred to as "*señora* Prudencia Linero" (the persistent honorific and her first name both suggesting an old-fashioned propriety). And her idiosyncratic penance of dressing regularly in brown Franciscan robes might also be taken as a sly, authorial wink at the Italian navigator who "discovered" the New World and was also wont to wear Franciscan garb. Finally, on a more universal, more human level, "Seventeen Poisoned Englishmen," while at first glance a tale of tabloid-style disaster, is also a wistful account of personal loss, an alien's loneliness, and provincial naiveté under challenge for the first time.

The title of "Tramontana" refers to a gusty wind that blows northeast-to-southwest over Catalonia, where the story takes place. What action there is occurs on the Costa Brava, which ordinarily fills up with summer tourists from northern Europe. The bulk of the piece actually consists of descriptions of the wind itself and of its corrosive effects on various individuals—the narrator (presumably García Márquez himself) and his family, the concierge of their building, and the hapless twenty-year-old Caribbean boy, a pop singer set upon by a mixed gang of Swedish revelers. The concierge's suicide by hanging foreshadows the Latin American's more dramatic end. The eleven Nordics, aiming to cure the expatriate vocalist of his "superstitious" fear of the tramontana, all but kidnap him for an upcoming performance in Cada-qués. Instead, en route he plunges from their van into the abyss.

Swedes are commonly reputed to be among the most rational, "civilized" people in Europe. Here, however, we see their golden youths behaving like barbarians. The narrator, perhaps playing on certain white travelers' clichés to the effect that Africans or Asians "all look alike," says of his Scandinavians that they're "difficult to tell from one another" (DCP, 179; SP, 133). In contrast with their acts of casual abuse and cruelty, the story takes place largely at a Barcelona club named after the Italian Renaissance fabulist Boccacio, where the narrator has shown up just after attending a concert by the great Russian violinist David Oistrakh. Hence we catch a glimpse of a couple of the best of Europe's high-culture treasures, though these cannot deter a mob of "ratio-nal," post-adolescent Swedes from engaging in nasty and destructive antics.

When "Tramontana" first ran as a personal essay in several Spanish-language publications in 1984, it bore the longer and more suggestive title "Tramontana mortal." The unsettling episode with the suicidal jump did appear, but the act occurred on a drinking binge among a group of local friends; there were neither abusive Swedes nor a helpless Caribbean songster in the picture. García Márquez has thus re-elaborated the original, true-life anecdote in order to have it fit the general, cultural, fictive themes of *Strange Pilgrims*.[17]

"Miss Forbes's Summer of Happiness" ("señora" = "Mrs." Forbes in the original) takes place on Europe's southern margins, on Pantelleria (Pantelaria in the Spanish original), Italy's volcanic island situated almost halfway between Sicily and Tunis. The two unnamed boys, ages nine and seven, come from Guacamayal, Colombia, a real town in the Magdalena department, about 200 kilometers south of Santa Marta, and not far from Sucre and Sincé, where a young García Márquez once lived. Such origins help establish that the father of the kids, a writer described as having "more presumption than talent" (*DCP*, 196; *SP*, 147) is *not* precisely Gabo. Moreover, the temporarily absent paterfamilias is the sort of South American intellectual who worships Europe, is ashamed of his own background, and entertains hopes of Europeanizing his two offspring.

The story is told retrospectively by the elder child, who, as a knowing adult, evokes the idyllic sensations of a distant, leisurely, Mediterranean summer—the beauty of the natural setting, the joys of deep-sea diving, and more. The actual time frame is left vague, though passing references to TV movies place it perhaps in the 1960s. The positive side of old Europe is represented by two of the local characters: the maid Fulvia Flamínea, who invites the two kids to her nearby home and there regales them with songs and stories; and Oreste, a fisherman by trade, whose ancestral Greek name links his moments with the boys together to a deeper and remote past. The boys' underwater discovery of a buried, meter-high Greek vase, bearing remnants of "immemorial" wine, adds to the overall feeling of olden times.

On the other hand, they also come upon a stock of undetonated yellow torpedoes, reminders of the ugly, less-civilized Europe of mechanized warfare. And of course there is their governess Miss (*Frau?*) Forbes, an almost stereotypically rigid and authoritarian German who moreover demonstrates "the most ancient, stale habits of European society" (*DCP*, 196; *SP*, 148). She in fact shows up wearing military boots and goes on to impose her will on the two kids, keeping tally points on their behavior and forcing them to eat in silence, sit upright, and chew ten times on each side of their mouths before swallowing. A snob as well, she limits their time with the plebs Fulvia and Oreste. At one time the narrator dubs her "a sergeant from Dortmund" (ibid.). (In García Márquez's film version of the story, made for Spanish television, Oreste once actually refers to her, casually, as "Hitler.") She nonetheless has a hidden, more complex side—swimming in secret, indulging a taste for cakes and wine, and taking in movies "forbidden to minors" on TV. Although Miss Forbes bakes superb desserts and has a love of the great German poet-playwright Schiller (declaiming him out loud), her admirable traits are hopelessly tainted by her domestic despotism.

The younger boy entertains childish fantasies of killing off their harsh governess. The ironic discovery, at story's end, of the woman's lifeless body in her bedroom, with twenty-seven knife wounds, in what will seemingly remain an unsolved crime of passion, makes the mysterious tyrannicide only slightly more disturbing than the foregoing account of Miss Forbes's unhappy, dictatorial regime.

Four of the stories—"The Saint," "I Sell My Dreams," "The Ghosts of August," and "Light Is Like Water"—represent García Márquez's signature narrative device and subgenre of magical realism. Their miracles, supernatural events, or at least amazing facts and occurrences are reported straight, as plausible happenings, sans doubts or uncertainties as to their believability.

"La santa" ("The Saint") starts out by introducing Margarito Duarte, a proper, taciturn fellow from the Andes and father of the eponymous potential girl-saint. For more than two decades he has resided in Rome in the hopes of a special papal audience. The miracle he has long lobbied for is multiple. When his unnamed daughter, dead at age seven, was exhumed eleven years hence during a cemetery construction project, her body was found incorrupt and weightless, and moreover the roses in her stiff hands had been, and have since remained, in bloom. Margarito's fellow townsmen duly raised funds for a canonization effort in the Holy See, where the Colombian pilgrim, with his daughter's body in what resembles a violoncello case, settled. Alas, what the traveler found in the Vatican was not the holy welcome mat but an impersonal bureaucracy that routinely brushed him off. One has to believe the church functionary who informs Margarito that, in the previous year alone, they had received 800 letters from across the globe regarding incorrupt cadavers.

The routinized magic further thickens in various ways. The participant narrator's friend Rafael Ribero Silva, a tenor presumably studying voice in Rome, sings high C's while practicing in his room and is regularly answered by a roar from a lion at the Villa Borghese zoo. On yet another, single occasion, as Ribero starts intoning the love duet from Verdi's *Otello*, he is joined from a distant house by a soprano who assumes the part of Desdemona, and who we later find out is Maria Caniglia (a real diva [1904–79], renowned in her lifetime). In yet another slightly eerie episode, on a visit to the zoo by some Colombians, the lion roars at the melancholic Margarito and avidly follows his movements. (The zoo guard attributes the targeted roars to "compassion.")

At the end of the piece, the nameless narrator revisits a Rome changed beyond recognition. There he runs into the doleful pilgrim still pursuing his cause; and it suddenly dawns on him that "the Saint was Margarito."

Given that not much happens beyond Margarito's endless waiting, the story features plenty of subplot and detail related to life in Rome—watermelon vendors, comical sex episodes, streetwalkers (including a prostitute who sees the intact little corpse and exclaims, "Mi si gelò il culo!"—"My arse froze!"), the summer heat, and the cavalcade of five popes from the 1950s on (including ill-fated Albino Luciani, better known as John Paul I, who offers Margarito a glimmer of hope yet dies following thirty-three days in office, as actually happened).

In addition, García Márquez inserts material from his own days in Rome as a late-twentyish enrollee at the Centro Sperimentale di Cinema, slipping in café banter with fellow students and also a private joke when his teacher Cesare Zavattini, responding to a suggestion that a film be made about Margarito's experience, dismisses it all as implausible. Later, however, a Greek student named Lakis suggests having the girl rise from the dead. This is precisely the ending given in the earlier movie version of the tale, *Miracle in Rome* (1988). The short story, then, is somewhat less magical yet more sad and brooding than the film.

When first published as an apparent essay in the Spanish-language press in the 1980s, "La santa" bore the title "La larga vida feliz de Margarito Duarte"—"The Long Happy Life of Margarito Duarte," with an obvious side glance at Hemingway's short story entitled "The Short Happy Life of Francis Macomber." The original focus, then, was more on the constant father than on his deceased daughter. Also, the title of the film *Miracle in Rome* inevitably evokes *Miracle in Milan*, the 1950 classic by none other than Cesare Zavattini, he of the cameo appearance in this piece. Cultural echoes and allusions thus resonate through the complex textual history of "The Saint."

The Spanish title "Espantos de agosto" (Terrors of August) already announces our being faced with a horror story in the vein of Lovecraft or Poe; the English title, "The Ghosts of August," has comparable connotations. The narrator, driving to Arezzo under the Tuscan sun with his wife and two young boys (clearly the novelist himself in this case) gets a foretaste of the uncanny when an elderly woman goatherd informs the travelers that the castle they are looking for is haunted. Naturally, the pilgrims in their car are amused at such superstition. Once they are there, the eighty-room structure is meticulously drawn by the narrator, and we read of one Ludovico, a Renaissance grandee who had built the edifice, knifed his lover in their bed, and then had himself devoured by his war dogs. The fateful bedroom and its furnishings are also described, along with the persistent scent of strawberries.

Under pressure from the kids and the late hour, the family decides to spend the night in two of the castello's ground-floor, updated bedrooms.

As the narrator awakes next morning, however, he realizes, shocked, that he and his wife are now on the upper floor, in Ludovico's bed, with his portrait on the wall, blood stains on the sheets, and again the smell of strawberries. We are indeed in a haunted house, where the ghosts of crimes past can alter present-day reality.

The reported host and owner of the castle, the Venezuelan journalist and writer Miguel Otero Silva, really existed (1908–85) and was a presence in his native land's print culture. Also authentic are the celebrated frescoes by Piero della Francesca in the nearby church of San Francesco. Both Ludovico and his castle, however, look to be inventions, vivid composites of the many such refined yet ruthless Renaissance princes, their mighty misdeeds, and sumptuous palazzo properties. Once again the story's title has undergone metamorphoses: in its initial incarnation within the Spanish-language op-ed pages it was called "Cuentos de horror para la Nochevieja" ("Tales of Horror for New Year's Eve"), reflecting merely the fact of its appearing on 30 December 1980.

The Spanish title of "Me alquilo para soñar" ("I Rent Myself Out for Dreaming") is more accurate, complex, and suggestive than the admittedly idiomatic English, "I Sell My Dreams." The Colombian woman, known solely by her nickname "Frau Frieda," is indeed described as having some gift for prophetic visions when sleeping. While still young she vaguely foretold her little brother's choking death, and as an adult she dreams the same dream dreamt by Pablo Neruda—to wit: a dream in which the poet was dreaming of her. In this regard the oneiric chain is further linked to Jorge Luis Borges as something the Argentine fantasticator himself might have composed (or, as it were, dreamt up). The narrator is a quasi–García Márquez figure, who looks back at his Austrian vacation from Italian cinema school.

The mysterious female expatriate, who had arrived in Vienna between the wars as a music student, reportedly was to earn her keep for decades as an interpreter of dreams for a local family she lived with. The enigmatic woman who dies at the start of the story in a Havana tidal wave may well be Frau Frieda, with her telltale serpent-shaped ring, though we readers are never fully and finally assured thereof.

"I Sell My Dreams" covers a wide geographic swath—first Vienna, then Frieda's retirement in Porto (with its spectacular ocean location), and in the end her possible association with Lisbon's ambassador to Cuba. Havana, with its own seaside promenade, the Malecón, frames the narrative. The lengthy, engaging, affectionate episode with Neruda (actually, yet another story of a Latin American pilgrim in Europe) reads very much like a memoirist's account, though only biographical research will determine whether the Barcelona stopover actually took place—and as reported. From a formal standpoint, however, the Neruda material gives the piece a stronger tie with reality: a flesh-and-blood poet sharing space with a professional dreamer-prophet (even if he dismisses her claims, saying, "Only poetry is clairvoyant").

Curiously, unlike the other eleven stories, Vienna's urban details are not spelled out, though its postwar, *Third Man*–type atmosphere is evoked. Still, the choice of city as initial setting may be significant: Vienna, the mecca of classical music, and also the home of Freud, whose most monumental work is *The Interpretation of Dreams* and whose name the Frau's nickname somewhat resembles.

"Light Is Like Water" builds on a fanciful conceit shared casually by the unnamed literary narrator, who in a Madrid poetry seminar compares electric light to water flowing from a tap. (What a nine-year-old Toto was doing at that seminar is not made clear.) The Colombian family of four, from the port of Cartagena, lives at 47 Castellana in Spain's capital, a landlocked city with just a small river. Nevertheless Toto and his little brother, in reward for their good grades, keep getting parental gifts of ever-fancier maritime gear— rowboat, fins, goggles, oxygen tanks—which they use for sailing and splashing in the full, high lamplight of their apartment. Three such navigational adventures occur. The first two, mom and dad never even notice. For the third one, however, the brotherly pair and schoolmates throw a house party with parental consent, yet they all end up drowning in the torrent of luminescence. The group tragedy is virtually overshadowed and cancelled out by the disproportionate magicality of the event, in which the light pours forth in a vast onrush onto the boulevard, and by the long list of floating debris items (including the father's condoms) that add a wistful, quirky humor.

The action takes place sometime after 1972, the year the film *Last Tango in Paris* came out (the parents go to see it during the kids' second sailing episode), and most probably well after the death of General Franco in 1975 and the subsequent end of movie censorship. Paseo La Castellana, 47, is indeed an apartment building, with a bank on the bottom floor.[18] The kids' school of St. Julian the Hospitator, by contrast, is pure invention, its name chosen, I gather, because that Catholic saint (chiefly known today as a result of Flaubert's short story with the same name) is reported to have ferried passengers across a river near his house, and is moreover the patron saint of rowers and boatmen.

The dominant conceit and the brevity of "Light Is Like Water" have helped make it a favored anthology piece, though it does lack in the richness and complexity of previous magical works by Gabo. The text contains a slight inaccuracy, moreover, in that at the end the narrator describes Madrid as a city "with no ocean or river," when in fact the small River Manzanares flows visibly through the older, western part of the town.

As one would expect from an avowedly left-wing author, two pieces—"Bon Voyage, Mr. President" and "María dos Prazeres"—deal with politics, not so much in the broad sense of cultural conflict and group power, but rather in the stricter, narrow domain of government and ordinary people's relationship thereto.

"Buen viaje, señor presidente," as the first story in the volume is originally entitled, is also the lengthiest. Set in the diplomatic, less-than-romantic, almost rootless city of Geneva, it brings together three unlikely characters: the nameless deposed president of a Caribbean banana republic, obliquely remembered as Puerto Santo;[19] his twenty-something compatriot, a fellow exile and hospital orderly with the wonderful handle of Homero Rey de la Casa (Homer King of the House); and the latter's wife Lázara Davis, a caramel-skinned Puerto Rican. The spouse—a "Yoruban princess," "intelligent and ill-tempered" though with "a tender heart" (DCP, 35; SP, 15) and fond of santería bracelets—fits perfectly the familiar mold of García Márquez's wise, feisty, strong-willed women. Homero will shadow and then befriend the ex-chief of state, partly out of ulterior motives—he having informal business ties with funeral parlors and with insurance firms that service less-than-wealthy foreign clients. In time, however, the tie becomes more affectionate and even familial.

The strongest and most enigmatic member of this trio is the seventy-three-year-old president himself. Little is actually said about his political stance or programs, yet they can be inferred. He was voted in democratically (Homero was a minor volunteer worker for his electoral campaign), then removed by an army coup. His friendship with the great, left-wing, Afro-French author Aimé Césaire, who in 1945 was elected the Communist mayor of Fort-de-France, marks him as a progressive. His law studies in Geneva and exile in Martinique (a part of democratic France) make the nameless president something of a cultured individual, and place him outside the cruder U.S. orbit. Although his late wife came from old colonial stock, his current economic situation approaches poverty, and with the murder of his only son he has no remaining kin. The narrator's veiled reference to the upcoming "harshest [winter] of the century" presumably means that of 1947, thus signaling a time when military juntas, generally with U.S. backing, were routinely overthrowing popularly elected, reformist governments in Latin America (as indeed happened with Venezuela's Rómulo Gallegos in 1947, Cuba's Carlos Prío in 1952, and Guatemala's Jacobo Arbenz in 1954). It was also a brief moment, pre–Cold War, when a coalition government that included leftist parties held power in continental France. (Incidentally, the narrator notes that Césaire "had just published his *Cahier d'un retour au pays natal* [*Notebook of a Return to My Native Land*]," his seminal first book, thus indeed placing the action in the 1940s.)

"Bon Voyage, Mr. President" is an unusually complex story, both in tone and structure. Besides three countries, it gives us three narrative points of view and close-ups of three highly different personal temperaments. The dominant emotion is one of wistfulness and loss, as this varied, improvised Caribbean threesome are shown to cope with uncertain life in an autumnal, somewhat cold Swiss metropolis. The city's geography—the lake, a statue of Calvin, street names, a restaurant—is sketched out, though the only interactions we see taking place with the native *Genevois* are business ones. In addition there are substantial doses of humor, as when Lázara is charged with selling the president's inherited jewels and discovers they are all fake; or when his excellency departs by rail, and Homero, realizing that the elder man has forgotten his walking stick, chases after the train and hurls the staff at him standing on the rear car's platform, only to see the cane crushed under the train wheels. The style, moreover, has its poetic touches, notably in the scene in which the couple entertains the ex-chief, and Lázara's adverse reaction to the man is conveyed by a fourfold anaphora with "Le pareció . . ." ("She thought him . . .").

Its everyday realism notwithstanding, "Bon Voyage, Mr. President" is something of a fantasy, or at least a wishful anachronism. To my knowledge, no major Spanish-Caribbean political leader from the mid-twentieth century ever studied in Geneva or would choose exile on the French islands. (The love affair of Latin American politicos with France was more of a nineteenth-century phenomenon, as exemplified by Mexico's Porfirio Díaz, who is buried in Paris's Père-Lachaise cemetery—and also as satirized by Alejo Carpentier in his comic novel *Reasons of State*.) In this regard García Márquez's magical-realist extravaganza *The Autumn of the Patriarch* is truer to the overall contours of Latin America's sordid state politics than is this sweetly touching story.

"María dos Prazeres" deftly intermingles radical politics with paid sex—in unusual ways. The protagonist (her Portuguese surname signifies "of the Pleasures") is a still-attractive, seventy-seven-year-old Brazilian mulatta who has spent over five decades as a prostitute in Catalonia, after having been sold as a teen in Manaos by her mother, and in time ditched in Barcelona by a Turkish seaman. As befits her advanced age, María at the start is seen preparing for death—receiving a house call by a mortician, choosing her cemetery lot (on the high ground, to avoid floods), visiting her future grave-yard, disposing of her possessions to various unidentified heirs, and, last but not least, readying her dog named "Noi" ("boy" in Catalan) for the ultimate transition.

The Franco regime is the indirect yet steady backdrop to the story. María has a long-standing, visceral relationship to Spain's 1930s Republican left. She attended the public burial of the renowned Anarchist leader Buenaventura Durruti (1896–1936), who had died mysteriously early on in the civil war. She would have liked her tomb to have been next to his unmarked grave; she now takes to secretly scribbling his name with her lipstick onto his blank tomb-stone. (The inscription always disappears overnight.) The aging Franco dic-tatorship shows its heavy hand when security agents shoot dead a student for painting a Catalan graffito that reads "Long live free Catalonia!" The regime in the end shatters her longest-standing relationship when her regular lover-client, a Count Cardona, defends at dinnertime the upcoming execution of some Basque separatists, and she responds by promising to poison the count's soup. (End of the affair.) The political reference helps place the final stages of María's story, most probably, in 1975. (Later that year, General Franco will breathe his last, as will María.)

The immediate plot of the story spans about a year and a half, starting out in April (1974?), going on to September, when María witnesses a burial; then autumn and Christmas with their jolly music and lights and street life; the harsh break-up with the count the following April; and finally the enigmatic ride in November (1975?). The changes of season help evoke the inexorable passage of time, one of the underlying themes of "María dos Prazeres," along with its more manifest subject of old age.

The mysterious concluding episode of the piece takes place during a raw and rainy November afternoon. On the face of it, a young fellow in a sump-tuous, almost noiseless automobile "the color of dusky steel" gives María a ride home, then starts walking up the stairs to her apartment. In the end she feels blissfully happy, living a moment she had been waiting for—having, one presumes, a man who simply cares about her. On the other hand, the strange nature of the scene also hints at an account of the arrival of death in the form of a dream-fantasy. The windows of the car lower "as if by magic" (DCP, 152; SP, 112). She informs the driver, "I'm going quite a distance," which could imply more than just her neighborhood. From the inside of the car, which smells of medicine, the city looks to have changed colors, and she compares the sheer size of the car to a dream. The youthful chauffeur has blond hair, recalling the stereotypical image of an angel. When exiting the car, María doesn't bother to close the door; later from her stair landing she overhears the sound of two doors slamming shut.

In sum, there is much that points to the possibility of these last pages being a hallucination in the Borges or Cortázar vein, as experienced by María in her dying moments. The story already features a previous quasi-magical element in María's beloved dog Noi, a small pet that miraculously sheds tears and also knocks on the door threefold whenever he wants in. "María dos Prazeres," in all, is one of the master's more complex and suggestive short narratives.

"I Only Came to Use the Phone" also has Franco's long tyranny as its broader setting, the regime serving as dimly symbolic of the story's quirky little tragicomedy. The piece actually consists of two narratives seamlessly interwoven into one. First is the main plot: María de la Luz Cervantes, a Mexican national residing in Barcelona, is driving on a highway through Aragón province's Monegros desert (located between Zaragoza and Huesca) when her rented car breaks down. She is picked up by a bus that is returning with some female patients to their single-sex mental asylum, where María hopes to use the telephone and get help. Once at the institution, however, the authorities treat her like just another inmate, and she finds herself locked up indefinitely with the rest of them.

The lithograph of General Franco that presides over the medieval dining hall casually suggests that we are witnessing an instance of the regime's arbitrary authority and powers of incarceration. María's clever use of the dictator's portrait to smash a window in an attempted escape may additionally be seen as a challenge to his autocracy. (It is worth passing mention that María's country, Mexico, was the only Latin American republic to deny diplomatic recognition to Franco's state.) The hardened female guards—one of whom bears the name "Herculina"—further bespeak a brutish system without their necessarily existing as allegorical stick figures. The "we" narrator who twice intervenes places the events in Francoism's twilight years, a time frame further reinforced by allusion to the young, waist-length-haired hippie, an earlier friend of María's. The unexplained, briefly reported demolition of the mental hospital in the last paragraph can be seen as anticipating or punctuating the end of the regime. Not that "I Only Came to Use the Phone" is an explicitly ideological narrative; the political details merely parallel and reinforce the private, human drama. Moreover, the underlying note of humor, with its banal, comical refrain, saves the piece from the trap of heavy-handedness.

Intermixed with María's bizarre mishap is a tale of wavering sentiment, romantic betrayal, and lover's revenge. María, a former actress who had conducted a number of casual affairs, has since done some growing up and settled into a permanent tie with Saturno, a magician by trade and a compatriot. Previously, however, she had managed to jilt a hapless Saturno three different times (and an unnamed first husband as well). Notwithstanding their current happy marriage, her accidental failure to return from Zaragoza leads Saturno to infer that she has ditched him for a fourth time, now with the hippie. When María at last tracks down her spouse by phone and he comes to see her, she assumes he will help her get discharged. (She treats him to effusive affection, addressing him with the term of endearment "conejo"—"bunny rabbit"—in the original.) Yet a devilish Saturno instead goes along with the official diagnosis and leaves poor María locked up—his revenge for her previous abandonments and for the more recent hippie affair that may or may not have happened.

"I Only Came to Use the Phone" is thus one of García Márquez's many accounts of the mysteries of male-female romance and the ways in which it can both grow and go wrong. It is also, just incidentally, the perfect consolation piece for those loving faithful who have found themselves blithely ditched sometime by a shallow and frivolous partner. Not surprisingly, in its original incarnation as a film script, the narrative bore the telling title "María de mi corazón" ("María of My Heart"), calling attention more to the love interest than to the darker comedy of errors. (Some readers might adjudge that the misunderstanding at the asylum, where the absence of written records or past history on María would surely have put her in the clear, strains credibility. Still, under dictatorship and in comedies, one might counter-argue, everything is possible.) On yet another level, "I Only Came to Use the Phone" tells of the ultimate frailty of all human ties, situations, and institutions—even of mental-health facilities.

The mysterious, irrational force of male-female attraction is ever among García Márquez's recurring topics, along with the fact and the effects of feminine beauty itself. "The most beautiful woman in the world" is indeed a superlative that has appeared more than once in the author's prose. These two subjects take center stage in "Sleeping Beauty and the Airplane." (The original Spanish title, "El avión de la bella durmiente," places a slightly unexpected stress on the means of transport that frames the plot.)

The entire piece revolves around a transatlantic flight, both the preliminaries and the actual trip, wherein a nameless narrator first notes an elegant, dark-haired young Venus at the check-in area of Paris's Charles de Gaulle Airport, and then by chance is assigned a seat next to hers in the jetliner's first-class cabin. The story captures some of the banalities familiar to all air travelers: the waiting-room boredom, the "commercial smile" of the employees, the delays occasioned by another passenger's multiple baggage or by bad weather, people stretched out on hallway floors, infants bawling. Then, on the plane, the contiguous narrator surreptitiously eyes the beauty—she initially awake and later asleep, he musing about it all in silence, with occasional interruptions for the in-flight movie, the toilet, or drinks. In the final sentence the exiting woman's reported, formulaic "excuse me" reveals her to be Latin American. The eight-hour delay due to a snowstorm allows for the poesy of an unforeseen nighttime narration and a long slumber. (Westbound transatlantic flights normally depart early in the afternoon and arrive during the day, well before sundown.) Other than this, not much happens here.

García Márquez adds some depth and substance to the story via a couple of cultural references. The first is a quotation, lines 9–12, from a love sonnet, "Insomnio," by Spanish poet Gerardo Diego (1896–1987). The original citation reads: "saber que duermes tú, segura / —cauce fiel de abandono,línea pura— / tan cerca de mis brazos maniatados." Diego's poem, significantly starts out as follows: "Tú y tu desnudo sueño. No lo sabes. / Duermes. No. No lo sabes. Yo en desvelo . . ." ("You and your naked sleep. You're not aware. / You sleep. No. You're not aware. I unasleep . . ."). The Spaniard's sonnet, moreover, features the equally relevant—unquoted—lines, "No hay vuelo / que alce hasta ti las alas de mis aves"[20] ("There is no flight / That will raise my bird's wings up to you").

Taking things a bit further, the story's narrative voice also evokes (without naming it) Yasunari Kawabata's *House of the Sleeping Beauties*, a novella about a curiously exquisite and isolated sex mansion where rich old men pay for the privilege of lying chastely next to comely young women from the house ranks. The Japanese Nobel laureate's book would later provide the inspiration and the epigraph for the Colombian disciple's own short novel, *Memories of My Melancholy Whores*.

Ultimately, "El avión de la bella durmiente" is a slight story that overly reflects its origins as a journalistic (puff?) piece. It is the only fiction in *Doce cuentos peregrinos* whose narrator assumes a prominent, almost leading role and can be too easily identified with the author himself. Perhaps García Márquez chose to include it among his "pilgrims" in order to have a suggestive total of an even dozen rather than the uncomfortable and incomplete prime number eleven.

"The Trace of Your Blood in the Snow" ("El rastro de tu sangre en la nieve") is the second-longest piece in the volume, by far the most intricate emotionally, and perhaps the richest, most evocative, and suggestive of them all. It is, moreover, one of the author's great tales of tragic, youthful, star-crossed love. The text's placement at story cycle's end could thus not be more appropriate.

Billy Sánchez de Avila and Nena (pronounced "NEH-nah") Daconte, the love-smitten, late-teens couple who suddenly marry, form an unlikely pair. While both are the offspring of Cartagena's old upper crust, their personalities stand poles apart: he a violent, roguish, beachcombing, good-for-nothing, macho lout interested solely in fancy cars and sex (a familiar enough type) and with no foreign experience; she a delicate, refined, cultured, multilingual, Europe-educated young lady, a serious reader and a saxophone player to boot. (Her innocence is suggested by her given name, which can mean "little girl.") Even their whirlwind courtship is something out of the ordinary, starting with the beach-hut scene in which Billy seeks to impress her with the size of his upright organ but she sagely deflates his ego instead. In time, though, Nena will seduce him, and they conduct a passionate amour, making love in cars, shelters, her parents' mansion, and even on their post-wedding flight to Europe. Amazingly, a warmly loving Nena succeeds in reaching the brash boy's scared, vulnerable side.

Their steamy romance, during as well as before the honeymoon, is told in flashbacks. The in-medias-res beginning concerns the newlyweds' Madrid-to-Paris ride in Billy's brand-new silver Bentley, with his bumptious machismo still in evidence, and without a single hospital, pharmacy, or hotel stop along the way—this despite Nena's steadily bleeding wedding-ring finger wounded by a prick from a rose thorn in Madrid. Finally, on a Tuesday, she is admitted to a Parisian hospital, Billy then spending a week astray in the City of Light, all but oblivious to his youthful bride's wrenching fate.

The last ten pages of the piece tell of utter desolation. We initially see Billy aimless in the French capital, ignorant of any foreign tongue and hopelessly nonplussed before such things as light-timers (the bane of all novice travelers to Europe), shared hotel bathrooms, newsprint toilet paper (we are probably in the early 1950s), complex parking rules, ordering meals in cafés (he eats multiple hard-boiled eggs because they're already sitting on the tabletop racks), the oppressively gray humid weather and January snow, the stand-offish Andean (i.e., *cachaco*) staff at the embassy, the distance to the Eiffel Tower, the enigmatic public telephones, the sheer spread of urban Paris. We see a rich, seventeen-year-old brat alone for the first time, sans the privileges of family wealth and status, not to mention only-sonhood. In his isolation Billy looks back nostalgically at his Caribbean world, his home, his foods, his mother—the narrator even granting the boy the wistful threefold anaphora, "He remembered . . ." (*DCP*, 236; *SP*, 180). During the intervening weekend he simply hides in his one-star hotel room across from the hospital. It is around this time, after Billy has been physically ejected when attempting to crash into the clinic, that we are informed, "he began to be an adult" (*DCP*, 238; *SP*, 182).

Billy's belated discovery that Nena has died, along with the retrospective information that follows, adds up to one of the saddest, most doleful moments in García Márquez's oeuvre, comparable to the episode of Aureliano Babilonia's terrible grief when his beloved Amaranta Úrsula bleeds to death in childbirth. The dry, objectively rendered account of the official postmortem activities only enhances the overall sense of Billy's loss, of mournfulness, as does the concluding description of a major snowfall descending over Paris.

In "The Trace of Your Blood in the Snow," the author performs a small miracle. He creates for us a situation in which we can feel profound pity for a spoiled, self-absorbed young whippersnapper whose lovely young bride succumbs to a trivial wound. It is the tragic side of García Márquez, noted in our chapter 5. Compassion for the beautiful, charming, cultivated Nena is all but expected; less so for her unsympathetic brash widower who, in some measure, bears responsibility for her sad fate (he refused to drive her to medical attention while on the road from Madrid). The emotion of the story is already anticipated in its title: the signaling of "blood" hints at a dire outcome, a human loss, and the unusual presence of the intimate adjective *tu* magnifies the sentiment and projects it onto the unstated survivor. (Within the story, of course, it is Nena who whimsically speculates on "the trace of *my* blood" [emphasis added] as a means to locate the couple should they lose their way.) The pain of remembrance of those events is further suggested halfway through when, on several occasions, the narrator inserts himself in order to report on the hospital's archives, on Billy's own recollections to him "many years later," and on the Colombian embassy officer who had dealt with Billy's case.

"The Trace of Your Blood in the Snow" has to it an almost fairy-tale quality. Despite its familiar settings and wealth of recognizable artifacts and routines, two of the story's key narrative facts would hardly pass muster within a more hard-boiled, down-to-earth, realistic piece of writing. The unnamed Parisian hospital's odd, Tuesdays-only policy for visitors (invented, I gather, so as to assign to Billy his harrowing six days lost and alone in the big city) is scarcely convincing in its role as crucial background material. Moreover, for all the dense details surrounding Nena's death, we are never informed as to the actual, specific, medical reason for the girl's demise. But then, only in a fairy tale could a beautiful young heroine die of a prick from a thorn on her wedding-ring finger—indeed from the thorn of a rose, the flower traditionally symbolizing love. The absence of chronological markers of any sort (motorcars and an airplane aside) helps give the story its timeless atmosphere of quasi-legend or folk fable. In all, García Márquez distills here a multiplicity of elements in what is one of his most heartfelt, emotionally charged short fictions.

Strange Pilgrims stands in an unusual relationship to García Márquez's two other mature books of stories. *Big Mama's Funeral* has a feeling of regional unity via its twin settings—Macondo and the nameless port "town," both located inland in northern, tropical Colombia. With the *Eréndira* volume, we saw above, García Márquez moves on and focuses on some minuscule villages around and about Colombia's north coast. The two earlier books thus reflect their author's personal shift, from the chronicler of ordinary life in his childhood towns to the poet of the Caribbean littoral.

By the time García Márquez started envisioning *Strange Pilgrims*, however, he had grown into an internationally renowned literary artist and seasoned cosmopolite. The third volume, with its pan-European spread, hence corresponds to the latter phase in his life. The geography is less localized, more scattered. And while the stories comprising the first two books do constitute something like organic totalities, *Strange Pilgrims* has a bit of a patchwork quality—the result, no doubt, of the highly varied origins of the texts themselves and the different shapes they had taken on over almost two decades. Most any collection of stories, of course, is bound to be uneven; and yet the strongest pieces in *Strange Pilgrims* can be counted among the Colombian's best fictions, long or short.

EIGHT

Juvenilia & Apprenticeship
(A Brief Interlude)

A still-developing Shakespeare wrote as his first tragic play the amorphous and sensationalistic *Titus Andronicus*. Faulkner in his thirtieth year published his thoroughly uncharacteristic and weak second novel *Mosquitoes*. Many a great author-to-be serves a public apprenticeship in the craft and fashions early writings scarcely suggestive of forthcoming triumphs in the art. The early work remains available only inasmuch as the subsequent growth and output of the same individual will dramatically surpass and supersede those trial efforts. García Márquez is no exception in this regard, having in his first twelve years as a writer produced nearly a dozen stories and two full-length novels, whose chief attractions today are the name and then-inchoate spirit of their maker, as well as their various hints and auguries of the masterpieces that are to follow.

Ten of the stories garnered in the volume *Ojos de perro azul* (included as Part I, "Eyes of a Blue Dog," in the English *Collected Stories*) were written by young Gabo between his nineteenth and twenty-fourth years. Another piece, "Monologue of Isabel Watching It Rain in Macondo," is a preliminary draft for *Leaf Storm* and was probably originally destined to be inserted into chapter 8 of that novel. The short narratives were not officially compiled as a book until as late as 1974, and this only out of expediency, in a move to counter the numerous pirated editions of García Márquez's work often issued by disreputable publishers throughout the Hispanic world.

Any readers minimally acquainted with a mature García Márquez, with his generous sense of humor and his loving eye for everyday life, will feel startled and disappointed at these stories. Brooding and morose, they deal overwhelmingly with death or isolation, and depict souls or bodies trapped in their respective graves or dreams. "The Third Resignation" gives us the musings of a young man buried in his tomb, "The Other Side of Death" the troubled thoughts of a surviving twin whose doppelgänger is about to be interred, and "Eva Is inside Her Cat" an account of a beautiful woman, tired of male attentions, who floats in an unspecified limbo, craves oranges, and tries to assume the shape of her cat, only to find out she has been dead three thousand years.

The "Eva" story is one of those clever, potentially rich fancies that, in the actual writing by their callow postadolescent creator, stand scarcely fulfilled. Other sweeter and more touching specimens ever so slightly anticipate the García Márquez who would evolve into a great novelist of love: "Someone Has Been Disarranging These Roses" portrays a dead boy who, in an affectionate signal to a former girl playmate, regularly messes up her flowers, and "Eyes of a Blue Dog" sketches a passionate amour that exists only in the male protagonist's nocturnal dreams, wherein his ardent woman invokes and everywhere scribbles the titular phrase (it is their private love-call) whenever she seeks him—alas, the man when awake remembers nothing. Some materials are simply bizarre without being magical, such as "The Night of the Curlews," with its point of departure a local folk myth about the curlew bird that pecks out the eyes of anyone who dares imitate its song, and the story tells of three men so victimized, who now feel their dark way amid the cruelly indifferent inhabitants of a small town.

The latter piece—all auditory, with no visual references, and narrated throughout in the "we" voice—shows the young García Márquez awkwardly trying his hand at modernistic technique and experimentation. In like fashion "The Other Side of Death" has surrealistic dreams suggestive of Yves Tanguy and even mentions the tearing of an eye with some scissors, probably at the instance of Luis Buñuel's early film *An Andalusian Dog*. "Nabo: The Black Man Who Made the Angels Wait" imitates Faulkner in its account of a decaying, rich, rural clan and their mentally retarded daughter and dedicated Negro manservant, while "Bitterness for Three Sleepwalkers," a portrait of a woman living in complete self-withdrawal, is composed of long Faulknerian sentences and probably has the Mississippian's "A Rose for Emily" as its model. "Dialogue with the Mirror" (perhaps the most forced of all these early narratives) has in turn a protagonist who, in his urgent need to get on to the office, and his utter isolation, vaguely recalls Kafka's Gregor Samsa.

Throughout most of these efforts one sees the twenty-year-old novice groping for formal virtuosity and purple prose, only to come up instead with strained conceits and pat endings. And while the stories do deal with some of García Márquez's more basic themes of human love and solitude, the narratives remain unrelentingly opaque and abstract, even cerebral, lacking in any palpable presence of things physical or social. Perhaps the one moment of humor recognizable as vintage García Márquez occurs in "The Third Resignation," when the doctor informs the boy's mother, "Madam, your child has a grave illness: he is dead." Otherwise little of the serenely poised artist we know from today glimmers forth in *Eyes of a Blue Dog*. If anything these stories help us see just how much any potential genius must grow in order to begin to qualify for the still-humble status of apprenticeship. They are, in a very real sense, student works—or, in the authoritative early judgment of Vargas Llosa, they belong not to the "canon" but to García Márquez's "prehistory."[1] The elder Gabo in his own memoirs considers his first story "a confused, abstract meditation made worse by my abuse of invented emotions" (*VC*, 300; *LTT*, 251), and adjudges every one of those short fictions as being "still in metaphysical limbo" (*VC*, 447; *LTT*, 372).

Of all these early pieces the best and only salvageable one is "The Woman Who Came at Six O'Clock," a Hemingwayesque fable of implied murder offstage, doubtless inspired by the U.S. author's renowned story "The Killers." In fact it is ingeniously narrated mostly in dialogue form; and its open-endedness furnishes a deft, subtly suspenseful final touch à la "Tuesday Siesta." The titular protagonist, a hardened, nameless hooker, marshals all her wiles toward cajoling the lovestruck restaurant owner in order to use him as a compliant tool and complicit alibi; she is thus an early study for the manipulative sort of female the author was to draw in full in the patriarch's wife Leticia. In the same way her generous admirer is an anticipation of that García Márquez array of unrequited innocents ranging from young Mina to Florentino Ariza. His first name José, cruelly played with and mocked by the hooker in various ways, suggests a docile but indispensable St. Joseph. And the title of the story, in the imperfect past tense in the original, really signifies not "Came" but "*Used to Come* at Six," and thus signals that day's untruth while also hinting that she no longer does come, for tomorrow she vanishes.

La hojarasca (*Leaf Storm*) was the novel that García Márquez wrote, on the back of U.S. customs forms, after hours at *El Heraldo* from 1950 to 1951. Submitted to Losada, the prestigious Argentine publisher, the manuscript was eventually turned down with a letter by Guillermo de Torre, a well-known literary critic (and brother-in-law of Borges), who noted García Márquez's meager talents and suggested that he try some other line of work. The book chanced to be put out in 1955 by a small house in Bogotá, S.L.B., presumably the initials of Samuel Lisman Baum, the owner (and the Israeli Embassy's cultural attaché), who then proceeded to disappear and leave the budding author with the job of peddling copies of *Leaf Storm* and paying off the printers himself. Sales on the market were few, as were the (albeit respectful) reviews. Only when it was reprinted at the time of the Colombian Book Festival in

1959 did its sales reach five figures and its journalist-author start to be taken at all seriously as a novelist.

Although García Márquez would subsequently try to deny it, *Leaf Storm* is clearly written under the youthful spell of the Faulkner of *As I Lay Dying*. The resemblances between the two works, in form as well as content, are fundamental and obvious: the continuous and key presence of a coffin, the problematical burials that each of the plots leads to, the role played in both narratives by small-town gossip, and, most of all, the use of different narrators with their varying psychological, spatial, and temporal perspectives on the events.

Of course, when Faulkner wrote *As I Lay Dying* he was a seasoned artist who knew exactly how to draw literary characters and highlight their essential traits—for example, Cora's righteousness, Darl's intellectualism, Dewey Dell's sultry femininity, Vardaman's little-boyishness. The García Márquez of *Leaf Storm*, by contrast, is a beginning novelist who assigns overly complex thoughts and sentences to Isabel's nameless boy, and whose Isabel herself lacks any stylistic features that would mark her as an abandoned wife and confused mother, age thirty. Moreover, where Faulkner creates a rich oratorio of fifteen voices fully interlinked, García Márquez has to make do with his apprenticeship trio of father, daughter, and grandson. Ironically, the Rabassa translation of *Leaf Storm* is something of an improvement over the original, is more "Faulknerian" even, inasmuch as the boy's monologues are simplified, while the author's own long, winding sentences, typical enough in Spanish, have a more distinctly "literary" flavor in English.

The novel has three time frames at work within its eleven multisectioned chapters. Its outermost temporal boundary we see in a separate preamble marked "Macondo 1909." These two pages in italics, very Faulknerian in their resounding cadences and visionary nostalgia, are a collective remembrance of the arrival of the banana company and its boom town, the "human leaf storm" that followed in its wake, engulfed the village, and reduced the original inhabitants to near-outsider status. (The original Spanish of the title is faintly pejorative and actually signifies "fallen dead leaves.") This voice is to reappear only in the first part of chapter 3, when a narrative "we" recalls the entry into Macondo, six years previously, of the good and courageous priest known as "Pup" (whose physical resemblance to the troublesome French doctor is a theme left undeveloped by García Márquez). In addition, the family maid Meme, via Isabel's recollections in chapter 2, part 3, will recall the "glory days" of Macondo at its founding, in which the unnamed colonel was a participant.

The second time span is a hot afternoon in October 1928, a fact we know early on via the colonel's observation that the doctor's latest bunch of French newspapers is "three months old: July 1928" (H, 28; LS, 16). That morning the Frenchman has hanged himself; his corpse now lies in a coffin; and the boy, the mother, and the old colonel are sitting around the gloomy house anxiously waiting for the mayor to bring official authorization to have the casket taken out for burial. Narrated in present tense, this frame covers just thirty minutes, from the sound of the whistle of the 2:30 train (acknowledged in the thoughts of each of the three family members), to the curlew birds that the boy reports as singing at three o'clock in his—and the book's—penultimate page.

The main body of *Leaf Storm* consists of a series of flashbacks piecing together the tortured history of the Frenchman and his relationship with the town, beginning with his arrival at the colonel's house in 1903 on through the complex and obscure ties that will persist between the two men even on the day he dies twenty-five years hence. One of those loner-adventurers who have a way of showing up and settling here and there around the Caribbean, the French doctor is a shadowy entity—his very name remains unknown. He is seen by us mostly through the compromised memories of the colonel, and sporadically through a neutral and weak Isabel, who is more concerned about any disgraceful repercussions from the funeral. In addition, she relays to us the harsher view of him taken by her snobbish stepmother Adelaida, who in turn scorns the Frenchman as a mere "animal" because of his diet of field grass.

The figure of the doctor may well have been inspired by a Faulkner character from *Light in August*, the lonesome Reverend Gail Hightower, whose early failures both as homilist and husband earned him local opprobrium and drove him into an isolation bordering on misanthropy, only to be brought back into the human fold when actively defending Joe Christmas (and giving his own life in the process). Somewhat similarly, during his first few years in Macondo the Frenchman starts out with a thriving medical practice, but in time loses it all to the banana company doctors and thenceforth turns into a sardonic and mean-spirited recluse who one night will curtly decline requests to tend striking workers wounded in government reprisals. The doctor's one and only redemptive act is his having performed surgery on the colonel's bad leg in 1925, thereby saving the old man's life (as revealed in the book's final chapter). Even this favor has its selfish motives, however: he frankly admits to the colonel that "a dead man wouldn't have been able to bury me" (H, 126; LS, 92). The irony, then, is that, for all the stuffy arrogance of the colonel's second wife Adelaida, her negative assessment of the Frenchman seems well justified. The man really does sponge off them and moreover refuses to attend their servant Meme when she falls ill. Were it not for the colonel, the doctor would in fact have had no one to bury him.

For the spiritual and narrative center of *Leaf Storm* is the colonel and his strong ties with everyone else—the family, the townsfolk, the corrupt mayor (whom he has to bribe), and of course the doctor. He is one of those tragic and contradictory figures familiar to us from García Márquez's later works: a military hero and a man of authority who inspires respect, but also a loyal soul and a moralist whose attachment to abstract principles and goodhearted tolerance, though admirable, are also in conflict with the best interests of his immediate loved ones. He gives full support not only to the less-than-humane doctor but also to Isabel's husband Martín, a slick, pretty-boy opportunist who abandons ship once his financial schemes have received the backing of the colonel, the latter then refusing to dismiss the man as a mere swindler.

Indeed, the colonel's stalwart loyalty would look foolish were it not for the unattractive qualities of most all of the other adult characters in *Leaf Storm*. In the few and brief appearances put in by them (in front of the church, at the barber's, etc.) the townspeople here are depicted as petty, gossipy, vindictive sorts who cannot elicit much sympathy, while Isabel and Meme, though not malicious, are scarcely more than passive victims. (The only other personage who comes off as clearly positive is the clergyman "Pup," who gallantly saves the delinquent doctor's house from being torched by the irate townsfolk.) The colonel thus stands for values and ties that exist beyond the narrow realm of immediate judgments and daily life, and the novel's epigraph from Sophocles's *Antigone* appropriately draws moral parallels between a nameless Colombian hero and a mythic Greek heroine (see chapter 5).

These links between a present burial and its hidden history, and between the colonel on one hand and a shady intruder, a banana company that ruins the doctor, and the ordinary Macondians on the other, are the basic stuff of *Leaf Storm*, its form as well as content. The rest either reinforces or exists in the shadow of this larger theme. Martín takes advantage of Isabel in a way that replicates the doctor-colonel relationship. And though the little boy's budding, mischievous sexuality may seem more or less gratuitous and included purely for its own sake, it does bring out the child's total indifference to the funeral at hand, while his latent homoerotic attraction for the body of his playmate Abrahán can be construed as a reenactment in little of the colonel's and Isabel's loving acceptance of—if not imprudent submission to—their respective despoilers.

As Regina Janes points out, much of the technique and the raw materials—including actual names and characters—that would be brought to full life in García Márquez's future masterpieces are found in *Leaf Storm*.[2] His projects were by then actively germinating in his imagination, even as his personal and artistic maturity still lagged behind. The result is this book that faithfully gives "promise" of what we now know was to come. One has to be impressed with the twenty-four-year-old's wealth of ideas; it is the work of a true novelist in the bud, a storyteller who has at last located his narrative ground and cast roots there—something that could not be said of *Eyes of a Blue Dog*. In later years García Márquez would continue to regard *Leaf Storm* with affection, but it is the affection that a mature man fees for the first intimations of what would become his true self.

In Evil Hour is García Márquez's most ambitious book prior to *One Hundred Years*, a thirty-year-old's attempt at forging a panoramic novel that broadly represents an entire municipality, from the corrupt powers to the festive poor. Accordingly, many of the characters we saw in the nameless "town" in *Big Mama's Funeral* resurface in these pages: the dentist, the military mayor, the widow Montiel and Mr. Carmichael, Mina and her blind grandmother. In addition, the shoebox containing dead mice, enigmatically brought over by Trinidad in "Artificial Roses," is clarified here: she trapped them at the church where, as a lay order member, she is employed at various maintenance tasks.

In the same way, the events narrated in *In Evil Hour* involve not just an adolescent girl or a benighted rich widow but rather affect the entirety of the population's lives. There is a heat wave and a two-year state of siege, and (as in the stories) a lull in the repression-rebellion cycle, shattered when some mysterious lampoons start appearing on people's doors in the mornings. Their source is never found, and, curiously, the sheets themselves merely state in writing what everybody in town already knows, or has heard before. And yet these "underground" media are subversive enough to spark bitter strife, causing an authority crisis in the local dictatorship. Moreover, the leaflets, dealing as they do with the not-so-secret lives of the well-heeled and powerful, are bringing mirth and glee to the shantytown slum dwellers, who periodically defy the gangsterish mayor to his very face. In the evenings he has this or that suspect arrested (a fiery woman; Mr. Carmichael), but somehow, curfew and all, the unsettling sheets still crop up at sunrise. Repression mounts; a youth, Pepe Amador, is tortured to death by onetime convicts now serving as military police; and in the end the political opposition takes to the hills to join the guerrillas.

The originally projected title of the novel was *Este pueblo de mierda* (roughly "This Shitty Town"), and in fact, for the first version published in Spain in 1962, the printers expurgated the vulgarisms and "purified" the style in the interests of "correct Castilian." Not until 1966 was a suitable edition printed in Mexico City. The manuscript of the novel did win the $3,000 Esso Prize in Colombia in 1961, though mostly (as the author often says) because the other entries were of such low artistic quality.

There are ten unnumbered chapters, all but two of them consisting of four unmarked subsections that narrate simultaneous or chronologically proximate events. The chief exceptions, chapters 5 and 7, add an extra subsection each, these having in common a character who is an outsider, a lovely and sensually accoutred fortune-teller, on leave from the visiting circus. Her name is "Casandra" (like the Trojan prophetess whose oracles were condemned to go tragically unheeded), and we see her in secret session with the mayor. The first of these supplementary sections contains a hint that the man (who declines Casandra's playful advances) may be impotent, or perhaps asexual, far more interested in his "business"; the second such section, in what is the key sentence and the moral climax of the book, has Casandra answering his request for the identity of the lampooners with her terse and conundrum-like "It's the whole town and nobody." (Chapter 4 in turn has only three subsections, for reasons unknown.) Every chapter, it bears mention, ends with an episode focusing either on the mayor or the priest as featured subject. In addition, the novel's opening and concluding sections finalize with materials and entire phrases shared between them (allusions to Father Ángel's blue eyes, the boxes of dead mice, the nervous smiles first of Trinidad and then Mina, and the lampoons) that thus show how the conflict goes on and on.

The lampoons, the mayor does speculate, may be the work of individuals acting separately. Still, all efforts to catch someone in the act prove unavailing—the prankster somehow eludes the most vigilant of officers on the night shift, and we can assume that even García Márquez had no particular "culprit" in mind. But then, as Vargas Llosa astutely points out, the leaflets should be seen not merely as "politics" but as magic, as intrusions of an unreal and fantastical world into a humdrum reality.[3]

Equally important, the spoofs serve as a means to help us get to know the town's principals and extras. The military mayor—the protagonist by far—is a colorful, voluble crook who extorts yearlings from César Montero, and also has the slum dwellers move from the flooded riverbanks up to his own higher grounds, then selling his squatted-on properties to the municipality. (At the same time, knowing his place in the hierarchy, he instructs his subordinates not to lay a finger on anyone from the ruling Asís family.) Judge Arcadio, who has just started out on the job, seems less interested in the law than in his sexual prowess—he boasts about making love to his wife thrice daily—and in fact he is conspicuously scarce once the situation turns dangerous. There are accounts of illicit amours (Nora Jacob and Roberto Asís), of the darker origins of Don Sabas's and the Asís clan's respective wealth, and of the clandestine roles played by the dentist, the doctor, and the barber, who in the end emerge as the book's subversive and nameless heroes.

And there is the pathetic Father Ángel, who cares less about the mounting political crisis and the murders than about couples who live in concubinage or the sexual content of that week's movie. Consistently ineffectual, at the one moment when his parishioners are expecting from his sermon a clearcut statement on the lampoons and their consequences, he lets them down and keeps silence on the matter. And in the climactic confrontation that he and Doctor Giraldo stage with the mendacious mayor on the ugly issue of Pepe Amador's death, the priest fails to muster any moral indignation or fury, makes whimpering pleas instead ("For the love of God" [*MH*, 199; *EH*, 180]), and finally succumbs to a coughing fit. As the doctor suggests to him in chapter 9, Father Ángel seems to be "trying to put bandages on morality" (*MH*, 183; *EH*, 165).

With its mosaic-like fragments comprising a sort of verbal mural, *In Evil Hour* takes its cue not so much from Faulkner as from the early Dos Passos of *Manhattan Transfer* (as Regina Janes pointed out).[4] Within each of the subsections the primary device is that of the "roving-camera," in which one of the characters functions as a human lens observing others and experiencing things in his or her own way.[5] And there remains the formative influence of the Italian neorealist filmmakers, seen previously in *Big Mama's Funeral* and *No One Writes to the Colonel*. Unfortunately the technical mix cannot accommodate García Márquez's populous cast and multiple brief episodes, the Italian model seeming to have worked best with his more intimate and smallscale dramas. In addition, because all of the characters stand more or less in the same relation to the author's "camerawork," and because no single personage figures prominently enough to serve as counterweight to mayor and priest, the book lacks a moral or artistic center. García Márquez himself has admitted that *In Evil Hour* is his poorest novel, "too geometric" in its overall shape and conception.[6] The final impression on the reader is cumulative rather than organic, and the narrative turns at best into a very sophisticated cartoon, a jokebook filled with numerous individual gags.

This latter weakness, let it be said, is also *In Evil Hour*'s strength. Indeed, what saves the book is its abundance of García Márquez's understated and mischievous humor. Examples proliferate on every page. The mayor, suffering from the fabled toothache we saw in "One of These Days," goes to the rebel dentist for an extraction, because "my teeth are above politics." At the barbershop he removes a "Political Discussions Prohibited" sign, on the grounds that "Only the government can prohibit anything. This is a democracy" (*MH*, 116; *EH*, 103). In a satire of literary criticism, Dr. Giraldo and his wife argue at some length as to whether the Dickens work she has just read qualifies as "a short novel," "a long short story," or "a short story, but a long one" (*MH*, 98; *EH*, 86). (The work in question, García Márquez revealed in an interview, is *A Christmas Carol*.)[7] Judge Arcadio sententiously announces, "In all of human history there's never been a barber who was a conspirator. On the other hand there hasn't been a single tailor who wasn't" (*MR*, 117; *EH*, 103–4). The solemnity of the statement becomes even funnier when the judge is proved wrong.

NINE

The Anatomy of Tyranny

We all know the stereotype: the Latino military general, with mustache and dark glasses perhaps, his chest colorfully adorned with stacks of medals and / or ribbons, a man crudely, grotesquely vicious, but also faintly clownish in his role as dictator-in-perpetuity of a mixed-race republic located somewhere in the Andes or the tropics. It is among the primary images of Spanish America held by countless news watchers the world over, many of whom may actually entertain few other notions about the continent's ways of life. It is a tyranny with connotations all its own, and certain words from its practices and its ethos — words like "junta," "incomunicado," "político," "número uno" — have managed to infiltrate the sidelines of the U.S. political lexicon as well.

It is also a painful, complex, long-standing historical reality all too familiar to the denizens of most Latin nations. As one might only expect, it figures prominently in the continent's literature. Not accidentally, the book universally considered the foundational prose classic in an independent Latin America — *Facundo* (1845) by the Argentine journalist, activist, and future president Domingo Sarmiento — is an account of certain aspects of the Rosas tyranny of 1835–52, a work that moreover defies all genre classifications, combining folklore, anecdote, biography, social analysis, fiery rhetoric, and political and military history all in one. Over the past century-and-a-half there have been a host of such works, for the story of a dictator is as much a tradition in Spanish-American writing as is the narrative of the rise of a capitalist — from Howells to E. L. Doctorow — in modern U.S. letters. When García Márquez wrote the concluding lines to *The Autumn of the Patriarch*, he delivered what is but a culminating instance of a continent's prime literary subgenre.

García Márquez's book, let it be said, is among the most difficult and forbidding of novels to face an uninitiated reader, consisting as it does of six unnumbered chapters, each a single paragraph, with syntax growing ever more sinuous and serpentine as the book progresses. By way of illustration, the first chapter of the novel has thirty-one sentences, the third nineteen, the fifth only fifteen, the sixth and final one being made up of a single 1,825-line sentence (in the Sudamericana edition).[1] Within any of those extended units the speaker and even the pronoun-subject can shift routinely and more than

ith no quotation marks, dashes, indentations, or other handy
fact the period and the comma are about the only punctua-
loyed throughout the text, the sole exception being the "aha!"
dictator in chapter 1, at the moment when he catches the op-
-handed on the day of his false "death." García Márquez actually
sp___ n entire session of proofreading of galleys that was dedicated exclusively to watching for and correcting commas![2]

The author first felt the inspiration for this book one night in Caracas in
January 1958. It was 4:00 A.M., and the eight-year dictatorship of General
Marcos Pérez Jiménez had just fallen. García Márquez and other journalists
were sitting in the foyer at Miraflores, the Venezuelan presidential palace,
anxiously awaiting word about the governmental transition. Suddenly there
burst into the room a soldier in combat fatigues, brandishing a machine gun.
Before everyone's astonished eyes the military man backed out, slowly and
silently, streaking the floor with his muddy boots—and then promptly fled
by car to La Guaira airport and safe haven abroad (OG, 117; FG, 81). García
Márquez knew at that point that he wanted to write a novel about a dictator, and the following year his budding imagination received a further boost
as he was covering events in revolutionary Cuba. Witnessing the political
trial of Batista henchman Jesús Sosa Blanco in a Havana stadium, he listened with horror both to the accounts of the army officer's brutal crimes
and to the death sentence passed on him by the tribunal before a hushed
audience.

García Márquez's originally conceived format for the book was, in fact,
that of a fallen dictator being tried in a people's court, with the tyrant's recollections being revealed to us via interior monologue. The author reportedly
worked along these lines on the project but gave up on it in Mexico in 1962,
discarding everything in its three hundred pages except—in his words—"the
name of the main character" (OG, 47; FG, 34). It was only in the wake of the
economic security provided by the sales of One Hundred Years that García
Márquez found himself free to experiment with the book at his own leisure
and come up with precisely the shape he wanted and deemed right for his
narrative.

The question often asked by first-time readers of Patriarch is, What possessed García Márquez to write the work this way? The answer clearly seems
to be "his artistic conscience." After the unimaginable success on all fronts of
his history of Macondo, by far the easiest thing would have been for García
Márquez to repeat himself and produce a sequel to One Hundred Years of
Solitude. Instead he chose to start anew and reinvent a novel that excludes

virtually all reminders, all vestiges either of that now-legendary world or its lucid, transparent art. The single noteworthy exception is the idealistic young foreigner who in chapter 3 comes to the dictator asking for help "to wipe out once and for all every conservative regime from Alaska to Patagonia" (*OPa*, 107; *AP*, 104). The phrase of course is lifted from *One Hundred Years* and identifies the visitor as none other than Colonel Aureliano Buendía. In addition, there is in chapter 6 a brief mention of the sextet of opportunistic lawyers dressed in black, ever for hire to the powers that be. This aside, the content of *Patriarch* shows no visible overlap with that of *Solitude*.

The geography too has shifted. Rather than the Macondo and "the town" of old, and the passing references to Riohacha and Manaure that had evoked García Márquez's north-coastal Colombia, we now have an entire country with vistas taking in the whole of the Caribbean. The capital city and port in which the action largely unfolds, with its place names like "Conde" and "San Jerónimo," has been said to resemble Santo Domingo, and the scattered allusions to Christopher Columbus would befit a town in whose metropolitan cathedral the admiral's remains allegedly lie buried.[3] At the same time the city has features suggestive of Cartagena, Colombia—for example, the old slave port, and more notably "the big house that looked like an ocean liner aground on top of the roofs" (*OPa*, 21; *AP*, 18), a precise description of Cartagena's Monastery of La Popa, so called because it resembles the stern—*la popa*—of a ship. On yet other occasions the dictator places certain "saltpeter deserts" recognizable as the Guajira to his *west*, not east (*OPa*, 122; *AP*, 120), and makes unequivocal mention of Bogotá ("the dismal and glacial city of the neighboring country . . . the eternal drizzle . . . the men in full dress on electric streetcars" [*OPa*, 106; *AP*, 103]) as if his perspective were Venezuelan. Caracas, it might nonetheless be recalled, is located in a high inland valley. The Patriarch's city and state are therefore best experienced as a pan-Caribbean composite.

The major difference between García Márquez's two greatest books, however, is without question that of approachability. *One Hundred Years of Solitude* is among the clearest of modern literary classics and is readily accessible to virtually anybody with adequate reading skills, from literate adolescents up. Its prose has a transparent anonymity, feels timeless and placeless, translates gracefully into English or Japanese or Italian, and can be skimmed with ease in flight or on a train. *The Autumn of the Patriarch*, by stark contrast, calls for a reader familiar with the workshop of modernist art and somewhat receptive to its procedures of interior monologue, temporal displacement, nonlinear form, abrupt transitions, and densely concentrated prose, all established earlier in the twentieth century by Joyce, Woolf, Faulkner, et al. But at the same time the ideal reader of *Patriarch* is a Caribbean-Hispanic who will easily recognize and respond to the book's manifestly Antillean flavor and smile at its countless regional colloquialisms, witticisms, proverbs, ditties, not to mention profanities ("qué carajo"), that make up its prose style. García Márquez likes to note that there are phrases in *Patriarch* comprehensible only to Barranquilla cab drivers (*OG*, 126; *FG*, 89). Language, an element that in most García Márquez works stays in the background and seldom calls attention to itself, here plays a far more active and prevailing role in the total experience of the book.

The paradox, then, is that so artful a text as *The Autumn of the Patriarch* is among the most *oral* and dramatic and local novels ever written, one whose words are best savored in the original Spanish, slowly and out loud. This of course is not casual bedtime reading, but its ways can be learned, and eventually *Patriarch*'s dense pages should become as much a shared artifact of the broader literary culture as are, say, *Ulysses* or *The Sound and the Fury*, works that once seemed daunting and now stand as indispensable items within the narrative repertoire. Whatever one may think of the new form fashioned by García Márquez, one can only admire the man's incorruptibility, his courage to put behind him the lucky fortunes of Macondo, isolate himself, and start all over again.

Still, one must not lose sight of the continuities between the later and the earlier novel, both of which interweave real history and narrative fantasy. In *Patriarch* there are traits and actions lifted wholesale from the biographies of actual Latin despots, in combination with the fictive tyrant's century or two of life, the reports of his healing powers (always from those he has cured), a magical eclipse of the sun, and the removal of an entire sea. Unbridled exaggeration is thus taken to further heights in this fantastical account of a tyrant. There is of course the same deft fusion of plebeian materials and high culture, and the area of style shows a similar line of development. The basic approach of *One Hundred Years*, after all, consists of long, leisurely paragraphs of narrative-anecdotal prose, interspersed every page or so with a brief quotation from a speaking character or two. The Buendías' solitude registers little talk, the only lengthy utterance being Fernanda's hilarious four-page harangue (chapter 16), presented without periods or dashes in a parody of stream-of-consciousness. *The Autumn of the Patriarch*'s narrative-anecdotal paragraphs in turn occupy a chapter each; the dialogue snippets are subordinated to and integrated within the "paragraphs"; and the comic monologues are broadly distributed among the entire cast of characters—the dictator plus his assorted loved ones, henchmen, courtiers, creditors, and more. In spite of the rift between the two books, the differences that make *Patriarch* do grow logically out of the format of *One Hundred Years*.

The Autumn of the Patriarch of course is a "novel" only by the widest possible stretch of the word's meaning. Indeed the book has almost as much in common with poetical and musical as it does with novelistic traditions. Moreover, if one stands back and contemplates the text whole one may see it as a prose "portrait" composed as a "collage." As we might expect, the fullest portion of this portrait is to be found in chapter 1, in which we see the man remembered at differing points from sometime during the second half of his career. By then he is a physical grotesque who drags around his gigantic "elephant feet" and later bears his herniated testicle on an orthopedic cart. Still quite rustic, he eats walking about and holding in his hand a plate of rice and beans and plantain; he sleeps face down on the floor with his right arm as pillow; and he keeps the presidential palace filled with cows and cow pies. In addition, he surrounds himself with weaker people whom he can lord it over: countless lepers, a thousand concubines, and a group of exiled former dictators with whom he plays dominoes and always wins. (The Spanish *dominó*, incidentally, can be taken as a pun—"he dominated.") Even his thousands of illegitimate children are born seven-monthers, that is, weaklings. Out on the street he attracts some crowds who view him with a mystical-populist regard; and he believes they "love" him. He in turn is a boyishly loving and devoted son to his mother Bendición Alvarado.

The only actual "plot" in that first chapter is the story of Patricio Aragonés, the exact double secretly employed to give an impression of the dictator's ubiquity. Like a court jester, Patricio can afford to tell his boss the naked truth—namely, that the true sources of the tyrant's power have been the British who first put him there and the U.S. Marines who have since supported him. The public jubilation at Patricio's (and the dictator's false) death, and the subsequent murderous retaliation at the hands of the utterly loyal presidential guard, serve to demonstrate both the extent of public discontent and the local basis of his support—the security forces whose officers he regularly buys off with promotions but also keeps off balance with parallel services and factionalism. Not accidentally the chapter opens with a remembrance of the artillery of William Dampier (a real British pirate who roved the Caribbean in the seventeenth century), has a constant U.S. presence either through the ambassador or the Marine destroyer ship, and ends with a fantastical reenactment of Columbus arriving with his trio of caravels. The European imperial powers that have historically shaped Caribbean tyrannies are thus alluded to from the outset.

This initial portrait is a flashback, as indeed are all of the accounts that pertain to the life of the dictator, for the tyrant is dead from the very first line of text and its apt mention of vultures. In fact the only portions of *Patriarch* that show a strictly linear and chronological structure, and that occur in an immediate narrative past, are the first few pages of each of the six chapters as well as the half-dozen lines that end the novel itself. As Regina Janes has beautifully demonstrated, those introductory sections "cover a period of twenty-four hours" lasting from Monday through Tuesday morning.[4] They sequentially recount the collective process whereby successive groups of people discover the dictator's corpse, identify it (so as to avoid a repeat performance of the Patricio Aragonés episode), arrange for embalming while they await fearful signs from heaven, prepare the corpse physically, plan strategy for a public announcement, and have the church bells toll. At the start of the final chapter, the body lies on the banquet table as the politicians and soldiers take their positions, and in the concluding lines everybody takes to the streets for a public celebration, the exhausting book ending with a pleonastic "había por fin terminado" (literally "had finally ended," though not thus rendered in the Rabassa translation).

Each of these preambular episodes leads imperceptibly into a chosen set of scenes from the dictator's life, arranged mostly thematically and chronologically, though with frequent breaks that transport us to more distant earlier times. Some of the crucial episodes from the tyrant's youth—episodes that help explain his mature pathologies—come up only in later chapters. García Márquez thereby reproduces the nonlinear ways in which we come to understand a dictatorial situation, inasmuch as the social and psychological quirks that motivate such a person's transgressions are generally learned about by victims and onlookers only when the process is well under way and even complete. If only for clarity's sake it may be worth our while to sum up in chronological form the "actual" biography of the Patriarch, separating the private from the public life only as a matter of convenience. In García Márquez's telling, the two are of a piece and inseparable.

The dictator was born of Bendición Alvarado, a bird painter and former prostitute who never knew which of her clients is his father (chaps. 4 and 6). Burdened from the start with a herniated testicle, he grew up illiterate and inland. "My name is Zacarías," he will scribble just once during a writing lesson with his wife (chap. 4). His first sexual experience was as a young army lieutenant, in a river with a camp follower who, feeling his hernia, said "go back to your mama and have her turn you in for another one" (chap. 4). For years thereafter he makes love fully clothed and only in the form of one-minute quickies or sudden rape—his normal practice with the palace concubines. Meanwhile his simple, rustic mother often says comically gauche things in public (approaching him in his limousine to have some soda bottles returned; wishing at banquets that he were not president), and has become an embarrassment. He has her put away in a suburban mansion, but will remain an ever-devoted son who communicates with her via telepathy, even after she is dead (chap. 6). For various reasons he also puts his enormous wealth under her name. He has no friends, only his trusted double Patricio (chap. 1) and his bodyguard Saturno Santos (chap. 2), a rebel general whom he was unable to capture and hence puts on the palace payroll instead.

In his midlife the general is smitten with love (sight unseen) for the slum dweller and beauty queen Manuela Sánchez, whom for months he will visit daily, never laying a hand on her, regaling her with huge gifts and grandiose gadgetry in her mother's presence, and even improving her tough neighborhood—until one day both women vanish during a solar eclipse. Bendición dies in chapter 4, a fact that causes much commotion, and he falls in love with defrocked nun Leticia Nazareno. From her he learns to really make love, to read and write, and to be a civilized man. After much cajolery and sexual blackmail on her part he brings back expelled church people, rids the palace of concubines and lepers, and marries her, she at their wedding ceremony giving birth to baby Emanuel. A seven-monther, the boy is trained for the military from the start and will be nicknamed "the little general." Leticia proves to be universally hated, and at one point she and the boy are devoured by fierce dogs. (There is some suggestion that the dictator may not have disapproved the murder.) The widower now brings back the lepers and concubines, his only significant amour thereafter to be a uniformed fourteen-year-old from the school next door; he gives and takes such pleasure in her that she will love him forever, whereas, aside from her state pension, he serenely forgets her. His advisors later replace the schoolgirls with uniformed whores who play for him the role of innocents. He finally dies, alone with his memories and infirmities.

The public life of the dictator began in the wake of the suicide of General Lautaro Muñoz, a classicist and a principled Liberal who refused to yield to the British. The latter then put into power the young patriarch-to-be, he expecting to last only a week (chap. 6). Starting out as a homespun populist who made direct contact with the people, curing their stud bulls of worms and fixing their sewing machines, his hunger for power led him to systematically eliminate all rival generals by getting them drunk and either putting them to ridicule or having them shot. The only person he kills with his own hands is the lady fortune-teller who predicts his minimum and maximum life spans. He gets Manuela Sánchez off his mind by taking charge of state matters after a hurricane wrecks the city. At some point there is a landing of U.S. Marines, on the pretext of stamping out yellow fever and civilizing the military (chaps. 1 and 6), and he "runs around like a cockroach" to wait on them while they treat him like a servant. He accumulates great wealth in cattle and communications, and wins the weekly lottery by having a little boy pick an ice ball out of the basket, but after two thousand of the children have accumulated in prisons, he dynamites them at sea, then executes those who obeyed the order. (The bizarre mock death probably occurs around this time.) A large-scale barracks revolt is quelled, but the dictator divines that the events were masterminded by his trusted aide General Rodrigo de Aguilar, whose body he has cooked and served for dinner at a posh banquet for the presidential guard.

There is great public mourning at the death of the tyrant's mother, on whose shroud is a Christ-like impression of her body. The dictator wants her canonized, but the papal nuncio, seeing in her sheet not a miracle but a painting, refuses; the Patriarch has the papal mission sacked and the nuncio sent sailing, naked, on a raft. A colorfully masculine Monsignor Demetrius Aldous, from Eritrea, is now charged with handling the patriarch's petition, but after months of nationwide research the cleric too concludes that the shroud is fake. The dictator declares war on the Holy See, announces his mother's "civil canonization," and expels all religious. They return during Leticia's "reign." After her murder, the tyrant hires the intelligence services of José Ignacio Sáenz de la Barra, a cultured aristocrat who will bring him bags full of severed heads and build an empire of repression far more airtight and ruthless than the dictator's. Disgruntled officers, after many aborted efforts, overthrow the ultrarefined top cop and publicly hang him. The country by now has vastly changed; outside the dictator's window he sees highways and glass towers, and the show is being run by his faceless advisors. But the national debt is enormous and, after much pressure from many a U.S. ambassador, he sells the Caribbean Sea to the Yankees. His only contacts with the outside world now are concocted newsreels, single-copy newspapers, and television soap operas to which he allots happy endings. Haunted by the ghosts of his victims, he nonetheless feels no final guilt, understanding, or self-knowledge, even in his final days.

As he prepared to anatomize a phenomenon so grotesque as Caribbean dictatorship, García Márquez found himself faced with a daunting problem of narrative voice, with serious limits inhering in any of the traditional approaches.

If recounted exclusively from the point of view of the strongman's enemies and victims, the resulting book would contain much suffering and gore—but few real tensions and surprises. The source of the suffering, moreover, would remain unspecified and unaccounted for; at best one could have expected a very good instance of protest literature. Among the chief flaws of Miguel Ángel Asturias's *El Señor Presidente* is the near-absence of the president himself, who, with but a single extended scene from close up—where he cuts a threatening figure, admittedly—never ceases to be more than a remote and shadowy entity. Asturias's is a novel of dictatorship in which what is most missing is the dictator. We see tyranny's effects but not its operating causes.

If narrated as a monologue by the dictator, as in fact García Márquez had first planned, the apparent effect would be one of tacit endorsement or obvious caricature, and in either case a narrow range of experience and emotions. There is also a problem of historical record: few Latin dictators have been all that interesting as people. Shallow, banal sorts, most of them have had manipulation, acquisition, and womanizing as their chief concerns—hardly enough of a repertoire around which to construct a varied human portrait. (One can imagine *The Sound and the Fury* made up exclusively of the thoughts of Jason Compson.) When fate has chanced to remove these ungentle men from the business of tyranny, they've proved to be singularly unheroic, unimposing, and small human beings. To depict his dictator in any other light would have been to stray from the essential truth—the latter a fundamental priority for García Márquez—while his sexual manias could not conceivably have sustained a long narrative without shading into voyeurism and soft porn. A minor fault of Alejo Carpentier's otherwise superb novel *Reasons of State* is that, in the last chapters, the unnamed First Magistrate, deposed and exiled in France, reverts to the nullity he basically is and thereby loses most of his narrative interest.

If the tale were told by a narrator more or less loyal to the dictator, there would have been the familiar difficulty in perceiving and being fair to the varied response of the larger population. Robert Penn Warren's *All the King's Men* recalls the political career of "Willie Stark" via the hardened prose of his cynical associate, former journalist Jack Burden, and throughout that novel in the shape of a memoir we see or hear very little of the ordinary folk on whose collective trust the demagogic populist gains the state governorship.

If composed by an omniscient onlooker, the tone of evenhanded objectivity toward both dictator and oppositionists would have produced an unconvincing and stillborn text. Neutral, noncommittal detachment is precisely the method of the great Spanish writer Ramón del Valle-Inclán, whose *Tirano Banderas*, an important precursor of *Patriarch*, depicts despotism and conflict in an invented Latin American nation, all conveyed by a surreal ambience of exaggerated grotesquerie, linguistic hyperbole, and a lexicon combining Mexicanisms and Argentinisms. (There are countless utterances from the common people, as in *Patriarch*, plus characters named Zacarías and Melquíades.) For all Valle-Inclán's virtuosity, however, his Spanish voice stands at a lofty remove from events and the book is ultimately rootless and cold, with no sectors arousing sympathy and the narrative itself degenerating into turgid mannerism. Finally, if García Márquez's novel had been told with overt sympathy for the victims and condemnation for the tyrant, we would have been treated to a literary artifact with predictable, textbook sentiments and inconsistent form, a failed romance posing as a novel.

As we know, the solution adopted by García Márquez was to bring in *all* voices, to compose a polyphonic text featuring the extensive solo arias of the dictator, accompanied in turn by the briefer recitatives and ariettas of his intimates and subordinates, contenders and followers, these ever-shifting ensembles further backed by a vast chorus of anonymous supernumeraries, who have their own once-in-a-lifetime stage entrances as observers, admirers, and sufferers of the patriarch, everything from ambassadors to concubines. From the dictator's detractors we hear surprisingly little, inasmuch as García Márquez wishes to avoid any of the usual emotions—while at the same time capturing the full totality—of the experience of dictatorship. Perhaps the one explicitly condemnatory phrase in the entire book is "the unity of all against the despotism of centuries," proclaimed at different points in the novel by the despot's successors (potential or actual), who of course have their own practical reasons for broadcasting such a slogan. Needless to say, the dictator's history of misdeeds provides a narrative record that is in itself more than sufficiently damning.

The net effect of this approach is that García Márquez deals with all sides equally objectively but also equally sympathetically. The suffering of the victims is not allowed to translate into hatred of the victimizer. Similarly, the vivid physical and mental ailments of the dictator, along with his declining years as puppet of youthful upstarts and later as isolated relic in the very nation he had long terrorized, all serve to arouse readers' sympathy without eliciting our forgiveness. In his final brooding monologues we share in the general's basic humanity as he endures his thorough, deaf solitude amid cows and fragments of ghosts, and bewails his senile incontinence, his stomach that rejects food, and his bodily betrayal and decay. In a dynamic that recalls the final scenes in *Macbeth*, *King Lear*, or *Boris Godunov*, we are moved to pity and fear for the Patriarch's incapacity to feel guilt or love, while at the same time we stop short of condoning his brutal and despotic reign.

García Márquez's all-perspectives procedure stems ultimately from the stream-of-consciousness novels of Joyce and Woolf, in which narrative voice routinely shifts from an objective third person to the intimate "I" thoughts of a Mr. Bloom or Mrs. Dalloway. The art was further refined by Beckett, who, in his novels *Watt* and *Molloy*, crystallized the device of integrating spoken dialogue within the very body of the narrative paragraph, omitting the quotation marks or dashes which had long conventionally signaled human voice, sometimes even dispensing with time-honored "he-said-she-said" formulas.

What García Márquez does in *The Autumn of the Patriarch* is to generalize the method across those six long paragraphs and expand the paradigm to bring in all grammatical persons; an "I" (*yo*) usually but not always the dictator; a vocative, affective, intimate "thou" (*tú*) that includes beauty queen Manuela and tyrannical spouse Leticia; a "he" (*él*) that, again, typically refers to the dictator but can also serve to signify his drunken rival Adriano Guzmán or the cultured thug José Ignacio Sáenz de la Barra, and a "he" moreover that may either signal the strongman objectively or evoke him through the imagined eyes of one of his women; a formal and respectful "you" (*usted*) with which the dictator—and, indirectly, the reader—is informed of matters by a wise but weak Patricio Aragonés, or by Vatican emissaries, or often by anonymous associates and interlocutors who relate key stories punctuated with "mi general" (such episodes are equally construable as *él* or *usted*, the verbs and other forms being identical: for example, chapter 4, recounting his fecal ejaculation with Leticia, ends with "pues era mierda, general, su propia mierda," an ambiguous possessive that is sadly lost in Gregory Rabassa's inevitable "it was shit, general, his own shit"); the broad "we" (*nosotros*) representing the citizenry, from the crowds that raid the palace to a small group of creditors who call on him in chapter 5; a plural "you" (*ustedes*) with which he gives orders; and a "they" (*ellos*) variously comprising, for example, his loyal presidential guards, the common people who "love" him in chapter 1, and the mob that, at the start of chapter 3, is recalled years later as having discovered a dead Patricio Aragonés.

The psychological shock of these constant displacements is felt especially strongly in Spanish, a language in which subject pronouns are normally omitted, the sudden shifts from *nosotros* to *él* (or any other) being discernible only in the verb conjugations or possessive forms. By unobtrusively yet dynamically marshaling the entire roster of grammatical persons onto the vast geography of his prose, García Márquez manages to convey a full sense of despotism and its both systematic and arbitrary network of relationships. Dictatorship is not only "I the boss," or "you Leticia," or "he the tyrant," or "we the citizens," or "you my lackeys," or "they my devoted people"—but all such subjects, and more, and all at once. These pronouns, floating signifiers, sometimes termed "shifters" for their infinity of possible referents, are what allow the author to piece together a total panorama that would have turned out less organic, less rigorous, had he adhered to a more traditional sentence and paragraph structure. *The Autumn of the Patriarch* gives its readers not just the broader politics of dictatorship, but the everyday linguistics and private erotics as well.

García Márquez on repeated occasions has characterized *Patriarch* as a long prose poem on the subject of power (*OG*, 122; *FG*, 86). In arranging his narrative along the lines just described above, he learned many a lesson from Virginia Woolf, whose novels, especially *The Waves*, also aim at the stylization and formality of the poetical genre. The lyrical, "poetical" qualities of Woolf's prose stem not so much from its legendary refinements as from its systematic use of verse devices like cadence, repetition, and occasionally even rhyme. *Mrs. Dalloway* is a sample storehouse in this regard, where, for instance, we find a paragraph in which "My name is Dalloway!" is iterated three times.[5] Of Clarissa Dalloway herself we read that "she never said anything specially clever; there she was, however; there she was"—rhyme and repetition both being present here (115). Later on Lady Bruton muses to herself anaphorically, "She sighed, she snored, not that she was asleep, only drowsy and heavy, drowsy and heavy, like a field of clover" (168). The latter example suggests verse meter, and also hints at the punctuation with commas to become generalized in *Patriarch*. (Woolf could also rely on the semicolon, a sign infrequently employed in Spanish.) Similarly, the narrative portion of Woolf's *The Waves* opens with six characters announcing in succession, "I see a ring," "I see a slab of pale yellow," "I hear a sound," and so forth, anticipating the anaphoric "vimos" ("we saw") of the first few pages of García Márquez's book.

Indeed, *The Autumn of the Patriarch* picks up on the poesy and rhetoric of "the great Virginia" and elaborates them to a logical but unprecedented extreme. Such a procedure no doubt grew out of necessity, given the author's absolute avoidance of reliable old landmarks such as paragraphs, blank spaces, or separate dialogue, and parentheses, colons, dashes, or quotation marks. García Márquez perforce is led to depend to a vast extent on rhythmic devices and on an informal scansion forged expressly for this book. The initial series with "we saw" is actually employed on several occasions in the course of *Patriarch*, and many casual formulas are stated more than once, for example, "bright January moon, he would sing, see how sad I am standing on the gallows by your window, he would sing" (*OPa*, 22; *AP*, 18). These brief "poetic" passages are myriad, as is the repetition of chosen phrases off and on throughout the novel, some of them political barbs ("infundios de apátridas," rendered by Rabassa as "lies spread by traitors"), others variations on pop-song motifs, such as "Manuela Sánchez of my misfortune" ("Manuela Sánchez de mi desventura").

Not surprisingly, it is at the more critical moments of the narrative that the poetical devices notably thicken. When in chapter 1 some balloons rise up to explode and drop thousands of leaflets over the city, we observe the Patriarch "seeing the colored balloons in the sky, the red and green balloons, the yellow balloons like great blue oranges, the innumerable wandering balloons" (*OPa*, 25; *AP*, 22). The old dictator's reading lessons, which are also his process of infantilization and submission to the wiles of Leticia, are "poetically" brought to life and given palpability by those hilarious first-grade jingles and tongue twisters he repeats to himself obsessively in the opening pages of chapter 5. And there are eloquent passages deploying the *ubi sunt?* motif in parodic form as when the Patriarch, now in the grip of henchman Sáenz de la Barra, on two different occasions longs for some of the most scabrous elements of his earlier reign: "Where are the puddles of dirty water of my foul-mouthed women . . . , where are my skinny seven-month runts who shat behind the doors" (*OPa*, 214; *AP*, 212). Among the phrases in this sequence is "qué se hizo mi escándalo de funcionarios" ("what happened to my uproar of clerks"), a lampoon of the line "¿Qué se hizo el rey don Juan?" ("What ever became of King John?") from Jorge Manrique's "Coplas por la muerte de su padre," a medieval elegy containing the most famous *ubi sunt?* in all Spanish verse.

The evident source for the formal shape of García Márquez's book is Woolf's *The Waves*, like *Patriarch* a novel entirely sui generis. Its basic scaffold consists of nine unnumbered chapters, each one initiated with an italicized preamble that depicts the course of a single day, as represented by the progress of the sun over the beach and a garden, from the opening line ("*The sun had not yet risen*") on through midday in chapter 5 ("*The sun had risen to its full height*") and the enveloping night of chapter 9 ("*Now the sun had sunk*"). These highly pictorial sections feature much evocative interplay between the movement of the sun and the incessant surge of the ocean's waves. The arc of that single hypothetical day frames the diverse lives of six cultured and refined English friends—three male, three female—from shared childhood through their several deaths. The longer final chapter is the monologue of a single, seventh character, Bernard, and the concluding lines of the novel read as follows:

"Against you I will fling myself, unvanquished and unyielding, O Death!"
The Waves broke on the shore.

The resemblances are so striking as to be inescapable. Woolf's descriptive passages about the sun correspond to the initial collective sequences at the start of each of García Márquez's chapters. The six English biographies suggest the Colombian's half-dozen narrative "blocks" focusing on selected aspects of the Patriarch's reign and character. Woolf's brooding chapter 9, set off by its exclusive focus on an aged Bernard, reminds us of García Márquez's morose single-sentence chapter 6, with its emphasis on the despot's dying alone and his sense of a life absurd and empty. *The Waves* finishes with Bernard confronting death, and is rounded off by a one-line echo of the italicized preambles. In similar fashion, after the dictator has finally faced "death's hooded cassock," *Patriarch* ends with a seven-line return of the images of collectivity with which the entire narrative had drawn its first breath.

Further continuity from Woolf to García Márquez can be seen in the formal manner in which the lives are rendered. *The Waves* is told to us not by a straightforward first- or third-person, but in quasi-declamatory fashion via the "voices" of its characters, each with his or her distinctive traits, while at the same time all carefully integrated into the structural arrangement of the book and, moreover, forming part of greater London, with off-and-on references to such standard landmarks as Regent Street, Piccadilly, and the Tube (subway). The many-sided story of the Patriarch in turn is told by the countless voices of himself and his compatriots, which convey his individuality as well as his relationship to others, all of it fitted into a grand narrative design and Hispano-Caribbean urban setting, complete with references to such typical spots as a beach, a coastal fort, a cathedral, a baseball stadium, a black ghetto, a barrio with dogfights in the streets, and (scores of times) a Plaza de Armas, which Rabassa translates simply as "the main square."

The "poetical" repetitions in *Patriarch* often have to do with an obscene word or deed: "He would allege that if God is the man you say he is tell him to rid me of this beetle that's buzzing in my car, he would tell him, he would unbutton the nine buttons of his fly and show him his huge tool, tell him to deflate this creature, he would tell him . . ." (OPa, 22; AP, 19). Of course profanities, as we have seen, have always played a key role in García Márquez's mature art. Now obscenity becomes virtually routine in this discourse of a dictator, thus symbolizing the man's earthy or boorish nature (readers will decide), while actions like defecation and fornication are common referents throughout the work.

The Autumn of the Patriarch thus performs the miracle of refining obscenity to a high and lofty state by integrating the whole vulgar lexicon and repertoire into the monumental rhythms and minutely crafted prose of a unique literary art. In this respect Patriarch—for all its modernist complexities—is also the most plebeian and "Rabelaisian" of García Márquez's texts. If in One Hundred Years he captured and made literary the omniscient voice of his small-town grandmother, in Patriarch he composed an art out of a broad Caribbean populace. Nevertheless, this "Rabelaisian" exuberance is also subjected to a "Woolfian" aesthetic of controlled novelistic shape and closely nuanced poetry. The book is equally oral and textual in its density.

One sign of the plebeian presence in The Autumn of the Patriarch is the occasional use of oral formulas from Caribbean popular song. As was noted earlier, Manuela Sánchez is regularly referred to via mock-affective tags—"my perdition," "my shame"—of the bolero (love-ballad) variety. Of the lovesick dictator himself, we read that "he searched out the solitary places in the building in order to sing . . . your first waltz as queen, so you won't forget me, he sang, so you'll feel you're dying if you forget me, he sang" (OPa, 74; AP, 71). Similarly, the Antillean-wide hunt for a vanished Manuela is conveyed by allusions to the dance forms respectively of Puerto Rico (the plena), Cuba (the rumba), Venezuela (the tune "Barlovento"), Colombia (the cumbiamba), and Panama (the tamborito). Any reader from the Caribbean will inevitably respond to and smile at the rhymes and rhythms the novelist brilliantly evokes in those fewer than ten lines.

There is also a European classical composer who, in a deeper and more subliminal way, governs the world of Patriarch. In his interviews García Márquez frequently states that among the prime influences in his dictator novel are the string quartets of Bartók. Actually there are some striking personal affinities between the great Hungarian composer and the Colombian Nobel-to-be. As a young man, Bartók traveled with his friend Zoltán Kodály around the rural areas of central Europe, where, gramophone in hand, they would record and then transcribe the folk tunes sung by willing peasants. Bartók would later integrate these melodies and measures into works of "high" art—sonatas, concertos, chamber pieces—synthesizing the original folk materials with his own harmonic and contrapuntal resources. There are any number of Bartók movements that sound remarkably like a band of Hungarian fiddlers livening up the local village dance. Similarly, as we saw in chapter 3 above, García Márquez would roam Caribbean Colombia as a kind of amateur anthropologist, observing folk customs and writing them up in his daily articles, with some particularly noteworthy reports on the music of the region. *Patriarch* represents García Márquez's fullest synthesis of plebeian forms and folk values with the concerns and pleasures proper to high literary art, and thus makes most evident the novelist's spiritual kinship with the composer Bartók.

Even more impressive are the structural parallels between the novel and certain Bartók compositions. The author personally admitted to me in July 1982 that "Bartók is one of my favorite composers; I've learned a great deal from him. My novels are filled with symmetries of the kind Bartók has in his String Quartets. . . . Although I've no technical knowledge of music, I can appreciate Bartók's use of form, his architecture."[6] (Actually, in our ninety-minute chat García Márquez showed himself to be extremely knowledgeable—however nontechnical—about the modern musical classics.) Given that *Patriarch* is a novel that casts aside virtually all of the familiar procedures and signposts of conventional narrative, it seems inevitable that García Márquez should have chosen to rely on the very art in which pure "form" and "architecture" play so central a role. And if in *One Hundred Years* the symmetries abound, in *The Autumn of the Patriarch* the formal architecture becomes of overarching importance.

The number of Bartók's String Quartets, like García Márquez's unnumbered chapters, is exactly six. All four movements of Bartók's Sixth Quartet begin with a kind of prelude in which a recurrent slow theme is stated and briefly developed, and then is followed by the principal body of the movement itself (a march, a scherzo, etc.); similarly, all six chapters of García Márquez's book start out with an episode relating to the discovery of the dictator's corpse, leading us thereafter to the actual chapter, consisting of incidents chosen from the tyrant's life. The initial movements of Bartók's Quartets tend to state certain basic rhythmic or melodic motifs that will figure prominently in the course of the entire work; in the same way, *Patriarch*'s initial chapter makes passing mention of characters and themes that will come up at various points in the narrative; the cows and concubines (palace life), Bendición Alvarado (affective life), Rodrigo de Aguilar (palace politics), Rubén Darío (literacy), and the foreign powers fittingly symbolized in William Dampier, the apostolic nuncio, the U.S. Marines and Ambassador Schontner, and the three fifteenth-century Spanish caravels.

Symmetry of design is the broad organizing principle of Bartók's greatest String Quartets. For example, the inner second and fourth movements of Quartet no. 4 share themes and are fast-moving scherzos, while in Quartet no. 5 the same two movements are expressive, songlike, and slow. In similar fashion, the even-numbered chapters 2 and 4 of García Márquez's novel concentrate primarily on the loving side of the tyrant. Both have long initial sections portraying his intense filial affection for his mother; from there they move on to depict the Patriarch in love as he courts Manuela Sánchez (chap. 2) and Leticia Nazareno (chap. 4), each of whom he relates to submissively, as remote and unattainable women of power. The two females are aptly described as robust, stocky peasant types, with large breasts and buttocks — obvious maternal figures meant as surrogates for Bendición Alvarado. For added symmetry, the preambular section of chapter 2 makes threefold mention of Leticia Nazareno, anticipating a character who will not enter the scene until the end of chapter 4. Pressing the musical analogy a bit further, one might say that these chapters 2 and 4 are like the slow, lyrical second and fourth movements of Bartók's Quartet no. 5, while at the same time, being the easiest and the more fast-moving chapters of the novel, they correspond to the two scherzos in Quartet no. 4.

By contrast, the harder world of politics takes full command in the book's odd-numbered chapters, 3 and 5. Chapter 3 in particular shows the man directly in control in various ways. On the positive and more benign side, we first see him as the homespun communicator who helps ordinary folk with their sewing machines or refractory husbands, and later as the master administrator who, in the aftermath of the hurricane, gets Manuela Sánchez off his mind by seizing on the task of urban reconstruction. On the negative side, in that same chapter he has the two thousand children murdered, and attains absolute power by crushing a series of military revolts and serving his closest aide Rodrigo de Aguilar for dinner.[7]

The corresponding chapter 5 inverts the symmetry, with the dictator now losing control to individuals wilier and trickier than he. First there is Leticia who, with her sexual and pedagogical powers, succeeds in restoring the church and, moreover, quickly becomes even more evil and corrupt than her patriarch husband. In the meantime we see the general evolve into a domesticated tyrant, a family man who wears gold-rimmed reading glasses and white uniforms, takes strolls in the palace garden, and sits in a white-walled office lined with dusty books and pictures of English horses. Following Leticia's murder, the power behind the throne slips into the subtle clutches of the soft-spoken and cultivated José Ignacio Sáenz de la Barra, he of the silk vests, French accent, Bruckner recordings, huge dog named after the cataloguer of Mozart, and heartless brutality that repels even the dictator himself. Chapter 5 thus stands chapter 3 on its head, tells of the absolute despot's personal comeuppance and political decline, narrates the undermining of his power by some close associates whom in earlier years he might well have summarily liquidated. (As the Patriarch actually notes in chapter 6, "I feel as if the reflection in the mirror is reversed.")

One more parallel with Bartók bears mentioning. The sixth and last String Quartet is capped with a slow and spacious finale in which fragments of earlier movements mingle and softly fade away. Similarly, the sixth and last chapter of *Patriarch* is a single spacious sentence that takes in the tyrant's physical deterioration, his ever-fading mind, and his fragmented memories of past incidents.

In the foregoing examination of musical and literary parallels, I have been fully cognizant of the abuses to which such analogies can be put when speculated upon gratuitously. Here, however, we have authoritative acknowledgment from none other than García Márquez himself. Once we are in possession of the Bartók "key" to *The Autumn of the Patriarch*, the formal clues and material evidence become too vast and too persuasive simply to be ignored.

The formal lessons García Márquez learned from Woolf and Bartók give *The Autumn of the Patriarch* its solidity and shape, while its plebeian language provides everyday tools and inexhaustible humor. In addition, some historical comment and literary parody are furnished through the imbedded presence of verses by the great Nicaraguan poet Rubén Darío and by excerpts from the diaries of Columbus. Darío is alluded to more than once in the novel, but the climactic moment comes in chapter 5 when the tyrant, picking up some culture, attends with Leticia a reading by the visiting poet (who in real life did become friendly with Latin despots). We see the character Darío reciting his "Marcha triunfal," a virtuoso paean to conquering heroes on parade, a technical tour de force if not a very profound lyric, though a favorite Darío anthology piece. (It is basically untranslatable.) And we "hear" entire stretches of the poem as experienced by the dictator, who is utterly moved ("this really is a parade, not the shitty things these people organize for me"), even stamping his feet in rhythm with the verse and later scribbling lines from the "Marcha triunfal" on his bathroom walls. In a Caribbean novel that aspires to the condition of poetry, it is fitting that one of the most renowned

Caribbean poets put in so glorious an appearance and even make a mental impact on the dictator.

The other crucial Caribbean figure who plays an important role in *Patriarch* is Columbus—with whom, after all, Hispanic Caribbean history begins. The fantastical vision of the three caravels at the end of chapter 1 is preceded by actual quotations from the admiral's account, in his diaries, of that momentous October Friday in 1492. With exquisite if unintended irony, only a few pages after he had remarked on the suffocating tropical heat, Columbus was to note condescendingly that "the inhabitants of both sexes in this island . . . go always naked as they were born" and later observed gleefully that the natives, "like idiots," bartered their gold for the Spaniards' glass beads and red bonnets.[8] These and many other lines are retained, often verbatim, in García Márquez's retelling of Columbus's narrative, with an obvious difference: the Spanish navigators here are seen as quaintly comical by the dictator's fellow "natives," who mock the archaic speech, heavy wigs, and jack-of-clubs dress of the newcomers, and accept the beads and bonnets only so as to please their greenhorn guests. As in *One Hundred Years*, European traditions of exploration and discovery are here stood on their heads.

Passing references to the Admiral of the Ocean Sea bob up occasionally in the novel, and by the final chapter he is only a pathetic phantom roving among the islands in his Franciscan robes (Columbus indeed used to wear them on ship), who exists in "a state of moral penury" (Columbus died poor and disgraced), and is reportedly "buried in three different tombs in three different cities," for Seville, Havana, and Santo Domingo all lay claim to his bodily vestiges. Here, then, Columbus has evolved into another version of the Flying Dutchman legend, a man "condemned to wander" as a result of his failed expeditions and because "he was a worse jinx than gold" (*OPa*, 258–59; *AP*, 256). It should be noted that throughout Spanish America, the 12th of October is a major holiday known as "El Día de la Raza" (roughly "The Day of Our Race"), whereby Spain's presence in the Americas is officially mythified and celebrated. In *The Autumn of the Patriarch*, by contrast, the "discovery" of America becomes a kind of antimyth, and Columbus and his followers are brought down to human size and spectral condition.[9]

In the end, however, what makes *The Autumn of the Patriarch* a significant contribution to human culture is its rigorous adherence to the essential history of Latin American dictatorship. For García Márquez's unnamed Patriarch is ultimately a complex and thorough redistillation of genuine facts and conduct from the actual lives of flesh-and-blood tyrants. In the pages remaining in this chapter I should like to take a passing glance at the colorful oddities and perversities of individual despots from whom the novelist created his memorable and "archetypal" composite of Latin authoritarianism.

When asked about the sources for *Patriarch*, García Márquez commonly cites biographers of Roman emperors — Suetonius, Plutarch — and hundreds of books about Latin American dictatorship. His creative use of the Roman materials is both fascinating and impressive. For example, in articulating the dictator's nightmare of being assassinated in chapter 3, García Márquez makes almost verbatim use of Plutarch's and Suetonius's accounts of the bloody murder of Julius Caesar, even retaining such precise details as the number of wounds (twenty-three) and the place of the fatal blows (the groin).[10] More generally, Suetonius furnished García Márquez a compelling series of portraits of absolute and arbitrary rule, the cruel degeneracy of which can shock even our benumbed twentieth-century sensibilities. In his legendary deadpan style Suetonius dwells on the physical and psychological maladies of his twelve Caesars, few of whom come off as positive. Coolly he alludes to the great Augustus's bladder pains and diarrhea (possibly the model for the Patriarch's herniated testicle) and recounts the tortuous relationship several of them had with their mothers (such as Nero's notorious passion for Agrippina). More striking still is the simply bizarre side of the Roman rulers. Caligula, for instance, grew up among the troops and as a child used to wear a miniature uniform (thus suggesting little Emanuel). On the matter of eliminating rivals and oppositionists, Domitian banned all philosophers from Italy, and Claudius executed thirty-five senators and three hundred knights.

The more monstrous emperors elevated their personal passions into collective concerns. When Caligula's sister-lover Drusilla died, he declared a period of mourning in which it became illegal to laugh or to bathe oneself, or to dine with one's own family; from then on he would publicly swear to Drusilla's divinity (saintliness and "canonization" not yet being among the religious ideals of Rome). The Patriarch's lottery schemes are anticipated by emperor-musician Nero, who set up frequent singing contests in which he bribed competitors to sing poorly and then would win all prizes for himself. There is in Suetonius's mighty subjects an infantilism that prefigures the Patriarch and his wide-eyed reading lessons — again Nero, who at the beginning of his rule used to play with model ivory chariots on a board (shades of those exiled dictators' domino contests that degenerate into tabletop war games), or Domitian, who would spend hours alone, snatching flies and then stabbing them with a pen point.

What García Márquez seems to have found in Suetonius's dozenfold narratives is, first, a pattern of power resembling those of many a Latin American despot: childlike viciousness and explosive passion combined with total control, a personal excess and flamboyant amorality surpassing any notions we may entertain of "normal" human conduct. At the same time, Suetonius's manner of presentation furnished the novelist an artistic model of fairness and impartiality, inasmuch as the Roman chronicler presents these awesome imperial horrors with a dry, lofty equanimity, never passing judgments or raising his voice, holding rather to a uniform, reportorial tone throughout.

On the other hand, the less remote realities of Latin American dictatorship provided García Márquez a vast array of experiences from which to choose, a field of referents *around* and *about* which he could design, engineer, and craft his narrative, building on and hyperbolizing the already grotesque deeds of those historical despots. As for my own researches, I can claim to have consulted only some dozen-and-a-half writings on Trujillo, Somoza, Gómez, and Perón (plus having some personal memories of life under Cuban and Venezuelan dictatorships in the 1950s). Even such elementary fare, however, can be an introduction enough to the biographical and psychological sources of García Márquez's fabulous autocrat. In the following analysis, a preponderance will be noted of materials from the life of Juan Vicente Gómez, who ruled Venezuela from 1908 to 1929 and 1931 to 1935 (and the basis for referring to which the author openly acknowledges [*OG*, 110; *FG*, 82]).

The Patriarch's uncertain origins, rustic background, and adult illiteracy. Gómez's date of birth is unrecorded, though as president he fixed on 24 July so as to coincide with Bolívar's birthday. Juan Vicente was the eldest of thirteen illegitimate children sired by one Pedro Gómez from various women; the purported father died when Juan was fourteen years old. Growing up illiterate in the Andes, the dictator-to-be never set eyes on a city of population larger than six thousand before he reached the age of forty-two.

The thousands of cows and cow pies in the Patriarch's palace. The personal tax collected for every head of cattle. The new species of cow being bred in his private provinces. This vivid reminder of the tyrant's enduring rusticity can be traced to several dictators. Even before he entered politics, Gómez expanded his cattle holdings by simple theft. Later he held the cattle and butter monopolies in Venezuela; until the final years of his presidency, cows were his preferred topic of conversation. Of Trujillo it has been said that he loved cows more than people. The Somoza clan monopolized the movement of Nicaraguan cattle, prohibiting their being transported without government permits, which were so expensive that a farmer had no choice but to sell his cows to Somoza.[11]

The Patriarch's harem and his fast, capricious, insatiable sex life. On his first journey to a large city, Gómez saw Dionisia Bello, the wife of an Italian merchant, and simply carried her off. As president, he would keep a mistress in another part of the house, while also visiting still other women around Caracas or bringing them briefly to his room. Twice a week, Trujillo used to have thirty new young "eligibles" line up in his office, choose one or two of them, take each to bed one or two times, and then set each girl free.

The tyrant's childish, submissive love of Manuela Sánchez, whom he treats like a queen and for whom he improvises amorous lyrics. Trujillo nourished a quasi-adolescent passion for socialite Lina Lovatón, and poured out some very bad love poetry in her honor. A sample: "She was born a queen, not by dynastic right but by the right of beauty, and so when the chords that filled the air during her splendid reign fell silent, she still reigned with the power of that right—her beauty. . . . The seductive power of Anacaona, the poetess Queen of Jaragua, abides in her eyes . . . as a remote enchantment."[12]

The despot's fascination with the schoolgirls next door. The fourteen-year-old who will forever treasure the memory of their passion together. After the death of his wife Eva, Perón converted the presidential home at Olivos into a sports center for high school girls. "He spent hours watching the girls play basketball, and he would ride around the grounds with them on scooters. . . . A pretty thirteen-year-old brunette named Nelly Rivas caught his eye and she soon became his mistress."[13] The Nelly Rivas scandal would long remain legendary in Latin America. (Incidentally, the Patriarch's adolescent lover remembers him as "la única razón de mi vida." Evita's autobiography was entitled *La razón de mi vida*.)

The Patriarch's maiden hands and satin glove. Gómez had small, delicate hands, and was never seen without gloves.

His holding court from a hammock. His common use of "Aha" as a response to lackeys or adulators. His fear of giving speeches from the palace balcony. At his Maracay residence, Gómez would surround himself with "friends," but never gave a public speech in his life. Among his most typical rejoinders was "Aha."

The Indian and former rebel Saturno Santos, who becomes the Patriarch's loyal and perpetually barefoot bodyguard, watching over his bedroom door. Gómez's personal valet, Tarazona, was "a short bowlegged dark-skinned Indian" who served the tyrant until death, tasting his foods, taking off his boots, and guarding his room.[14]

The total control the dictator establishes after the hurricane. The plasma sold by government ministers to their ministries, and sold in turn to hospitals. After a hurricane in 1930, the Dominican Congress passed an emergency law that transferred the full power of the state to Trujillo. Following the 1972 Managua earthquake, a blood bank owned by Cuban emigrés was buying blood from poor Nicaraguans at $5.25 a pint and making huge profits from foreign sales. Speculation exists that Somoza was involved.

The single-copy newspapers, the made-to-order television movies, the news made by pasting together the tyrant's older pictures and current sayings. Gómez used to spend every evening in his private theater, watching the same set of news-reels, learning from them and from his educated courtiers everything he knew about the rest of the world.

The close relationship with his mother. Her suburban house. The pilgrimage of the body nationwide. The canonization attempts. The only woman with influence over Gómez was his mother Hermenegilda, for whom he built a mansion at the beach resort Macuto. When Evita Perón died, the Argentine food workers' union cabled the pope to request her canonization. One Perón courtier proposed a prayer to Eva; another suggested capitalizing all pronoun references to her. Later, her embalmed corpse was secretly spirited away to a false grave in Milan, Italy. In 1971 her body was retrieved by a Perón agent and put on a train to Perpignan, France, whence, in a box labeled "radio sets," it was driven by car to Madrid.

The harassment of the apostolic nuncio and the closing of the convents. Over the last 150 years, many Latin governments have launched demagogic attacks on the church. Guzmán Blanco of Venezuela expelled bishops and shut down convents. When the ecclesiastics declined to name Trujillo "Benefactor of the Church," he closed parochial schools, spread rumors of priests on assassinations lists, had bombs and noxious substances thrown at church property, and hired prostitutes to do lewd dances in churches during mass. Perón exiled the auxiliary bishop of Buenos Aires and his aide, with nothing but the clothes they were wearing.

Vicious, predatory Leticia. Her relatives who get rich from the salt, water, and tobacco concessions. Her blue fox stoles (in a tropical country). Trujillo's mistress, María Martínez, was "astute, audacious, egotistic, proud, hotly ambitious, and without a trace of scruples. Unlike Trujillo, she had no moments of generosity."[15] She became rich with a hardware business and the army laundry concession. Eva Perón appointed her mother's boyfriend, a mail clerk, to head the Argentine postal system. On her visit to Spain and Italy in 1947, she regularly wore a white fox cape in the hot summer sun. Filipina First Lady Imelda Marcos's "raids" on Neiman-Marcus and her three thousand pairs of shoes, and Mme. Duvalier's fox stoles, continue Leticia's tradition. (Somoza himself owned ten thousand uniforms, some equipped with neon lights.)

Emanuel, the only child recognized by his tyrant father. Born a major general. Wears mini-uniforms, attends diplomatic receptions, practices with a recoil cannon at age six. Of his many children, Gómez recognized only those with Dionisia Bello. Ramfis, the eldest son of Trujillo, had real pistols for his first toys. The boy's fourth birthday was attended by the president's cabinet. At age four he was named colonel, brigadier general at age nine. Servile toasts honoring the boy were normal government protocol.

The shadow-president Patricio Aragonés. The powerful hatchet man Sáenz de la Barra, who upstages the military brass. Many Latino tyrants have set up weak heads of state while continuing to hold the real power — Gómez's Juan Bautista Pérez in 1929, Somoza's René Schick in 1963, Perón's Héctor Cámpora in 1973. On the other hand, some henchmen turn out so crude and evil that ruling circles come to prefer the actual dictator, as was the case with Trujillo's number two man in the 1940s, Anselmo Paulino Alvarez. In yet other instances, the henchman succeeds in getting subtle control over the boss, as did Perón's close aide José López Rega, a crackpot mystic and occultist who claimed powers to revive the dead.

The dictator's honorifics: "protomacho," "the stud," "the Magnificent," "General of the Universe," etc. Among Generalissimo Trujillo's countless titles: "Superman," "Super-Great Citizen," "Greatest Illustrious Creator of Generations," and the slogan "God and Trujillo."

The tyrant's brutal kinds of punishment: throwing prisoners to the crocodiles; having them publicly drawn and quartered. His recurring comment: "poor man." Gómez used to hang up certain enemies on meat hooks on trees beside a road. About the victims, Gómez as well as Trujillo was wont to say, "poor man." Somoza amused himself by throwing baby calves to the crocodiles in his moat.

The attack by British and German gunboats. The deal with Ambassador Traxler to have the United States take over European debts in exchange for lifetime subsoil rights. In 1902, European gunboats blockaded Venezuela, demanding payment of debts. Ambassador Bowen mediated for then-dictator Cipriano Castro and had the European blockade lifted. Later, during high-level rivalries between Castro and Gómez, the latter requested and got U.S. warships to show their support, keeping Castro out of the country and thereby allowing Gómez to seize power.[16] Gómez was to levy low taxes on the oil firms and place no restrictions on their land holdings.[17]

The dictator's personal conference with the U.S. Marine commander to decide the future of the nation. The unrelenting pressures by Yankee ambassadors. Trujillo began his political career by ingratiating himself with the officers of the occupying U.S. Marines. Somoza attached himself to then–Secretary of War Henry Stimson, and worked as a translator for the Marines, who created the National Guard and named Somoza its director. From the twentieth century onward, U.S. embassies in Latin America have materially supported dictatorships and encouraged coups against "unfriendly" governments. Earl Smith, who served in Cuba during Batista's rule, recalls that the U.S. ambassador was then regarded as "the second most important personage in Cuba."[18]

The sale of the Caribbean Sea and its transferral to Arizona. During the nineteenth century, two Dominican dictators offered to sell the enormous inlet at Samaná Bay to the United States. In the early 1970s a U.S. magnate purchased London Bridge from the City of London, had it disassembled into marked stones and then reassembled for $7 million in Lake Havasu City, Arizona.

The key trait that these and other like Latin despots show in common is an innate political genius and an uncanny gift for leadership, manipulation, and control, as well as for spotting and destroying enemies. The episode at the cockfight, where the Patriarch accurately senses that the tuba player in the band is preparing to shoot him, has its counterpart again in Gómez, who reportedly in his sleep or during strolls would "hear voices" and intuit that certain individuals were plotting against him. (He was therefore known as *el brujo*—"the sorcerer.") Indeed, this crafty intuition has often been the single outstanding talent of these dictators, who otherwise remain tactical virtuosos and idiots savants with few intellectual or other depths worth note. In the twentieth century the only non-Communist *caudillo* who manifested any ideological complexity or subtlety, any approach to politics that went beyond short-term manipulation, was Perón, who, not being a servant of foreign powers, had to think up a party strategy and mass political programs of his own.

Latin dictators have achieved the status of a kind of world myth, as García Márquez himself likes to remark, and his novel beautifully sums up the historical roots, the felt qualities, and the "spiritual" essence of that myth. And where corresponding novels by Carpentier and Roa Bastos work with the Europeanized mentality and cultured veneer of nineteenth-century "enlightened" despots such as Dr. Francia and Guzmán Blanco, García Márquez performs the perhaps more difficult task of recreating a tougher, cruder, more philistine and "American" sort of human and political animal.

Beyond that, however, *The Autumn of the Patriarch* is a meditation on the larger theme of power itself, an imaginative grid and model that can be applied to tyrants at all levels and to tyrannies of many a kind. Hence, though *Patriarch* is by no means "psychological" fiction, it does novelistically what

T. W. Adorno did as psychological researcher for his now-classic portions of *The Authoritarian Personality.*[19] If we put aside the Patriarch's intensely Antillean world for a brief moment, we will recognize familiar character traits such as combined servility and resentment toward the powerful, corresponding contempt toward those who serve him, incapacity to deal with love in any terms other than submission/control, the occasional self-conception as victim, the unctuous pat statements of false grieving and "concern," the profound conventionalism and conformism (Eichmann's notorious "banality"), the psychopathic lack of moral conscience, the almost pitiful absence of self-knowledge, the childlike dependence on surface charms, and the chronic conniving, deceit—including self-deceit—and Machiavellian manipulation. Anyone who has had a tyrannical boss, parent, love-mate, or friend will know immediately what it is I am talking about.

The Novelist of Love

It was only when he was in his late fifties that García Márquez came to be regarded as one of the great writers of romantic love. While Caribbean magic and politics stand out as the subjects most commonly associated with his art, the truth is also that few novelists have written as wisely and in such full depth about that banal yet elusive world of male-female attraction, courtship, and love, with all its attendant pleasures and frustrations, its commitments and ambivalences, its private certainties and public prejudices, its erotic force and everyday suppressions, its subjective, complex subtleties and objective, simplifying ritualizations, its expectations and surprises, and its entire ensemble of ups and downs—its vastly contradictory textures—as has the Colombian novelist. Love in García Márquez's fiction is as it is in real life: both fearsome and joyous, all-consuming yet creative, ecstatic and serene, glorious yet somehow sad and funny as well.

The interest had long been with him. Some of García Márquez's most imaginative and touching early articles tell of lovers reunited after undergoing many trials, or of the ways in which the telephone has transformed old courtship habits (*OP*, 1:684 and 702). Commenting in February 1955 on the romance that had blossomed between renowned bullfighter Dominguín and an Italian beauty (who had written the Spaniard one of those innocent fan letters, "filled with the expressive and nonsensical foolishness of love"), the young journalist would conclude his brief column with the wry observation that "love remains, through the end of time, more powerful than a [raging] bull" (*OP*, 2:971). These insights he was to include and develop in his magisterial "total" novels; *One Hundred Years of Solitude* is not only a town-and-family chronicle but also, as we saw earlier, a compendium of love stories; and *The Autumn of the Patriarch* anatomizes the tyrant's erotic disorders and ill-fated love life as much as it does his political history. To his interviewer for *Playboy*, a jolly García Márquez characterized himself as "a nymphomaniac of the heart."[1]

The novella or short novel "The Incredible and Sad Tale of Innocent Eréndira and Her Heartless Grandmother" depicts successively love for sale, young love, and love unrequited, all amid the desolate sands of the Guajira desert. The lengthy title suggests a carnival barker's high bombast, and its two women in fact live mostly in tents (a circus tent, eventually). Save for "Big Mama's Funeral" no García Márquez narrative evokes with such fervor the atmosphere of plebeian festiveness and street revelry as does "Eréndira" (its shorter title). The basic plot, ironically, is as sad as the title indicates: a fourteen-year-old innocent is prostituted for two years by the "handsome white whale" of her grandmother, in payment for a million-peso "debt" incurred when the girl accidentally burned their house down. The novella thus first concentrates on the act of love commercialized and extorted by power.

For the grandmother, herself a whilom whore, love is and always has been just a business, and she typically reduces everything to (in Marx and Engels's phrase) "the icy water of egotistical calculation." When she first offers Eréndira to the widowered shopkeeper, the girl is examined for her dimensions and treated like so much merchandise — there is an entire page of haggling as to her "price." Throughout the story we see the old vixen computing labor costs, going to such absurd extremes as having Eréndira do the Indian servants' dirty wash so as to discount it from their pay, or trying to browbeat an ambulant, feisty photographer into defraying a fourth of the musicians' wages. The rotund adventuress shows that unctuous, informal, backslapping amicability ("'Because I like you," she explains to the photographer [*CE*, 139; *CS*, 294])[2] or the capacity for unwitting projection and false outrage (for example, accusing the widower of "lack of respect for virtue" [*CE*, 104; *CS*, 268] or calling Eréndira's overeager customers "perverts" and "an inconsiderate bunch of slobs" [*CE*, 115; *CS*, 277]) ordinarily associated with unscrupulous businesspeople. On one level, then, "Eréndira" is a comic caricature of capitalism at its rawest, most "underdeveloped," and most interpersonally predatory. The matriarchal pimp and domestic tyrant even gives orders in her sleep.

Eréndira on the other hand is a classic portrait of pure innocence in absolute thrall to worldly power. Having fully internalized her oppression, the heroine *follows* orders and does housework in her sleep, routinely replying with a formulaic "Sí, abuela" ("Yes, grandmother") to the old despot's every utterance. These are in fact the only two words the oppressed will ever address directly to her oppressor (the sole exceptions being three scattered brief complaints to the malevolent matriarch about pains from overwork). When the grandmother, in order to retrieve Eréndira from the convent, pulls the trick of marrying her off to a pliable Indian boy, the victim "willingly" returns to her victimizer's clutches even while pointing at her nominal husband. Further along in her "career" Eréndira toys mentally with pumping boiling water into the evil ogress's bath but suddenly repents when called by her, and later, to her lover Ulises she will confess being incapable of murdering the old harridan "because she's my grandmother." In the end, in a kind of magical Freudism, Eréndira's face takes on instant maturity the moment her male-factress plops dead at the hands of Ulises. And yet she abandons her loving redeemer, for the sordid injustices she has endured have made her selfishly individualistic and opportunistic rather than compassionate or sympathetic (a common enough real-life result). The young maiden, it turns out, never loved her wooer and rescuer.

"Eréndira" is in fact a shrewd and very funny love story cum swashbuck-ling tale. Much of its wild humor, appropriately, derives from its being a broad parody of some venerated traditional genres: ancient myth, medieval romance, and above all fairy tale, along with movie melodrama (a kind of twentieth-century avatar). Numerous conventions are plundered from these formats and turned upside down. The "hero" Ulises, an angel-faced naïf and occasional bungler, is the farthest thing possible from the wily adventurer of Homeric fame. Neither is this tropical Ulises a navigator, nor a woman-izer; indeed he is a virgin, and on their first night his experienced damsel has to teach *him* about love after he goes limp.[3] Similarly, Eréndira's late father and grandfather share the noble name "Amadís," an obvious echo of the most celebrated of medieval Spanish romances of knight-errantry (famously satirized, of course, by Cervantes). García Márquez's Amadises were smug-glers on the hot Guajira desert rather than gallant knights in an idealized Europe. The first Amadis rescued not a pure maiden from a tower but a heartless whore from an Antillean brothel, while the second was actually shot in a fight over a woman (*CE*, 99; *CS*, 264). The aging moll now lives re-enacting past glories, dining at her long table decorated with silver candelabra and set for twelve, an empty aristocratic ritual aptly symbolizing her fake elegance.

It is the fairy-tale nature of "Eréndira," however, that most gives the no-vella its distinctive details and flavor. The characters are instantly recognizable types. Eréndira herself is a kind of Cinderella, a paragon of girlish innocence, slaving under a tyrant who is cruel stepmother, wicked witch, and evil queen (indeed she sits on a throne, borne aloft by Indian servants) all rolled into one. Max Lüthi, a renowned expert on the genre, notes that the fairy-tale hero frequently "breaks away from his home and goes out into the world."[4] Like-wise, when on a moonlit night Ulises's father demands to know where the boy is going, the latter responds, precisely, "Into the world," and moreover elicits a requisite paternal curse from his stereotypically ruddy, pipe-smoking,

Bible-declaiming Dutch progenitor. The parting is further comically undercut when, in a follow-up scene, the paterfamilias declares sententiously, "He'll be back, beaten down by life," and his wise Guajiro Indian wife snaps in reply, "You're so stupid. He'll never come back" (CE, 151; CS, 303).

The adventures involving the three principals are the familiar stuff of fairy tale, played by García Márquez for laughs. The youthful, wealthy enough "hero" falls in love at first sight with the young "maiden in distress"—in fact ends up in bed with her on their first meeting, she actually charging him her full fee (thereafter half, finally nothing) for her tender reciprocities. Later in the story an anguished Eréndira calls out Ulises's name (like Rapunzel in her tower) into the night, and from his distant orange plantation he miraculously—yet expectedly—hears her cry. His successive ordeals on her behalf culminate, true to form, in the final scene when he slays the dragonlike virago with a knife (though he could have simply shot the cad in her sleep), setting Eréndira free. But alas, there is no final wedding or "happily ever after" for this gallant, tearful paladin so casually abandoned by his ladylove. Indeed, only in the safety of the convent, in chapter 4, will Eréndira admit to being happy. She actually does marry—not at the end, however, but exactly midway through the novella, when the grandmother arranges the instant wedding with the Indian boy in order to spirit her away from the missionaries. The forced marriage-of-convenience lasts not forever but a few ceremonial minutes.

Fairy-tale narratives show a marked preference for the numbers three and seven.[5] "Eréndira," accordingly, has seven chapters containing some fundamental threes: three different men who first "initiate" the heroine; three "abductions" of Eréndira (by missionaries, by rival whores, and by Ulises); three oranges pilfered from the family farm by the hero just before the couple's abortive flight; and his three attempts at slaying the ogress, the third, with its hand-to-hand combat, being typically the fiercest.[6] The naturalness with which the miraculous and fantastical are incorporated into the text, as simply one more element in the story, is another fairy-tale trait.[7] Ulises's ability to change glass objects to blue is diagnosed by his sagacious mother as a symptom of lovesickness, on the same order as his lack of appetite for bread; the oranges that grow with diamonds inside of them are appropriate for a social milieu of professional contraband; and the moribund grandmother's oozing green blood helps highlight the vixen's not being exactly human. (Possible associations: green is the color ordinarily attributed to dragons; and, in Spanish, *verde* is a common synonym for the sexual.) The special role assigned in "Eréndira" to hard objects—the gilded piano, the diamond-oranges, the gold vest—replicates the fairy-tale genre's bias for palpable mineral presences: gold rings, metal swords, glass slippers.[8]

Moreover, with its purehearted lovers struggling against a slick and grotesque villain, "Eréndira" plays on the conventions of silver-screen romance and Perils-of-Pauline melodrama. Ulises utters lover's vows perfectly imaginable in the corniest celluloid tearjerker—for example, at his first encounter with Eréndira: "Everyone says you're very beautiful. And it's true" (CE, 117; CS, 278). Or later, at Eréndira's request that he kill the witch: "For you, I'll do anything" (CE, 154; CS, 305).[9] The sordid context of these lines gives them their unmistakable parodic flavor. The story in fact was first drafted in 1968 as a film script, though a cinema version, directed by the Brazilian Ruy Guerra, did not appear until 1984.[10] The garish decor of the novella's opening does suggest a set by Fellini,[11] and Ulises in flight is actually described as brandishing a pistol "with the confidence of a movie gunfighter" (CE, 136; CS, 292). (The revolver, naturally, turns out to be a hopeless dud at the height of the chase.) The final lines of the story are clearly inspired by the ending to Truffaut's 400 Blows—in 1959, we might recall, García Márquez wrote an awestruck review of that landmark film (OP, 4:773). In "Eréndira," however, the device too is altered: whereas the French youngster's long rush toward the sea ends on a quizzical freeze-frame there, García Márquez's adolescent girl first runs alongside the ocean and then heads back into the desert—still running.

Other moments in the story suggest the farcical rhythms and raw physicality of the animated cartoon genre. When a virginal Eréndira resists the widower's lusts by screaming and scratching at him, he slaps her off the ground, and she "with her long Medusa hair" floats momentarily in space—just as happens to cartoon characters before falling off some cliff (CE, 105; CS, 269). In his surprise initial visit to her, Ulises at first is seen sticking out his face from behind her bed, and she rubs her head with the towel "to prove that it wasn't an illusion"—humorous gestures recognizable to any comic book fan (CE, 116; CS, 277). The cruel murder of the hapless photographer in chapter 5 is told with a pratfall rapidity ("He flipped into the air and fell dead on top of his bicycle" [CE, 142; CS, 297]) that helps attenuate the sheer horror of the event. And the silent detonation of the gilded piano, along with the evil woman's caricaturesque understatement (she observes, "Pianos don't explode just like that" [CE, 159; CS, 309]) are reminiscent of the well-placed sticks of dynamite in countless Tom and Jerry short features. García Márquez thereby raises cartoon conventions to the level of a high art—appropriately, for in some of his earliest articles he wrote favorably of comic strips and promoted their literary legitimacy (OP, 1:153).

Like many of García Márquez's shorter works, "Eréndira" deftly combines a profound sadness with a (literally) explosive humor. On one hand, the sufferings of real-life Eréndiras admittedly go on by the thousands in our world day after day, just as devout lovers also exist who are abandoned once their good works have been completed. But the author also understands that, in literature, tales of woe make no converts and that social evils are often better lampooned knowledgeably than excoriated morally. Where righteous indignation would have failed, the narrative is saved by its funny side. The grandmother no doubt is malevolence incarnate, heartlessness made flesh, but she is also ridiculous both visually and psychologically—her honey-tongued hypocrisy being unforgettable. Similarly, the lovers' first-night chat consists of a series of one-line jokes only García Márquez can have dreamt up—such as Ulises's comparing the sea to "the desert but with water," or his alluding to a man who could walk on the waves, "but that was a long time ago." With its formal wizardry, its tropical adventures on the road, and its seriocomic, bittersweet flavor, "Eréndira" stands as one of García Márquez's most delightful and perfect shorter creations.

Chronicle of a Death Foretold also contains a parody love story—though little to laugh about. This is García Márquez's darkest book by far, the only major volume of his that isn't funny (while being thick with ironies). Its amorous element in turn comes enmeshed within a broad network of collective concerns such as class, rituals, honor, religion, and guilt—but also, in a twist of fate, finally exists for itself. The plot couldn't be simpler: Bayardo San Román, a mysterious, attractive, rich young man, shows up in August at an unnamed small town, seeking a wife. He takes a fancy to Ángela Vicario, who resists at first but is eventually talked into it by her middle-class parents. A monumental wedding feast is held six months later; that night, however, Bayardo returns Ángela to her family because she is not a virgin. Brutally interrogated by her mother as to the culprit, Ángela mentions Santiago Nasar, the only son of a locally successful Arab family. In revenge her twin brothers Pedro and Pablo murder Santiago with machetes in front of his house before the eyes of most townspeople, who remain shaken by the crime long thereafter. Following three years in prison the twins are acquitted on grounds of justifiable homicide; Bayardo drops out of sight; and Ángela suddenly falls in love with, and for the next seventeen years writes a weekly letter to, her "husband," who one August day shows up with her two thousand letters, unopened, and says, "Well, here I am."

Its seemingly simple plot and prose notwithstanding, the five unnumbered chapters of *Chronicle* form a narrative in its way as complex as is *The Autumn of the Patriarch*. The impending crime is anticipated in the initial seven words; hearsay reports it at the end of chapters 1 and 3; the autopsy takes up the start of chapter 4; the terrible social aftermath to the crime opens chapter 5; and the actual murder—preceded by a breathtaking suspense sequence—is only rendered in all its horrific detail in the final five paragraphs of the text. We see the consequences of the murder long before the murder itself, and the immediate buildup to the murder, in turn, only toward the end. In the same fashion, each of the first three chapters ends with an allusion to Santiago by name, while the last of course tells of his annihilation.

The organization, as in *Patriarch*, is not as much chronological as by subject. The first chapter concentrates on Santiago's final ninety minutes of life; the second, on Bayardo and on the wedding night; the third, after some legal matters, on the Vicario brothers; the fourth, following the autopsy and a report concerning the fate of the respective families, on Ángela's late-budding love; and at last, the fifth, after an account of the townspeople's reactions, on the tense few minutes of pursuit and murder. The "Faulknerian" juggling of time is by now a seamless and perfectly natural literary device in García Márquez's arsenal.[12]

The other literary artifice in *Chronicle* is in the telling itself, for it is a novel not only about a horrendous crime but about the narrator's task of piecing together the crime. While the volume could simply have been called *The Death of Santiago Nasar*, the chosen title signals the book's being someone's account of that death too. The "Crónica" of the Spanish original is a standard journalistic term denoting a reportorial article, usually of a nonpolitical and even sensationalistic kind. It's a genre familiar enough to García Márquez the journalist, who in fact serves as the "chronicler'" for this mock report and includes as "informants" his own real-life parents, four of his younger siblings, and his wife-to-be Mercedes. Self-portrayed as a resident of the town at the time of the murder, who now reconstructs the events after a twenty-seven-year interval, the novelist manages to evoke an immediate suspense as well as a serene hindsight in his readers, who in turn find themselves experiencing those febrile episodes from the two perspectives at once.

From the first page to the last, the various concentric and remote times that surround the murder alternate with the more recent testimony from the surviving witnesses. The text bristles with such indications as "he said to me," or "she admitted," or "many agreed that," and the like.[13] One scholar has counted thirty-seven speaking characters who directly contribute to the narrator's investigation, their combined statements adding up to 102 such quotations, on average almost one per page.[14] Another scholar tallies up nearly eighty characters putting in some sort of appearance[15] — the equivalents of those countless fleeting street voices that comprise much of *The Autumn of the Patriarch*. Here, however, the lack of an omniscient narrator makes discrepancies inevitable. In an obvious instance, some witnesses remember that fateful morning as sunny and breezy, others as gray and drizzly. On the other hand, though most of them consider Santiago innocent of the drastic charges (as does, fairly emphatically, the chronicler), a large variety of contradictory speculations emerges as to why Ángela would frame him.

As is often pointed out, *Chronicle* shows many of the conventions of the classic detective story.[16] Besides a crime, a motive, a victim, and an investigator, there is the role of the judiciary — a trial complete with judge, attorney, and an extensively-cited legal brief. In the same way, the autopsy scene enumerates Santiago's multiple wounds with a clinical exactitude. The text deploys certain other precise details typical of the genre. The unfolding clock time — 5:30, 6:45, 6:58 — is carefully spelled out; Santiago's gun collection — with brand names and models — is dryly enumerated; and the twins' two sets of knives are meticulously described as to type and size. And there is, toward the end, the customary explanation and summing up of the crime and its consequences.

But this is a whodunit with a difference. The normal sequence of events, after all, is reversed. The identity and motive of the criminals is fully revealed halfway through the opening chapter; the criminal act is withheld until the closing pages. Santiago's formidable weaponry proves to be useless, and precisely because of his own state of bewildered innocence. Though the twins are legally acquitted, their honor killing has most probably visited its summary justice on the "wrong" party. An enormous gap thus remains in this detective story; the murder, strictly speaking, is no mystery at all, yet it gives rise in turn to the unsolved mystery of the sexual "culprit."[17] The unrepentant killers turn themselves in, but it is their taciturn sister, unreliable and unforthcoming as a witness, who has in a sense pulled off the perfect crime.

What could have been just a naturalistic thriller about bloody deeds and rustic chivalry is given special depth and resonance through the intimations of Greek tragedy, religious ritual, and other archaic residues woven into García Márquez's text. Following the classic unities of place and action, the novel opens and closes inside the victim's home, and the book's every page bears the stamp of that one murder.[18] Concerning unity of time, the central events cover the twelve hours that unfold between the wedding feast the day before (presumably about sundown, though there are no concrete indications) and next day's sunrise. The outer time frame of the physical novel is just over ninety minutes, from Santiago's arising upstairs at 5:30, to his falling dead in the kitchen at 7:05.

As in Sophocles's *Oedipus Rex*, there are dark omens and foreshadowings, some of them unwittingly from the victim-to-be. When the housemaid Victoria throws the rabbit's entrails to the dogs, a shocked Santiago exclaims, "Don't be a savage. What would it be like if those guts were from a human being?" (*CM*, 20; *CD*, 10). And in fact Santiago at the end is clutching at his entrails. At the wedding, moreover, he compares its floral decorations to those for the dead and says, "I don't want flowers at my funeral" (*CM*, 69; *CD*, 42). The terse observation, "That was the last time *x* saw him," appears four different times in the text, and the twins of course go announcing their plans, eight times in chapter 3 alone.[19]

The almost incredible series of chance misses, in which countless individuals set out to forewarn Santiago yet are detained, misinformed, or simply ignored, seems, in the heat of the narrative, one of those bitter instances of every possible thing going mysteriously wrong. Seen whole, however, the random accidents add up to a chain of inevitability. Like King Oedipus, who only too late in the game realizes that the machinery he set in motion leads inexorably to him, a rich Santiago is sealed in his fate, seems moreover destined to remain oblivious to what is happening, and in his distraction even spurns armed assistance from the father of his fiancée. There are some additional and familiar ambiguities. Though he may not be specifically guilty of the deflowering, Santiago does impress us from the start as a proud and arrogant young man who casually abuses the maid's daughter, and later, to the narrator, mocks Ángela as "your cousin the ninny" (*CM*, 53; *CD*, 32). In keeping with his social and sexual hubris, there is also in Santiago's dying moments a tragic and heroic grandeur—the way he walks a hundred yards with his usual good carriage, smiles at the astonished neighbors whose house he traverses, tells his aunt across the river that he has been killed, and arrives faithfully home before dropping finally dead.

Chronicle tells of two great collective events—the joyous wedding (complete with a serenade to the deserted mansion) and later the tragic murder, witnessed by the townsfolk who gather in the plaza as if for a parade. "We" is in fact the grammatical subject of the opening paragraph to chapter 5, after which the narrator recalls the effects of the crime on many of the individuals concerned—for example, the prompt death of Ángela's traumatized father, or the prostitution that was to be the lot of Santiago's fiancée. Here the cast of characters—with unique names such as Celeste Dangond and Poncho

Lanao—fast multiplies as we learn of their respective involvements with the crime and/or their eventual fates. The communal ties with Santiago's death are thereby established and made real, are shown and itemized as well as told—and the murder looms more and more as a collective rite of sacrifice. Indeed the word "sacrifice" is actually employed on earlier occasions in referring to the Vicario twins' work as cattle slaughterers, a repeated usage that predisposes us to view the murder as another sacerdotal act by self-appointed ministers (their last name hinting at this role).

The ritualistic nature of the events is further underscored by the novel's religious intimations. The death in the Spanish title is "anunciada," with overtones of the Annunciation. The morning of the murder is at first dominated by the collective excitement over the arrival of the bishop, whose brief and perfunctory blessing disappoints them, and their emotional high pitch is retained for the deeds shortly to follow. Most of the key names in the book seem chosen for their religious connotations: Ángela, Pedro and Pablo (as in the apostles), their mother Purísima, their father Poncio ("Pontius"); Bayardo San Román (who is no saint); the Nasar hacienda *Divine Face* and their maid Divina Flor (with a parallel irony in the name of Santiago's sweetheart Flora); and the medical student Cristo (short for Cristóbal) Bedoya, who is unable to save his best friend.[20] The combination "Santiago Nasar" is a striking paradox, Santiago being St. James, the Spanish slayer of Moors, here applied to an Arab (albeit a Christian).[21] Of the García Márquez siblings, the one who most sees Santiago that day is his sister the nun (never mentioned by name), while Ángela herself is compared at one point to a nun. In all, the roster reads like a devotional gathering.

The archaic flavor of the action in *Chronicle* is heightened by its elusive remoteness in time and the presence of earlier sorts of technology. Though not specified, the period appears to be the 1920s, when Model-T Fords would be something novel. In addition, Bayardo's father had once waged war against Colonel Aureliano Buendía (that is, in the 1890s), and at the wedding there are waltz ensembles playing. Significantly, the only two automobiles mentioned are those belonging to the San Román outsiders; the only communications medium alluded to is the telegraph; and the bishop sails past in an old-fashioned paddleboat of a kind American readers would associate with Mark Twain and that were out of use in Colombia by 1950.

Chronicle's very first glance at ancient traditions is its epigraph ("the pursuit of love / is like falconry"), which comes from a seventeen-line lyric by the great medieval Spanish-Portuguese poet Gil Vicente (1456?–1536?). Though the disturbingly beautiful and deceptively simple poem of origin is all but untranslatable, its basic idea is to liken love to a sport that, with ill-chosen prey, can bring dangers, battles, and woes aplenty. The original Spanish, moreover, contains an important pun, for "altanería" signifies not only "falconry" but also "arrogance, hauteur."[22]

From the start it is hence hinted that *Chronicle* will tell of the romantic chase as well as of human pride and power. Each of the two romantic males in the book is in fact characterized initially as arrogant and haughty. Santiago, a falconry expert, is even referred to once as "a sparrow hawk" (*CM*, 144; *CD*, 90). This lively and imaginative set of notions receives a further twist halfway through the novel, when the narrator recalls warning Santiago at the brothel by citing to him (without identifying) the first three lines to Gil Vicente's same poem: "Halcón que se atreve / con garza guerrera / peligros espera," well rendered by Rabassa as "A falcon who chases a warlike crane / Can only hope for a life of pain"; nevertheless, "heron" rather than "crane" is the more accurate prey here (*CM*, 105; *CD*, 65). The second quotation within the book (and the opening of the poem) therefore emphasizes the conflictual side of romantic love, its "politics" as it were. As we have seen, for all their might and power, both Santiago and Bayardo will be unwittingly brought to heel by the warlike heron Ángela.

For indeed at the core of *Chronicle* is a love story, a narrative about the customs, clashes, illusions, and emotions of love. Briefly ignoring the Santiago material, we could summarize the novel thus: wealthy and attractive male courts local girl; estrangement occurs; reconciliation later follows. The initial portions of the love narrative are highly evocative of fairy-tale romance. With his narrow waist, silver buckles, and kid gloves, Bayardo at first resembles a medieval seigneur. His given name inevitably recalls the famous "knight without fear or blame" of fifteenth-century France. His personal traits are heroic—he hails from the highest local military stock, knows church Latin and Morse code, and is a champion swimmer. And his courtship is all pomp and ceremony—he buys Ángela's favorite house as her bridal gift, and their wedding feast harks back to society's most hallowed of shared erotic dreams.

These and many other romantic formulas are to be seriously subverted in the course of *Chronicle*. The trouble begins with Ángela, who at first does not like Bayardo, thinks him "conceited" and "stuck up" (*CM*, 49; *CD*, 29) but, feeling intimidated, also finds him "too much of a man for me" (*CM*, 56; *CD*, 34). And of course she doesn't love him, but her mother Pura, seeing economic gain, informs Ángela, "Love can be learned too" (*CM*, 57; *CD*, 35). The disastrous night and the honor killing, in turn, elicit from the narrator's wise mother Márquez the resigned and telling equation, "Honor is love" (*CM*,

155; *CD*, 97), to which most townsfolk agree. Ángela, however, proves to be a feisty, resilient sort who, though hard-pressured into the marriage, subtly resists—for example, she refuses to don her wedding gown until Bayardo's two-hour-late arrival. And of the chief actors she is the only one not to succumb to death or degradation, acquiring in her solitude as a seamstress in Riohacha a self-knowledge and a quiet dignity all her own.[23]

In the process Ángela grows as a woman. She begins to feel for Bayardo precisely when being punished by her opportunistic mother, and the sentiment thereafter becomes an entity potent and enduring enough for her to write and mail to him the two thousand letters. Ironically, her flabby and balding Bayardo will prove to be an egotistical man less than worthy of the warrior "heron" he comes back to, while Ángela's belated passion turns out to be the only true and lasting bond of romantic sentiment depicted in the book. Love, an emotion in *Chronicle*'s initial stages closely bound up with such matters as social prestige, virginity fetishism, and family honor, finally blooms as a genuine personal feeling, with its own internal dynamic and history, only after the entire paraphernalia of power and control has been swept aside and superseded—and also when the woman, now on some equal footing with the man, consents to him from the depths of her inner being.

Though Ángela's two thousand letters reportedly run the full gamut of emotions from those of secret lover and proper fiancée to abandoned wife, the only quotation furnished from those pages is the almost cliché-novelesque, "As proof of my love I send you my tears" (the spot being not tears at all but spilled ink). Love-by-letters is of course the most basic of amorous written traditions, with literary roots in the epistolary romance and with real-life implications of distance and deferred passion. The fact that here the recipient saves but never even opens his beloved's correspondence adds to the whole dark joke, and the one statement we see when the couple finally meet again in the flesh is not some joyous term of endearment but Bayardo's banal and fatuous, "Well, here I am."[24]

These letters and what they stand for are among the many other amorous conventions more or less undermined and parodied in *Chronicle of a Death Foretold*. There are Santiago's parallel love letters to Flora, violently thrown back at him in her misinformed hysteria minutes prior to his death. There is the bereaved love of the widower Xius, his own noble sentiment no match for Bayardo's flamboyant machismo. At the wedding there is a prelude to another such union in the narrator's impulsive proposal to the young girl Mercedes (which, by contrast, will lead to a long marriage in real life). One might normally consider the bottom end of the love scale to be the brothel of María

Alejandrina Cervantes, but the whorehouse is actually a kind of refuge and erotic "school." The madam herself, her long name resonant with old heroic and literary echoes, is affectionately depicted as a woman of some authority, one with whom an adolescent Santiago could have fallen in love. If anything it is Santiago and his father who, in their dealings with the domestics and the lesser whores, are the most exploitative of their sexual power as rich males. In *Chronicle*, as in other García Márquez novels, the erotic takes on many forms, from the most spiritual and selfless to the most abusive and base.

The impact of *Chronicle of a Death Foretold* is further heightened by our knowledge that the narrative is based in part on some true events close to the author. The original crime occurred on Monday, 22 January 1951, in the town of Sucre, where García Márquez's family had been living for ten years. Here is a rudimentary summary of the real-life incidents.[25]

After a year's romantic involvement, Miguel Reyes Palencia, twenty-nine, the scion of a landowning family, married a local schoolteacher named Margarita Chica Salas, twenty-two, on Saturday the twentieth at 7:00 A.M. He loved her, but had also been pressured into marriage by threats from Margarita's older brothers (not twins) José Joaquín and Víctor Manuel, commercial fishermen, who had heard slanderous rumors about the young couple. At the wedding night Miguel got completely drunk, then slept the entire day and night following the festivities. Early on Sunday the twenty-first he awoke in a bedroom at the Chica household, saw Margarita naked at his side, and found out she was not a virgin. He beat her, demanding her deflowerer's name, but she refused. He then returned her to Mrs. Chica, who, on her knees, implored him to wait a few weeks in order to avert scandal. Margarita's brother Víctor now showed up and asked; she named Cayetano Gentile and burst into tears.

Cayetano, twenty-four, tall, elegant, and good-looking, the son of successful Italian immigrants, was a third-year medical student. He and Margarita had been engaged once in the past, though this had not prevented him and Miguel Reyes Palencia from being drinking partners and close friends. On the morning that he was to die, Cayetano went down to the river port to see Miguel and Margarita off on their honeymoon trip, but the couple, strangely, had never showed up. There he also posted a letter to García Márquez's father Eligio in Cartagena, and ran into Gabo's brother Luis and sister Margot, who invited him over for breakfast. Cayetano graciously declined the offer, he being due at the family farm *El Verdún* that same day. He then went by to see his sweetheart Nydia Naser, not yet aware that José and Víctor Chica were at the general store across from his two-story house, waiting to hack him to death.

A crowd was gathering near Cayetano's home. His mother Julieta was inside, having been warned about the death threat by a little boy she knew. Seeing one of the Chica brothers running toward the house, but not her son approaching rapidly from the corner opposite, she slammed shut and locked both doors. Cayetano arrived at the front door and started banging and screaming. Julieta, thinking it the pursuers, scurried inside for protection. Cayetano now fled, curiously bypassing the hotel next door (where there was a policeman), and dashed into the following house, but Víctor reached his prey and knifed him fourteen times. The victim managed to rise up and walk home, his entrails dangling out. He died there amid relatives, saying "I'm innocent." The Chica brothers turned themselves in immediately, spent a year in jail, and were finally acquitted. Meanwhile the Chica family moved away, and Margarita, feeling disgraced, did not venture out for two years. Miguel in turn remarried, became an insurance agent, fathered twelve children, and nourished no regrets on the matter. Thereafter he saw Margarita just twice, first for the annulment, and years later on some obscure financial question. The townsfolk mostly thought Cayetano guiltless.

The crime would have a lasting impact on young Gabo, who was in Cartagena at the time. He knew all of the parties involved; Cayetano had been a friend since childhood, and Julieta was godmother to one of Gabo's younger brothers. A practicing journalist of three years, García Márquez considered writing an article or a novel about the incident, but his editor friend Germán Vargas suggested that he let the whole thing settle in his mind, and his mother also asked him to wait, not wanting to see her relatives and personal memories written up in a book of his. Besides, the apprentice author had not yet found an organizing principle for the narrative, and to this end he often rehearsed the story with friends, feeling that the plot still had, in the words of Álvaro Cepeda, "a leg missing." In fact it was Cepeda who, a couple of decades later, suggested adding the estranged lovers' reunion, and at that point it all fell into place for the novelist, who realized that it was not so much the account of "an atrocious crime" as "the secret history of a terrible love." In other words, a love story waiting to be told.

The love element is in fact what gives the recast plot its imaginative dimension. Both the groom and the accused lover become highly romanticized entities. Santiago's Arab origins, for one, make him additionally remote and exotic, as also does, for Ángela, her exile in faraway Riohacha. Geographically the real Sucre lies quit a ways inland, but from *Chronicle*'s unnamed town the shimmering Caribbean Sea, with its pirate legends and romantic ocean cruisers, is sighted more than once. The bride's avenging brothers are reborn as twins, a "magical" sort of condition, and their profession as butchers allows for their skill with the machetes and that repeated early use of the word "sacrifice." The bishop's visit is of course totally invented for the sake of religious "atmosphere."

Countless other details have been altered, and space permits us to cite only a few. In a perfect reversal, it is the narrator's mother who now becomes the victim's godmother, he even bearing her middle name, the mutual ties thereby being thickened, while it is Mrs. Vicario and not Ángela who has been the schoolteacher. Cayetano's sweetheart's last name "Naser" is actually retained in a variant form, but given to Santiago. The judiciary aspect, for artistic reasons, is also greatly magnified. Rather than the 322 out of 500 pages assiduously studied by the novel's sleuth-narrator, the only legal document that the author in reality managed to consult was the seven full pages of the brief for the defense. To add to the ironies, although García Márquez did converse with the Chica brothers' defense attorney, the man by that time was advanced in years and could scarcely remember the trial, which for him was just another honor-killing case—a far cry from the continued amazement that the learned and literate judge expresses (for us) in Chronicle.

It is precisely this rustic code that Chronicle of a Death Foretold evokes, a code that, to younger and more modern readers (the author's own two children included) seems as remote as science fiction.[26] In this regard the book is a subtle indictment of the machismo that forms part of such a code. García Márquez in his interviews often declares himself antimachista,[27] and the novel contains some passing attacks on such an ethic, notably from the shopkeeper Clotilde, who complains of women's solitude before men and specifically mentions Pedro's act of shaving with a butcher knife as "the height of machismo." Doing what the Andalusian Lorca also did with real nuptials and a peasant vendetta in Blood Wedding, the Colombian novelist brings off a poetical and quasi-"anthropological" reconstruction of a ritual murder, treats it with such dignified objectivity as to create from it a work of tragedy—but one that conveys its own moral critique as well. As we have seen, true love is depicted as coming into its own only when machismo and its associated values have been scrapped.

Love in the Time of Cholera is García Márquez's most extensive narrative—five hundred pages in the original, Spanish-language, Bruguera edition. Of its six unnumbered chapters, the final one occupies a fifth of the entire novel and is by itself longer than all of Chronicle of a Death Foretold. On many counts the book comes as a surprise. It is in some ways a good old-fashioned love story (as the phrase goes), a fact established in the title, which Hispanic readers in conversation habitually shorten simply to *El amor.* (We in turn shall abbreviate it *Love.*)

The book is also an intentional return to nineteenth-century realism, the outright fantasy we associate with García Márquez now being mostly absent. Among the few clear-cut exceptions are the ill-omened, colorful parrot that can speak French and Latin and even bark like a mastiff, and the forlorn ghost of a woman waving her handkerchief from the riverbank at passing ships. The narrative geography is thickly textured with descriptions worthy of Balzac, and the unnamed city in which the action unfolds is clearly modeled after the lovely, stately colonial town of Cartagena, with its old viceroys' quarter and cobblestoned streets.

At the same time the city has aspects of Barranquilla and Santa Marta,[28] for instance, the mention of a visit by aviator Charles Lindbergh, who on a 1929 goodwill tour of South America made a stop in Barranquilla (not Cartagena). Still, when the Urbinos go on their ballooning trip, Cartagena is the only place described not in terms of a site that "they flew over" but rather as one that "they could see" (*A*, 330; *L*, 226). In addition there are invented landmarks—the Gospel Park and the Arcade of the Scribes (where Florentino respectively reads poetry books and writes amorous missives for non-literate lovers), and also such imagined towns as San Juan de la Ciénaga and Puerto Padre.[29] On the other hand, the long boat journey up the Magdalena River seems true to the different stops familiar to a lonely adolescent Gabo of 1943, including the terminus at La Dorada, where one caught the train to Santa Fe (as Bogotá used to be known).

The action covers approximately sixty years, from circa 1875 to circa 1935. Fermina Daza is thirteen when she starts her first, secret engagement to Florentino, aborted three years hence. Not too long afterward, she and her newlywed husband depart on their honeymoon journey and will attend the premiere of Offenbach's *Tales of Hoffman* (1881). The day before Dr. Urbino's absurd death the couple went to see the Hollywood version of *All Quiet on the Western Front*, from 1930 but probably screened a year or so later in Colombia. Because Fermina is seventy-two when widowed and her second courtship by Florentino lasts about a year and ten months, the closing moments of the book can therefore be placed somewhere between 1933 and 1935.

The plot, again, could not be simpler: Florentino Ariza, seventeen, falls in love with Fermina Daza, and she reciprocates, if somewhat drily. Their relationship will be broken off as a combined result of pressure from Fermina's socially ambitious father and her own mysterious caprice. She then marries

Dr. Juvenal Urbino, of the old aristocracy, and slips with some effort into the role of great lady, while Florentino rises to the top of a local river-transport firm and has at least 622 love affairs. Fifty years later Dr. Urbino dies; Florentino after the funeral boldly professes his enduring love to the widow; a complicated push-and-pull courtship ensues; and their love is finally consummated on a riverboat trip.

Many elements, both experiential and literary, went into the making of this García Márquez novel. It is, as we shall see, a love story with many a difference, telling not of the all-too-familiar romantic fulfillment of two youths but of a couple in their seventies (something of a first in literature). For the second larger theme in *Love in the Time of Cholera* is that of aging and its difficulties, a process not easily romanticized. García Márquez in his interviews concerning *Love* mentions having read Simone de Beauvoir's *The Coming of Age* (in the British edition, *Old Age*), and his novel is consciously and profoundly informed by the Frenchwoman's classic study of the subject.[30] *Love* narrates, as de Beauvoir first does, the physiological changes typically accompanying aging: Florentino's loss of hair and teeth in chapter 5; his broken leg from a minor fall in chapter 6; Fermina's sudden condition of deafness in one ear aboard ship; the undegradingly honest description of her bare wrinkled shoulders and froglike skin; and the general odor of human fermentation.[31] There are also the memory losses—some slightly comical, some heartrending—suffered by Dr. Urbino and by Florentino's mother Tránsito. And there is Florentino's subjective psychological sensation of seeing time pass for others without realizing that it is passing for him too (*A*, 292, 319; *L*, 199, 228), a discrepancy to which de Beauvoir dedicates many pages.[32]

At the same time *Love* dramatizes a lively debate on elderly sexuality. The eighty-one-year-old Dr. Urbino, who has found his consolation in "sexual peace," embodies an antierotic high rationalism extolled by Plato, Seneca, and other of history's wise moralists. More, the concluding chapter reveals that the Urbino couple had not made love in two decades, while their own joyless daughter Ofelia thinks love "ridiculous" in one's middle age and simply "'revolting" among the elderly. All this stands in clear contrast to Florentino's unflagging sexual vigor at seventy-eight and his consummating the love of his life at that time. Florentino and Fermina serve as eloquent rebuttal to the many long-standing forms of conventional wisdom that cruelly mock eroticism in the sunset years and doggedly claim that "the idea of sexual relations . . . between elderly people is deeply shocking."[33] *Love* hence joyously celebrates sex among the aged and nullifies those silly though persistent stereotypes about "dirty old men." Not accidentally, the author first got the idea for *Love* from the touching nocturnal memory of an elderly couple dancing aboard a ship, a vision he would make into the exhilarating high point of this novel.

The book of an author approaching old age, *Love* is in some ways a serene compendium of García Márquez's life experiences and wisdom. Two such experiences are worth noting for the essential raw material they provided him. The earlier Florentino-Fermina relationship is based largely on the courtship of García Márquez's own parents.[34] His father, Eligio García, played violin, as does Florentino, and the story of the telegraphic communications that kept their stubborn romance alive is preserved almost "word for word," in "rigorously historical" form, in this novel.[35] Decades later, when the author was pursuing researches for the book, he chanced to find out that his septuagenarian parents "were still—at that time—making love!"[36]

The other real-life incident that had an influential impact on the author was a news item he read in the 1960s, in Mexico, about two Americans, a loving couple in their seventies, who for four decades had been meeting yearly in Acapulco, where they would frequent the same hotel and restaurants. The amour was clandestine, for they were happily married to other people, a fact that happened to become known only when a boatman murdered the couple for their pocket money.[37] Both chilling and astounding, it is one of those stories that elicits our empathy for an absurd death at the same time that, ironically, it allows us a glimpse of eroticism and romance alive and well among the world's aged. Not for nothing does the author have Fermina hear of such an incident on the radio and come close to weeping over it, further dwelling on it in her mind during the reunion with Florentino (*A*, 461; *L*, 318).

Love and aging, then, constitute the double focus of this novel, the former being present in countless ways throughout.[38] As has often been commented, there is almost every possible sort of male-female tie in *Love*—older-younger affair and vice versa, female-on-male rape and vice versa, adultery, masturbation, prostitution, jilting, crime of passion, suicide for love, conjugal affection, unconsummated sexual attraction, young love, elderly love, and a formal courtship complete with chaperone and go-between.[39] There are serenades, references to hundreds of love letters, many subtle little tricks and gestures of pursuit, and the braid of Fermina cherished by Florentino. The cheapjack pop culture of love is alluded to in copious quantities—bad poetry, tearjerker serials, the soap operas that Fermina listens to—and often parodied. The epigraph to the novel comes from "The Crowned Goddess," a love tune from the 1970s, which García Márquez dares to insert anachronistically into his narrative and—as former president López Michelsen suggested—lends a substantial role, comparable to that assigned by Proust, in his celebrated Swann-Odette amour, to the fictional sonata by Vinteuil.

At one point, in a comment on the elderly Florentino's letters, there arises a passing phrase about "el perfume de una gardenia" (*A*, 424)—an unmistakable echo of "Perfume de gardenias," one of the most renowned of *boleros*, those Caribbean love songs whose spirit permeates much of this novel. Many other lines in the book seem lifted right out of dime-novel prose or *bolero* lyrics. Dr. Urbino's dying words, "Only God knows how much I loved you" (*A*, 72; *L*, 43), would fit perfectly either in a sentimental song or a *True Confessions*-type paperback (the Latino equivalent). On more than one occasion an amorous Florentino is described as speaking under the inspiration of the Holy Ghost—to Anglo ears a farfetched notion but perfectly conceivable in Hispanic culture, where folk-Catholicism and folk-romanticism often merge. The boat on which Florentino and Fermina finally become lovers bears the appropriately "allegorical" name *Nueva Fidelidad*. And needless to say the final line in the book—Florentino's absolutely certain "Toda la vida," "Forever"—is the well-worn conclusion to thousands of facile songs and stories, the humorous twist here being that Florentino is talking not to Fermina but to the captain, and refers not to his love but to the comings and goings of the riverboat.

On occasions the more solemn love rituals are wickedly parodied, simply in order that they will not be taken too seriously. Three key romantic moments in *Love* become tinged with Rabelaisian ribaldry in García Márquez's hands. In the long-awaited scene in which young Fermina at last accepts from Florentino his very first letter of courtship, a bird turd happens to drop right onto the embroidery frame she employs in receiving the crucial missive (*A*, 97; *L*, 61). Three years hence her father is about to send her safely away from her lover, and Fermina hides in the bathroom where she composes for him a brief farewell note—on a square of toilet paper, which she sends along with a braid of her hair (*A*, 128; *L*, 82). As tensions mount, the spoofing turns to outright farce: when five decades later a nervous Florentino for the first time dares to drop in on Fermina, he is suddenly seized by an uncontrollable need to defecate, and rather than run the risk of spoiling this long-awaited reunion, he cuts short his visit after a few formulaic exchanges, arranging a future date (*A*, 442; *L*, 304–5). Though love and its associated forms may be celebrated in this book, they are also indulgently and outrageously satirized when necessary.[40]

As one might expect, the realist novel *Love* includes all kinds of period detail—types of carriages, literary works, Strauss waltzes, new technologies such as crank-operated telephones and that wonderful ballooning trip, and cameo appearances by Urbino's teacher Dr. Proust (father of the novelist) and by Joseph Conrad *né* Korzeniowski, who spends several months in the unnamed town and makes a gun-running deal with a shady Mr. Daza. And there is the social fabric of the city, with its varieties of public space, and two dominant class "blocs" represented by the Social Club (aristocracy) and the Commercial Club (bourgeoisie). The three chief characters similarly embody their respective backgrounds—Dr. Urbino, with his two resonant family names, from the old colonial elite; Fermina, the beautiful scion of the new breed of rough-hewn buccaneer capitalists who seek high standing in the young republic; and Florentino, illegitimate but connected by birth to a more modern and reputable shipping enterprise that nevertheless ravages the forest environment whose populations it largely serves. There are the accounts of hacienda life with the Sánchez clan, perhaps a nod at the milieu of Isaacs's romantic novel *María*.[41] The novel's traditionally omniscient narrator also speaks as a member of the community, shifting on occasions to the use of "we" or "us" or "here" (A, 24, 76; L, 10, 45).

In preparing for the writing of *Love*, García Márquez diligently read or reread certain European realist works, among them Alessandro Manzoni's *I promessi sposi* (1840; *The Betrothed*). The classic historical novel of Italy, it tells of a young rural couple who are ready for marriage, only to find their wedding plans repeatedly thwarted by political thugs and a cowardly priest, plus riots, wars, and, especially, a bubonic plague epidemic—yet are joyfully reunited some years later. García Márquez of course has always been fascinated by accounts of plagues, and he admits to having studied with particular care the corresponding episodes in Manzoni. The influence can be seen in the plot of *Love*.[42] In one instance (in the Spanish original), the chaperone Escolástica is reported as dying in the Agua de Dios "lazareto" (A, 123), the latter an institution that figures prominently in *The Betrothed*.[43]

An even more important influence is Flaubert's *Sentimental Education* (1869). The phrase actually appears early on in the narrative of Florentino, when we read of the affective wisdom he would achieve "at a more advanced stage of his sentimental education" (A, 100; L, 63). García Márquez admits to having first set out to emulate the French author and combine historical panorama with love story, but in time he scaled down his objectives out of concern that the public sphere would overshadow the private, as is sometimes the case with Flaubert.[44] Still, there are striking parallels between the two novels (both of which, coincidentally, were likened by some reviewers to albums of photos). *Sentimental Education* in fact starts out on a riverboat journey, during which the protagonist, Frédéric, a sensitive if undistinguished young man, falls in love at first sight with Mme. Arnoux, a charming, pure-hearted lady "who looked like the women in romantic novels," and who in her heart will respond positively to Frédéric's affections while remaining steadfastly faithful to her flighty bourgeois husband.[45]

Frédéric in turn will continue lovesick for Mme. Arnoux throughout the book, indulging many a familiar affective formula: "Every word that fell from her lips seemed to Frédéric something new, something exclusively hers"; "he was in love with everything connected with Madame Arnoux—her furniture, her servants, her house, her street."[46] At the same time, over a ten-year period Frédéric entertains unfulfilling liaisons with the vulgar if sensual courtesan Rosanette and with the stolid heiress Mme. Dambreuse. His sole true love nevertheless remains Mme. Arnoux, whom after a gap of almost two decades he will see once again, in an affectionate though unpassionate reunion, for both are now too old and disillusioned to live the sentiments of their youth. Their lovers' reunion is hence neither a consummation nor a fresh start. The similarities with *Love in the Time of Cholera*, then, are obvious—as are the differences. Whereas Flaubert's novel ends in bleak desolation, Florentino throughout all his affairs will sustain his romantic dream and succeed in making it reality. (There may also be an intended parody of the famous carriage scene in Flaubert's *Madame Bovary* when Dr. Urbino plays a little stripping game in his own coach with Hildebranda and Fermina.)

The major difference between *Love* and its nineteenth-century prototypes, however, lies in its frank descriptions of sex. The difference has to do not only with the greater sexual tolerance of our times but also the ways in which sex is dealt with in the narrative. Physical love in most nineteenth-century fiction, when it plays any role at all, usually forms part of a sordid power struggle (Balzac's *Cousin Bette*, for instance), or is an expression either of women's wiles or of male control. In García Márquez's novel, by contrast, the erotica is depicted as delectable and positive for its own sake. To put it quite simply, Florentino and his many bedmates enjoy each other without a trace of shame or guilt. Moreover, throughout *Love* it is the women who tend to take the initiative, and their aggressive, pantherlike sexuality is implicitly acclaimed rather than prudishly maligned. Even female masturbation arises in *Love*, and Fermina's adolescent cousins gleefully compare the number of times that they are able to engage in autoeroticism daily and orgasm per session.

The contrast is especially dramatic when one considers those nineteenth-century heroines—for example, Merimée's Carmen, sinful and destructive in her sultry eroticism; or Emma Bovary, a pitiful and exploited adulteress and "fallen woman"; or Dorothea Brooke (in *Middlemarch*) or Mme. Arnoux, among whose positive attractions is the very fact that they keep their sensuality under control. In *Love*, on the other hand, female sexuality is given free expression. Not accidentally, all but one of Florentino's sexual partners are experienced women—widowed, separated, or still married. This is partly in order to reflect the Hispanic mores of the time, when premarital sex in respectable society was largely out of the question (as demonstrated in *Chronicle*), but also because the author surely intuited that pretty girls in their teens would probably not feel attracted to a sad and homely Florentino, whose look of pained melancholy is precisely what his older paramours like about him. One of the most moving moments in this novel is when Florentino and Fermina make their serene, septuagenarian love in her cabin aboard ship, an eroticism so wise and highly distilled it takes them "beyond love."

Various temporal patterns and structural symmetries—those García Márquez trademarks—have their indispensable role in shaping *Love*. As in *The Autumn of the Patriarch* and other of the author's works, the narrative starts out with a death in the "present," in this case circa 1931; a long flashback of over fifty years takes up chapters 2–4 and most of 5, the concluding pages of which then pick up on the dangling thread from chapter 1; chapter 6 now proceeds with the final courtship and romance. Concerning parallelisms, among the most important is the set of deflowerings of Florentino and Fermina, both of them in chapter 3, on his and her respective boat trips, and in each case with more experienced and aggressive sexual partners; their elderly consummation will likewise take place on board ship, three chapters and five decades hence. The opening suicide of Jérémiah de Saint-Amour, motivated not by love but by dislike of old age, is contrastively echoed by the love suicide of América Vicuña toward the end. That the given names of both protagonists start with the same letter *f*, and that their last names each contain a striking intervocalic *z*, is an obvious linguistic fact worth passing mention.

The triangle of chief characters forms a configuration around which the novel's major themes are to revolve. The opening chapter is Dr. Urbino's, and the inevitable first impression is that he is the hero of the book. A weighty individual, he has had a brilliant career as doctor and professor; as civic leader he has performed such admirable services as starting a men's corps, reviving the local theater, and ridding the town of cholera epidemics. He is patrician in lineage, is used to giving orders, and is well connected—the archbishop and the governor both attend that afternoon's banquet, and upon his death there is a three-day period of official mourning. Dr. Urbino's urbane manners are impeccable. Indeed he is all manners, and in time he will strike us as a bit complacent, too sure with his European ways—with his library of acceptable French books, all uniformly leatherbound (though no Zola), his English furniture, and his lofty rationalism. Despite the hint of youth in his name "Juvenal," the good doctor—invariably referred to by his professional title—appears never to have been a young man.

In chapter 3 we find out that Dr. Urbino was among the most eligible bachelors in town, figuring in many a young woman's dreams—was, in short, the very image of a "catch." And his wedding with Fermina was one unmatched in the century. While chapter 1 gives us a portrait of the resulting elderly affection, subsequent chapters tell the history of a long, stable companionship seriously shaken just once by the doctor's inept dalliance with a black Protestant preacher's daughter. Out in society Dr. Urbino and Fermina are the picture of poise, seen usually arm-in-arm, "the two of them in perfect harmony" (A, 334; L, 229). García Márquez quite deftly evokes this public idyll as well as those inevitable small tensions in private—the discords over the husband's wetting the edge of the toilet bowl, their harsher quarrel over an absent bar of soap, and his disastrous attempt at housework at the end of chapter 5. Still, as marriages go it is a good one, the kind we might read about today in glossy magazines.

So positive is this initial portrait of the doctor's marriage—the wife first being mentioned only a third of the way into the chapter—that an unsuspecting reader might be led to think it the central focus of the novel. As one reads of the intimate history of their relationship, however, a more complex reality emerges. The doctor is many things, but a romantic person he is not—his letters to Fermina are serious and to the point, with none of Florentino's perfumed fire. When he serenades her, he hires a concert pianist to do the job; unlike Florentino, he plays no musical instrument. Most important of all, on their first night as spouses in bed he is perfectly "aware that he did not love her" (A, 236; L, 159), for theirs is a bond originating partly in Mr. Daza's opportunistic dreams and partly in the doctor's need for "a social adornment" (A, 216; L, 145). Later, to his aging wife's casual complaint of unhappiness, the wise doctor replies sententiously, "Always remember, the most important thing in a good marriage is not happiness, but stability" (A, 435; L, 300). In retrospect, then, Dr. Urbino's dying words of love seem said because they are the expected protocol—conjugally proper rather than deeply felt.

In a darker vein there is the conjugal life as lived and perceived by Fermina, who vaguely senses herself having developed into "a deluxe servant" employed "in [Dr. Urbino's] holy service" (A, 323; L, 221). The poet Sara

Noriega—a lover of Florentino's—takes an even harsher view, dismissing the grande dame as a mere "whore" who has married a man for his money (*A*, 293; *L*, 200), though the judgment is one clearly motivated by malice. An extended key passage shows a middle-aged Fermina passing in review her own many doubts and anxieties, such as her prenuptial inner questionings as to what made the doctor any more preferable to Florentino; her later seeing her spouse as "the creature of a paternal plot"; her hellish first six years' coping with certain bitter, doltish, or narrowly prejudiced in-laws; and her suspicion that her high-and-mighty husband may be a weakling at heart (*A*, 300–306; *L*, 205–9).

And indeed, the entire flashback and final aftermath constitutes—through the characters of Fermina and Florentino, and the experience of their love regained—a sustained and subtle refutation of the premises and conventional values so skillfully established and duly honored in the opening chapter of *Love*. Fermina herself, a natural rebel, will be described throughout the book as a stubbornly mulish sort who bristles at any hint of arbitrary imposition or control. Her first three utterances to young Florentino, not accidentally, are brisk commands; and even when bedding down with her two different sexual partners it is she who finally decides on consummation. And yet, as the author himself once noted, Fermina becomes more bourgeois than she realized.[47] In the end she fully accepts Florentino only after too many of her upper-class supports have crumbled or proved unreliable—what with scandals in the press concerning her husband and her father, the unctuous prudery of her daughter Ofelia, and her friend and confidante Lucrecia del Real del Obispo abandoning her in time of need.

Florentino for his part stands for everything that Dr. Urbino is not. Where the doctor is rationalistic, academic in tastes, and soberly antipassion, Florentino is spontaneous and emotive, likes all romantic poetry good or bad, and will fulfill himself as a women's man and ultimately as one woman's man.[48] Though he does rise up in his profession and becomes a successful river transport administrator, this matters to him only insofar as it will help make him worthy of Fermina. In pointed rebuttal to the to-be-arranged marriage, moreover, during that suspenseful confrontation between Florentino and Mr. Daza when the latter orders him to stay away from his daughter, Florentino counterargues, "It seems to me that she is the one who has to decide" (*A*, 126; *L*, 81). Thus besides living for love, he is ready to die for love and to defend a woman's right to choose her mate. A romantic hero in the tradition of Goethe's Werther or Benjamin Constant's Adolphe, his sentimental excesses are ironically offset both by his erotic virility and by his eccentric homeliness.

The episode of Jérémiah de Saint-Amour in the opening pages is—as critics often complain—soon forgotten and never again mentioned. But it too forms part of the broad debate that runs throughout *Love*. The Afro-Frenchman calculates his suicide long beforehand, refusing to live past sixty (seventy in the English version, apparently because of a typing error), out of a principled opposition to aging. What we see dramatized at the end of the book, by contrast, is the possibility of genuine passion and romance in old age. In addition, Saint-Amour has a devoted lover (whom we meet but whose name we never learn), yet has kept her clandestine and steadfastly refused to let her share in his day-to-day life. His last name notwithstanding, Jérémiah de Saint Amour is not a man for whom love is sacred. Worse, Dr. Urbino finds out that Monsieur Saint-Amour was not a political refugee but an escaped convict, a fact that casts a pall over the affection in which the doctor had held him. In this light the later suicide of América Vicuña, however tragic (and however reprehensible Florentino's treatment of her), takes on a certain nobility, for it is motivated by love rather than calculation, and has the virtue of honesty, unlike the enormous shadow play set up by Jérémiah.[49]

Love in the Time of Cholera shows many of García Márquez's most admirable traits—grand sweep, hints of tragedy, and robust humor—in combination with the best qualities of the nineteenth-century novels it consciously emulates—a feel for the lived textures of everyday existence, an intuitive grasp of society and its ways, and lots of good story telling. However, it also succumbs to the notorious faults of that genre, notably an overabundance of detail (of "metonymy," as theorists might say), a discursiveness that at times becomes long-winded, and, in the middle chapters particularly, a somewhat loose and episodic structure. The author's exuberant imagination often flows to excess in the pages of *Love*, such as those lengthy lists of house pets in the first chapter and of European consumer purchases in the third. And though each one of Florentino's many depicted women friends is a delight individually, the instances accumulate in sufficient numbers so as to muddy the narrative. Other, nonsexual stray episodes appear similarly gratuitous—for example, the account of Florentino's ill-fated attempt, in chapter 3, at raising a sunken Spanish galleon.

It is perhaps no paradox that *Love* is García Márquez's most joyous book—and also his least disciplined or rigorous. Yet it is a novel that stays in the mind, producing a deep and lasting glow of satisfaction *after* being read, and the outer chapters are as beautiful and artful as anything ever fashioned by the author. Moreover, García Márquez's millions of readers can only applaud his courage and originality in writing a novel of love (a subject traditionally thought of as the preserve of younger authors) when on the verge of old age, a bit like Verdi composing his single comic opera, *Falstaff,* when in his seventies. The Colombian literary wizard's capacities for independence and self-renewal inevitably move us to admiration.[50]

ELEVEN

The Bolívar Novel

In the decades that followed his Nobel Prize, García Márquez showed no sign of settling into high complacency, contenting himself with past achievements, or becoming a public mouthpiece. On the contrary, as an artist he continued to astound his readers by taking on subject matters as grand and risky as those depicted in his previous works. Every book he has published since *Love in the Time of Cholera* stakes out some new territory, opens our eyes to an array of experiences hitherto seldom treated either by himself or by other literary authors.

In 1989, García Márquez surprised everyone with *The General in His Labyrinth*, a novel that has as its protagonist none other than Simón Bolívar (1783–1830; pronounced See-MONE Boh-LEE-bahr), the supreme commander whose forces freed Venezuela, Colombia, Panama, Ecuador, Peru, and Bolivia from Spanish Imperial rule. Here, however, rather than the heroic soldier and statesman, what we see is the defeated politician, wasting away during his final months of life, outdone by allies and rivals, discredited among large segments of the New Granadian populace, and thoroughly dejected as he prepares to emigrate to Europe but ends up sailing to his unforeseen death near the coastal town of Santa Marta.

To pen such a book was an audacious step indeed. Throughout much of Hispanic America, but especially in García Márquez's native land and its neighbors, the figure of Bolívar enjoys cult-like status. Children in school are taught to revere him quasi-religiously, while in adult public life the man inspires high-flown political rhetoric beyond measure. Parks and plazas, boulevards and buildings, schools and universities bear either his name or the honorific title *El Libertador* (as did a broad avenue near my home in 1950s Caracas). Postage stamps by the hundreds have commemorated him and his accomplishments. There is an entire country named after him; and the *bolívar* is the currency unit of the nation of Venezuela, where, in the early twenty-first century, President Hugo Chávez launched a project dubbed the Revolución Bolivariana.

In the academic and information sectors, generations of scholars and scribblers have produced books and articles about him. Over a hundred biographies exist,[1] as well as specialized volumes commenting on every conceivable aspect of Bolívar's thought, career, and even love life. Educators seek ways to present him to malleable young minds, and in such contexts the laudatory language can reach breathless heights. A Venezuelan fourth-grade text says of him, "He was an admirable man—without doubt, the best in our history, and also the crowning figure of [Latin] America."[2] Another grade-school reader by Emilio Peña, weighing in on Bolívar's final testament in the final rivalry between Venezuela and Colombia, notes:

> From his heart as Father of our Country, from this noble and abnegated heart, there poured forth, then, gentle words of forgiveness for those who, driven by the infamous serpent of envy, with a parricidal hand, had ignominiously struck against his life and his untitled reputation as leader and warrior. Before the angel of glory opened to him the gates of immortality and granted him the triumphant laurels with which he would appear, in the eyes of future generations, it was Bolívar's lot to drink of the bitter cup of vituperation and misfortune, of abandonment and poverty, of ingratitude and scorn.[3]

Latin American literati have also shared in and contributed to this hero worship. The Ecuadorian lyrist José Joaquín Olmedo (1780–1847), whose "La Victoria de Junín: Canto a Bolívar" is considered one of the first reputable poetic works of an independent Latin America, has the last Inca emperor and the forces of nature proclaiming the general the "arbiter of peace and war" and "a living mirror of glory." Guillermo Valencia (1873–1943), who during his lifetime was the unofficial poet laureate of Colombia, in his "Oración al Libertador" hails Bolívar as "Immortal Father," "New Hercules," "Achilles," and "Sacred and Heroic Man." Even the great Chilean bard Pablo Neruda (1904–73) could fall in line in his own "Canto para Bolívar," where, in an echo of "The Lord's Prayer," he starts out by addressing the leader, "Padre nuestro que estás en la tierra / en el agua en el aire . . ." ("Our Father who art on earth / in the waters, in air").[4]

For a Colombian author—the Liberator's avowed enemies and detractors aside—to write about Bolívar in any terms other than the official, established, "canonical" ones, then, already constitutes a path never taken.

Both Bolívar the myth and the man himself are scarcely known or understood outside Latin America. A look at the man and his trajectory are therefore in order.[5]

There is no doubt that, in numerous respects, Bolívar qualifies as a remarkable individual. A superb horseman and swordsman, he possessed great physical endurance and could swim long stretches even when ill. At social gatherings he dazzled guests with his facility and grace as a ballroom dancer. Though relatively short (5′6″), the good-looking Bolívar was attractive to women. Tragically widowed at the tender age of twenty, he went on to have lovers across Europe and South America, yet the only one to remain close to his heart was Manuela Sáenz (about whom, see below). Born into enormous colonial wealth and privilege, he had no particular interest in money and in fact gave away much of his riches to war widows and orphans, even turning down a state pension in his final year.

Bolívar was extremely cultured and quite conversant with the work of thinkers such as Hobbes, Locke, Montesquieu, Voltaire, and Rousseau; he carried cartons of books wherever he went and used to read every morning. He had an uncanny facility at remembering people's names (a key skill in politics) and was a gifted orator and prose stylist. While his fellow officers had attended some of Spain's best military academies, Bolívar surpassed them as a battlefield tactician and strategist through sheer intuitive genius. Ambidextrous, he could shave with either hand even as he chatted.

Among the back-of-the-book materials in *El general en su laberinto* is a "Sucinta cronología" of the life of this multifaceted man, put together by Vinicio Romero Martínez, a Venezuelan historian. The decision to include such an outline, one gathers, came from García Márquez himself, and the synopsis indeed provides a readymade framework for the plot, along with a reminder that much of what we have read has its basis in historical fact. At this point, meanwhile, it might be helpful to furnish a brief bio-narrative in order to help place the events of the novel within something like a familiar context.

Simón José Antonio de la Santísima Trinidad Bolívar y Palacios was born in 1783 near Caracas, in an outpost of the Spanish Empire. (Venezuela until 1776 had been part of the viceroyalty of Nueva Granada, then becoming an administrative unit with Imperial offices of its own.) The family's roots harked back to early Iberian settlement of the colony, where the Bolívars eventually owned gold and copper mines—from which Simón would later help finance the Independence Wars. In his veins there coursed some African blood, the result of an illicit liaison between a remote Peninsular ancestor and a black slave. Orphaned by age ten, he was then raised by an uncle who provided him with an influential (and subsequently legendary) tutor, Simón Rodríguez, a passionate though eccentric disciple of the Enlightenment and Rousseau.

In 1800 Bolívar set sail for Spain in order to complete his education as a young gentleman. While there, in 1802, he courted and married María Teresa Rodríguez del Toro y Ayala, she also the offspring of a Venezuelan father. Unfortunately, only eight months after the couple's prompt return to their homeland, María Teresa perished of yellow fever. Bolívar, who was scarcely ever to speak of the loss, went back to Spain in 1803. Finding Iberian ways too limiting, he soon was in Paris, where he met the renowned German-born scientist and explorer Alexander von Humboldt. According to legend, Humboldt in Bolívar's presence praised the South American continent and saw it as ripe for separation from Spain. The leader-to-be also toured the south of France and much of Italy with his former tutor, Simón Rodríguez. On a visit to Rome's Monte Sacro (Aventine Hill) on 15 August 1806, Bolívar experienced an epiphany that would become legendary in its own right: clasping his teacher's hands, the twenty-three-year-old swore to free his country from Spanish rule.

The Napoleonic occupation of Spain in 1808–16 sparked independence revolts and provisional juntas throughout the Americas, including an 1810 patriot declaration in Caracas. That year, Bolívar, already involved somewhat in the events, was sent to London on a three-man diplomatic mission to engage in the intricate high protocol of making independence-related contacts. In the meantime, Francisco de Miranda, a seasoned, respected, sixtyish activist, had been organizing radical if premature actions against Spanish power, first in London and then in the Venezuelan colony; battlefield defeat and surrender at La Victoria in 1812, however, resulted in Miranda's arrest and deportation by Royalist forces. Bolívar, now back in Venezuela to prepare for war, collaborated in complicated and subtle ways with this official reprisal, even labeling Miranda a "coward" for having lost. The Miranda affair is among the less honorable moments in the Liberator's career.

Spain's armies offered stiff resistance to the rebels, with military hostilities lasting until the early 1820s. In 1813, Bolívar started emerging as a distinguished commander among the patriot forces and their fluctuating fates. A series of reverses led him to flee to Jamaica in 1815, where he wrote the now-famous "Jamaica Letter" that contains astoundingly prescient reflections on the continent's bleak future. There he was almost assassinated, surviving only by sheer happenstance in a case of mistaken identity. Later, with logistical help provided by the president of Haiti, Bolívar and his troops set sail from the Afro-French island and landed in Venezuela, the beginning of a long series of campaigns that would free Venezuela, Colombia, Panama, and Ecuador, in a joint federation, from Spain.

With further military cooperation from his closest (and perhaps only) friend, Marshall Antonio de Sucre, Bolívar's forces liberated Peru and the Alto Peru region, the latter being renamed Bolivia. The Bolivian constitution, which initially called for a lifelong presidency, became a temporary template for governmental organization in the rest of the federation. A darker moment in Bolívar's final campaigns was his one-on-one meeting in Guayaquil, in July 1822, with José de San Martín, liberator of Argentina. Following that two-day encounter, attended by no one else, San Martín mysteriously withdrew from the struggle and went into exile in Europe, dying there in 1850.

After Spain's final capitulation in 1824, Bolívar was assigned the presidency. Peace, however, proved to be a tougher enterprise than war. His official life in Bogotá now became a losing battle to maintain his original vision of a single South American state. Regional, ideological, demographic, and economic rivalries of every sort soon laid siege to his leadership. In a prime instance, Venezuela's military commander José Antonio Páez, an illiterate and rude yet charismatic *caudillo*, was to spearhead separatist tendencies and at last secede from Colombia in 1830. Bolívar, reviled by the new neighboring authorities and declared persona non grata throughout Venezuela, had lost his very homeland. And in Colombia itself, factions led by Bolívar's personal and ideological rival, former vice-president Francisco de Paula Santander, ended up repeatedly outmaneuvering him. During these (and previous) years there were several assassination attempts on the Liberator, and in one close call he was saved by his mistress, Manuela Sáenz.

It is on the next, final phase of the Liberator's life that García Márquez's novel focuses. On 27 April 1830, weary of all the intrigues, Bolívar resigned from the presidency and soon set sail on the Magdalena River for European exile. In the course of his six-month journey, the Colombian Congress chose the unmemorable Joaquín Mosquera as his successor, and his friend Sucre was murdered on the way to Quito in the mountain forest of Berruecos, near Pasto. Meanwhile Bolívar had contracted tuberculosis, and on 17 December, after having reached the Atlantic coast, he died at the Quinta de San Pedro Alejandrino in Santa Marta. On his deathbed he had asked his trusted aide Gen. Daniel O'Leary to burn all his papers. O'Leary, though a good soldier, disobeyed; the archives survive to this day as a treasured primary source. Today the Quinta de San Pedro is a Bolívar museum.

As a military leader, Bolívar on occasion could be as ruthless as the worst of them. In 1818, partly in response to Royalist atrocities, he ordered hundreds of Spanish prisoners of war summarily executed. Another disturbing instance concerns Manuel Piar, among his more brilliant officers, a charming, blue-eyed mulatto from Curaçao. When Piar became implicated in anti-

Bolívar activities, the leader had him summoned. Piar fled, but, after his capture by a Bolívar aide, he was court-martialed, demoted, and shot by a firing squad.

Of Bolívar's many female companions, only Manuela Sáenz is now remembered. Bolívar met her in Quito in 1822, when he was thirty-nine and she was in her early twenties, and they eventually became long-term lovers. Illegitimate and originally from Lima, Manuela had been espoused when quite young to an English physician twice her age named James Thorne. Manuela, an extremely witty and colorful individual, was, like Bolívar, a first-rate fencer, shooter, and equestrian—in many respects his equal. She wore a dragoon uniform whenever she accompanied Bolívar in public and in time earned the popular sobriquet "La Libertadora." Bolívar for his part wrote Manuela many beautiful love letters that have since been printed and reprinted. They are filled with tenderness and passion, though he never commits himself completely to her.

Manuela not only gave the Liberator much-needed love and companionship; she would literally save his life. Whenever there were disturbances against Bolívar, she would jump into the fray, fully armed in battle gear. In the most celebrated incident, on 25 September 1828 the presidential palace was attacked by a band of conspirators led by an ambitious Venezuelan, Pedro Carujo. Bolívar was asleep, and, when first being woken up, considered fighting them personally. Manuela, by contrast, suspected the worst, and had Simón get dressed and jump out the window. Carujo and his henchmen now broke in the door and Manuela, sword in hand, faced up to them, giving Carujo false leads as he searched each room. In due time official reinforcements arrived and routed the rebels. Throughout the three-hour ordeal, Bolívar hid in the San Agustín River, under a bridge.

Manuela broke with her English husband in 1823, telling him in a respectful letter that his compatriots were too stuffy for her. When Dr. Thorne died in 1847 she was denied any inheritance. She survived Bolívar by twenty-six years, wandering in Jamaica and about the Pacific coast, and finally ended up in the port city of Paita, Peru, where she eked out an existence selling cigars and translating letters written by U.S. sailors to their Latina lovers. Among her visitors was the Italian patriot leader Giuseppe Garibaldi.

One more historical figure deserves a glance. To some extent, Bolívar's later career and posthumous reputation were shaped by Francisco de Paula Santander (1792–1840), a key ally in the Independence struggles and later the leader's chief nemesis. A lawyer by training, and an able, almost obsessive administrator, Santander was in temperament the precise opposite of Bolívar: reserved, almost pedantic, a desk man at heart, and in love with money. A convinced federalist and hence a foe of centralization, he was nonetheless designated Bolívar's vice-president in 1821. Yet he disagreed with his boss on virtually every major policy issue and intrigued against him constantly. In time Bolívar's fall from grace would be Santander's political and ideological gain. To this day, the Bolívar-Santander rivalry and schism is a major topic in Colombia's historical discussions and debates.

Many of the signal moments from these three lives are recalled and/or dramatized in the flashback portions of *The General in His Labyrinth*, notably in the later chapters, by which time we readers have come to know Bolívar and his accompanying allies.

A rough map of the Liberator's final voyage closes the Spanish editions of the novel. A somewhat improved map opens the English-language edition, though it omits the town of Tenerife, presumably a printing oversight. In order to orient readers who wish some sense of the progression and geography of the journey, here follows a brief outline of the ports of call, by chapter.[6]

> Chap. 1. Final day in Santa Fe de Bogotá, 8 May; departure by land with six close allies (for their names see chap. 2, *GSL*, 47; *GHL*, 42).
> Chap. 2. Stops and spends a night in Facatativá; another night near Guaduas; arrives at Honda.
> Chap. 3. Visits Honda; sets sail by barge after three days.
> Chap. 4. Visits and departs Mompox; debarks in and visits Zambrano; reprovisioning in Tenerife (again, omitted from the English-language map).
> Chap. 5. Two days in Barranca Nueva; twenty-nine days in Turbaco.
> Chap. 6. Arrival and sojourn in Cartagena.
> Chap. 7. Transferred to Villa de Soledad.
> Chap. 8. Travel by land; passes through Barranca de San Nicolás (modern Barranquilla) and Ciénaga Grande (Great Swamp). Travel by sea to Santa Marta; stays in the old Customs House there. Transferred to a nearby hacienda, San Pedro de Alejandrino, where he dies.

The barebones plot of *The General* is quite simple: Bolívar leaves Bogotá, ready to emigrate to Europe. With a small retinue he sails down the Magdalena River toward the Atlantic coast, making various stops along the way. In time his health weakens and he breathes his last. End of story. What will make this plot much more complex are the day-to-day details of the journey itself, in combination with the many flashbacks that add up to a retrospective—if highly selective—biography of the Liberator.

From the opening line, with Bolívar lying naked in his bathtub, we see a man who has figuratively and literally been stripped down. He is thoroughly dispirited and preparing for his final exit. He has been ousted from office; popular unrest is spreading. He will bid adieu to Manuela. Next, he and his manservant José Palacios ride past a slum, where street urchins shout out his nickname *"Longanizo"* (rendered as "Skinny Shanks," but more akin to "Sausage") and pelt him with a cow pie. Anti-Bolívar graffiti adorn many an outer wall. At some river ports he will not even be recognized by local notables or will be confused with disreputable elements. A local celebration in his honor at Honda is rained out, but he also encounters Miranda Lyndsay, the beautiful daughter of a British diplomat he had met in Jamaica (who now asks for a political favor—to get her father out of prison). Other individuals encountered en route include a son of former Mexican independence emperor Iturbide, a German hitchhiker, war widows, occasional admirers, a chauvinistic French intellectual called Diocles Atlantique, a Gallic count with his cocky-sarcastic Martinican mistress, and the bishop of Santa Marta.

The increasingly hot, humid lowlands weather disagrees with the General. His residual well-being is further eroded by the official prohibitions against Manuela's mailing him letters, and by the reports of Venezuelan secession and of Sucre's death. The sounds of birds console him somewhat, yet he also notices the ecological devastation along the way, as well as the deterioration of Cartagena. At one point he even talks about a new military push to fight Venezuela's separation—in vain, inasmuch as events have taken on a life of their own. Finally, he pens his last testament and other documents regarding future care of his relatives and retainers (of whose several fates we readers are duly informed). The General spends his last two weeks prostrate, attended by a French and a U.S. doctor, and then by Bishop Estévez for last rites, before he dies on 17 December.

Starting with chapter 2, we hear of Bolívar's past history through numerous flashbacks recalling his public life and personal experiences (these latter episodes seldom factual). Among them:

> Military campaigns; a brief fling with a mulatta slave woman, Reina María Luisa, whose freedom he purchased from her master; the plot against him by Carujo, from which Manuela saved him; the attempt on his life in a hammock in Jamaica (chap. 2).
> The fateful meeting with Humboldt in Paris (chap. 3).

The tensions with Venezuela's General Páez and with Colombian rival
   Santander; his ten nights' fling with the beauty Josefa Sagrario; his
   European years and his oath in Rome (chap. 4).
The long amour with Manuela; the Peruvian campaign (chap. 5).
The youthful lover in Lima whose bodily fuzz he thoroughly shaved off;
   General Piar's insubordination and execution (chap. 6). The General's
   relations with prelates; more military campaigns (chap. 7).
And finally, the young man's brief, tragically truncated marriage
   (chap. 8).

The General of course is fiction, and should be treated in that light. In the broadest sense it resembles such established works as Tolstoy's *The Death of Ivan Ilyich* or Carlos Fuentes's *The Death of Artemio Cruz*, both of whose central characters' final days provide a vantage point from which to look back on a life and take stock of its full trajectory. It can also be likened to García Márquez's own *Chronicle of a Death Foretold* and *The Autumn of the Patriarch*, where the respective protagonists' impending deaths serve literally as "pretexts" to recall their divers stages via a series of narrative flashbacks.

In addition the dying in this novel unfolds over a six-months' journey and thus helps structure a "road narrative." The Magdalena, it should be noted, was in 1830 the sole transport link between Colombia's central highlands and the Atlantic littoral. García Márquez, needless to say, knows the river intimately, having traveled the same route, round-trip, eleven times during his youth, and he would affectionately evoke that world of alluvial navigation in *Love in the Time of Cholera*, the Bolívar novel's immediate predecessor. Hence there is a personal, authorial tie here as well. Still, what is curious about *The General* is how little actual description it provides either of the Magdalena milieu or of the boat trip itself.

Instead, *The General* introduces select, well-placed sense-impressions of nature that serve to punctuate the journey's various stages.[7] We read of the sweet-smelling flowers in private gardens and the herds of horses on the savannah, the many violent downpours at Honda and on the river, the malignant and foul-smelling vapors of the swamp, the snow-capped peaks of the Sierra Nevada, and the rough seas on the way to Santa Marta. Similarly, as a means of fleshing out the day's ordinary details, there is much emphasis on the foods that are prepared and consumed along the way. We thus witness the sumptuous "American breakfast" shared by Bolívar with former colleagues on the day of departure, the red wine and venison stew in Guaduas, the glass of port and turtle soup in Honda, and so on. Once in a while the narrator pauses to make a list, as when the Bogotá families take advantage of sunny weather one Sunday and head for the savannah, bearing "baskets of roast suckling pig, baked brisket, blood sausage with rice, [and] potatoes with melted cheese" (*GSL*, 78; *GHL*, 72). All these combined facts of nature and cuisine help convey a river journey without having to focus on the mechanics of travel itself.

In deciding to portray via fiction so larger-than-life a figure as Bolívar, García Márquez must have faced a challenge beyond measure, one even greater than when he was figuring out how to depict his imaginary, plebeian Patriarch. Almost any extended look at the great man would have run the risk of ringing false or coming off as incomplete, and moreover would have found itself competing with the thousands of other, well-established versions that live within millions of South American minds.

García Márquez hits upon a number of artful ways in which to "frame" the character Bolívar as well as place him at a safe and manageable narrative distance. Only once, in the concluding paragraph of the first chapter, is the protagonist referred to by name—and in this case by all seven of them, in flowery, rhetorical, old-Spanish style. (The surname itself will appear just one more time, when a sad, stray dog picked up by the entourage is ironically christened by the leader as "Bolívar.") Otherwise the illustrious figure is alluded to simply, by the narrator and by other characters, as *"el General."* Moreover, in the original Spanish, a language in which subject pronouns are infrequent, the man's reported acts—the verbs—are seldom even preceded by an *"él"*—"he." In another, passing detail, Bolívar's heroic stature is already questioned when we see him leaving Bogotá without insignias and mounted not on a white steed but a mule (albeit a good one).

García Márquez's Bolívar is further situated within a geographical polarity—examined in my chapter 2—of coastal peoples vs. highlanders, of *costeños* vs. *cachacos* (though the novel contains neither word).[8] Hence, when Bolívar is at an official delegation that is seeing him off, he goes through the ceremonial motions but, we read, is "a total stranger" to "that ambiguous city" about which he has repeatedly remarked, "This isn't my theater." And regarding his speech patterns we also find out about "his Caribbean accent . . . which . . . had not softened, [and] sounded even harsher compared to the lush diction of the Andeans" (*GSL*, 41; *GHL*, 34). This early characterization places Bolívar within the regional distinctions given dramatic shape by *One Hundred Years of Solitude*.

In addition García Márquez is exceedingly cautious about how he presents his Liberator in the ever-shifting narrative arena. Throughout the book,

Bolívar is regularly accompanied, scarcely ever appears alone.[9] There are no descriptions of his face or facial gestures, and moreover we are never given so much as a glimpse of his inner life and private consciousness. Whatever intimate thoughts or feelings he may have are relayed to us through other characters' perceptions or memories of him, or are communicated via his manservant José Palacios, who functions as a kind of sounding board for the General, a squire to the knight[10] — and of course a conduit to us readers. As the faithful Palacios himself remarks early on, "Only my master knows what my master is thinking" (GSL, 22; GHL, 14).

Adding further to the author's artistic distancing of Bolívar, he utters no lengthy statements. Actually, long quotations are rare in the best of García Márquez's works (the scarce instances thereof being humorous in intent), and he largely avoids dialogue. As it happens, the format he crystallized in One Hundred Years, consisting of extensive narrative stretches interspersed with minimal speech, suits his Bolívar fiction to a T. The General talks strictly in one- or two-liners, occasional snippets that, when not plot-related or part of an encounter, fall mostly into three categories. They are sometimes laments about his current state ("I have no friends" [GSL, 15; GHL, 7]). Or they can be snipes at his enemies (on Santander: "That one's a really slippery bastard [truchimán]" [GSL, 62; GHL, 57]). And, in many an instance, the General resorts to profane language, the Spanish equivalents of the strongest, crudest, four-letter Anglo-Saxon vulgarisms — which, it must be said, sound much more authentic and even "classic" in the original Spanish. Casual outbursts of pendejo and carajos seem quite plausible from a Bolívar who is, after all, a seasoned, hardened South American soldier. As García Márquez observed in an interview, "Bolívar was a foul-mouthed Caribbean."[11]

By far, the means the author employs most frequently in order to characterize Bolívar objectively are the recorded words of Bolívar himself. According to García Márquez, virtually everything that is stated by the Liberator, or paraphrased by the narrator, comes from Bolívar's own letters or from third-party documents reporting on and remembering him. A few examples should suffice. Shortly before departing Santa Fe, Bolívar tells Manuela, "I love you a great deal, but I will love you even more if you show more judgment than ever before" (GSL, 14; GHL, 6). This comes from a letter the man wrote to his lover, dated 7 May 1830, in which he declares, "I love you a great deal, but will love you more if you now show more judgment than ever."[12] Later, toward the end, the General dictates some dark thoughts to José Laurencio Silva: "America is ungovernable, the man who serves a revolution plows the sea, this nation will fall inevitably into the hands of almost indistinguishable petty tyrants of every color and race" (*GSL*, 257; *GHL*, 257). These bleak statements are culled almost verbatim from an oft-cited letter that, on 9 November 1830, Bolívar addressed to Gen. Juan José Flores, then-president of the newly independent Ecuador.[13]

A more youthful Bolívar was an eager admirer of the United States, and he paid the country a visit on his return from Europe in 1806. He later grew disillusioned—a shift here demonstrated when the character notes to Iturbide that that new nation's "tale of liberty will end in a plague for us all" (*GSL*, 225; *GHL*, 223). The dire prediction plays on one of Bolívar's best-known opinions, conveyed by letter on 5 August 1829 to British chargé d'affaires Patrick Campbell; it reads, almost casually, "the United States, which seems destined by Providence to plague [Latin] America with miseries in the name of liberty."[14]

On occasions the author fabricates subtle human turns for the sake of drama. For example, on 20 January, Bolívar is cited as extolling Marshall Sucre as "the worthiest of generals" (*GSL* 28; *GHL*, 21). We then read of the loyal General Urdaneta feeling stung by this passing encomium for a fellow officer, and carrying the slight forever in his heart. There is no record, though, of the real Urdaneta having been affected by these formulaic words of praise, which he saw simply as a slip of the tongue.[15] On the other hand, sometimes García Márquez intermingles fact with fiction and vice versa. Virtually all of the "other women" recalled or encountered during the General's journey are made up (including the memorable Miranda Lyndsay). However, the brief dalliance with Anita Lenoit in chapter 4, which the Liberator himself denies, exists at least as an unconfirmed legend among Colombian lovers. One particularly vivid mixture can be found in the attempt on Bolívar's life in Jamaica, when a paid assassin thought he had knifed the General in his hammock but instead killed the hapless compatriot Félix Amestoy, who had chanced to be sleeping there. Where Bolívar actually was at that moment seems to be undocumented, and so García Márquez has a clever Miranda diverting the Liberator with an innocuous, humorous errand (delivering a cake), thereby saving his life.

Indeed, García Márquez's fundamental procedure in this book is to flesh out real incidents for which actual, full documentation is slight. Of Bolívar's brief stopover in Veracruz, for instance, next to nothing is known. And so, in a flashback in chapter 7, García Márquez assigns to the sixteen-year-old traveler a two-month visit to Mexico City, in which, over a couple of exquisitely wrought pages, the imperial capital's clear air, resplendent canals, and public markets with exotic wares (armadillos, river worms, grasshoppers) are wondrously, poetically evoked. And of course, as the author himself has noted, for Bolívar's last trip the available personal information is scarce, with perhaps three of the Liberator's letters extant. Such a gap in knowledge is precisely what García Márquez takes advantage of to dream up the journey's surrounding affective, human, and narrative details, without any danger of being upstaged or challenged by the harder, solid facts of history.

One immediate source for this historical fiction is, reportedly, another fiction: a short story—actually a preliminary sketch for a novel—called "El último rostro" (His Final Countenance), by the author's close friend and compatriot, the writer Álvaro Mutis. García Márquez indeed starts out his concluding "Gratitudes" ("My Thanks") by signaling Mutis's sketch as the inspiration for *The General in His Labyrinth*. Scarcely fifteen pages in length, and purportedly discovered at a London auction in the 1940s, "El ultimo rostro" contains a fragment of an alleged diary kept by a Polish colonel and veteran of Napoleon's wars named Miecislaw Napierski. The supposed manuscript's entries, dated 29 June through 10 July 1830, add up to an account from Colonel Napierski about a dispiriting visit to Cartagena in the company of Bolívar on the final leg of his journey.

Unlike García Márquez's novel, Mutis's first draft refers to Bolívar by name from the outset, devotes nearly a paragraph to describing the Liberator's face and hands, and treats us readers to lengthy, disillusioned disquisitions from Bolívar's lips. *The General in His Labyrinth*, in turn, alludes to Mutis's unfinished draft by inserting in chapter 6 a visit by Napierski with his journal, which, the narrator notes, "a great New Granadian poet would recover for history one hundred eighty years later" (*GSL*, 194; *GHL*, 190–91). The novel, moreover, is dedicated to Mutis, who is generously credited with giving García Márquez "the idea for writing this book."

The factual accuracy of García Márquez's novel with respect to historical references is a trait typically noted by scholars and critics of his work. The author made every effort to clear his manuscript of any possible anachronisms. In an almost humorous example, he remarks in his afterword that he originally had shown Bolívar eating mangoes, but later needed to change it on finding out that, back then, the fruit had not yet been introduced in Colombia. (On the other hand, at one point in chapter 4 the narrator highlights "the aluminum light of noon" [*GSL*, 108; *GHL*, 102])—an unlikely comparison, given that aluminum was still under development in the laboratory and would not be commercially produced until the 1860s.)

The narrative voice prevailing throughout García Márquez's book is that of a concerned, late-twentieth-century Hispanic man of letters who has transposed himself to 1830 and there assumed the role of dispassionate (though not detached) observer. There are nonetheless certain issues raised in *The General* that, though legitimate and true enough, function rather as projections of twentieth-century concerns onto Bolívar's times. A digression on artistic renderings of the Liberator observes that earlier representations were faithful to his mixed-blood ancestry; but as the leader's posthumous fame grew, the artists "began to idealize him, washing his blood, mythologizing him until they established him in official memory with the Roman profile of his statues" (*GSL*, 184; *GHL*, 180). (Having recently seen an 1839 portrait by Antonio Salas that depicts Bolívar still as a dark-skinned *mestizo*, I can attest to the difference.) In our time, of course, to question white racism is commonplace, but to do so in the nineteenth century was well-nigh unthinkable. Similarly, while facing Dr. Gastelbondo, Bolívar lashes out at foreign debt as a burden to national independence, saying, "I despise debt more than I do the Spaniards . . . [D]ebt will destroy us in the end" (*GSL*, 222; *GHL*, 221). Although the critique may be an actual quotation, the crippling consequences of debt would emerge as a point of contention only in twentieth-century polemical literature.

Some Europeans have looked upon the young Latin American republics with a certain condescension — which some Latin Americans, in turn, resent. The lengthy encounter between the French traveler Diocles Atlantique (his surname is suggestive) and the General serves to highlight this split in a dramatic, almost "allegorical" way. When Monsieur Atlantique subtly questions Bolívar's thought and policies, the latter is shown, for over two pages, citing instance upon instance of a violent, barbaric, unjust Europe. He concludes his rebuttal by saying, "So . . . don't attempt to teach how we should be, . . . don't try to have us do well in twenty years what you've done badly in two thousand. . . . Dammit, please let us have our Middle Ages in peace!" (*GSL*, 129–30; *GHL*, 120).

In sum, white-skin prejudice, foreign debt, and Europe's arrogance are issues that seem more suitable for discussion in 1989 than in 1830. Still, *The General in His Labyrinth* is not unique in this respect. Historical novels such as Tolstoy's *War and Peace* and E. L. Doctorow's *Ragtime* also revive the events of past generations via the preoccupations, the lens, of their authors' immediate present — and their works indeed gain from the perspective.

At only one brief juncture does the novel's serenely poised and objective point of view become an explicitly collective voice speaking for an entire people and their ill-fated history. When General Urdaneta stages a coup d'état at the start of chapter 7, the narrator refers to it as "the first of the forty-nine civil wars we would suffer in what remained of the century" (*GSL*, 201; *GHL*, 199). Assuming just once the first-person plural, García Márquez here links the aftermath of the fall of Bolívar to the sequel of military conflict and instability that came to characterize his native land.

Though in some degree personal, such interpolations also grow directly and naturally out of Colombia's history. And conversely, whenever sources allow, the author is true to the documentary facts of the case, all the way down to the men who attend to Bolívar in his final days. The Doctors Révérend, (Mac)Night, and Gastelbondo (referred to as Gasterbond by one historian),[16] the visitor Colonel Luis Perú de Lacroix, Bishop Estévez (who administers last rites), and Spaniard Joaquín de Mier (in whose mansion the General expires) are all well-documented figures. It is the humble folk, their existence preserved by no extensive records, whom the author has had to invent. The cause of Bolívar's death is left unspecified, presumably to reflect the uncertain state of medical science at the time, though today's doctors would infer tuberculosis.[17]

Owing to the nature of the action depicted, *The General in His Labyrinth* does not build on the rigorous structural symmetries typical of the author's previous major works. For similar reasons of subject matter, neither does it present thematically arranged chapters that ignore chronological sequence and instead flatten time into a kind of spatial collage. Indeed, for the very first time in his fiction, García Márquez in this book furnishes the precise years and dates of events.

Still, being a conscientious craftsman, the novelist utilizes various other organizing tools. The many flashbacks tend to be triggered when a port of call brings to mind Bolívar's previous experiences there. Moreover, as Seymour Menton points out, in each of the eight chapters Bolívar is shown either coughing, running a fever, vomiting blood, breaking wind, afflicted with headaches, or losing weight and height.[18] On the other hand, in every chapter there is also the recollection of at least one former romantic encounter with a woman. These are the logical building blocks with which to construct a novel about a terminally ill patient who has also lived numerous amours. They represent current bodily dying along with the erotic vitality of yore.

Several García Márquez scholars have noted parallels between *The General* and his previous works. The Bolívar book tells of "the autumn of a patriarch" whose "chronicled" death is already known, if not exactly "foretold." Its last lines recall the ending of his dictator novel, and the liturgical phrase "por los siglos de los siglos" ("for ever and ever")[19] — itself echoing the final words of the Spanish version of the Catholic prayer, the *Gloria patri* (in English, "world without end")—harks back to the closing sentence of his great short story "Big Mama's Funeral." And like so much of García Márquez's writing, *The General* deals with issues of political power.

In many ways, though, the Bolívar project constitutes a radical departure from García Márquez's customary and familiar artistry. It is the only novel in which he acknowledges the background documentation and the individuals who helped him with research—in addition to providing the map and the chronology. And of course it's a narrative very much involved with unvarnished fact and day-to-day reality, albeit from another era. As Larry Rohter observes, whereas García Márquez had previously transformed the ordinary into something mythical, here he "renders a mythical figure as a man of ordinary attributes."[20]

When *The General in His Labyrinth* first appeared, it quickly became throughout much of Latin America a "must-read, the subject of countless café, dinner party and television round-table discussions,"[21] with attitudes ranging across the spectrum. As one might expect, the book sparked fervid debate among historians, especially those in the Academia Colombiana de Historia, some of whom (including the eminent writer Germán Arciniegas) adjudged the novel "irreverent" and repudiated it for showing both a Bolívar in constant pursuit of women and a Liberator with a body laid to waste by disease and pain. Rohter similarly quotes Carlos Ramos, a Salvadoran journalist living in Mexico: "By writing this book, García Márquez has stripped Latin Americans of one of the few heroes we have," yet also admitting that he enjoyed reading it.[22] The novel was enough of an event for Belisario Betancur, President of Colombia (1982–86), to issue his own reflections, seeing in its pages an "inexhaustible feeling of emptiness, of lack of direction and of fear in the face of the incoherencies we suffer and inflict on others."[23] Fidel Castro, for his part, lauded the work for its "pagan" image of the Liberator.[24]

García Márquez, then, has done an admirable job of "humanizing" Bolívar, of affectionately bringing the great man down to earth as had never been done before. For so singular an achievement the novel will long be remembered, in particular by the educated denizens of Colombia and the neighboring region. After having read *The General in His Labyrinth*, one cannot *think* of Simón Bolívar, or encounter his name or a picture or a statue of him, without the Gabo version welling up as a major response, a counter-model, in one's mind.

Precisely because of the book's topic, methods, and purposes, however, there are in it no "magical" moments, and the Colombian fabulist's renowned wit and bawdy humor are conspicuously absent, other than in Bolívar's own brief interventions and escapades. Some of the flashbacks at times read like straight biography, prompting critic John Leonard's observation that, "What we get here is information instead of art."[25] Moreover, García Márquez leaves out from his revisionist account two highly important yet less savory moments in Bolívar's life: the repudiation of fellow patriot Francisco de Miranda in 1812 and the mysterious private meeting with San Martín, in Guayaquil, in 1822. This pair of episodes does not reflect well on the real-life Liberator; they show him to be not just sinned against but sinner too. By omitting them, the author tilts the scales ever so slightly in favor of the national hero. From this warts-and-all portrait, a few warts are missing.

The General in His Labyrinth, one must finally concede, does lack somewhat in the signal literary virtues of its creator, and for such reasons the novel can ultimately leave a bit of a flat impression. In addition, for those not raised within the daunting shadow of the Bolivarian myth, the book loses political and especially emotional impact. The very subject matter of *The General* makes it García Márquez's most strictly *local* work of fiction, and hence not a work for those non-Colombian or non-Venezuelan readers just venturing into his rich, imagined universe. *Caveat lector.*

TWELVE

The Unending Love Story

Well into his sixties and seventies García Márquez continued his narrative explorations of the subject of male-female attraction and love. The result was two brief yet luminous novels that push the customary boundaries of romantic experience, plumbing hitherto unknown emotional depths and coming up with some strange surprises along the way.

García Márquez's earlier love novels, we saw in chapter 10, all tell of romantic amours with a difference. His are not the fables of handsome-fellow-meets-and-weds-attractive-young-lady, the standard stuff of countless classic novels and formulaic films. In "Eréndira" the author openly spoofs the old fairy-tale plot of courtship and happily-ever-after. In *Chronicle of a Death Foretold* he explodes the expected outcome for the newlyweds, giving their postnuptial future new twists beyond imagining. And in *Love in the Time of Cholera* the central couple unites only when well into their seventies. In these works, the various familiar love story conventions are mercilessly parodied and subverted. And yet, in the end, the *emotion* of love is what is most powerful, most authentic of all.

The writer's two latter-day novels of romance, *Of Love and Other Demons* (1994) and *Memories of My Melancholy Whores* (2004), bring with them yet another slant on the male-female story. Both of them depict an amorous entanglement that emerges between an older man and an early-adolescent girl. (They have a passing precedent in the tragic liaison between the septuagenarian Florentino and the youthful schoolgirl América Vicuña toward the end of *Love in the Time of Cholera*.) In this regard both of the later works inevitably suggest parallels with Nabokov's *Lolita*, a book that, in 1957, set the model and the template for any such imagined alliances.

Unlike most of García Márquez's previous major works, *Of Love and Other Demons* drew relatively little fanfare when it first appeared. While the initial printing of 100,000 copies sold out within weeks and the reviews were, as expected, glowing, there was precious little of the excitement that had accompanied *The Autumn of the Patriarch* or *Love in the Time of Cholera*. One possible reason was simple public fatigue. His Nobel Prize was in the past; and the attentions lavished on the author and on his various literary and political activities had played themselves out. With the sudden end of the Cold War and of the bloody conflicts in Central America, moreover, García Márquez's provocative stances had been rendered somewhat less newsworthy among his ideological allies and his detractors both.

Yet another factor in the diminished attention may have been the book's recondite contents. Set in Cartagena during the twilight years of Spain's empire, it fleshes out in some detail such subjects as black slavery, African folk-beliefs and religious practices, church-state relations, Catholic hierarchy politics, and, most tellingly, an intense amour between a love-struck thirty-six-year-old Jesuit cleric and an alienated twelve-year-old girl. These are not matters that most book critics—foreign, non-Hispanic ones in particular— might feel able to discuss comfortably or authoritatively.

Deceptively short, *Of Love* is quite complex and multilayered, with a varied cast of characters, a broad experiential range, and numerous flashbacks. Moreover it is the first García Márquez novel to start with a preface—an untitled, italicized, three-page remembrance that serves to introduce the action. In it the author recalls a demolition job on a Clarissan convent in Cartagena, in 1949, where work crews have found the tombs of colonial personages, several of whom we will soon be reading about: the bishop, the abbess, the Marquis, and the latter's first wife. This liminal account culminates with the workmen's discovery of twenty-two meters (sixty-five feet) of copper-colored hair from the head of a dead child named Sierva María de Todos los Angeles. The author ends his evocation with his own grandmother's recollections of such a legendary, long-haired, aristocratic little girl—a tale that he signals as inspiration for the narrative to follow.

Time in *Of Love and Other Demons* is a constant zigging and zagging. Here is the main plot, followed next by flashback portions.

At a market, while accompanied by a servant, twelve-year-old Sierva María is bitten by a black dog. The girl, who had been born prematurely and was then unloved and neglected by her Marquis father and mixed-blood (*mestiza*) mother, grew up mostly in the slaves' quarters, there learning to dance before she could talk and then picking up three African languages. She remained illiterate and innumerate. Dominga Adviento, a slave who served as her surrogate mother, promised not to cut the youngster's hair until the day of her wedding. Her biological father, now somewhat concerned about the dog bite, takes her for treatment to several white medics, whose remedies only worsen her condition. He's then summoned by the local bishop, who believes Sierva María to be possessed by demons and officially orders her transferred to a cell at the convent of the nuns of Santa Clara. When first confined, she hardly speaks and fights back if bothered or attacked, yet once again finds solace with the black folks who work there.

The bishop's librarian, Cayetano Delaura, who has already dreamt of Sierva María before knowing her, is charged with the task of exorcising her demons. During his visits in her cell she is physically hostile to him. But Cayetano, entertaining doubts about the alleged possession, is soon in love with the prisoner. Over time, he wins her heart, partly by reciting romantic poems of Garcilaso to her. Eventually he happens upon an old tunnel leading from outside the convent to Sierva's quarters. They take to seeing each other secretly at nights, hugging and kissing, though never consummating their passion—and hoping for a legitimate future bond. She suggests they flee; he (foolishly) insists on pursuing legal means. Alas, the tunnel one day is discovered, and Sierva María is moved to another cell. A frustrated Cayetano in turn loses control over himself and is publicly condemned to work and cohabit with the chronically sick. Sierva, abandoned, facing losses on all fronts, and with her head having been shaved, is finally found emaciated and "dead of love" on her cell bed.

Like all of García Márquez's major works, *Of Love* features flashbacks and subplots aplenty. In addition, to an extent that is unusual for the author, it is populated by a wide array of vivid, fully drawn, memorable characters who stand out as much as do the two lovers. These other personages are far more than "secondary"; they fill out the immediate as well as broader contexts of the amour, providing necessary information for readers to understand the main plot, which in itself occupies only about a fourth of the entire book.

Let us for starters consider the family, the parents of which constitute a self-contained, grotesque soap opera in themselves.

The father, Don Ygnacio de Alfaro y Dueñas, second Marquis of Casalduero. He grew up a slow, sickly, scared child. His first female interest during adolescence was Dulce Olivia, an inmate at the insane asylum next door to the family palace. Ygnacio's father, to "rescue" him, sent him off to stay on the family haciendas, but the boy was horrified by country life. Later, seeking prestige, the elder Marquis forced his son to marry a Spaniard, doña Olalla de Mendoza, who on a group outing was unfortunately fulminated by lightning. Decades hence, the widower Ygnacio was pursued and raped in a hammock by Bernarda Cabrera, daughter of a socially ambitious foreman who, when she got pregnant, literally shotgunned the second Marquis into marriage. The couple frankly hated one another and were utterly indifferent to their lovely child.

The mother, Bernarda Cabrera. She ended up conducting a long-term, torrid affair with her handsome, bought slave, Judas Iscariote. After his death she would sate her lust with any black man she could. In the meantime she prospered through the trade in slaves, and later in flour shipments. Now the crisis with her daughter has her worried about gossip; she departs for the countryside. During her absence Ygnacio attempts to win back the affections of the asylum inmate, Dulce Olivia, an initially idyllic re-encounter that ends in a vicious quarrel. Then he takes off to woo Bernarda, but she openly confesses to him the fact of her countless bedmates and her loathing for her life. (He leaves silently; his vulture-consumed remains are found two years hence.) With her many vices — her breaking wind, her addiction to chocolate, and more — Bernarda is one of the truly repulsive female characters in literature. Her first name echoes that of Bernarda Alba, the joyless, tyrannical materfamilias in García Lorca's last play, though she's far more repugnant.

Sierva María. Given this desolate family background, that the child turns out as she does has a sad, wrenching logic to it. Shunted aside and given precious little education (which she resists anyway), Sierva has become in some measure a feral, unsocialized child, unfit to live in the Creole milieu of which, by virtue of her skin color, she is nominally a member. And while both parents feel some remorse over her confinement and Ygnacio suddenly decides to be an attentive father, by then it is too late. The African slaves, by contrast, have long offered her reliable company, affection, a sense of belonging, and a rich cultural environment. *Of Love* may not be, strictly speaking, a "psychological" novel or a book about child rearing. Yet it shows, via an almost exemplary case, what can go wrong when a youngster grows up unloved, even despised, at home. As Cayetano observes to the bishop in a very modern, enlightened, and then-subversive comment, "[W]hat seems demonic to us are the customs of the blacks, learned by the girl as a result of the neglect her parents kept her in" (*DA*, 120; *OL*, 91; translation altered slightly).

Don Ygnacio "rotting in his hammock" represents a Creole aristocracy existing "one thousand three hundred nautical leagues from a king who had never heard his [Ygnacio's] name" (*DA*, 65–66; *OL*, 47). Ever fearful of being murdered by his slaves, he keeps them at bay with his herds of mastiffs about the palace. Bernarda and her aggressively, upwardly mobile father, for their part, stand for the "shopkeeper aristocracy" ("aristocracia de mostrador") that compensates for the lack of a local bourgeoisie. Outside of this chronically dysfunctional upper-class family, the bulk of events takes place under the absolute sway of the church — its Catholic doctrines, ecclesiastical might, and diverse individual members — whose cast of characters is as follows:

Bishop Don Toribio de Cáceres y Virtudes
Josefa Miranda, Abbess of the Clarissan convent
Father Tomás de Aquino Narváez
Martina Laborde, convent prisoner

The bishop. The preeminent force in this constellation. His second sur-name—"Virtudes"—hints at a high moralism. (Also, a "y" in Spanish double last names usually denotes blue blood.) An army lieutenant in his youth, now an enormous hulk who, from his throne, inspires an almost magical awe, he is "weighty" in both senses of the word. He sounds very like a bishop when issuing pronouncements, such as his judgment on the Indies: "[A] kingdom menaced by sodomy, idolatry, and anthropophagy. Like the land of the Moors" (*DA*, 103; *OL*, 78). Unforgiving, and obsessed with the idea of Sierva María's demonic possession, he, speaking for church and Inquisition, is the one who ultimately determines her terrible fate even after the Vice-roy's doctors have examined her and seen no sign of rabies. In certain ways a perceptive and even wise man—he reluctantly grants that Galileo was right about Earth's rotation and provisionally tolerates librarian Cayetano's emo-tional attraction toward "the girl"—as high prelate he nonetheless stands for church control and dictates that a dangerous Sierva must be locked up and "exorcised."

Josefa Miranda. Farther down in the hierarchy yet more unbearably author-itarian. Born in the Peninsular town of Burgos, itself a bulwark of religious traditionalism, she is a harsh, austere, resentful, power-hungry woman who denies all legitimacy both to the local bishopric and the Creole aristocracy, dismissing the latter as "gutter nobility." For her own reasons she challenges the bishop about Sierva's presence at the cloister. She construes the mysteri-ous death of the venerable Father Tomás de Aquino Narváez (see below) as one more sign of "demonic animosity" toward the nunnery. (Interestingly, when Cayetano suggests privately to the bishop that *she*, Josefa, is the one truly possessed, his boss all but agrees.) Where Bernarda Cabrera is bound-less, worldly spite, and Bishop Toribio is lofty, vested, Olympian might, Ab-bess Josefa is meanness incarnate, decked in spiritual garb.

Father Narváez. His given names are the Spanish version of "Thomas Aqui-nas," the most renowned medieval theologian and philosopher, a quotation from whom serves as epigraph to the novel. He represents another, more open and more humane sector within the powerful Holy Church. Notwith-standing his severe, past prosecutions of European heretics and pagans, he now lives among the local black slaves and knows their languages. Gallantly he restores to Sierva her African necklaces; speaks to her in Yoruba, Congo, and Mandinga; treats her with tenderness; and wins her over. She in response shows him a sweet side that surprises even the abbess. The heroine thus acquires an ally who might have given her support and understanding and saved her from the very worst. Alas, the good father's unresolved demise (one of the many intentional loose ends in the book) deprives her of any possible relief or respite.

Martina Laborde. Another dissident element within the religious community. Sierva's next-door neighbor at the convent. In the original Spanish version she is characterized as a "vulneraria," a technical term denoting a person of the cloth accused of murder. A former nun herself, she's serving a life sentence for allegedly having knifed to death two fellow residents, though she claims innocence. Cayetano during a visit notes that she is physically unattractive, even grotesque. And yet Martina is a charismatic presence — the priest further observes that "her seductive power was a material current that could be felt at once" (*DA*, 122; *OL*, 93). Her surname hints both at French origins and the Spanish word for "edge," suggesting some marginality within the world she inhabits.

Martina is the only inmate of the cloister to give comfort and support to Sierva María, teaching her embroidery and providing much-needed company. A lonely Martina for her part finds hope and solace in the young girl's "demons," the African ones included, and when Sierva suffers one of her "demoniacal" attacks, it is the accused murderess who calms her down. In a terrible irony, Martina's unexpected flight, via the same tunnel utilized by Cayetano to meet with his beloved, is a fatal blow to her protégée and — inasmuch as she has neglected to seal the tunnel's entrance — deals the coup de grâce to the clandestine romance as well.

The above characters (in addition to Cayetano, discussed below) serve to represent the various aspects and spaces of official, late colonial life: the convent with its gardens, kitchens, and cells; the ever-threatening Inquisition and its surveillance; the stunted intellectual milieu and the somehow less than fully effective prohibitions; the delicate, complex relations between church and viceroyalty; the works of charity with the infirm; and the ultimate power of the episcopal seat. At the same time, we get from these venues an impression of decay. The bishop's palace is in ruins, its grounds overgrown with weeds. The enormous bishop is usually seen either seated on a throne or reclining in a hammock, his speech undermined by the irregular breathing and coughs of asthma.[1]

Similarly, the palace of the Marquis is "a melancholy ruin" with "large empty spaces and . . . many objects out of place" (*DA*, 19; *OL*, 10). The dilapidation is further stressed during Ygnacio's last-ditch effort at winning back Bernarda at the rural hacienda, a place also "in ruins," with plants breaking through the floors, "chairs devoured by termites," a broken clock, and dust-filled air (*OL*, 140; *DA*, 180). Some hopes are raised halfway through the action with the arrival of a new viceroy, appointed by the new Bourbon reformers then at work in Madrid, but the bishop easily overrides the man's more worldly, up-to-date vision. The spiritual authority thus holds greater sway and can trump the crown's very deputy, yet both religious and secular power present an image of physical and psychological decrepitude, as befits a system that is in its final decades and will be swept away by the emerging forces of the Enlightenment—to be led by, among others, Simón Bolívar.

Abrenuncio de Sa Pereira Cao. Standing thoroughly outside the established church and Creole elite, Abrenuncio is a Portuguese Jew (thus twice an outsider), settled in Cartagena to evade the long reach of Peninsular law and prejudice. The best-known physician in the city. He employs treatments that his peers deem unorthodox but that nonetheless have proved effective, such as playing a harp at the bedside of the sick (in a word, music therapy). A local mouthpiece of rising Enlightenment thought, he sees no difference between African and Catholic exorcisms, save that Christian methods are more brutal and murderous. His personal library, one of the town's best, contains the banned works of Voltaire—symbols of his erudition and his defiance of Inquisitorial control. He diagnoses, rightly, that Sierva by now is probably free of any health risks, due to the time elapsed and the location of the dog bite. And he deplores the use of exorcisms in "curing" the girl.

At one point Abrenuncio even intuits (as a Dr. Freud later might have) that Cayetano has shown up for a visit solely out of a need to pour out his grief about Sierva—a need for a talking cure, as it were. Frankly admitting to being an atheist (like many of his contemporaries in France, the *philosophes*), Abrenuncio also sees in Cayetano a potentially free intellect to whom he can loan subversive texts (including Voltaire in Latin). His avowed indifference to sexuality is appropriate for a man fully committed to the exercise of reason. The last words he will speak in the book, even as he reflects in Cayetano's presence on "the religion of death," are that "the only essential thing is to be alive" (*DA*, 188; *OL*, 145). Abrenuncio thus stands as a serene counterweight to, an intelligent and absolute negation of, the society whose margins he inhabits. His true country, in the long term, is the future.

Father Cayetano. By far the most complex character in *Of Love*, Cayetano is first introduced in passing as the bishop's aide during the Marquis's episcopal visit in chapter 2. He comes into his own as a full-fledged male protagonist only in chapter 3, halfway through the book, at which point he is identified as *Cayetano* Alcino del Espíritu Santo *Delaura* y Escudero. His two principal names, one scholar argues, may allude to the Catholic reformer St. Cajetan of Thiens (1480–1547), who as a youth maintained a correspondence with an Augustinian nun, *Laura* Mignani, and even paid her a mysterious visit in 1523 at the Santa Croce monastery where she was cloistered.[2] Other commentators have seen in Cayetano's surname a clear echo of the Laura immortalized by Petrarch in his love sonnets. It bears mention that, in Spanish, "Cayetano" is not that unusual a handle; there was in the 1950s a jaunty Caribbean pop tune with "Cayetano" in its title, and among the leaders of the Salvadoran insurgency in the 1970s and '80s was a seasoned fighter named Cayetano Carpio.

García Márquez's Cayetano, born to and raised by a Creole mother in Spain, will eventually succeed in understanding his mother's nostalgic longings for her native New Granada. A serious intellect, like the Portuguese doctor, he has already built up under the bishop's auspices yet another of the top libraries in the Indies. Fittingly, his life's ambition is to achieve the post of librarian at the Vatican, and indeed he is one of three candidates for the job before his fall from ecclesiastical grace. Though educated at Salamanca, a center of theological training and orthodoxy, he appears scarcely interested in doctrinal issues and even less so in power or control. As a seminary student he had actually read, without realizing it, the *Amadís of Gaul*—a chivalric novel, the best-known instance of the genre, mercilessly spoofed by Cervantes's *Don Quixote* and banned in Spain's colonies. Given all the contending influences on his being, it is not surprising that, at an important juncture, Cayetano can admit to Abrenuncio, "At my age . . . I am no longer certain where I came from. Or what I am" (*DA*, 147; *OL*, 110).

What turns Cayetano's existence around, of course, is his falling hopelessly in love (or whatever one decides to call it) with Sierva María. From their first encounter he puts up with the girl's violent rejections, and he finally wins her over with patience, tenderness, and poetry recitations. The cultured cleric's ardent and unconsummated passion stands among literature's great depictions of genuine, obsessive, all-giving yet tragically illicit love. And his opting not to flee with Sierva when she urges it bespeaks a stubborn and foolish attachment to church rules and practices. As one scholar observes, "Cayetano's sin is not that he loved too much, but that he failed to love when it counted."[3] In the end, Delaura has lost both his true beloved and his elevated status as a man of books.

But the character for which and thanks to whom *Of Love and Other Demons* exists is the lithe and enigmatic Sierva María. Unforgettable with her knee-length, copper-colored hair and her clear eyes, perfect teeth, and shapely, about-to-flower physique, she is almost fairy-tale-like in her beauty. Other-worldly and ethereal, she is at the same time no shrinking violet, no helpless waif. When, at the convent, some novices attempt to rip away at her African necklaces, she fights back, biting as a threatened viper would; later, when going behind a tree to urinate, she brandishes a stick to fend off any beasts. Perfectly capable of slaughtering a goat for an African ritual, Sierva María will become beast-like herself when the horrific exorcising siege pushes her to the brink.

For all her vitality and strength, Sierva María is nonetheless the absolute victim of her dominant, Creole milieu—victimized first by her squalid, infra-human, upper-class parents, and finally by the nuns and bishop of the church. At the end she further succumbs as a tragic victim to chance and circumstance; with the demise of Father Aquino, the closing of the tunnel, and the fall of Cayetano, she will die wrenchingly abandoned and alone. The only sector in which, when alive and healthy, she moves comfortably and feels "at home" is that of the slaves, assuming with them the name "María Mandinga." (The African element in the book will be examined below.) Her given name sums up her dual identity: "María" for the illusory Iberian-Catholic background, "Sierva" for the servants who function as the young girl's "family."

Despite the vividly dramatic nature of her role, throughout the book Sierva María remains largely remote and mysterious, a cipher. In the first half of the narrative she is quoted exactly twice, and both instances convey untruths. When Dr. Cao, while examining her injury, asks if she has fallen, she says, "From the swing" (DA, 45; OL, 31). Later, in chapter 3, in reply to the black servants who inquire about her wound, she states, "My mother did it with a knife" (DA, 86; OL, 64–65). In the second half of the novel, Sierva's third direct quotation, in rejoinder to Martina's query about her confinement, is also untrue, albeit now presumably gleaned from the church exorcism of her: "I have a devil inside" (DA, 112; OL, 86).

Only with the caring, selfless treatment of Cayetano does Sierva María begin to express herself more freely and frankly. About the cruller given to her by the priest, she notes, "It tastes like swallow shit!" And, laughing "for the first time" on seeing Delaura's own wound, she declares, "I'm worse than the plague" (DA, 114; OL, 87). As their unique relationship evolves, she will start holding real conversations with her loving suitor.

Her alienation notwithstanding, Sierva María is seldom depicted by herself, appearing regularly in others' company instead. Moreover, in a characterization technique we noted in *The General in His Labyrinth*, her personal thoughts and innermost being remain out of reach to us. There are three brief exceptions to the pattern, two of them slight and perfunctory. The first is when some novices leave Sierva sitting momentarily on a bench, at which point she gets up to sip some water from a cistern and then goes behind a tree to pee. Next comes the initial night in her isolation cell, where the narrator focuses not on her solitary psyche but on the awful convent food and on the sounds of the sea outside. Sierva María's single major episode all alone is her dying scene, yet the action is conveyed obliquely, in a summary sort of way. Finally, in the concluding paragraph she is described as dreaming of a snowy landscape as seen through a window, where she consumes a bunch of golden grapes—a dream cited previously in the novel, now somewhat transformed, and the only intimate thought of Sierva María's ever made visible to us. Otherwise she exists as an alien, all but unattainable presence—as she must indeed appear to her many Creole associates, Cayetano included.

What gives the barely adolescent Sierva María a glimpse of possible salvation, and her devoted Cayetano a taste of extramural, earthly joys, is, of course, the passionate feeling that emerges and evolves between the two of them over a period of a couple of months (at most). García Márquez in these pages far surpasses his amorous evocations from writings past, and achieves heights of simply wondrous beauty. We see Cayetano become thoroughly consumed by emotion, tolerate Sierva's spitting and scratching at him, yet finally gain her affections via every means from bringing her candy to teaching her basic literacy. And we see a slowly yet surely tamed Sierva María reach a state of high bliss wherein she will present to her constant suitor her cherished Oddúa necklace, recite love lyrics to him in return, and keep her cell clean besides. From the moment he first kisses her lips, they discover together, as one, the raptures and pleasures of physical (however incomplete) intimacy.

Indeed, the evolving relationship between Cayetano and Sierva follows the standard love story conventions. There is the suitor's initial fascination with a beautiful female, love almost at first sight (an attraction further reinforced when, in "ecstasy," he watches her, in regal garb, posing for a portrait). There is Cayetano's simple, unembellished declaration of love. There is a stormy, push-pull, clandestine courtship in which, as often happens, she resists him. There is their first kiss, followed soon thereafter by his "anticipating the happy day when they would be free and married" (*DA*, 167; *OL*, 128). There is the exchange of gifts—the poetry, the necklace. (He even brings candy.) And there are the nights of sheer bliss. But alas, Cayetano's long-term marital hopes are not to be—the rest of the story is about their ties' tragic deterioration, all due to circumstance. (Not coincidentally, the undoing of their great romance occurs in counterpoint with the lonely Marquis's woeful attempts at reconciliation, first with mad Dulce Olivia, then with a depraved Bernarda.)

In telling of so powerful an amour—which, surprisingly, takes up less than ten pages of the entire work—García Márquez taps into the traditions of what is known as courtly love. This literary current first appeared and flourished among Provençal troubadours of the eleventh century and remained capable of inspiring artists over the next millennium. In the courtly love narrative, a male suitor submits to his lady (much as does a vassal to his feudal lord), who in turn makes unusual demands on the would-be lover and can even be cruel and distant to him. The sentiment, passionate and intense, aims ultimately at the fusion of the lovers, even if the cherished goal is never to be achieved. The lady indeed may sometimes be already married and thus unavailable for lifelong companionship. Still, the feelings aim neither at the common run of matrimony nor at the practical purpose of procreation. In all, it adds up to a kind of religion of love.

C. S. Lewis, one of the leading scholars of courtly love, sums up in five sentences certain aspects of the tradition that could have been written to describe Cayetano:

> The lover must be truthful and modest, a good Catholic, clean in his speech, hospitable, and ready to return good for evil. He must be courageous in war (unless he is a clerk) and generous of his gifts. He must at all times be courteous. . . . The rule of secrecy in love . . . is strongly enforced. . . . But perhaps no rule is made clearer than that which excludes love from the marriage relation.[4]

Yet another literary topic to be discerned in the Sierva-Cayetano bond is that of the *Liebestod*, literally "love-death": the tragic demise of one or both of a pair or lovers, a loss that, paradoxically, can render their love eternal. The emotion will not turn stale, banal, or ordinary, nor will it degenerate into ambivalence, indifference, or hate, inasmuch as the fact and memory of pure Eros will live on as the most potent reality. We see this in such vivid instances as *Romeo and Juliet* and in the final, illicit love affair between Amaranta Úrsula and Aureliano Babilonia in *One Hundred Years of Solitude*. The libretto of Wagner's *Tristan and Isolde* dramatizes, through its eponymous protagonists, the courtly love plot, and moreover the work gave currency to the German composer's idea and term, *Liebestod*. Though Sierva María dies terribly forsaken and unaware of Cayetano's inability to meet with her again, their star-crossed love stays in the mind of the reader precisely because it ends at the very peak of their mutual passion.

Throughout many of the love scenes Cayetano recites lyric verse to Sierva María. The poems he quotes are by Garcilaso de la Vega (1500?–36), the great author-cum-soldier who is credited with founding Spanish Renaissance poetry. Garcilaso, though married, fell in love at one point with a Portuguese lady named Isabel Frayre, who herself had a husband; she died young in childbirth. It is generally assumed that Isabel was in some way the muse and inspiration for Garcilaso's many love lyrics, which tell of combined devotion and suffering in terms familiar to us from courtly love traditions. Perhaps not coincidentally, Garcilaso—from whom the amorous priest claims direct descent—died sometime near his thirty-sixth birthday, the same age at which Cayetano discovers love and loses both it and his high standing.

The beautiful ending to chapter 3 contains, in close succession, two passages from Garcilaso. The first of them, however, is somewhat deceptive: "Bien puedes hacer esto con quien pueda sufrillo" ("Well canst thou do this to one who might endure it" [DA, 114; OL, 87]).[5] These words come not from a sonnet; nor are they addressed to a loved one. Rather they are from the third of three Canciones that tell about being imprisoned on an island in the Danube (as indeed befell the hapless poet). In addition García Márquez alters the original text, which is structured as two short, separate lines, and actually reads, "Bien *pueden* hacer esto / *en* quien *puede* sufrillo" ("Well can *they* do this / To he who *can* endure it"). One could say in justification of the poetic choice that its autobiographical context corresponds to Sierva's plight, though of course readers unfamiliar with Garcilaso will not sense the connection, and the alterations come to light only with a bit of research.

The chapter concludes, appropriately, with the very simple declaration from the last lines of Sonnet V: "Por vos nací, por vos tengo la vida / por vos he de morir, y por vos muero" ("For thee was I born, and do have life / For thee shall I die, and am now dying").

The citations are not resumed until chapter 5, by which time the lovers' passion has grown full fire. We see Cayetano reciting the famous first line from Sonnet X, "¡Oh dulces prendas. . . !" ("O sweet treasures. . . !" [DA, 162; OL, 124]). Thereafter the quotations are in numerical order. Two come from Sonnet I, "Cuando me paro a contemplar mi estado" ("When I stand and contemplate my fate" [DA, 164; OL, 126]). These are followed by the opening line from Sonnet II, "En fin a vuestras manos he venido" ("Into thine hands at last have I arrived" [DA, 165; OL, 127]), wherefrom three more lines are aired. The final excerpt from Garcilaso appears immediately after Sierva's luxuriant hair has been shaved in the cruel exorcism ritual. Back in her cell the girl weeps as she hugs Cayetano, he in response exhorting, "No more tears," then glossing his injunction with a line from the second terzet in Sonnet II: "Bastan las que por vos tengo lloradas" ("They do suffice, those that I've wept for thee" [*DA*, 170; *OL*, 131]). Here again the novelist has made a slight change, for the original line is in the subjunctive: "*Basten*" (and hence "*May* they suffice"). The newer line, now in the indicative, makes a statement rather than a wish.

These quotations help show both how rigorous and how free García Márquez is with the poetic originals. More important is the way in which the lines of verse serve as a kind of amorous reinforcement and quasi-religious liturgical backdrop to the unfolding love story.[6] Indeed, just before the first of the quotations, we read that "Delaura responded not with the Gospels, but with Garcilaso" (*DA*, 114; *OL*, 87). In the religion of love that emerges in the privacy of Sierva María's dark cell, the classic lyrics give it shape, tradition, even a soundtrack as it were. Moreover, Sierva herself ends up learning the poems by heart; and the two lovers' reciting the verses antiphonally to each other further strengthens and enriches their unnamable trysts. An amour gains in depth and stature from the presence of the poetry.

It is not redundant to note that García Márquez's novel is a love story. Cayetano quite simply and touchingly sums up this fact when, to a still-feral Sierva's asking why he's trying to heal her, he declares himself, almost offhandedly, with a statement that has been uttered by countless millions throughout history: "Because I love you very much" (*DA*, 122; *OL*, 93). For Sierva María, the love will bring her profound emotions without which her short, besieged existence would have been still poorer. For Cayetano, who can only imagine a life with Sierva, it means a world of possibilities that, sadly, he is incapable of seizing when he should. Yet despite their dolorous fate, the unlikely couple are the only ones in the book who are blessed with a true, deep, however fleeting happiness. And if love is indeed a "demon," as both title and Cayetano's fatal trajectory suggest, its course is ultimately more authentic than what we see at work in the society that surrounds (and condemns) them.

By the same token the book demonstrates the converse, the negative consequences of love's absence. Bernarda lives for lust and power, not love. Ygnacio's own genuine love for Dulce Olivia is nipped in the bud by his aristocratic father, and the rest of his affective life will be a loss, a void. Toward their own daughter neither of them shows much capacity for parental tenderness. (At one point in her last year Ygnacio tries to be the caring father, but the time for that is long past.) Bishop Toribio and Abbess Josefa, in turn, are depicted as being concerned solely with ecclesiastical infighting and control rather than with any emotional ties. Only Abrenuncio has gained a certain serenity, and this by ignoring all Eros for a life of pure rationalism. *Of Love and Other Demons*, then, is a love story that dramatizes the demons and dangers of *not* being able to love.

On yet another level that goes beyond the stated theme, García Márquez's novel portrays an archaic world in which individuals, owing to the limits imposed on them by their society, find their deeper potentials ultimately blocked and frustrated. Under more favorable conditions, Cayetano could have been both a man of letters and a caring spouse. In France or England, Abrenuncio's scientific and philosophical aptitudes might possibly have found opportunities to flourish. Had the viceroy taken heed of Martina's request and pardoned her, she may well have quietly reconciled herself to her existence and become less bitter. And were it not for a horrendous home life, followed by the policies of church and Inquisition, the beauteous Sierva María might at the very least have been able to develop into a normal, attractive adulthood and a warm, stable domesticity. Finally, the slaves, had it not been for their assigned legal status, might have taken on human roles other than those of decorative beauties, exploited menials, and prized sex studs.

Of Love is the first and only García Márquez novel that gives some close attention to the African presence and the history of slavery in Caribbean Colombia. The latter topic appears on the opening pages of chapter 1, where we read about a ship belonging to the Compañía Gaditana de Negros, from which unspecified numbers of African cadavers are being thrown overboard, these then washing up ashore. The cited company actually existed; it was charged in the seventeenth century with shipping slaves to the major slave ports of Cartagena and Veracruz.[7] ("Gaditana" means simply "from Cádiz," a port city in southern Spain.) The book accordingly depicts certain key details from the local slave trade—the methods for display and sale of "merchandise," the competition with traders in Havana, and the contraband in other black flesh from England's Caribbean colonies.

In the novel, Ygnacio's father, the first Marquis, made his fortune with 5,000 slaves and two barrels of flour per slave. Bernarda in turn gets actively involved in the slavery traffic, later turning to flour when the market for it appears more lucrative. This in fact is what the Compañía Gaditana did in 1765 when it sought permission to import two barrels of flour per slave, thereafter shifting to flour exclusively (because there was a greater risk of blacks dying than of flour spoiling).[8] A more eager Bernarda will up that quota to three barrels per, and finally, in a record smuggling operation, to twelve barrels full. The family's wealth and prestige is thus founded originally on slave sales, and upkeep of the palace is the task of house slaves. Were it not for the herds of mastiffs standing guard inside, the serfs might have risen up or slit the indolent Marquis's throat. Meanwhile Bernarda's sole human interest in male bondsmen—first the quite colorful Judas Iscariote (a traitor to his race), later any nameless stud she can lay hands on—is to satisfy her animal prurience. And in an analogous instance for the opposite sex, we read on the narrative's second page about a stunning Abyssinian woman put on sale for her weight in gold, a sum paid by the high secular authority, the governor. (Blacks can be beautiful as well.)

In all it is a system of naked power, ruled by brute force (captivity in West Africa, transport in chains), the free market (money exchange in America), security measures (e.g., dogs), and racial legislation. Yet in a profound irony, it is among slaves that young Sierva María finds herself. As the narrator states quite explicitly and eloquently about the slave community: "In that oppressive world where no one was free, Sierva María was: she alone, and there alone. And so that was where her birthday was celebrated, in her true home and with her true family" (*DA*, 21; *OL*, 11–12). The ultimate paradox: Sierva is free only with her enslaved friends. Moreover, in the absence of any family life of her own, the slaves function and have functioned as "her true family."

Sierva María's close ties to the slaves and their culture go back to her earliest babyhood, when Bernarda loathed the infant from its first suckling and feared she might kill it—whereupon a caring slave, Dominga de Adviento, took charge, then both baptized the child and "consecrated her to Olokun, a Yoruban deity of indeterminate sex" (*DA*, 59; *OL*, 42). Olokun, one of the sixteen *orishas* (gods and goddesses) of the Yoruba religion, is indeed seen by the orthodox faithful as male, but by other elements as female. He/she is owner of the totality of waters and symbol of the seas, and is moreover the highest *orisha* after Obatalá (the latter in turn being the father of all the *orishas* and of all humanity).[9]

Learning from early on the languages, dances, and sacrificial rites of the slaves (for example, drinking rooster's blood), Sierva María at one point startles Bernarda by swearing at her in Yoruba. The girl is also raised with African ablutions and is "purified . . . with the Verbena of Yemayá" (*DA*, 60; *OL*, 43). The goddess Yemayá, whose name shows several variants across the African diaspora (among them "Iemanyá"), personifies motherhood as the very source of "plant, animal, and human life."[10]

Eventually Sierva María wears sixteen collars—a key number in Yoruban religion, with its sixteen deities. Later on those neckpieces will become tokens of caring and love. Early one morning (in a scene noted previously), after Cayetano has recited to her all forty of Garcilaso's sonnets, as he departs Sierva makes him a gift of "the beautiful necklace of Oddúa" (*DA*, 163; *OL*, 125). Oddúa, as a source puts it, is "the oldest of Obatala's avatars, the one who created Obatala himself. Oddua [no accent in the source] is the creator and administrator of justice. He represents the mystery and secrets of death, and has power over solitude."[11]

A few pages hence, Father Aquino, in an act of affection and solidarity, hands back and places around Sierva's neck her previously confiscated collars: "The red and white of the love and blood of Changó; the red and black of the life and death of Eleggúa; the seven aqua and pale blue beads of Yemayá" (*DA*, 171; *OL*, 132). Again, within the Yoruban pantheon, Changó (also Shango and Xango) is the god of wrathful illumination and retribution, bringing forth truth via thunder and lightning.[12] Eleggúa (also Elegba) is the deity of choices, a trickster who brings the balance of nature and also guards crossroads.[13] Yemayá we have already seen as the mother-goddess. The colors that García Márquez associates in this passage with each *orisha* are generally accurate, though one source that I consulted identifies Shango's colors as red and black instead.[14]

In an added detail, García Márquez assigns, to certain slaves, names suggestive of their mixed backgrounds. That of Dominga de Adviento, Sierva's first nursemaid, combines the ritual holy day of Sunday ("Domingo") with the sacred season of Advent. The young girl's current domestic, Sagunta, bears in feminine form the toponym of the legendary Iberian city, Sagunto, that heroically resisted Hannibal's siege before going down to defeat in 218 B.C.

While García Márquez purposely avoids overwhelming his text with an abundance of local color, he incorporates just enough allusions to African artifacts, beliefs, and practices to capture the human milieu in which Sierva María feels "at home." For modern, twenty-first-century readers, that world is alien; for Sierva it is the only constituted world she has known and lived in comfortably before chancing upon true love. During her last days, deprived of both Cayetano and her African community, the forsaken girl understandably starves herself and dies alone.

Of Love and Other Demons qualifies as a historical novel in that it takes place in a relatively remote past era. When reading it, John Leonard observes, we are "reminded how long the Inquisition lasted, even in the Americas, and what it *felt* like."[15] The broad, circumambient social realities—slavery, aristocracy, women's condition, race—are rendered in sensuous detail. As is typical of the genre, the book seamlessly mingles individual story with objective fact, particularly the traceable, hard facts of late Imperial Spanish times.

The novel's specific time frame is conveyed via select historical markers that help draw a rough chronological outline for the events in the plot. One clear instance is Abrenuncio's library, which contains Voltaire's complete works in French (and some in Latin translation). Though it is not stated whether the renowned author (who died in 1778) is still alive at the time, in the narrative his writings remain fresh enough to be considered a subversive element in the colony. In addition the good doctor has in his possession a copy of Padre Isla's satirical-didactic novel *Fray Gerundio*, first published in Madrid in 1757 and subsequently banned by the Inquisition.

As we shall see momentarily, though, García Márquez takes some liberties with obscure historical facts. In chapter 2, of the Marquis's first wife we are informed that "Doña Olalla had been a student of Scarlatti Domenico [*sic*] in Segovia" (*DA*, 52; *OL*, 36–37). This item, besides giving the doña a colorful background and a detail-rich activity for her to build on in Cartagena, is a first step toward situating the larger chronology of the novel. Scarlatti, the great composer of keyboard sonatas (and still a joy to pianists and harpsichordists today), lived in Spain as Royal Music Master, from his arrival in 1729 to his death there in 1756.

Let us assume (for reasons to be elucidated below) that, during her childhood and teens, Olalla was Scarlatti's pupil sometime from, say, 1730 to the early 1740s. This would take her to Nueva Granada and her marriage at the nubile age of twenty or so. Following Olalla's early death by lightning, the time span of Ygnacio's widowhood is not specified, but we do know that he is fifty-two when the twenty-three-year-old Bernarda rapes him and then gets pregnant from the encounter. Sierva would thus have been born around 1769.

There is one slight problem with the author's having placed Scarlatti in Segovia: no biographies record the composer as having resided or worked in that town. He lived initially in Sevilla, then in Castile, and did spend summers in the royal, French-style palace at La Granja, which is near Segovia —but that is about all. García Márquez either has made a clerical error or is having some mischievous fun with history.

The other chronological marker is the solar eclipse that opens chapter 4. My research into such astral phenomena as would be discernible from eighteenth-century Cartagena show exactly two candidates: a total eclipse on 25 September 1745 and the margins of an annular (that is, partial and ring-like) eclipse on 23 April 1781.[16] The former occurred too early for the novel's Scarlatti and doña Olalla episodes. The latter date, on the other hand, fits the events just right, giving Cayetano and Sierva some weeks of loving prior to the girl's death in May. It also places us less than a decade before the French Revolution, a cataclysmic event that has not exploded yet lurks in the back of any historically conscious reader's mind.

Again, a minor historical discrepancy: the eclipse in *Of Love and Other Demons* is characterized as total—not annular or incomplete, as it indeed was. Obviously a thorough darkening of the skies carries considerably more dramatic impact, and García Márquez thus presumably chooses to alter the astronomical record for his artistic ends. The eclipse provides a dark and shimmering backdrop to the intimate conversation between Delaura and the bishop, wherein all sorts of sensitive issues are aired, among them the unending debate between science and religion.

But where García Márquez most mixes historical fact and fiction is in his untitled preface. Selected investigations have led me to the conclusion (also entertained by other scholars) that his novelistic invention begins then and there, rather than in his subsequent chapter 1. None of the proper names, whether sonorous or banal, are to be found listed in the standard documentation sites where one might expect to encounter them. Scattered references do exist to a "Cristóbal de Eraso"—not, however, the ceiling craftsman cited in the book but a military engineer and/or admiral. And though García Márquez reports having been assigned by Clemente Manuel Zabala, his real-life boss at his first news job in Cartagena, to write about the demolition, there is in the author's early journalism no record of his having worked on such a story. Moreover, according to one critic, the Clarissan convent was dismantled in the early 1990s, not the late 1940s.[17] Finally, the very notion of a human corpse growing gorgeous hair to a length of sixty-six feet seems the stuff of legend and even fairy tale rather than objective chronicle. (One physician informed me that it is "medically impossible.")

The preface thus exists to lend an air of reality to the personages and the narrative to follow. It should best be interpreted as a kind of "chapter zero."[18]

Two other names in *Of Love* merit a brief look. Early on in the first chapter, Abrenuncio is described as being a disciple of "the physician Juan Méndez Nieto, another Portuguese Jew who had emigrated to the Caribbean because of the persecution in Spain" (*DA*, 29; *OL*, 18). Here the narrator alludes to an actual, historical doctor, author of the first Spanish medical treatise in the New World. The only minor problem is that Dr. Méndez died in 1666, more than a full century before the unfolding of the novel's chief events! On a related note, in chapter 4 we read of a visit to Cartagena by the new, reformist viceroy, don Rodrigo de Buen Lozano. I have looked up a list of viceroys for eighteenth-century Nueva Granada and not come up with any name remotely resembling his. "Lozano," it bears mention, means "healthy-looking" in Spanish, and "Buen Lozano" reads almost like the semi-allegorical name of a literary character. In this historical novel, then, the chronology and individuals from that focused-on past have a somewhat fluid existence.

One subtle way in which the author imparts an aura of historical authenticity to his account is via diction, vocabulary. Every three or four pages, at most, there appears a Spanish archaism, or perhaps a word pertaining to, say, navigation or to household goods from that past era. Hence we have *gorgotero* (22) instead of *vendedor* ("street hawker"), *beque* (37) instead of *bacinilla* ("chamber pot"), *ergástula* (31) instead of *cárcel* ("jail"), *carcavera* (81) instead of *prostituta* ("prostitute"), and *marear* (109) instead of *navegar* ("to navigate," "to sail"). At one point the narrator employs the antiquated, feminine gender *la color* (54) rather than the current, masculine *el color*, and also uses the now-defunct future subjunctive when saying "cuanto le hiciere falta" (130). In all, just enough chosen lexicon to evoke a period flavor through his prose.

The romance between a thirty-six-year-old adult male and a twelve-year-old pubescent female raises unavoidable comparisons with Nabokov's *Lolita*. The resemblance is perhaps not accidental. Besides the obvious subject matter (which in each case includes a deep and desperate love of the grown man for the young girl), there is the death of Ygnacio's first wife Olalla by lightning at a picnic—precisely as befalls Humbert Humbert's parents. Equally important, the purported preface by García Márquez has certain practical functions analogous to those of the alleged foreword by Dr. John Ray in Nabokov's book. Besides creating what Roland Barthes calls a "reality effect," it also introduces key characters by name, and in particular spends a paragraph on the fact of Sierva's ravishingly long hair. This latter saves the author from the task of having to present so extreme a trait until he is well into the narrative, and that only in passing—much as Dr. Ray's initial text serves to inform us in advance about the fate of Lolita and her classmates. The parallels between the two love stories thus appear to be more than casual.

Finally, the novel itself contains many of the hidden structuring features that Nabokov was so fond of. As an instance, the ashen dog that bites Sierva has a white blaze on its forehead. Cayetano in turn is described as having a streak of white on his forehead (*DA*, 76; *OL*, 56). Completing a triangular relation, Abrenuncio's second surname, Cao, is Portuguese for "dog," and his first one, Pereira, brings to mind the Spanish "perro"—"dog."

A supernatural atmosphere permeates much of *Of Love and Other Demons*. To a limited degree, the book is a return to the García Márquez who made "magic realism" a celebrated byword. Shortly after Sierva María arrives at the cloister, novices report having seen her fly about with transparent wings; and her presence in their midst produces wild rumors of poisoned pigs, prophetic waters, and a chicken that flew to the horizon. This of course is the "magic" of Catholic demonology and of folk superstition—yet it is also the mental universe inhabited by the convent's devout inmates.

Meanwhile Sierva coyly plays along with the role they've assigned her, imitating voices of the beheaded or of satanic monsters. In the wake of Martina's escape, the girl claims to the abbess that she has watched six demons with bat's wings transporting the accused murderess across the seas. Sierva thus resorts to dark miracles having diabolic content and imagery reminiscent of the fantasies of Hieronymus Bosch. On her last days Sierva behaves like one possessed, speaking in tongues and mimicking the shrieks of birds. The mythology of demonic seizure has thus claimed a young victim of the society's lore; she has become what they say she is. Much as García Márquez did in his great works of the late 1960s and 1970s, he here gives flesh to the magical thinking shared by the dominant sectors of a traditionalist society.

Two sets of events, however, can be counted as pure magic. At the end of chapter 4, in a stormy meeting between the two lovers-to-be, Delaura witnesses a "fearful spectacle of one truly possessed. Sierva María's hair coiled with a life of its own, like the serpents of Medusa, and green spittle and a string of obscenities in idolatrous languages poured from her mouth" (*DA*, 152; *OL*, 118). Even here, however, the occurrence is qualified by its reportedly being seen through the eyes of Cayetano.

The other magical incident is more complex, and comprises three distinct episodes of a similar kind. In chapter 3, Cayetano tells the bishop about a dream of his: he sees Sierva (this before having met her) seated at a window watching heavy snow fall over a field in Salamanca, Spain, while she eats some grapes in the knowledge that the final one spells death. (The fruits in this otherwise incongruous narrative are presumably a reference to the Spanish custom of rapidly swallowing twelve grapes, just before the bells strike twelve, at old year's end.) Then, in the following chapter, the magic continues when Sierva, unprompted, tells Cayetano about her having experienced that same dream (sans the Salamanca setting), even though she had never seen snow before. Finally, in a highly poetical climax, on the night of her death

Sierva once again dreams that snowy dream, this time consuming the grapes two by two, desirous of reaching the last one.

Dreams, of course, have been customarily linked with various sorts of magic throughout history. We also know that certain prosaic dreams are in fact widely shared (e.g., dreaming of going to school barefoot or naked, or of forgetting to show up for a test or for work). But they also can have romantic associations. Indeed, one occasional casual fantasy is that of two loved ones dreaming the same unique dream, and here we see the two virgin lovers briefly attaining the exalted point of Sierva sharing Cayetano's dream, not just once but twice, the second time even as she breathes her last (death being in García Márquez a typical context for magical occurrences). The author, incidentally, further gathers his compatriots into this shared meteorological experience when, using the first-person plural, he reminds them that "we had [snow] right next to the sea, in the Sierra Nevada" (*DA*, 139; *OL*, 107).

Of Love and Other Demons breaks new ground for García Márquez in his actively including the presence of cultures and ethnicities other than Colombia's dominant, Hispanic ones in his narrative geography. His audience thus gets a vivid glimpse of the world of Afro-Colombian slavery and its myths and customs, on almost equal standing with those of white Catholicism. At one point the bishop even reflects in passing on the cathedrals that were built in Yucatán in order to hide the pagans' (i.e., Mayans') pyramids—a backward glance at yet another key component of Spain's overseas colonialism. In *Of Love*, then, we see García Márquez as a wise multiculturalist who shows that a complex society is far from monolithic and is made up of more than just one ethnolinguistic group.

In countless ways, *Of Love and Other Demons* is among García Márquez's more special books. An impressive range of human experience comes to life in its less than 200 pages. More than any other novel of his, it delves deep into the human heart, both the wondrous and the darker sides of our feelings. An unusually serious and tragic work, it nonetheless offers many smiling specimens of the author's signature irony and humor, notably in the exaggerated portraits of its less-lovable characters. His objectivity, however, is astounding. He neither sentimentalizes Sierva nor stigmatizes Bernarda nor condemns the bishop; on the contrary, they all have their full, fair say on the novelist's stage. And the narrative prose is distilled down to a maximum spareness—to a point where the transitions can at times appear a bit brusque and incomplete. Not surprisingly, the novel went through eleven manuscript versions—seven on the computer and four in page proofs.[19]

Though unfashionable to say so in our time, *Of Love* is perhaps García

Márquez's most beautiful work. It is also his saddest. As Julio Ortega notes, "ésta es su primera novela para llorar" ("This is his first novel to cry to").[20] There is no happy ending here, yet the book evokes a profound empathy. While the similarly brief love novel, *Chronicle of a Death Foretold*, is horrifying in the crime it recounts, such honor killings are now perceived as archaic, pre-modern, strange; and its atrocious events summon up more fear and frustration than commonality of feeling. By contrast, most of us know instances of genuine love shattered by circumstances; likewise many of us have known a hellish childhood, or an empty and desolate upbringing. The simple human content of *Of Love and Other Demons* can thus still speak to us today.

A full ten years after *Of Love and Other Demons*, García Márquez came out with *Memoria de mis putas tristes* (translated as *Memories of My Melancholy Whores*). The brash Spanish title is both a bit of a shocker and a joke. The Castilian term *puta*, short for *prostituta*, has a highly colloquial flavor, something like "hooker" in American English. Moreover, the book, appearing not long after García Márquez's personal memoirs in 2001 and also bearing the suggestive rubric *memoria* on its front cover, surely led many of the author's unsuspecting fans to think it the yearned-for sequel to *Living to Tell the Tale*. They were soon disabused: *Memories* is a novel, perhaps the author's last. The gag is taken still further, though, when readers find out that this remembrance of whores past contains not a single sex scene! The harlots in these pages chat, reminisce, give counsel, serve as intermediaries—and not much more.

Much of the novel's dynamic derives from the interplay between the protagonist's quirky personality and oversized life span on one hand, and the current, rather slight if unusual plot on the other.

The unnamed narrator is a unique creation, even for García Márquez. A cultured, refined, even precious ninety-year-old bachelor, he resides on the second floor of his long-deceased parents' mansion, with no surviving kin or domestic company (save for the family maid, Damiana). He survives on two pensions, one from his decades as a frankly poor teacher of high school Latin and Spanish, another from his forty years as a cable editor for a local daily. "Ugly, shy, and anachronistic" (in his words), he keeps himself active by crafting—longhand and in ink, since he never learned to type—a weekly column for the Sunday paper. The essays give him a modest following; cab drivers and teenaged girls recognize him. And his fellow office workers seem to like him as a venerable presence, the women even flirting with him. For pastimes he dips into Latin literature and thrills to classical music. His one attempt at marriage, in his twenties, crashed when he refused to issue out of his room for the wedding ceremony. Since then, his sole affective tie has been occasional stand-up sodomy with the servant (who once harbored for him an unrequited passion), and twice- or thrice-weekly visits to brothels. In a log he kept between his twenties and fifties only, he tallied up some 514 sexual partners.

At this point it bears explaining that, in the Hispanic world, there is no stigma attached to men seeing prostitutes, and indeed it is considered acceptable, normal behavior. Many a Latin youngster has had his initiation with a paid sex worker (as was the case with the narrator at age twelve). Moreover, in García Márquez's novels, as we've seen previously, brothels often function as social centers, privileged spaces where men of all ages seek refuge, solace, friendship, and, if not love, then some sort of surrogate. As the nonagenarian himself puts it, "Sex is the consolation you have when you can't have love" (MPT, 69–70; MMW, 58).

As is his wont, García Márquez starts things off with a memorable first line. Says the narrator, "The year I turned ninety, I wanted to give myself the gift of wild love with an adolescent virgin." And so Rosa Cabarcas, a similarly withered madam and a friend of the protagonist, finds him a suitable candidate and calls him with the good news. A droll odyssey-by-taxi transports the oldster to Rosa's business, she leading him to a secluded bedroom, where, that evening, there unfolds a romance like no other. The lover-man finds and observes a "molasses-colored" damsel stretched out naked on the bed, fast asleep and with her back turned to him. Thus she will remain all night long as he contemplates her, sometimes strokes her, and finally dozes off at her side. As the suitor departs at sunrise, the young beauty still slumbers.

The situation repeats itself while growing more intricate over an entire year's time. He dubs her "Delgadina" ("delgada" means "slender") and at various points addresses her in her sleep, recites to her the first drafts of his weekly articles, reads The Little Prince and Arabian Nights to her deep slumber, and so forth. He pens his columns for her, fashioning them as oblique letters to her, and they cause a sensation among his devotees. Delgadina for her part will smile at him just once and utter a single, cryptic sentence.

The ghastly murder of a banker at the brothel and the ensuing legal mess temporarily shut down Rosa's shop, putting the strange liaison on hold. As the suspenseful months tick by, the don chastely visits a former bedmate (now married to a Chinese immigrant farmer), tries to pawn off his Italian mother's jewels, and simply remembers, waiting for the girl's return to her moonlighting job. (By day she sews on buttons at a factory, location unknown.) For the first time in his life, he experiences suspicion and jealousy.

When the twosome does finally "meet" again under the same conditions, her body has grown in height and blossomed out. Shortly afterward, Rosa lets him know that "the poor creature is head over heels in love with you" (*MPT*, 95; *MMW*, 109). So the old guy finally has love — and an heir for whom he can remodel the brothel (to be bequeathed to him by Rosa). The final paragraph is a veritable celebration, a hosanna to the beauties of the new day and to the joys of ordinary living.

Memories thus depicts the potentially redemptive power of a love relationship, however peculiar it may be. Pre-Delgadina, the nonagenarian had lived thoroughly caught up in his private, isolated little world. His parents have been dead since his twenties. No siblings, cousins, nieces, nephews, late uncles, or other next of kin are mentioned. Nor do there appear to have been any male buddies in his long history. (His friendships with the whores, like his multitudinous sexual episodes, have all been paid for.) Incapable of long-term love or affection, he froze when faced with his planned marriage, which he aborted. The old coot, it seems, may function adequately in society, but his personal existence, his soul, is barren and quite pitiful. Perhaps the bizarre bond with a virgin teen is the only sort of tie that he, a kind of virgin of the heart, is ultimately fit for. Like Delgadina, he is a novice, a rank beginner.

Several women readers have expressed to me their distaste for the elderly narrator's personality — his proclivities, his treatment of his loyal maid, his self-centered and far-from-mature romancing. It should be said that, in drawing such a character and his actions, the novelist is not implying approval thereof but rather showing what can happen far off on the utmost edges of the spectrum of human behavior. By way of comparison, in *The Autumn of the Patriarch*, García Márquez fashioned an infinitely more repugnant figure, a lowbrow head of state who rapes and murders victims by the thousands. And yet the author succeeds in capturing the tyrant's common humanity, makes him comical, even evokes our pity for him. (As García Márquez remarked to me in an interview, "[I]n that book I tried to achieve a serene vision. I don't condemn him [the dictator].")[21] Similar criteria are applicable, mutatis mutandi, to *Memories of My Melancholy Whores*. No doubt, countless men of power as well as ordinary male folk have mistreated or abused women. We've also learned that many a solid citizen might lead a secret life (the latter the title, in fact, of a notorious Victorian sex memoir). This fictive private confession thus suggests what could be taking place behind the most respectable of bourgeois exteriors, without necessarily passing judgment on those happenings.

Memories, as a love story, shows some of the genre's classic rites and symptoms, scattered among its huge, outré differences. There is actually a regular, chaste, old-Hispanic-style courtship, with visits, gifts, flowers (albeit stolen ones), and all. There are love letters and love declarations, even if not aimed directly at the love object. Just past the book's midpoint the inamorato writes of his desire to join a student demonstration with a placard confessing, *"I am madly in love"* (*MPT*, 67; *MMW*, 55). The life-changing sentiment alters the nature of the now-happy scribbler's weekly essays, and in his lovesickness he forgets about showering and shaving. For the first time the veteran word-smith knows the sheer bliss of sharing a tie that is erotic yet also transcends Eros. We must believe our remarkably self-knowing memoirist when he an-nounces that his life now feels different. Besides, he might yet be saved from dying alone—the latter the worst misfortune, as melancholy whore Casilda Armenta remarks to him on one of his visits to the brothel (*MPT*, 95; *MMW*, 82). And who knows? Perhaps he and his beloved will complete the cycle and life happily ever after . . .

Meanwhile, *Memories* presents us with another courtly love situation, though taken to parodic extremes, whereby every detail about the "trysts" adds up to a spoof, a kind of send-up of that scene in which Tristan and Isolde lie side by side in a cave, fully clothed, with Tristan's sword between them. Readers can only speculate as to what will become of the couple once Delga-dina wakes up and they embark on their domestic routines together. In real life outside the brothel, of course, the girl is a simple, illiterate factory hand whom poverty has driven to potential whoredom. (Julio Ortega describes her as a "barbarian" to whom her cultivated wooer serves as a Pygmalion figure.)[22] At the same time, there is here a tendency to idealization along with the cult of unspoiled virginity, much like Don Quixote transforming the peas-ant girl Aldonza Lorenzo, in his mind, into his high lady Dulcinea del Toboso. (Coincidentally, "Delgadina" and "Dulcinea" both begin with the "d" sound, and are long, tetrasyllabic names, a trait the aged beau much desires.)[23]

Comparisons with *Lolita* are inevitable, if with signal differences. The oldster-youngster affair is utterly chaste and still-budding. Unlike Humbert Humbert, García Márquez's scribbler, while self-absorbed and hitherto in-capable of deep emotion or intimacy, seems personally sane, not cruel, un-calculating, and, within the limits that his nature allows, socially integrated. Moreover he woos his fresh damsel with gifts and caring rather than devious-ness or trickery. Indeed if things work out after the novel ends, Delgadina can at least expect some upward mobility, an escape from poverty and pros-titution, and not the sad, sordid fate that is the lot of Nabokov's Dolly Haze Schiller.

Old age, needless to say, is an essential component in García Márquez's slim book. Earlier we examined *Love in the Time of Cholera* as a detailed account of the aging process. *Memories* takes this several steps further; it tells of already *having aged*, of having reached the ranks of the "extremely old." It is about looking back in solitude and realizing that most of one's human ties—erstwhile sex providers included—are gone. It is about glancing casually at a group photo of the office personnel and noting that just four of one's former colleagues still remain. It is finding solace in the cultural icons of one's bygone youth and reviewing each of one's decades as distinct. It is visiting the fortyish doctor-grandson of one's former physician and seeing virtually the same face now speak a sentence that grandpa-doc once spoke. It is approaching an ex-fiancée—as does the nonagenarian with Ximena, she wheelchair-bound—at a concert, and hearing her innocently ask who one might be. It is saying to Casilda, "I'm getting old," and having her reply, "We already are."

It is this overarching narrative fact that gives *Memories* its wistful, nostalgic, at times regretful (not to mention melancholy) tone. Such feelings are to be expected in what is presented as the narrator's own memoir, which he dubs with García Márquez's bold title and purportedly is composing right in his long-deceased parents' library. Most of his text is hence retrospective, though with the unusual feature of a new, prospective happiness currently beckoning him. The entire plot takes place in the seven decades sometime before 1960, further giving the text the atmosphere of a lengthy backward glance. Not surprisingly, the novel comes filled with markers that help frame the different actions. Indeed, for so short a tale, *Memories* is highly allusive, with multiple references—local, pan-Hispanic, and international.

Early on we learn that the protagonist's father died at age fifty, on "the day the Treaty of Neerlandia was signed" (*MPT*, 16; *MMW*, 10), that is, 24 October 1902. (This is the same historical treaty that brings to an end the civil wars in *One Hundred Years of Solitude*.) One can thus assume that the memoirist was born around 1870 and began his amorous pursuits in the 1880s. He refers to a big event at the Teatro Apolo as "Fábregas season"; Violeta Fábregas was a renowned Mexican actress of the 1920s. Of the dictionaries in the elderly journalist's possession, the first three he lists are classics dating back centuries. What he calls the "innovative [*novedoso*] *Diccionario Ideológico*," however, first came out in 1942, while the Italian dictionary by Zingarelli initially appeared in 1922, with subsequent editions to follow. On his ninetieth birthday the old guy gets a pile of gifts from his newsroom colleagues, among them a recording of Stefan Askenase (a Belgian-Polish pianist) playing Chopin's

Preludes—an LP from the 1950s (which I and a Caracas schoolmate listened to at the time).

On the night of his birthday the music lover attends a recital by Jacques Thibaud and Alfred Cortot, in which they perform César Franck's violin and piano sonata. Cortot (1877–1962) was in his time a very famous pianist, and Thibaud (1880–1953)—his name misspelled "Thibault" by the narrator or the author—a celebrated violinist. (The pair in fact recorded the Franck piece in 1929. With cellist Pablo Casals they constituted a world-renowned trio.) After the concert, the blissful narrator is introduced to the two musicians by Maestro Pedro Biava—a real-life Italian immigrant from early in the twentieth century who, in 1933, went on to found the Symphony Orchestra of Barranquilla. Later on, in chapter 4, when the columnist writes an essay on whether or not to sacrifice his pet cat, he cites Pablo Neruda's delightful "Oda al gato" ("Ode to the Cat") and its unforgettable line, "mínimo tigre de salón."

In the wake of our Romeo's second session with his somnolent Juliet, he fantasizes about their singing as a duet the *boleros* of Agustín Lara (from Mexico, among the most famous and artful of popular-song writers) and tangos by Carlos Gardel (Argentina's legendary tango singer and composer). For their third encounter he brings the object of his affections a picture by Orlando Rivera (d. 1960), a Barranquilla artist, known as *Figurita*, who painted murals, designed carnival floats, and drew cartoons (among these latter the only known caricature of the Barranquilla Group of writers). As the romancer approaches her room, he overhears "Pedro Vargas, el tenor de América" (as the Mexican pop singer [1906–89] was, in fact, commonly designated), singing a tune by *boleros* composer Miguel Matamoros (1894–1971). And for a yet later meeting he brings her an ink drawing by Cecilia Porras (an avant-garde painter from Barranquilla, d. 1972), along with *Todos éstabamos a la espera* (*We Were All Waiting*), a book of stories by Álvaro Cepeda, one of García Márquez's closest buddies, honored as "Álvaro" in the final chapters of *One Hundred Years*.

And yet . . . The same chronological discrepancies we saw earlier in *Of Love and Other Demons* also crop up here in *Memories*. As it turns out, Álvaro Cepeda's volume of stories saw light in 1959, and violinist Jacques Thibaud had already died in 1953! The cultured old coot thus could not conceivably have attended a Thibaud recital in 1959 or later. Once again, García Márquez utilizes some real names and genuine icons in order to evoke a general era rather than to demarcate time frames with absolute exactitude.

The name "Delgadina" with which the nonagenarian rechristens his paramour has its own layered history. Several Spanish *romances* (traditional ballads) and Mexican *corridos* feature a "Delgadina" character in their narratives. The protagonist of *Memories*, however, is more specific, referring as he does to "the song about Delgadina, the king's youngest daughter, wooed by her father" (*MPT*, 58; *MMW*, 47). This is in fact a real ballad, "El rey tenía tres hijas," about a monarch who imprisons the beautiful youngest of his three daughters and then falls in love with her. The song in question, in 3/4 time, begins,

> Cuando salían de misa
> su papá le platicaba
> Delgadina, hija mía
> yo te quiero para dama
>
> (As they left church
> Her dad was telling her
> "Delgadina, my daughter
> I want you as my lady")

At the end of the tale, Delgadina, alas, dies in captivity—a fate that, we assume, is not what García Márquez's old codger has in mind.

The epigraph that graces *Memories* provides an initial, hidden clue to the book's contents. The citation is the very first line from *House of the Sleeping Beauties* by Yasunari Kawabata. The Japanese Nobel laureate's haunting short novel tells, in third person, of a secluded country inn where elderly men pay money to lie down and sleep—and sleep only—next to a slumbering, post-adolescent girl. A certain amount of touching is permitted, within strict limits. The girls cannot ask the house madam about their clients, and vice versa. The male protagonist, sixty-seven-year-old Eguchi, who sleeps with five of the young charges, differs from García Márquez's narrator in that he is married, with three grown daughters (though his wife is scarcely mentioned). The secret meetings serve as a springboard for Eguchi to recall past events, and at one point out on the street he runs into an ex–girl friend who is carrying a baby girl.

As in *Memories*, there are in Kawabata's book five chapters; the young damsels occasionally utter something vague in their sleep; a man dies at the inn; and Eguchi absents himself for a few months before a final return. On the other hand, unlike the tropical ambiance of *Memories*, *House* has more "typically" Japanese nature imagery of butterflies, camellias, and maple leaves. Still, the parallels between the two texts are close enough for us to assume that the Asian writer planted the seed in the Colombian's mind for *Memories*, similarly to what we saw earlier with "One of These Days" and its episode borrowed from Graham Greene.

Memories of My Melancholy Whores is the first García Márquez novel to be set in Barranquilla, a coastal city for which the novelist feels special affection, having flourished as a journalist and made lifelong friends there when in his twenties and moreover having lived in brothels alongside sex workers, whom he also befriended. Not surprisingly, the text alludes in passing to many a Barranquilla landmark—the Parque de San Nicolás, Paseo Colón (later Paseo Bolívar), Calle del Crimen, Teatro Apolo, Loma Fresca bus, Puerto Colombia (the city's sea port), and of course *El Heraldo*, where the author once labored as a daily columnist. (By contrast, the local *Diario de la Paz*, which runs the ninety-year-old loner's Sunday columns, is pure invention.)

From the occasional references to military patrols in the streets and to the official resident censor, one gathers that the characters are living at the time of *La Violencia* and in particular during the 1953–57 dictatorship of General Rojas Pinilla. (The secret nickname given to the censor, "the Abominable No-Man" in the translation, is actually "the Abominable Nine O'Clock Man" in the original, an indication of his arriving ever punctually at 9:00 P.M. in order to clean up everybody's prose for the next morning's paper.)

As in *Of Love and Other Demons*, the author works in some region-specific lexicon here and there—for instance *guaricha* instead of *prostituta*. A few of the words are so local they do not even appear in dictionaries, including that of the Royal Spanish Academy—notably *camaján* ("hanger-on" in the translation [*MPT*, 22; *MMW*, 15]) and *filipichín* (rendered as "dandy" [*MPT*, 25; *MMW*, 18]).

Its brevity and sordid subject notwithstanding, *Memories of My Melancholy Whores*, as we have been seeing, is among García Márquez's more elaborately crafted novels. Each one of its five chapters contains an abundance of subepisodes—the delightful birthday party thrown at the office for the colleague just turned ninety; the present of a pink angora cat he is given by the typesetters (and with which he develops a relationship parallel to that with Delgadina); the lovesick narrator's visit to the morgue and abortive attempt at seeing Delgadina's factory from inside; his pedaling around town, singing with joy, on Delgadina's brand-new bike gift; his fruitless attempt at pawning off his mother's prized jewels.

And there are even a couple of brief moments of near-magic. One is the mysterious graffito in lipstick that the old fellow finds on the brothel bathroom's mirror, "The tiger does not eat far away," an inscription the protagonist attributes to Delgadina—wrongly, since, as he later finds out, she is illiterate. The other quasi-magical passage concerns the young girl's only and quite enigmatic, almost surrealistic utterance, "It was Isabel who made the snails cry" (*MPT*, 76; *MMW*, 64).

Aside from the less-than-attractive narrator and his emotional shortcomings, the wealth of anecdotes and insights to be found in *Memories of My Melancholy Whores*, along with the prose style, combine to make it a mesmerizing little piece of fiction. It is befitting that, for what may well be the author's valedictory novel, he should have composed an extended aria on being very old and a love song to one of his most treasured towns, giving us this book of autumnal (if somewhat skewed) beauty.

THIRTEEN

The Journalist & Memoirist

García Márquez, we saw in chapter 3, started his professional writing career as a journalist, first churning out personal columns and, later, news stories for the daily press. In many ways he was to stay with the job and its craft. "A reporter," he noted in a *Playboy* interview, "is something I've never stopped being."[1] At different moments in his long life as a narrative artist he would take a break from fiction and produce an item for the leading print media on some signal current event—for example on the case of Elián González, the six-year-old Cuban boy who ended up on U.S. soil in 1999 and, following a vast and bitter legal, political, and popular controversy, was reunited with his father Juan Miguel on the Antillean island. García Márquez wrote eloquently on the topic, vividly reconstructing the sea journey and ultimately, subtly siding with Elián's father. One version of the account appeared as an op-ed piece in the *New York Times*.

Much of García Márquez's journalism, his youthful work particularly, has been gathered in book form and/or studied by scholars. (As an instance, see chapter 4 of this volume.) In addition, prior to 1990, two of his more delightful and exciting short volumes of reportage had consisted essentially of transcriptions, recorded accounts of unusual experiences as recounted to Gabo by the concerned parties themselves—the seaman Alejandro Velasco who survived for ten days in a life raft on the open sea in the Caribbean (*The Story of a Shipwrecked Sailor*, 1970; English translation, 1986), and the left-wing Chilean filmmaker Miguel Littín, who, while disguised and underground, shot a documentary right under the noses of the leaders of General Pinochet's fear-wracked dictatorship (*Clandestine in Chile: The Adventures of Miguel Littín*, 1986; English translation, 1987).

In 1996, however, García Márquez came out with a major work of investigative journalism entitled *Noticia de un secuestro* (*News of a Kidnapping*). Worthy of any sleeves-rolled-up, tobacco-consuming, streetwise reporter from a city newsroom, the book at the same time bears the seasoned novelist's mark of literary craftsmanship, with a rigorous formal architecture, frequent and well-placed flashbacks, and even brief moments of strangeness and magic. Chock-full of real-life detail, *News* qualifies as one of the Nobel laureate's more complex opuses, containing as it does hundreds of individual personages, actors, and operatives from all layers of Colombian society.[2]

And *News* is by far the most *Colombian* of García Márquez's works, fully comprehensible only to reasonably educated and informed Colombian readers. The many government officials as well as the media-star captives who populate its pages were, in their time, routine presences in the local news outlets, even before the kidnappings, which is presumably why the novelist dispenses with any physical or psychological sketches of the book's celebrity figures. Such information would have taken up precious space and, for Colombian readers, been redundant. Only the ever-present kidnap guards and personnel (over a dozen of them in total) are actually granted anything like distinctive personalities, voices, and physiques (though not faces, inasmuch as they always wear ski masks).

Any extended look at *News of a Kidnapping* requires some brief historical background.[3] Starting in the 1970s, Colombia's drug capitalists had been accumulating enormous wealth and power, building up an alternative economy that challenged the nation's old-guard, legitimate elite. They also launched ambitious social programs of their own and, in the process, garnered considerable respect and prestige among the general public. Meanwhile, in a totally separate development, in the 1980s the Marxist guerrilla group M-19 won government amnesty in exchange for laying down their arms and participating peacefully in the electoral process (a move that backfired when a thousand of their candidates were assassinated by paramilitary forces).

During these decades, official Washington convinced itself that the best way to end sales and consumption of recreational drugs in the United States was to track down and arrest *foreign* drug capitalists. The U.S. government began pressing for the extradition of Colombian drug kingpins for trial in U.S. courts. One of them, Carlos Lehder Rivas, was in fact captured in 1987 and duly sent to the United States, where he ended up sentenced to life in federal prison.

The remaining drug-trade Extraditables, as they became known, now wished to avoid Lehder's fate, aiming instead to secure more lenient terms within the Colombian justice system. Seizing the initiative, Pablo Escobar, the most notorious of the drug *capos*, started demanding for himself and his cronies the same amnesty privileges gained by the M-19 guerrillas, along with official promises of nonextradition to El Norte. Kidnapping and occasionally murdering prominent Colombian citizens were his eventually successful means of extracting precisely such a guarantee from the government, then headed by President César Gaviria.

The sheer abundance of events and people in *News* makes summarizing the plot well-nigh impossible. Suffice it to say that the volume recounts the kidnapping of six men and four women by salaried thugs, followed by the lengthy ordeal of captivity, the seemingly endless and ineffectual government responses to the horrific situation, the mysterious deaths of two of the female hostages, the daily anguish of the victims' kin, and at long last the freeing, suspensefully, in stages, of the remaining abductees. The book's odd-numbered chapters focus exclusively on the captives and on their grim, claustrophobic, uncertain plight. The even-numbered chapters, by contrast, depict the other, "normal" world outside, where life unfolds and twists and turns without direction in government offices or in family members' homes. As the story moves along, the author's narrative scheme becomes a bit more fluid. Chapters 7 and 11, for instance, report on the liberation of hostages and hence fuse the two realms. And chapter 2, via a flashback, relates the forcible seizures of Diana Turbay (daughter of an ex-president) with her TV crew, and also of the aging, elegant restaurateur Marina Montoya.

For the sake of clarity, here follows a time line of the chief events in *News of a Kidnapping*:

— 1990 —

30 August. Diana Turbay is kidnapped, along with TV crew members Azucena Liévano, Richard Becerra, Orlando Acevedo, and Juan Vitta, as well as German journalist Hero Buss.

18 September. Marina Montoya and Francisco "Pacho" Santos are kidnapped, in separate actions.

7 November. Maruja Pachón and Beatriz Villamizar are kidnapped together.

29 November. Juan Vitta is released.

11 December. Hero Buss is released.

16 December. Azucena Liévano is released.

17 December. Orlando Acevedo and Richard Becerra are released.

18 December, 15 January and 16 February, 1991. Three different members of the drug-trafficking Rodríguez Ochoa family surrender to the police and are subsequently imprisoned.

— 1991 —

24 January. Marina Montoya is executed in an empty lot.

25 January. A police operation results in Diana Turbay's accidental death in a crossfire.

8 February. Beatriz Villamizar is released.

20 May. Maruja Pachón and Pacho Santos are released, two hours apart.

19 June. The Colombian Constituent Assembly votes to outlaw extradition. Alberto Villamizar (Beatriz's husband) goes to meet with Pablo Escobar, who now willingly hands himself in to the authorities.

— 1993 —

2 December. After more than two years of luxurious imprisonment, an untimely escape, and life on the run, Pablo Escobar is shot dead by the Colombian security forces.

— 1991 (final flashback) —

Some unspecified time after 19 June, a stranger shows up at Maruja Pachón's apartment and dutifully returns her engagement ring, its gem slightly damaged.

In contrast to the foregoing dry, factual chronology, the very gist of *News of a Kidnapping* is the day-by-day agony of the abductees crammed into tiny spaces, sometimes two to a small mattress, with foul air and with the constant presence of armed guards, who rigorously monitor their charges' every toilet break and morning shower. (Pacho Santos moreover is kept chained to the frame of his bed.) The hostages have just one available garment change (sweat clothes provided by the kidnappers), eat terrible food (mostly beans), are allowed limited reading fare (mostly entertainment magazines) and sporadic access to radio and TV, and live in unending fear of being shot dead (as indeed will happen to Marina). In addition there are the many occasions when hopes for release are raised—only to be cruelly dashed. *News of a Kidnapping* thus has all the makings of a gripping suspense thriller; its story simply happens to be true.

For the female hostages there is the added terror of being raped by the ever-present guards. Still, other than an armed youth's occasionally peeking at a woman in the bathroom, the book features virtually no reports of sexual molestation or assault. (One set of guards watches porn videos together, though that is another matter.) The young toughs, we readers infer, seem to be under strict orders from on high not to abuse their captives sexually.

Indeed, the complex personal ties with the guards and the allied personnel (the presumed landlords, consisting of the so-called "butler" and his fun-loving, always-singing wife Damaris, for instance) constitute a major portion of the book's hostage chapters. The rotation of guard groups makes for a great deal of character diversity and subplot material. Some individual guards are polite and considerate, others brusque and nasty. Some are deeply religious, others thoroughly nihilistic in their views.

The relationship between hostages and guards provides further human content and drama within their chapters. On occasion the prisoners and the toughs quietly play cards or chess together. At one point the guards actually throw a birthday party for Maruja, who later gets into some serious talk with them about their attitudes and personal backgrounds (from broken homes, largely). And there are even hugs and farewells whenever an abductee is finally released. Furthermore, Marina Montoya, in a textbook instance of what is known as Stockholm Syndrome, is seen fraternizing and identifying with the guards, crying on their shoulder and even defending them before her co-prisoners. A guard nicknamed "Barrabas," in turn, comes to "adore" Marina and bestow affectionate caresses upon the lady. (An odd detail concerning the sixtyish Marina is the care she lavishes on her fingernails, a way of remaining active and maintaining dignity through her ordeal.)

One unusual insight that emerges in the course of the narrative is that the guards too, in a sense, are also hostages of the situation. At any given moment they just as well could find themselves liquidated, either by the police or by Escobar's own salaried henchmen. For a good chunk of the day they share in the horrendous living conditions of the abductees, doing so only for the money. Virtually none of them, it must be noted, comes across as necessarily evil, even though they are in the employ of an evil cause.

Still more dramatic tensions grow out of the oft-shifting emotional bonds between the hostages themselves. Early on, the abductors of the two women offer to release Beatriz, who instead chooses to remain with Maruja out of solidarity. Later, in chapter 5, however, she will angrily—and perhaps inevitably—reproach Maruja, saying, "Don't you dare talk to me like that! Not when it's your damn fault I'm here" (*NS*, 131; *NK*, 113). The Maruja and Beatriz pair, for their part, will resent Marina's passively submitting to the guards, yet this rancor is later replaced by Maruja's compassion for the elder lady's terrible fate. By the same token, Diana Turbay voices enormous guilt to her crew members about having led them on such a dangerous and ill-fated misadventure. Conversely, her staff writer Juan Vitta will admit to having deeply hated her when he realized that they had fallen into the hands of the dreaded Extraditables. The emotions in these captivity episodes—the unavoidable result of people cohabiting in extreme and precarious circumstances—form an essential part of the plot of *News of a Kidnapping*.

In evoking and portraying this cauldron, this roiling brew of human emotions, García Márquez focuses on the most gut-wrenching aspects of the captivity experience. Given that relatively little actually *happens* during the victims' time as abductees, their daily round of inner feelings takes on a special narrative importance. Being kidnapped, the book shows, consists of more than physical deprivation. It also inflicts ceaseless suffering on the mind and spirit; and moreover it involves lengthy, tentative, sensitive negotiation with captors and fellow captives both. This complex admixture of brutality and diplomacy, compounded by the basic struggles to keep one's sanity, to live with an unbearable anxiety at the nebulous prospects for release, and to face the sudden relevance of ultimate issues such as total isolation and possible death—all these are major components in the fearsome events conveyed here by a great novelist.

The even-numbered chapters concentrating on the world outside are a necessary flip side to the contents of *News of a Kidnapping*. A narrative made up solely of the hostages' point of view would have been potentially limiting and claustrophobic as literature. Those "outside" sections, by contrast, come teeming with people, places, and actions, with hundreds of subepisodes and telling details. Here we witness the suffering and distress of the abductees' intimates, juxtaposed with the impotence of the central government and its functionaries in the face of the Escobar emporium's skilled if horrific tactics, and the necessary delicacy of the steps to be taken, the methods to be pursued. The chapters abound in memorable characters, most of them from high government and media circles. The intricate ties that bind these individuals suggest just how small and all but incestuous that Colombian inner circle happens to be.

These chapters are considerably harder to follow for a foreign reader unacquainted with the countless Colombian public figures, who bob on and off the page, talking, jockeying, and maneuvering to the best of their abilities. The reader should simply stay and slog along, however, inasmuch as the pieces eventually fall into place with the piling-up of events. Pointedly, it is in these public chapters that García Márquez, speaking to and for his fellow citizens, twice chooses to employ in passing the first-person plural "we." The first such moment appears halfway through the book, the other toward the end. As he weighs in on the chilling situation in January 1991, immediately following the murder of Marina Montoya, the narrator observes, "Since 1984, when Minister Rodrigo Lara Bonilla had been assassinated, *we had experienced* all kinds of abominable acts, but it was not over yet, and the worst was not behind *us*" (NS, 149; NK, 128 [emphasis added]). Later, on the antepenultimate page of the volume, reflecting on the primal cause of it all, the author's Colombian voice notes, "Having become the biggest prey in *our* history, Escobar could not stay more than six hours in one spot . . ." (*NS*, 325; *NK*, 289 [emphasis added]).

These shifts in point of view, brief and transient though they may be, show us a García Márquez stepping outside his role of objective reporter and assuming the stance of concerned citizen, of informed participant in his country's woes. With these strategically placed if fleeting gestures, he ventures just momentarily into the realm of *testimonio*, the nonfiction literary genre that, over the past few decades, has emerged among literate Latin Americans as a means of conveying some of the adversities, struggles, and deeper longings of a much-afflicted continent.

Among the many vivid personages populating these chapters is the tele-priest Father Rafael García Herreros, a man who might easily have stepped out of a novel, with his eighty-some years of age, his daily *one-minute* devotional telecasts, and his "indispensable" secretary Paulina (the only human being on earth who knows how to extract, each day, the cleric's contact lenses). Regarded as a saint by the broad masses (including the kidnapping guards), the right reverend and his selfless efforts ultimately make possible the final surrender of Pablo Escobar. On a differing note, one of the more unforgettably positive moments in the book occurs when the eight-month captivities of Maruja and Pacho at long last come to an end on 20 May, their private releases then prompting a public celebration of collective joy, with automobile horns honking wildly in the streets.

Worth passing mention is the fact that, amid his account of very physical horror and its attendant naturalistic details, García Márquez is not above occasionally resorting to magical elements and supernatural concerns. Hence María Victoria, the wife of victim Pacho Santos, is shown meeting with a seer who had predicted the death of Diana Turbay and who now happily informs her that her husband is still alive. The novelist gives an entire page, moreover, to an astrologer named Mauricio Puertas, who has prepared Escobar's astral chart and foresees only four possible fates for the drug entrepreneur: namely, hospital, graveyard, jail, or (of all things) a convent. An Escobar on the lam finds his curiosity so piqued by these divinations that he comes quite close to seeking out the astrologer, a plan eventually frustrated by his precarious circumstances. In these reports, as in the author's more magical fiction, García Márquez depicts how ordinary folk live these prophecies rather than assigning any special privileges to such lore.

The primal force behind all these horrific events, needless to say, is the notorious and legendary Pablo Escobar, who does not appear in the book until its epilogue, ten pages from the end. When he finally comes down out of a helicopter, ready for incarceration—with his shoulder-length hair and thick, chest-length black beard, his sun-tanned skin and tennis shoes, his easy gait and "chilling" sang-froid—the effect is startling, electrifying. He is unique, resembles no one previously seen by the auxiliary middleman and witness Alberto Villamizar (the spouse of Beatriz). Such is Escobar's authority and charisma that he can order the *policemen* to lower their arms—and they duly comply. The beautiful pistol that he yields, with its gold monogram inlaid on a mother-of-pearl handle, befits the professional outlaw and successful businessman perfectly. To top it all, he cordially offers family help to Villamizar—a man whom he had once tried to assassinate. The six-page scene of Escobar's surrender is the stuff of high drama, worthy of a scene from classical tragedy.

Putting together so much raw material involved enormous amounts of journalistic spadework and heavy lifting for the author. The book itself was taken up at the behest of Maruja and her husband; and although Maruja at first simply wanted to forget and repress those awful months, she finally poured forth some twenty hours of oral testimony. Around fifty individuals were interviewed in total—and in utter secrecy. García Márquez at times had a journalistic colleague, Luz Ángel Arteaga, stand in for him to do data-gathering at official organizations, while his cousin Margarita Márquez "transcribed over four dozen cassettes in absolute silence."[4] To interview the three Rodríguez Ochoas, he visited them alongside a delegation of U.S. journalists and managed to speak with the trio separately—all this in order to avoid the spotlight, which would have placed his book project at center stage and blown his cover. So much information did García Márquez compile in the course of his investigations that the original draft of the manuscript consisted of 700 pages, an impossible bulk which he pared down to 300.

The biggest journalistic scoop of all, needless to say, would have been for García Márquez to land an interview with Pablo Escobar himself, who reportedly had gotten wind of Gabo's new work in progress. Unfortunately the drug kingpin died in the early phases of the literary venture, and for his intimate portrait the novelist ended up having to depend on the many letters that Escobar had penned "to the authorities, to the families of the hostages, and to his own lawyers."[5] García Márquez expresses repeated amazement at the high quality of the narco-entrepreneur's prose style—yet another field of endeavor in which this evil genius appears to have excelled.

News of a Kidnapping, by the very nature of its genre and contents, is a somewhat local book, closely bound up with its time and circumstances—literally a work of "news." It nonetheless attains a status of high art via the masterful way in which it evokes, at every level, a sordid world of suffering, intrigue, power, politics, and crime. It has in the Colombian author's oeuvre a standing analogous to that held by such nonfiction reportages as *The Armies of the Night* and *Miami and the Siege of Chicago* in the late Norman Mailer's work. (Just incidentally, one reason García Márquez settled on the word "news" was that previous works of his had already featured the terms "chronicle" and "story" [*relato*] in their titles.)[6] Ezra Pound once defined poetry, aphoristically, as "news that stays news." Though the news matter in *News of a Kidnapping* might not remain forever new, the book will most likely be read so long as García Márquez's writings are savored, studied, and (dare I say?) enjoyed.

As often happens with cancer patients, García Márquez's long, alarming bout with the disease in the late 1990s led him to take stock of his existence both as a human being and as a writer. And so, in the wake of his double ordeal of life-threatening illness cum arduous treatments, he turned for the first time to yet another nonfiction genre: autobiography, confession, memoir (or whatever one chooses to call it).

The result was *Vivir para contarla* (2002; *Living to Tell the Tale*, 2003), an extensive backward glance in which the author pours forth remembrances of his early years for the eager eyes of his millions of admirers. The book can thus be seen as the possible final reckoning of a man who had confronted the abyss and now feels compelled to "tell" all before it's too late. At 577 pages of text in the Grupo Norma edition, *Vivir* is García Márquez's heftiest single tome. In terms of sheer human content, and as a singular exercise in recollection, it is arguably his richest and most multilayered piece of writing.

Presented as the first of three projected volumes, *Vivir* takes us into Gabo's mid- and later twenties, starting with the eight years of uncertain if idyllic childhood in the home of his maternal grandparents in Aracataca and moving on through his arresting phase as a rising staff writer for the respected Bogotá daily *El Espectador*. Hence we witness the small-town past and its many ups and downs, and then, along the way, we share in the continuous and complex growth pangs of a young whelp's writing vocation—both as salaried journalist and as apprentice artist.

Given the multiple strands that comprise the total tapestry of *Living to Tell the Tale*, to sum up its story would amount to a futile pursuit. Moreover, goodly portions of its major facts and broader outlines are in some measure already familiar to us from previous sources. What distinguishes the book's contents, aside from its greater wealth of details, is their evocative quality and the attention given to personal emotions. As the epigraph to the volume suggests, *how* one remembers one's life matters more than the raw data of the life itself.

And so, northern Colombia's Caribbean ambiance is vividly conjured up, with its luxuriant, suffocating heat, its bewitching folklore, and its dense meshwork of familial and quasi-tribal ties. We get a concrete feel for the towns where Gabito dwelled—sleepy and impoverished Aracataca, gossip-ridden yet comely Sucre (with its river), entrepreneurial Barranquilla, chilly and proper Bogotá, and dazzlingly beautiful Cartagena.

The ever-widening narrative comes teeming with accounts of Gabito's ten younger siblings—so many that, as an adolescent, he could not keep them straight or even recognize them all when back from boarding school every summer. And there are his dreamy, homeopathic-pharmacist father Gabriel Eligio, ever-absent as he chases one money-making scheme after another, and his once-rebellious mother Luisa and her heroic efforts at creating order amid chronic household chaos, not to mention his aunts, uncles, cousins, and half-brothers beyond counting. Add to the populous clan García Márquez's long succession of buddies, classmates, colleagues, and fleeting, one-time acquaintances, and we find, as in *News of a Kidnapping*, a cast of characters in the three figures, though this time each one is fleshed out by the verbal sculptor with loyalty and loving care.

Among the many tales retold here is that of the special, rich relationship enjoyed by little Gabito with his grandfather, Colonel Nicolás Márquez, referred to on occasion by the man's affectionate nickname "Papalelo." The Colonel, we've seen in chapter 3, was himself a remarkable individual and public figure. Here by contrast we get to know grandpa Nicolás in the role of substitute parent, and few interpersonal ties are as positively memorable as this one. In the author's words, "my grandfather was complete security for me. My doubts disappeared only with him, and I felt I had my feet on the ground and was well established in real life" (*VC*, 97; *LTT*, 77). The two-some go out on leisurely afternoon strolls, discovering the world's wonders together, albeit—for reasons of height—from differing perspectives. At one point in their conversations Papalelo introduces the young boy to the figure of Simón Bolívar as "the greatest man in history"; another time, at home, he places a dictionary in Gabito's lap, characterizing it as the book that "knows everything" and is "never wrong" (*VC*, 112; *LTT*, 90).

Judging from García Márquez's retrospective account, theirs seems to have been the perfect father-son (so to speak) bond. Understandably, the grown novelist would always hearken back to that cross-generational tie as the most crucial in his life. The boy in *Living to Tell the Tale* naturally thinks of their unique alliance as the prevailing norm; and following the Colonel's death from throat cancer a growing Gabo will spend years sorting out and grasping the significance of that sudden full stop and termination.

Equally important are the dozen or so women who have a place in the Márquez household, and not just the blood kin but also the colorful live-in maid and the washerwoman and their female offspring. Of course there are the assorted aunts who bear quirky names or nicknames, notably Wenefrida ("tía Nana"), the seventy-nine-year-old Francisca ("tía Mama"), the ever-silent Elvira (a kind of model for Santa Sofía de la Piedad), and blind Petra, among others. From all of them comes the "thread of secret communication" that Gabo will always sense with women, his generally feeling "more comfortable and secure" with them than with men (*VC*, 89; *LTT*, 70).

Though the author never spells it out in explicit terms, the eight-year-old's inevitable transplanting to his biological parents' turf appears to have had some difficulties. There are signs of incompatibility. At grandpa's, the little boy used to like to spin tales for the folks gathered around the table, where the women and the Colonel, delighting at such inventiveness, would applaud his narrative bent. The father, by contrast, now dismisses these yarns as "lies," and, harsh taskmaster that he is, even disciplines the kid for them. Moreover the time spent with his parents is that of a too-huge family treading water day after day in unrelenting poverty. Hence on one occasion a choice has to be made between a potato or the Sunday newspaper, and on another a frightened Gabito is sent by *mamá* to request a handout (unsuccessfully) from a local moneybags. Throughout all this a prolific paterfamilias worships and fantasizes about wealth, and uproots his wife and brood periodically. Gabo's growth amid his immediate kin thus comes off initially as a bewildering new life-stage, a disorienting limbo after his first eight years in a now-lost paradise.

Also inevitable in this account of youthful growth is the matter of adolescent sex and sexual escapades, both inside brothels and out. Male postpubescence, as is well known, is a stage when sex looms at its most potent, surprising, and mysterious; and memoirist García Márquez does justice to that phase. Among the incidents worth mentioning here is Gabito's erotic initiation, when he is avidly disrobed, bodily lifted, and tenderly violated by an affectionate, nameless prostitute (much like the very first time for José Arcadio with Pilar, or Florentino with an anonymous sex worker). There are the youth's months-long, afternoon affair with Martina Fonseca, a white woman married to a huge, 6'2" black sailor, or a later liaison with "Abyssinian" beauty Nigromanta, who will entertain the teenager during the absences of her police sergeant husband, leading eventually to an armed confrontation between illicit lover and cuckolded spouse (who spares Gabito only because the kid's pharmacist father had once cured him of a bout with gonorrhea).

These ribald episodes serve to liven up and bring comic relief to what is a mostly sad and lonesome late-boyhood. Though the author has never owned up to it in interviews, nor has it been noted in biographical works, Gabito in post-puberty seems to have been attractive to older, experienced women, some of whom aggressively sought him and seduced him—a dynamic he would later capture in his novels. Meanwhile, scattered throughout the pages of this book is the elusive figure of his wife-to-be, Mercedes, familiar enough from previous writings, whom he meets halfway through the volume and proposes to, and whose unopened letter will have the final word, as it were, in these spirited remembrances.

Politics inevitably crop up as a subject in a memoir penned by an avowedly left-wing writer. Already the first chapter touches frequently on the United Fruit Company, a topic familiar to all devotees of *One Hundred Years of Solitude*. The massacre of striking workers and its undetermined number of dead, the nostalgia that some Aracataca townspeople feel for the company, and the harshly divided attitudes concerning the possible return of the Yankee firm—these are issues passionately lived and relived from early on by the grown-ups in Gabito's childhood. On another note, Venezuelan exiles from the tyranny of General Juan Vicente Gómez—who will subsequently serve as the principal real-life model for the dictator in *The Autumn of the Patriarch*—wend their way in and out of adult conversations here recaptured.

But by far the most extensive political narrative in *Vivir* tells of the rise of the great Liberal firebrand Jorge Eliecer Gaitán, his absurd and tragic assassination on 9 April 1948, and the apocalyptic revolt that sweeps through Bogotá in response to the atrocity. Among those so swept up is a twenty-one-year-old Gabo, who, seeing countless electrical appliances and other merchandise strewn all over the streets, joins in with the feverish looters and grabs for himself a brand-new leather briefcase. In addition, as a good journalist he expertly depicts the virtual collapse of the central government as well as the presence of a student named Fidel Castro among the visitors at a Pan-American Conference. In all, García Márquez's account of those enormous events takes up a full twenty pages of his fifth chapter.

Within this cataclysm remembered, the most striking single moment occurs at the very scene of the crime. There, amid the rioters clamoring for the head of alleged culprit Juan Roa Sierra, the author reports having witnessed something extraordinary: a "tall man, very much in control of himself and wearing an irreproachable gray suit" (VC, 335; LTT, 281), inciting the mob to seize and kick the suspect to death. Later on, García Márquez sees the same mystery man picked up by "too new a car as soon as the assassin's corpse was dragged away" (VC, 339; LTT, 283). In his words, "the man managed to have a false assassin killed in order to protect the identity of a real one" (ibid.).

If Gabo's story and interpretation are accurate, he has essentially demolished the official, established version of one of the most notorious assassinations in Latin America's blood-soaked history. Still, even if the budding author really did observe such a scene—and we have no reason to doubt his veracity—his re-vision is just one of dozens that have been proffered by all sorts of people, from respected researchers to sheer crackpots (e.g., certain right-wingers who argue that, actually, the murderer of Gaitán was Fidel Castro).

Some readers from across the ideological spectrum may have felt disappointed at the relative absence of politics—notably left-wing politics—from these memoirs. But then, García Márquez has not been one to issue general pronouncements or credos in his prose. Issues of doctrine, ideology, policy— these are not the world in which his mind typically moves and operates. Even in his long career as a journalist his views have always come embedded within anecdotes. Similarly, in *Vivir para contarla* we read about childhood poverty, the United Fruit Company, and the Bogotá riots, all via stories thereof—from which we can infer his politics. True, he could well have said something about his youthful ties with leftists and Communist Party members, yet to a great degree that is privileged information; to name names or even hint at identities would have endangered past associates and their families. In any case, García Márquez is not, and never was, a strictly political writer. He is rather a writer who happens to be left-wing.

The central lifeblood of *Living to Tell the Tale* is, in fact, Gabito's long struggle with his literary vocation. The book actually starts out with a family disagreement concerning that calling. In a meeting with his mother on her mission to sell off grandpa's house, she then and there confronts him: Gabo's father wants him to stick with his law studies, for economic reasons. Gabo in turn wants to write, period. And so it goes—the issue of the boy's emerging talents, their fitful manifestations and growth, and the assorted obstacles to them, will dominate much of the rest of the book. A Dr. Barboza who had lived across from the family in Aracataca once encouraged young Gabo's writing side. Also, following the suicide of a Belgian friend of the family, the five-year-old observes, "The Belgian won't be playing chess anymore" (*VC*, 115; *LTT*, 93) — a neat conceit, celebrated in the Colonel's household and described by the author as "my first literary success." At the Liceo de Zipaquirá, he will pen love poems for his schoolmates' objects of desire (as does Florentino Ariza). And the adolescent's wild, imaginative notions that compensate for his weaker points are rewarded with good grades from his teachers.

Becoming a writer of course means doing lots and lots of reading, as well as building up necessary knowledge and craft. We see young Gabo discovering the Modernist and other classics, texts he studies intently, taking them apart in a "surgical disemboweling" (*VC*, 441; *LTT*, 367) in order fully to figure out their inner workings. One can only be amazed at the extensive literary education the apprentice picks up from his friends, from local poets and poetic movements, and from his esteemed mentor Ramón Vinyes, who first teaches him about the complex matter of structuring time in narrative.

In addition we bear witness to Gabito's growing awareness of the verbal minutiae of prose. Early on he decides to steer clear of adverbs that end in "-mente" (equivalent to "-ly" in English), a suffix he considers "a bankrupt habit" ("un vicio empobrecedor" [*VC*, 316; *LTT*, 265]). And when he first encounters, in an old pamphlet, an account of a mustachioed war veteran called "Buendía," he is taken with the name; though he worries that it might occasion unwanted rhymes with imperfect tense verbs ending in "-ía," he sticks with it anyhow. Along the way we see him sweating mightily to create stories and a first novel, and eventually realizing that his beginner's fictions are confused and abstract attempts that exist in a "metaphysical limbo" (*VC*, 447; *LTT*, 372).

Throughout his life as a public figure, García Márquez has praised journalism as a legitimate artistic medium, particularly the reportorial side of the trade. Here in the latter chapters of *Living* we are able to track Gabo's rise to journalistic prominence in his homeland. The memoirist thus lavishes loving attention on the job's regular news-gathering routines and procedures, expresses sheer delight at the everyday life and ambiance of the newsroom, and later conveys the uniquely dynastic atmosphere of his years at *El Espectador*, with the three different generations of the Cano publishing clan present at all levels of Bogotá's number-two daily. It is a touching and memorable portrait of a family-run business driven by a precise cultural mission.

On his beat Gabito comes upon some astounding true stories (a few of which I have discussed in earlier chapters). In one case, reporter Gabo actually helps stage events for the sake of some demonstrators in the Chocó, a region near Panama then struggling to maintain its territorial and legal integrity. A particularly heart-wrenching account involves 3,000 little children, forcibly separated from their blood kin in an army campaign against guerrillas. Few of the toddlers are old enough to utter either their own names or those of their parents (among the children is a pair of thirteen-day-old twins), and they will mostly end up as accidental orphans. It is a terrible instance of government reprisals causing far more suffering than the armed rebels might have inflicted or even imagined. Perhaps the bizarre event served as the ultimate inspiration for the 2,000 children who are ordered blown to bits by the desperate tyrant in *The Autumn of the Patriarch*.

Vivir para contarla both starts and ends with a journey: back to Aracataca in the first instance, on to old Europe in the second. Still, owing to the chronological constraints of the genre, the book shows few of the symmetries with which the author has meticulously structured so many of his major works. His experimental bent nonetheless comes forth in assorted ways. The volume begins not with his birth and infancy—as memoirs are wont to do—but with an almost twenty-three-year-old Gabo's return visit to his hometown along with his mother, and their disputes over his plans to be a full-time scribbler. Throughout *Living*'s first half the narrator will flash back and forth between his later literary development and some chosen early moment in his childhood. The book, moreover, contains precious few mentions of specific years, time being kept in a more or less general, mythical state. The master who plays with time in his great works of fiction retains to some degree the same approach in this true-life memoir.

In addition the volume ends inconclusively on a note of suspense, with a letter from Mercedes in reply to a kind of ultimatum Gabito had previously sent her, now awaiting his arrival in his hotel in Geneva. As with the ending of the short story "Tuesday Siesta," the book cuts short and leaves it to readers to imagine (at least for the time being) what the outcome might be. The technique actually goes back to the serial novels of the nineteenth century, although in those cases constant readers could look forward to relief and new information within a month's time. Here, by contrast, Gabo's faithful will have years to wait—assuming a sequel is forthcoming.

Also worth noting in *Vivir para contarla* is its immense vocabulary, a lexicon vast in recondite, learned, literary words as well as in local, everyday, colloquial items. The book, moreover, is suffused throughout with its author's signature traits of levity and joy—no anger or despair in these pages. As novelist Tomás Eloy Martínez remarks, "Instead of *Vivir para contarla*, this book should have perhaps been called *Vivir para gozarla* [Living to Enjoy/Rejoice in the Tale], for even the worst misfortunes of wretchedness, hunger, and disease are told with an invincible humor."[7]

Gabo fans will marvel at finding here so much raw material—names, phrases, incidents—that would make its way into his major works of fiction. His grandmother Tranquilina Iguarán will hand down her last name to matriarch Úrsula Iguarán in *One Hundred Years*, while her nickname, Mina, becomes that of the innocent, heartbroken teen in the author's beautiful short story "Artificial Roses." The countless people in the region whose name is "Cotes" provide him the family handle for Aureliano Segundo's mistress, Petra Cotes. A movie-house owner, Antonio Daconte, will have a literary off-spring in Nena Daconte, the hapless, star-crossed protagonist of "The Trace of Your Blood in the Snow." The resonantly named María Alejandrina Cervantes, a sex worker encountered by young Gabo, will later be retained and promoted to a madam in *Chronicle of a Death Foretold*.

As for the quotations: as his dad departs for new business, the author recalls, "Only then . . . did I realize how much I loved him" (*VC*, 164; *LTT*, 134), a reflection kept almost verbatim in describing Aureliano Babilonia's reaction to the violent demise of the last José Arcadio, the effete seminarian. Similarly, the boy's Aunt Mama is remembered as saying to a nun, "Usted es de las que confunden el culo con las témporas" (*VC*, 91; "You're one of those women who doesn't know her ass from a day of fasting" [*LTT*, 72]), an insult later hurled at the infamous prude Fernanda del Carpio. (The sentence, I assume, is of a proverbial nature; in English one might say "her ass from her elbow" or "from a hole in the ground.") And then there is Gabo's sister Rita, who learns her school lessons by intoning out loud their rhymes and alliterations (*VC*, 470; *LTT*, 392), much as does the elderly dictator with his comical literacy sessions in *The Autumn of the Patriarch*.

Even more striking are the episodes and situations instantly recognizable as key moments in the fiction. Regarding *One Hundred Years of Solitude* only: The grandma makes and sells animal candies (Úrsula); the grandpa hides in a workshop, crafting little fishes (Colonel Buendía). The author's mother, still a girl, invites her classmates to a house party, for which her parents purchase seventy chamber pots (Meme). Gabito's baby sister Margot eats dirt (little Rebeca). A former servant shows up for the burial of Colonel Márquez, even though the man's death is as yet unannounced (Cataure and José Arcadio Buendía). In another instance: Papalelo tumbles down when trying to grab his 100-year-old parrot, much like Dr. Urbino in *Love in the Time of Cholera* (grandpa survives, however). There are many, many more.

From a larger perspective, these episodes are simply among the countless anecdotes that abound and proliferate in *Living to Tell the Tale*. It has long been a critical commonplace that García Márquez thinks in terms not of ideas but of stories, and a memoir is the perfect venue for him to give free rein to this tendency. Just as the novelist shows a knack for portraying individuals via some telling idiosyncrasy, the memoirist can also string story upon story and weave thereby a worthy total tapestry. One anecdote that stands out tells of the petrol dealer who, at one of Colombia's airports, accidentally fills the storage drums not with aviation fuel but with automobile gasoline—an oversight that causes a public relations nightmare for Gabo's friend and fellow author Álvaro Mutis, at the time a successful oil company executive.

Certain close parallels between *Vivir para contarla* and Proust's master-piece *Remembrance of Things Past* are unavoidable. Indeed, just as the youthful memories of adult narrator Marcel are conjured up by the flavor of a mad-eleine biscuit being taken with a cup of tea, Gabo the memoirist, recalling a tropical meal that he savored on his return visit to Aracataca, remarks: "From the moment I tasted the soup I had the sensation that an entire sleeping world was waking in my memory. Tastes that had been mine in childhood and that I had lost when I left the town reappeared intact with each spoonful, and they gripped my heart" (*VC*, 39; *LTT* 28).

In this respect the epigraph to *Vivir*, often remarked upon by critics, is worth citing in full: "La vida no es lo que uno vivió sino lo que uno recuerda y cómo lo recuerda para contarla" ("Life is not what one lived, but what one remembers and how one remembers in order to recount it"). The last two words of the original Spanish sentence echo those of the title, "*para contarla*"—"to tell it," "it" in this case being the *life* rather than the "tale" found in the English-language idiom.

Such a quasi-aphorism calls attention to the twin roles of selective mem-ory and choice of form in setting forth any personal history. There is no pure, unadulterated past; it is always filtered via the recollector's mind and medium. So profound if obvious a truth has led some critics to assert that, actually, *Vivir para contarla* is yet another "novel" by the Colombian master. Such a notion, though, does violence to the most fundamental categories of knowledge. García Márquez's novels and short stories, while inspired by real places and real people, are nonetheless fictions. A memoir such as *Living*, by contrast, purports to be the truth, and its readers approach it in that spirit and expectation. The Buendías are an invention, whereas the idyllic house of Colonel Márquez, and later the chaotic household of Gabriel Eligio García, really existed, and that is why the author chooses to memorialize them in print.

In 2005, García Márquez surprised interviewers by stating his sudden decision to cease writing, along with his frank relief at not having to write any more. If such is the case, his many devoted readers will no doubt experience disappointment, especially those who had looked forward to the projected second and third volumes of his memoirs. With respect to the recollections unwritten, however, one can see some logic in his choice. Many of the details of Gabito's early youth were not known to his audience and thus constituted brand-new material for volume 1. On the other hand, as he enters his years as a recognized writer and later as a celebrated public icon, a great deal of the biographical data would be well-trod from previous studies (including this one). Besides, writing about one's triumphs and one's friendships with the rich and powerful can lack in narrative suspense, and can even seem unintentionally boastful.

Perhaps García Márquez has made a wise resolution in discontinuing his memoir project. Perhaps some day, by other means, we will find out the mysterious contents of Mercedes's letter to him at a hotel in Geneva, Switzerland.

FOURTEEN

The Legacy

Because of the enormous reach of his reputation, García Márquez is now seen not just as another major author, but as the prime symbol of the surge of creativity in Latin American letters in our twentieth and twenty-first centuries. Doubtless there are other novelists who at the very least came close to equaling the Colombian's achievement: Alejo Carpentier from Cuba, Julio Cortázar from Argentina, Carlos Fuentes from Mexico, and the Peruvian Mario Vargas Llosa all come readily to mind. But it is García Márquez whom readers have come to perceive as standing for that ongoing literary ferment, much as the names "Tolstoy" or "Dostoevsky" are at times employed as a kind of retrospective shorthand for the arrival and impact on the world cultural scene of extraordinary writing from a backward and barbarous Russia.

Of course it is in great degree the accessibility and translatability of this shy Colombian's art that has made possible a world readership so astonishing in its scale. An erudite and conscientious craftsman, García Márquez has nonetheless fashioned an oeuvre that, with the exception of *The Autumn of the Patriarch*, can be savored and comprehended by readers having no especial literary sensibilities or skills. He is that phenomenon rare in our time—a writer both sophisticated and popular, the latter in the sense not only of "widely purchased" but also "of the people." In this regard García Márquez stands in the tradition of the nineteenth-century novelists, whose high art combined the common touch and thus enabled them to speak to large audiences, and who, in the notable case of Hugo, by representing a progressive and humane politics, could inspire genuine affection among their millions of devotees and serve as a positive example to them.

As I suggested in chapter 1, García Márquez's public presence in Colombia and Latin America resembles that of Hugo in the France of his time. Virtually every ordinary Colombian knows who García Márquez is, and tens of millions of Latin Americans have read at least something by the man—a newspaper article, a story, or the one hundred years of Macondo. So much is his work in the public realm that in the 1980s the fine Panamanian salsa singer, composer, and (more recently) screen actor Rubén Blades recorded an entire album of songs with lyrics based on eight García Márquez short stories.[1] And although *One Hundred Years of Solitude* would later spawn certain pale if commercially successful imitations (magical realism "lite," as it were), that landmark novel now exists as a glorious instance of literature's possibilities, of what prose narrative can do for our imaginations and emotions, our politics and pleasures, our knowledge of life and our sense of humor.

At the same time García Márquez's writing joyously flouts and challenges all manner of social and academic proprieties—no doubt one of the reasons for its lively sales in his native land, a country notoriously stuffy in its officially sanctioned values. By ignoring or defying a host of orthodoxies of left, right, and center, García Márquez has freed literature from some shopworn if prestigious rules and, correspondingly, given a solid boost to the grass-roots life of imaginative letters. As a young Bogotá business executive once commented to me, Gabo's book proved to many Colombians that great novels can be fun, and that good literature is not for intellectuals only but for anybody who comes to it seeking enjoyment. García Márquez himself likes the anecdote of the grateful Buenos Aires student who said to him, "Now we're going to show the world that you don't have to be either proper or a big shot or an academic to make literature."[2] Few works resist the authority of monumentalization and sanctification as does that of García Márquez.

The sway of the Colombian author's writing example, moreover, is being felt outside of Latin America, particularly in the United States. In an almost surprising development, in early 2004, *One Hundred Years of Solitude* served as the chosen title for Oprah Winfrey's highly influential TV book club; and in 2008, the same show selected *Love in the Time of Cholera*. The impact of García Márquez's work can even be detected at the level of ordinary, day-to-day printed prose. Newspapers in the Americas and Europe now commonly employ such formulas as "X Years of Solitude" (or "of X"), or "Love in the Time of X," or "Chronicle of an X Foretold" as templates for their headlines.

Moreover, for some three decades, virtually every publishing season north of the Mexican border brought with it at least one volume of fiction that was influenced by García Márquez. The relationship can be discerned at its most fruitful in some of the work of our more outstanding authors. The aura of magic that hovers over such novels as Toni Morrison's *Song of Solomon* or John Nichols's *The Milagro Beanfield War* or even the film *El Norte* would not have been possible without the originating instance—now practically proverbial—of *One Hundred Years*. There are characters in *Milagro* and in William Kennedy's *Ironweed* who routinely chat with the attentive dead or with ghosts, the sort of material that, before Macondo, was confined exclusively to fantastical fables or fairy tales such as *A Christmas Carol*. The narrative repertory of U.S. novelists has thus been visibly enriched by the phantoms of Melquíades and Prudencio Aguilar and their exchanges with select Buendía family members.

The poetical unreality and artful exaggeration with which García Márquez can tell of wars, strikes, and repression have in turn enabled American novelists to write of larger historical forces and collective battles in ways that help transcend the notorious limits and naiveté of 1930s proletarianism. The memory and the specters of a strike of tramway workers haunt the down-and-out hero of *Ironweed*, and a struggle of Hispanic villagers for their land rights in New Mexico is the actual plot line of *Milagro*. Alice Walker's *The Color Purple* beautifully mingles a decades-long story of the fluid life and emotions of a rural Southern black family along with distant reports of British colonialism and imperialism in Africa, in terms roughly analogous to those of the banana firm's arrival and actions in *One Hundred Years*. Robert Coover in *The Public Burning* dreams up a vast panoply of quasi-magical spectacle along with a zany character named "Uncle Sam," the better to convey the sordid atmosphere surrounding the execution of Julius and Ethel Rosenberg. In this regard it is worth mentioning that Coover knows good Spanish — as do Kennedy, who worked as a journalist in Puerto Rico, and also Nichols, who spent some time in Guatemala. Kennedy himself published in 1973 an interview with García Márquez that is something of a minor classic, while Coover's own essayistic tribute to the Colombian, from 1977, is entitled simply "The Master's Voice."

The hand of García Márquez is particularly evident in Paul Theroux's *The Mosquito Coast*, a strangely compelling account of Yankee adventurism in the Caribbean, one that harks back to those nineteenth-century romances of travel and intrigue but also touches on certain deep issues of American imperialism, innocence, and obsessiveness. The New England family that sets out to start anew in the Central American bush is led by a visionary tinkerer of a father who hopes to bring salvation to the tropics with his ice-making invention. In the Edenic utopia of their founding there is no need of a priest, and at one point the family actually posts signs on the jungle trees in order to remember their names. All this is clearly suggestive of José Arcadio Buendía and Macondo, as is the apocalyptic destruction in the novel's concluding scenes. *Mosquito Coast*, let it be said, is a fine novel in its own right, and the fact that a good deal of its plot and ideas owe their existence to García Márquez in no way detracts from the book's artistic strengths.

Still another, more recent U.S. novel that shows the García Márquez imprint is *Cellophane*, by the Peruvian-American editor and memoirist Marie

Arana. The book tells of an engineer-adventurer who, in an unspecified twentieth-century decade, moves from Lima to the jungle with his kin and there launches a cellophane factory (a paper substance that throughout will possess a mysterious, semi-"magical" aura). His populous family includes an eccentric and quite mad daughter-in-law, and his counselor is a wise native shaman by the name of Yorumbo (a kind of equivalent to Melquíades). Among *Cellophane's* more significant narrative elements are a prophetic monkey, some animal spirits, epidemics of truth-telling and of erotic longing, a flock of yellow butterflies with sexual implications, and an endless rain. Portrayals of comic misperceptions and of the power of sex are recurrent topics in its pages. An apocalyptic Nature—in the form of a mighty conflagration together with the jungle—will finally consume the settlement. ("It was the end" are the concluding words.) In addition to these "Macondian" parallels, the book contains an episode of exorcising of demons, as in *Of Love and Other Demons.*

These works from talented U.S. authors illustrate the extent to which Gabo's themes, subjects, and moods have become part of the workshop and the repertory of fiction writing, just as, in music, the innovations of Ravel and Stravinsky once reshaped jazz, and the lush, distinctive harmonies of Astor Piazzolla have more recently become a standard style for crossover tangos and even film soundtracks.

"Who is the living author you most admire?" was the question the *New York Times Book Review* asked of twenty English-speaking writers in 1977. Three of them—Norman Mailer, Lois Gould, and Anne Tyler—mentioned García Márquez. Tyler's statement is especially worth citing. In her view, the Colombian "has somehow figured out how to let time be in literature what it is in life: unpredictable, sometimes circular, looped, doubling back, rushing through sixty years and then doddering over an afternoon, with glimmers of the past and future just beneath the surface."[3] A case in point is Tyler's best-known novel, *Dinner at the Homesick Restaurant,* the very moving chronicle of a Baltimore family whose loving matriarch, Pearl Tull, eventually goes blind. Its first chapter begins in medias res, and consists of a series of flashbacks and flash-forwards, with the thread of the initial scene then picked up on at the end—much the way the opening chapter of *One Hundred Years* works. The novel has love situations that repeat themselves—Pearl is left by Beck, Jenny by Sam—and the book concludes with the sudden reappearance of a long-forgotten past through Beck's surprise return. Most important about *Homesick Restaurant,* however, is its folkish and "balladlike" quality. Conceived at a surprisingly high level of generality, it furnishes very little local description—a few Baltimore street names; and the characters come as close as possible to being essences without becoming allegorical stick figures—not unlike the method of the Colombian author. We read not of Buicks or Hitachis in Tyler's book but simply of "the car" or "the radio." And as narrator she dares to say of Cody Tull, on first hearing Ruth Spivey's last name: "He thought it the loveliest sound he had ever heard in his life"—precisely the sort of sentence that García Márquez has made into his own personal trademark.[4]

The changing narrative theories of novelist John Barth exemplify certain later shifts in American literary values. In 1967 Barth published in *The Atlantic Monthly* his highly influential essay "The Literature of Exhaustion." Singling out the work of Jorge Luis Borges as the writing model for our time, Barth praised the Argentine author for having breathed new life into some tired old forms through the fruitful use of self-reflexiveness and parody. Barth's speculations elicited some incomprehension and controversy when first published, but, in one of those familiar ironies of history, ideas such as his soon rose to dominance in the "postmodern" ethos that settled into certain areas of U.S. letters during the 1970s.

Hence those artfully self-referential metafictions that deal primarily with their own fictionality became the fashion, among campus-based authors particularly. And even before Barth's essay, Borges's own hand was being detected in the fictions of Donald Barthelme, Thomas Pynchon, Robert Coover, and John Gardner.[5] In a parallel development, the antirealist theories of Jacques Derrida and Roland Barthes, among others, achieved a status of quasi-orthodoxy in academic criticism, their highly intellectualized texts seized upon as chief sourcebooks for the new graduate-school clerisy. Polemicists like Rosalind Krauss could even go so far as to see Derrida et al. as the true "*authors*" of our time precisely because their innovative texts did *not* deal with "love or money or the July Monarchy."[6] For the new postmodern "establishment," literature was no longer about life or indeed about anything at all, but rather about itself, and any notion that a writer could address and depict major human concerns was dismissed as embarrassingly outdated and naive.

In 1980 Barth expressed if not exactly a change of heart, then a contrasting outlook that envisioned newer and wider horizons for narrative. The very title of his new essay, "The Literature of Replenishment"—also first published in *The Atlantic*—clearly signaled a reply and a revision to his 1967 piece. And now Barth singled out for highest possible praise none other than *One Hundred Years of Solitude*, citing its "synthesis of straightforwardness and artifice, realism and magic and myth, political passion and nonpolitical artistry, characterization and caricature, humor and terror." More important, the Colombian's novel was "humanly wise, lovable," and gave proof to our own jaded sensibilities that "new fiction could be so *wonderful* as well as so merely important." To the Barth of the 1980s, García Márquez is "that enviable succession [to Borges]: an exemplary postmodernist and a master of the storyteller's art."[7]

As Barth rightly emphasizes, García Márquez restored to fiction that aspect long slighted by official modernism and postmodernism alike: telling stories. More, in defiance of regnant aestheticist claims whereby there is nothing to write "about" and all is text, García Márquez's book joyously spun tales that depict good old-fashioned matters of the heart like love and loss, and tell of fundamental human experiences like time, growth, and death — whole areas that, in our hyperintellectualized postmodern culture, are becoming endangered species. At the same time García Márquez enabled our novelists to rediscover those public and social themes of power, imperialism, and resistance to domination that, in U.S. fiction since 1950, had been more or less taboo subjects. In this regard it is interesting to note the boundaries that, at García Márquez's prompting, were being crossed. Raymond Federman, one of the best known of American metafictionists, could deal fantastically and poetically with wars, student demonstrations, and the Holocaust in his novel *The Twofold Vibration* — in which the opening sentence from *One Hundred Years* is specifically quoted early on.[8] On the other hand John Updike, the bard of America's largely apolitical and intensely private suburban middle class, could venture into new territory in *The Coup*, a novel that tells of a dictator in an imaginary African nation, and is inconceivable from Updike's pen without the example and encouragement of *The Autumn of the Patriarch*.[9]

"Mythic" is one of those facile pat terms often applied to García Márquez. The word "myth," of course, would acquire a certain status in literary criticism in the postwar decades, and a great deal of inspired high nonsense was often evoked in its name. Suffice it to say for our specific purposes that the ancient Greek noun *mythos* meant simply "story" or "tale," and in modern times would denote "a traditional story of unknown authorship, ostensibly with a historical basis, but serving usually to explain some phenomenon of nature, the origin of man, or the customs, institutions, religious rites, etc. of a people" (*Webster's New World Dictionary of the American Language*, 1959). In short, a myth is a narrative that treats fundamental and substantive issues of human existence and purports to furnish some intuitive understanding thereof through its telling. And it is precisely that which García Márquez, with his broad vision, ideological sophistication, and superb story-telling gifts, has furnished his many readers in the Americas and throughout the world.

The influence of Latin American authors on U.S. ones is a fact that invites special attention. Until fairly recently, the prime foreign models for Yankee writers were French. Flaubert/James, the Symbolists/T. S. Eliot, the Naturalists/Dreiser, Céline/Henry Miller, Beckett/Albee: these and other Franco-American literary disciplineships stand in the public record and are the subject of many a scholarly study. Imaginative literature has not been among France's strongest points in the current decades, however, Gallic letters having ushered in their own triumphal "age of criticism" (to cite Randall Jarrell's still-pertinent postwar phrase). Parisian literary life since 1960 has found its crowning heights dominated not by novelists or poets but by theorists of various stripe, and their impact on our American shores is a phenomenon restricted all but exclusively to the rococo realm of the academy. In the absence of vital and inspired innovators in French literary art, the most fertile lessons in U.S. writing over the last few decades have been learned from Latin Americans such as Borges, Cortázar, and particularly García Márquez.[10]

This Latin American narrative sway north of the Rio Grande, then, is a first in our history. What previous cultural influences there were from south to north had made themselves felt rather in the nonverbal arts: in music and—less so—in painting. The Argentine tango, the Brazilian samba, and the wealth of Afro-Caribbean rhythms have repeatedly left their mark on U.S. popular music and on the jazz repertory (including pieces by Dizzy Gillespie, with Spanish titles such as "Con Alma"), while composers in the European tradition such as Copland, Bernstein, Stravinsky, Milhaud, and Virgil Thomson have at different points incorporated Latin forms into works of their own. Similarly, in a now all but forgotten episode, the grand historical wall paintings of Mexican muralists like Diego Rivera would inspire artists of the caliber of Thomas Hart Benton and Ben Shahn, and serve as model for countless instances of public art in the United States during the leftish 1930s.[11] Today for the first time it is the Latin American fiction writers who have been having a creative impact as they remind North Americans of certain deeper, long-term realities, certain basic facts of life and art that, in our late, baroque, overwrought and overly technified civilization, have become dimly remote from our common experience.

Of the Latin American authors it is García Márquez whose presence in *yanqui* letters has proved at this time the most potent and enduring by far. So fruitful an influence must inevitably invite applause, and one can only hope that, despite his recent announcements about putting down the pen and writing no more, he will furnish us a few more magisterial instances of his superb craft. The 1980s saw and lamented the inevitable passing of such major literary figures as Carpentier, Cortázar, and Borges, whose works nevertheless remain. The narrative ferment in Latin America, moreover, has continued into the next generation, notably via the Argentinian Tomás Eloy Martínez, the Colombians Fernando Vallejo and Laura Restrepo, the Chileans Ariel Dorfman, Antonio Skármeta, Diamela Eltit, and, in particular, the dazzlingly inventive Chilean-Mexican-Spanish experimentalist Roberto Bolaño (who, alas, died prematurely at age fifty in 2003)—to cite only a random few.

Meanwhile, himself now past eighty, García Márquez can look back at six decades of marshaling his strengths toward fashioning some lasting narratives of history, politics, and love. These writings—ranging from four-page short stories to five-hundred-page novels—now belong to Colombia, to the Americas, and to those readers worldwide who take pleasure in savoring his distinct set of virtues. Literature is different after *One Hundred Years of Solitude*; so are our thoughts about life and fiction.

Notes

CHAPTER ONE

1. Bruce-Novoa, *Chicano Authors*, p. 243.
2. See "Gabo," "Gabo Nobel de Literatura," "Gabriel García Márquez, el octavo escritor de habla española que obtiene el Nobel," and "Premio Nobel a García Márquez."
3. Santamaría, "El Nobel de Gabo" and "Quiero recibir el Nobel con Vallenatos."
4. Santamaría, "Quiero recibir el Nobel con Vallenatos." See also *El Tiempo*, 22–25 October 1982, passim.
5. Quoted in Fischer, *The Necessity of Art*, p. 92.
6. See Koning, "They also Serve," and Hardwick, "The Fictions of America."

CHAPTER TWO

1. Reichel-Dolmatoff, *Colombia*, pp. 167–68.
2. Granda, "Toponimia de origen bantú," p. 276.
3. Friedemann, *Carnaval en Barranquilla*, p. 79.
4. Granda, "Un afortunado filónimo bantú: *Macondo*," p. 641.
5. Gilard, "El grupo de Barranquilla," passim.
6. Perrin, Introduction to Wilbert and Simoneau, *Folk Literature of the Guajiro Indians*, pp. 2–3.
7. Chomsky, *Linked Labor Histories*, chap. 7, pp. 264–93.
8. Interview with Osorio, "Poco café y mucha política," in Rentería Mantilla, *García Márquez habla de García Márquez*, p. 182.
9. "El viaje a la semilla," interview with *El Manifiesto*, in ibid., p. 164. Also translated in Bell-Villada, ed., *Conversations with Gabriel García Márquez*, p. 86.
10. Oquist, *Violence, Conflict, and Politics in Colombia*, p. 79.
11. Fluharty, *Dance of the Millions*, p. 48.
12. Ibid.
13. For a first-rate account of these events, see Braun, *The Assassination of Gaitán*, pp. 132 ff.
14. Oquist, p. 119. Sánchez, "La violencia y sus efectos," p. 219.
15. Hobsbawm, "La anatomía de La Violencia en Colombia," p. 21.
16. Fluharty, pp. 110–16.
17. Sánchez, p. 220.
18. Oquist, pp. 178, 184, and 155–95.
19. Ibid., p. 225.
20. Sánchez, p. 246.
21. Oquist, p. 186.
22. Sánchez, pp. 231–34. Fluharty, pp. 246–48, 288, 307, 314.

23. Hobsbawm, p. 22.

24. Fals Borda, "Lo sacro y lo profano," pp. 41–42. Fluharty, p. 311.

25. Henao and Arrubla, *History of Colombia*, p. 95.

26. Ibid., p. 156.

27. Kline, *Colombia*, p. 88.

28. Kepner, *The Banana Empire*, pp. 290–327.

29. Valverde, "La nueva respuesta de la literatura colombiana," pp. 854–56.

30. See the excellent "Introducción" by Gustavo Mejía in his edition of Jorge Isaacs, *María*, pp. 7–31.

31. Concerning the artistic value of *María*, see the chapter on that book in Menton, *La novela colombiana*.

32. The spelling of his second last name is uncertain. Variants include Freyle, Freire, Freile, and even Fresle. An English version of *El carnero* exists; see Rodríguez Fresle, *The Conquest of New Granada*, trans. W. C. Atkinson.

33. Rodríguez Freire, *Conquista y redescubrimiento del nuevo reino de Granada*, pp. 244 and 305 respectively.

CHAPTER THREE

1. No complete, current biography of García Márquez exists to date, though Gerald Martin's official life of the author is scheduled for publication in the United States the same year as this book. Still, there is ample biographical information scattered about in journalistic pieces, general-interest critical works, and the hundreds of interviews granted by the novelist since 1967. The following narrative of his life pretends to be neither final nor complete, but synoptic, relevant, and useful to the immediate purposes of our study. It has been pieced together from these sources: Oscar Collazos, *García Márquez: La soledad y la gloria*; Gabriel García Márquez, *El olor de la guayaba: Conversaciones con Plinio Apuleio Mendoza*; Stephen Minta, *Gabriel García Márquez: Writer of Colombia*; Mario Vargas Llosa, *García Márquez: Historia de un deicidio*; and a great many interviews, particularly those compiled in Alfonso Rentería Mantilla, ed., *García Márquez habla de García Márquez*. Last but not least, I must express my scholarly debt to Professor Jacques Gilard for the lengthy biographical "Prólogo" he includes in each of the three main volumes of García Márquez's collected *Obra periodística*, a pioneering project that first helped expand our knowledge of the life, development, and background of the Colombian author. Finally, there is Dasso Saldívar's grand and beautifully written *García Márquez: El viaje a la semilla: La biografía*, a major scholarly contribution, though it stops at around 1970, shortly after *One Hundred Years of Solitude* was published.

2. Collazos, p. 16.

3. Interview with Cobo Borda, "Piedra y Cielo me hizo escritor," p. 34.

4. Collazos, p. 21. This anecdote is placed in Gabo's adolescence in the biographical sections of both Vargas Llosa's and Jacques Gilard's mammoth studies of the author. However, García Márquez at the beginning of his memoirs recounts a similar though much-expanded tale as occurring in his twenty-third year.

5. Cobo Borda, p. 34.

6. Vargas Llosa, p. 33.

7. Gilard, "Prólogo" to *OP*, 1:8.

8. Minta, pp. 42–46.

9. Cobo Borda, p. 35.

10. Vargas Llosa, pp. 37–38.

11. Gilard, "Prólogo" to *OP*, 2:8–13.

12. For a detailed examination of García Márquez's work as film critic, see Gilard, "Prólogo" to *OP*, 2:26–60.

13. Ibid., p. 34.

14. Gilard, "Prólogo" to *OP*, 2:83 and 86.

15. Gilard, "Prólogo" to *OP*, 3:25.

16. Plinio Apuleio Mendoza, "18 años atrás," in Rentería Mantilla, p. 91.

17. Collazos, p. 44.

18. Literally "Pliny Apuleius." Classical first names are still fairly common in Latin America, Colombia in particular.

19. Gilard, "Prólogo" to *OP*, 3:33–36.

20. Gilard, "Prólogo" to *OP*, 3:60–62. Vargas Llosa, pp. 58–59.

21. For detailed examinations of some of those film scripts, see Vargas Llosa, pp. 67–73, and Collazos, pp. 91–95.

22. Saldívar, pp. 428–30.

23. Vargas Llosa, p. 75.

24. Ibid., p. 77.

25. Saldívar, pp. 430–46, traces in loving details this process of creation and composition, along with the circle of friends and literary comrades who gave Gabo sustenance and solace during the entire feverish period.

26. González Bermejo, "Ahora doscientos años de soledad," p. 55. Trans., "And Now, Two Hundred Years of Solitude," in Bell-Villada, ed., *Conversations with Gabriel García Márquez*, p. 13.

27. This phase of García Márquez's journalistic activity is itemized and commented on in Benson, "García Márquez en *Alternativa* (1974–1979)" and "García Márquez en *Alternativa* (1978–1980)."

28. Mera, untitled preface to *Aracataca Estocolmo*, p. 60.

29. Collazos, p. 233.

30. The address, "The Solitude of Latin America," is included in McGuirk and Cardwell, *Gabriel García Márquez*, pp. 207–11.

31. Nereo López, "Testimonio del fotógrafo," in *Aracataca Estocolmo*, p. 95.

32. Collazos, pp. 256–46.

33. Caballero, "El amor en los tiempos del Nobel," p. 32.

34. Gerald Martin, *Gabriel García Márquez: A Life*, pp. 558–59.

CHAPTER FOUR

1. Gilard, "Prólogo" to *OP*, 2:72–73. Collazos, *García Márquez*, pp. 33–34. Vargas Llosa, *García Márquez*, p. 45.

2. In *OP*, 3:483–523, 647–52, and 669–760. Compiled in the shorter volume, García

Márquez, *De viaje por los países socialistas*. Because of its greater accessibility to most readers, I will be using the latter volume for page references.

CHAPTER FIVE

1. Interview with Pereiro, "La revolución cubana me libró," in Rentería Mantilla, *García Márquez habla de García Márquez*, pp. 205–6.

2. "El viaje a la semilla," interview with *El Manifiesto*, in ibid., p. 161. Also in Bell-Villada, ed., *Conversations with Gabriel García Márquez*, p. 82.

3. Interview with Urondo, "La buena hora de GGM," in ibid., p. 73.

4. "El viaje a la semilla," p. 161. In Bell-Villada, ed., *Conversations*, pp. 81–82.

5. Interview with Sarret, "Estoy tan metido en la política," in Rentería Mantilla, p. 215.

6. Interview with Cobo Borda, "Piedra y Cielo me hizo escritor," p. 35.

7. Interviews in Norvind, "Intelectuales interrogan a GGM," in Rentería Mantilla, p. 152.

8. Sophocles, *Oedipus the King*, pp. 128 and 133.

9. Sophocles, *Antigone*, p. 205.

10. Bradley, "Hegel's Theory of Tragedy," passim.

11. Roses, "A Code of Many Colors."

12. Palencia-Roth, *Gabriel García Márquez*, p. 219.

13. Rabelais, *The Histories of Gargantua and Pantagruel*, p. 74.

14. Bakhtin, *Rabelais and His World*, p. 452.

15. Ibid., pp. 6, 11, 45, and 90.

16. Oberhelman, *The Presence of Faulkner in the Writings of García Márquez*. Irby, *La influencia de William Faulkner*.

17. Fuenmayor, *Crónicas sobre el grupo de Barranquilla*, p. 30.

18. The novelist once recalled how "intensely dazzled" he felt "when I first discovered *Light in August*" and "especially *Absalom*." Prego, "Conversación con Gabriel García Márquez," p. 71.

19. Cited in Minter, *William Faulkner*, p. 87.

20. Woolf, *Orlando*, p. 34.

21. Ibid., p. 18.

22. Woolf, *Jacob's Room*, p. 160.

23. Camus, *The Plague*, p. 16.

24. Defoe, *A Journal of the Plague Year*, pp. 136 and 186.

25. Ibid., p. 41.

26. Malaparte, *The Skin*, p. 217.

27. Saldívar, *García Márquez: El viaje a la semilla: La biografía*, pp. 410–12.

CHAPTER SIX

1. Janes, *Gabriel García Márquez*, pp. 61–62.

2. The noun *ternera* means "veal," but here may rather suggest *ternura*, "tenderness." It is worth nothing that, on a visit I made in 1982 to the cemetery in García

Márquez's boyhood town of Aracataca, the first two gravestones I saw were for two women with the family name of Ternera!

3. For a fuller discussion, see Bell-Villada, "Names and Narrative Pattern in *One Hundred Years of Solitude*."

4. Vargas Llosa and García Márquez, *Diálogo*, p. 30.

5. Lévi-Strauss, *The Elementary Structures of Kinship*, pp. 119 ff.

6. Ibid., pp. 9 and 12.

7. Harss and Dohmann, "Gabriel García Márquez, or the Lost Chord," p. 327.

8. Arenas, "En la ciudad de los espejismos," in Martínez, *Sobre García Márquez*, p. 143.

9. Henao and Arrubla, *History of Colombia*, p. 551.

10. Minta, *Gabriel García Márquez*, pp. 14–19.

11. For a detailed account both of the historical events and of García Márquez's treatment of the facts, see Bell-Villada, "Banana Strike and Military Massacre."

12. Castrillón, *120 días bajo el terror militar*, p. 33.

13. Kepner, *The Banana Empire*, p. 320.

14. Bell-Villada, "Journey to Macondo," p. 26.

15. Friedemann, *Carnaval de Barranquilla*, pp. 79–89.

16. Monsalve, "Una entrevista con García Márquez." Quoted in Peel, "Short Stories of García Márquez," p. 165.

17. Maturo, *Claves simbólicas de García Márquez*, p. 155.

18. Monsalve, p. 4.

19. "El viaje a la semilla," interview with *El Manifiesto*, in Rentería Mantilla, *García Márquez habla de García Márquez*, p. 164. "Journey Back to the Source," in Bell-Villada, ed., *Conversations with Gabriel García Márquez*, p. 87.

20. Columbus, *Four Voyages to the New World*, p. 11.

21. Vespucci, *The Letters*, pp. 8, 42, and 47.

22. Pigafetta, *Primer viaje en torno del globo*, p. 48.

CHAPTER SEVEN

1. Benedetti, "García Márquez o la vigilia dentro del sueño," p. 184.

2. Ibid., p. 182.

3. Vargas Llosa, *García Márquez*, p. 58.

4. Ibid., pp. 65 and 73.

5. Benedetti, p. 183.

6. See Bell-Villada, "What the Apprentice García Márquez Learned from the Master Graham Greene," passim.

7. Vargas Llosa, p. 43.

8. René Prieto, "The Body as Political Instrument," pp. 37–38.

9. Ibid., p. 37.

10. Durán, "Conversaciones con Gabriel García Márquez," in Rentería Mantilla, *García Márquez habla de García Márquez*, p. 31. Torres, "El novelista que quiso hacer cine," in ibid., p. 46.

11. Vargas Llosa, p. 476.

12. Cobo Borda, "Piedra y Cielo me hizo escritor," p. 36.

13. Hemingway, "After the Storm," in *Short Stories*, pp. 374–75.

14. For a fine discussion of this story see McMurray, *Gabriel García Márquez*, pp. 120–24.

15. For an examination of possible mythic sources for this story, see Speratti-Piñero, "De las fuentes y su utillización."

16. Michael Palencia-Roth, in his article "Los peregrinajes," notes that only three of the stories do *not* feature a García Márquez–type narrator. They are "Bon Voyage, Mr. President," "María dos Prazeres," and "Seventeen Poisoned Englishmen."

17. For example, in Madrid's *El País*, 1 February 1989. It is widely available on the internet.

18. I am grateful to my friend and colleague Antonio Giménez for verifying this fact for me.

19. There is on Guatemala's Atlantic coast a city called Puerto Santo de Castilla. However, it is only remotely possible that the author had this place in mind when conceiving the story.

20. Gerardo Diego, "Insomnio," *Primera antología de versos*, p. 158.

CHAPTER EIGHT

1. Vargas Llosa, *García Márquez*, pp. 217–32.

2. Janes, *Gabriel García Márquez*, p. 26.

3. Vargas Llosa, p. 426.

4. Janes, p. 35.

5. McMurray, *Gabriel García Márquez*, p. 34.

6. Interview with Monsalve, "La novela, anuncio de grandes transformaciones."

7. Cobo Borda, "Piedra y Cielo me hizo escritor," p. 30.

CHAPTER NINE

1. Williams, *Gabriel García Márquez*, p. 119.

2. Caballero, "Érase una dictadura," in Rentería Mantilla, *García Márquez habla de García Márquez*, p. 121.

3. Nemes, review of *El otoño del patriarca*, p. 176.

4. Janes, *Gabriel García Márquez*, pp. 88–89.

5. Woolf, *Mrs. Dalloway*, p. 92. Subsequent references to this edition appear in the text.

6. Bell-Villada, "Building a Compass" (interview), in Bell-Villada, ed., *Conversations with Gabriel García Márquez*, p. 138.

7. This horrific scene might best be interpreted as a literal dramatization of the political cliché about "tyrants devouring their rivals."

8. Columbus, *Four Voyages to the New World*, pp. 6–8.

9. For a thorough examination of this subject, see Palencia-Roth, "Prisms of Consciousness: The 'New Worlds' of Columbus and García Márquez," and the same author's *Gabriel García Márquez*, pp. 191–201.

10. Palencia-Roth, *Gabriel García Márquez*, pp. 185–90 and 201–15.

11. Unless otherwise indicated, references to dictators in this account come from the following biographies: Thomas Rourke, *Gómez: Tyrant of the Andes*; Robert D. Crassweller, *Trujillo: The Life and Times of a Caribbean Dictator*; Bernard Diederich, *Somoza and the Legacy of U.S. Involvement in Central America*; John Barnes, *Evita, First Lady: A Biography of Eva Perón*; and Robert D. Crassweller, *Perón and the Enigmas of Argentina*.

12. Crassweller, *Trujillo*, p. 134.

13. Barnes, pp. 171–72.

14. Rourke, p. 140.

15. Crassweller, *Trujillo*, p. 129.

16. Pocaterra, *Memorias de un venezolano de la decadencia*, 1:193. Ewell, *Venezuela*, p. 47.

17. Ewell, p. 57.

18. Smith, *The Fourth Floor*, p. 23.

19. Adorno et al., *The Authoritarian Personality*, pp. 654–783.

CHAPTER TEN

1. Dreyfus, "*Playboy* Interview," p. 178. Also in Bell-Villada, ed., *Conversations with Gabriel García Márquez*, p. 132.

2. In the Rabassa translation, "it's because of the liking I have for you." I have offered my own version of this line in the interests of vernacular rhythms.

3. Morello-Frosch, "Función de lo fantástico en . . . *Eréndira*," p. 328.

4. Lüthi, *Once upon a Time*, p. 141.

5. Ibid., p. 53.

6. Hancock, "Gabriel García Márquez's 'Eréndira,'" p. 49.

7. Lüthi, p. 45.

8. Ibid., p. 51. See also Meneses, review of *Eréndira*.

9. I have again slightly altered Rabassa's translation of these lines.

10. The final movie version was faithful enough to the story's plot and atmosphere, and Claudia Ohana was well cast in the title role. On the other hand, the movie was far too slow paced and not very funny, and Irene Pappas as the grandmother looked neither evil nor obese enough.

11. Vargas Llosa, *García Márquez*, p. 634.

12. Donald L. Shaw, "*Chronicle of a Death Foretold*," pp. 96–98.

13. Ruffinelli, "*Crónica de una muerte anunciada*," p. 278.

14. Williams, *Gabriel García Márquez*, p. 137.

15. Ávila, "Una lectura," p. 37.

16. March, "*Crónica de una muerte anunciada*," p. 61. Rama, "García Márquez entre la tragedia y la policial," p. 17.

17. March, p. 65. Rama, pp. 16–21, argues from internal evidence that Ángela Vicario's perpetrator may have been the narrator himself. It is a compelling yet ultimately less than convincing argument, inasmuch as it goes against the larger spirit and themes of the plot.

18. Palencia-Roth, *"Crónica de una muerte anunciada."*

19. Rama, pp, 10–11.

20. Solotorevsky, *"Crónica de una muerte anunciada,"* p. 1090.

21. Jarvis, "El halcón y la presa," p. 226.

22. For an excellent examination of the epigraph and its relation to the novel's themes, see Jarvis, passim. Her article helpfully cites the poem in full. The following awkward translation is mine.

Halcón que se atreve	A falcon taking chances
con garza guerrera	With any fighting heron
peligros espera.	Is simply looking for troubles.
Halcón que se vuela	A falcon that was flying
con garza a porfía,	With a heron, was so stubborn
cazarla quería,	He wanted to hunt her
y no la recela.	And didn't suspect her.
Mas quien no se vela	But he who won't feel wary
de garza guerrera.	Of any fighting heron
peligros espera.	Is simply looking for troubles.
La caza de amor	The hunt for love
es de altanería;	Is like falconry / arrogance;
trabajos de día,	Hardship by day,
de noche dolor.	At night, sheer pain.
Halcón cazador,	Hunting falcon
con garza tan fiera,	With that wild heron,
peligros espera.	You're just looking for troubles.

23. Rama, p. 14.

24. Solotorevsky, p. 1090. López de Martínez, "El neorrealismo de Gabriel García Márquez," p. 246.

25. For the following account, I have relied chiefly on García, *La tercera muerte de Santiago Nasar*, pp. 39–88. See also Grossman, "Truth is Stranger than Fact," which includes photographs of Miguel Reyes Palencia and of Cayetano Gentile.

26. Dreyfus, p. 178. Also in Bell-Villada, ed., *Conversations*, p. 130.

27. Guibert, "Gabriel García Márquez," p. 316.

28. López Michelsen, "López presenta la novela," p. 7.

29. Ibid.

30. Marlise Simons, "Love and Age: A Talk with Gabriel García Márquez," in Bell-Villada, ed., *Conversations*, pp. 143–44.

31. Cf. Beauvoir, *Old Age*, the first chapter, "Old Age and Biology," pp. 17–37.

32. Ibid., chapter "The Discovery and Assumption of Old Age," pp. 283–361.

33. Ibid., p. 317.

34. See chapter 3 above.

35. Arroyo, "El amor, la vejez, la muerte," p. 2. Font Castro, "Las claves reales," passim.

36. Hamill, "Love and Solitude," p. 192.

37. Simons, "García Márquez on Love," p. 23. Also in Bell-Villada, ed., *Conversations*, pp. 156–57.

38. Arroyo, pp. 2–3.

39. Palencia-Roth, "La primera novela de García Márquez después del premio Nobel," p. 7.

40. In this connection it is worth recalling that Flaubert's father was a doctor, while García Márquez's had studied medicine.

41. See chapter 2.

42. Simons, "García Márquez on Love," p. 23. Also in Bell-Villada, ed., *Conversations*, p. 156.

43. In her otherwise fine translation, Grossman semantically narrows "lazareto" to "leprosarium" (*L*, 79).

44. Arroyo, p. 2.

45. Flaubert, *Sentimental Education*, p. 22.

46. Ibid., pp. 59 and 65–66.

47. Simons, "The Best Years of His Life," p. 48. Also in Bell-Villada, ed., *Conversations*, p. 165.

48. For an excellent discussion along these lines, see Minta, *Gabriel García Márquez*, pp. 138–41.

49. Ibid., pp. 142–43.

50. The 2007 film version by the British cinéaste Mike Newell was beautiful to look at, and the sound track featured some fine music by Colombian singer-composer Shakira. The decision to have the actors deliver the dialogue in English with Spanish accents, however, was an unfortunate one. Moreover, the humor of the novel was totally absent. Hence the final line, which in García Márquez's book is ironic and parodic, something of a joke, is played straight by Javier Bardem.

CHAPTER ELEVEN

1. Llácer Llorca and Enjuto Castellanos, "Historia novelada o novela histórica," p. 152.

2. Quoted in Werz, "Reflexiones sobre la imagen de Bolívar y la enseñanza de la historia en Venezuela," p. 115.

3. Quoted in ibid., pp. 116–17.

4. Discussed in Vargas, "*El general en su laberinto*: Una subversión del discurso de la proceridad," p. 75. For a wider-ranging discussion of this topic, see Conway, *The Cult of Bolívar in Latin American Literature*.

5. This portrait and sketch are compiled from the following sources: Lynch, *Simón Bolívar: A Life*; Masur, *Simón Bolívar*; Madariaga, *Bolívar*; and Rourke, *Man of Glory: Simón Bolívar*.

6. For an initial draft of this itinerary, I am indebted to Vargas V., "Biografía, historia y literatura," p. 46.

7. Vargas Vargas, "*El general en su laberinto*: Hacia un verosímil latinoamericano," p. 42.

8. Kline, *Los orígenes del relato*, p. 303.

9. Oviedo, "García Márquez en el laberinto de la soledad," p. 77.

10. Ortega, "The Reader in the Labyrinth," p. 90.

11. Samper, *"The General in His Labyrinth* Is a 'Vengeful' Book," p. 180.

12. Cited in Klooster, "La versión garciamarquiana," p. 59.

13. Cited in Lynch, p. 276.

14. Cited in ibid., p. 264.

15. Llácer Llorca and Enjuto Castellanos, p. 158. Weldt-Basson, "The Purpose of Historical Reference," p. 104.

16. Madariaga, p. 644.

17. Lynch, p. 277, mentions that the Drs. Révérend and MacNight did diagnose "a serious lung condition."

18. Menton, *Latin America's New Historical Novel*, p. 101.

19. The Latin original reads *"in secula seculorum."*

20. Rohter, "García Márquez Portrays Bolívar's Feet of Clay," p. C13.

21. Ibid.

22. Ibid., p. C15.

23. Kline, p. 320.

24. Rohter, p. C15.

25. Leonard, "García Márquez versus Simón Bolívar," p. 248.

CHAPTER TWELVE

1. Kerk, "Patterns of Place and Visual-Spatial Imagery," pp. 774–76.

2. Cussen, "García Márquez's *Of Love and Other Demons*," p. 53.

3. Ibid., pp. 53–54.

4. Lewis, *The Allegory of Love*, pp. 34–35.

5. I have slightly altered Edith Grossman's translations in order to make them conform to Elizabethan diction and verse rhythms.

6. Camacho Delgado, "La religión del amor en la última narrativa de Gabriel García Márquez," p. 169.

7. Fajardo Valenzuela, "El mundo africano en *Del amor y otros demonios*," p. 105.

8. Ibid., p. 106.

9. Edwards and Mason, *Black Gods*, p. 60. Deaver, "Obsesión, posesión y opresión en *Del amor y otros demonios*," p. 82.

10. Edwards and Mason, p. 66.

11. ⟨http://w3/lac.net/-moonweb/Santeria/Drum/Oddua.html.⟩ Just incidentally, there is in San Francisco a small company called "Oddua Records," that specializes in world, jazz, hip-hop, and fusion music.

12. Edwards and Mason, p. 42.

13. Ibid., p. 8.

14. ⟨http://en.Wikipedia.org/Wiki/Shango⟩.

15. Leonard, review of *Of Love and Other Demons*, p. 838.

16. Espenak, *World Atlas of Solar Eclipse Paths*. I am grateful to Professor Jay Pasachoff of Williams College for helping me secure this information.

17. Camacho Delgado, p. 159.

18. Ibid.

19. Lopez de Abiada, "La niña, el exorcista y el amor demonizado," p. 153.

20. Ortega, "Del amor y otras lecturas," p. 273.

21. Bell-Villada, "Building a Compass" [interview], p. 137.

22. Ortega, "*Memoria de mis putas tristes*," p. 74.

23. Coetzee, review of *Memories of My Melancholy Whores*, p. 6.

CHAPTER THIRTEEN

1. Dreyfus, "*Playboy* Interview: Gabriel García Márquez," in Bell-Villada, ed., *Conversations with Gabriel García Márquez*, p. 99.

2. For an in-depth look at the many personalities, major and minor, that populate García Márquez's book, see Ángel Díaz Arenas, *Reflexiones en torno a "Noticia de un secuestro*," passim.

3. I am greatly indebted to Professor Bruce Bagley of the University of Miami for providing necessary background information. For a readable, if slightly one-dimensional, journalistic account, see Bowden, *Killing Pablo: The Hunt for the World's Greatest Outlaw*.

4. Cato, "Gabo Changes Jobs," in Bell-Villada, ed., *Conversations*, p. 186.

5. Ibid., p. 187.

6. Pombo, "García Márquez habla de su nuevo libro," p. 455.

7. Martínez, "La imagen ante el espejo," p. 198.

CHAPTER FOURTEEN

1. Recording by Rubén Blades, *Agua de luna*, Electra 9 60721-1.

2. Vargas, "El nuevo Quijote de la literatura española," in Rentería Mantilla, *García Márquez habla de García Márquez*, p. 19.

3. Statement by Tyler in "Writers' Writers," *New York Times Book Review*, 4 December 1977, p. 70.

4. Tyler, *Dinner at the Homesick Restaurant*, p. 151.

5. On the matter of Borges's influence on U.S. writers, see Bell-Villada, *Borges and His Fiction*, second edition, pp. 278–81.

6. Krauss, "Poststructuralism and the 'Paraliterary,'" pp. 37 and 40 (emphasis in the original). See also my comments on Krauss's essay in Bell-Villada, "Criticism and the State," pp. 124–25.

7. Barth, "The Literature of Replenishment," in *The Friday Book*, pp. 204–5.

8. Federman, *The Twofold Vibration*, p. 11.

9. Updike, *The Coup*.

10. The impact of García Márquez's work on literary culture in the Middle East and Asia is a subject that has only begun to be explored. In this regard, see Carlos Rincón, "Streams out of Control: The Latin American Plot," in *Gabriel García Márquez's "One Hundred Years of Solitude": A Casebook*, edited by Gene H. Bell-Villada, pp. 153–69.

11. O'Connor, "The Influence of Diego Rivera," passim.

Select Bibliography

Even before his Nobel Prize, secondary writings on Garcia Márquez had constituted something of an annual flood. Since October 1982 that flood has grown into an ever-present deluge. To consult everything—good, bad, and indifferent—about the Colombian author would be to embark on a journey without end. (The most complete bibliography on García Márquez now takes up four very fine volumes from Greenwood Press.) Inevitably one ends up choosing those books, articles, and interviews most suitable to one's general needs and approach. Gaps are inevitable; that somewhere in our libraries there is a first-rate but unrecognized study of García Márquez is a suspicion that ever lingers on.

In compiling the following select bibliography, I necessarily restrict myself to those major and minor sources that 1) I have at any time read or consulted and also that 2) I have incorporated in some way into the general thinking of this book (whether or not the works are cited in my text and notes). I express my sincerest apologies to all the good journalists, scholars, critics, and theorists whose work—due to reasons either of my neglect or their incompatibility with a general-interest study such as this one—may not be listed here.

WORKS BY GABRIEL GARCÍA MÁRQUEZ

In Spanish

El amor en los tiempos del cólera. Barcelona: Bruguera, 1985.
La aventura de Miguel Littín, clandestino en Chile. Madrid: Ediciones El País, 1986.
La bendita manía de contar. Barcelona: Ollero & Ramos, 1998.
Cien años de soledad. With an Introduction by Joaquín Marco. Madrid: Espasa Calpe, 1984.
El coronel no tiene quien le escriba. Mexico City: Editorial Era, 1972.
Crónica de una muerte anunciada. Buenos Aires: Editorial Sudamericana, 1984.
Del amor y otros demonios. Barcelona: Mondadori, 1994.
De viaje por los países socialistas. Cali, Colombia: Ediciones Macondo, 1980.
Diatriba de amor contra un hombre sentado. Barcelona: Grijalbo Mondadori, 1995.
Doce cuentos peregrinos. Buenos Aires: Editorial Sudamericana, 1992.
Los funerales de la Mamá Grande. Buenos Aires: Editorial Sudamericana, 1970.
El general en su laberinto. Bogotá: Editorial Oveja Negra, 1989.
La hojarasca. Buenos Aires: Editorial Sudamericana, 1972.
La increíble y triste historia de la cándida Eréndira y de su abuela desalmada. Barcelona: Barral Editores, 1972.
La mala hora. Buenos Aires: Editorial Sudamericana, 1972.
Memoria de mis putas tristes. New York: Vintage Español, Random House, 2004.
Noticia de un secuestro. Barcelona: Mondadori, 1996.

Obra periodística. Vol. 1, *Textos costeños*. Edited with an Introduction by Jacques Gilard. Barcelona: Bruguera, 1981.

Obra periodística. Vol. 2, *Entre cachacos I*. Edited with an Introduction by Jacques Gilard. Barcelona: Bruguera, 1982.

Obra periodística. Vol. 3, *Entre cachacos II*. Edited by Jacques Gilard. Barcelona: Bruguera, 1982.

Obra periodística. Vol. 4, *De Europa y América (1955–1960)*. Edited with an Introduction by Jacques Gilard. Barcelona: Bruguera, 1983.

Ojos de perro azul. Barcelona: Plaza y Janés, 1979.

El olor de la guayaba. Conversaciones con Plinio Apuleio Mendoza. Barcelona: Bruguera, 1982.

El otoño del patriarca. Buenos Aires: Editorial Sudamericana, 1975.

Relato de un náufrago . . . . Barcelona: Tusquets, 1970.

Vivir para contarla. Bogotá: Editorial Norma, 2002.

In English Translation

The Autumn of the Patriarch. Translated by Gregory Rabassa. New York: Harper & Row, 1976.

Chronicle of a Death Foretold. Translated by Gregory Rabassa. New York: Alfred A. Knopf, 1982.

Clandestine in Chile. The Adventures of Miguel Littín. Translated by Asa Zatz. New York: Henry Holt, 1987.

Collected Stories. Translated by Gregory Rabassa and J. S. Bernstein. New York: Harper & Row, 1984.

The Fragrance of Guava. Plinio Apuleio Mendoza in Conversation with Gabriel García Márquez. Translated by Ann Wright. London: Verso, 1983.

The General in His Labyrinth. Translated by Edith Grossman. New York: Alfred A. Knopf, 1990.

In Evil Hour. Translated by Gregory Rabassa. New York: Harper & Row, 1979.

Leaf Storm and Other Stories. Translated by Gregory Rabassa. New York: Harper & Row, 1972.

Living to Tell the Tale. Translated by Edith Grossman. New York: Alfred A. Knopf, 2003.

Love in the Time of Cholera. Translated by Edith Grossman. New York: Alfred A. Knopf, 1988.

Memories of My Melancholy Whores. Translated by Edith Grossman. New York: Alfred A. Knopf, 2005.

News of a Kidnapping. Translated by Edith Grossman. New York: Alfred A. Knopf, 1997.

No One Writes to the Colonel and Other Stories. Translated by J. S. Bernstein. New York: Harper & Row, 1968.

Of Love and Other Demons. Translated by Edith Grossman. New York: Penguin Books, 1995.

One Hundred Years of Solitude. Translated by Gregory Rabassa. New York: Avon Books, 1979.

The Story of a Shipwrecked Sailor . . . . Translated by Randolph Hogan. New York: Alfred A. Knopf, 1986.

Strange Pilgrims. Translated by Edith Grossman. New York: Alfred A. Knopf, 1993.

INTERVIEWS WITH GARCÍA MÁRQUEZ

Algazal. "Diálogo con Gabriel García Márquez. 'Ahora que los críticos me han descubierto.'" *Lecturas Dominicales* in *El Tiempo* (Bogotá), 26 May 1968, p. 5.

Arroyo, Francesç. "El amor, la vejez, la muerte." *Los Libros* in *El País* (Madrid), 12 December 1985, pp. 1–3.

Azancot, Leopoldo. "GGM habla de política." *Indice* (Madrid) año 24, no. 237 (November 1968): 30–31. Reprinted in *García Márquez habla de García Márquez*, edited by Alfonso Rentería Mantilla (q.v.), pp. 37–39.

Bell-Villada, Gene H. "Building a Compass." *South: The Third World Magazine*, January 1983, pp. 22–23. Reprinted in *Conversations with Gabriel García Márquez*, edited by Gene H. Bell-Villada (q.v.), pp. 133–40. Reprinted as "A Conversation with Gabriel García Márquez" in *Gabriel García Márquez's "One Hundred Years of Solitude": A Casebook*, edited by Gene H. Bell-Villada (q.v.), pp. 17–24.

———, ed. *Conversations with Gabriel García Márquez*. Jackson: University Press of Mississippi, 2006.

Caballero, Oscar. "Érase una dictadura." *Cambio 16* (Madrid), 1975. Reprinted in *García Márquez habla de García Márquez*, edited by Alfonso Rentería Mantilla (q.v.), pp. 119–25.

Castro, Rosa. "Con Gabriel García Márquez." *¡Siempre!* (Mexico City), no. 739 (23 August 1967): 6–7. Reprinted in *Sobre García Márquez*, edited by Pedro Simón Martínez (q.v.), pp. 26–30.

Cato, Susana. "Gabo Changes Jobs." Translated by Gene H. Bell-Villada. In *Conversations with Gabriel García Márquez*, edited by Gene H. Bell-Villada (q.v.), pp. 184–90.

———. "García Márquez regresó a Bolívar al campo de batalla." *Proceso* no. 648 (3 April 1989): 51–55.

———. "'Soap Operas Are Wonderful: I've Always Wanted to Write One.'" Translated by Gene H. Bell-Villada. In *Conversations with Gabriel García Márquez*, edited by Gene H. Bell-Villada (q.v.), pp. 148–53.

Cobo Borda, Juan Gustavo. "Piedra y Cielo me hizo escritor." *Cromos* (Bogotá), 28 April 1981, pp. 30–36.

Couffon, Claude. "Gabriel García Márquez habla de *Cien años de soledad*." In *Sobre García Márquez*, edited by Pedro Simón Martínez (q.v.), pp. 26–30.

Dreyfus, Claudia. "*Playboy* Interview: Gabriel García Márquez." *Playboy* 30, no. 3 (February 1983): 65–77, 172–78. Reprinted in *Conversations with Gabriel García Márquez*, edited by Gene H. Bell-Villada (q.v.), pp. 93–132.

Durán, Armando. "Conversaciones con Gabriel García Márquez." *Revista Nacional de Cultura* (Caracas), año 24, vol. 29, no. 185 (July–September 1968): 23–34. Reprinted in *Sobre García Márquez*, edited by Pedro Simón Martinez (q.v.), pp. 31–41. Reprinted in *García Márquez habla de García Márquez*, edited by Alfonso Rentería Mantilla (q.v.), pp. 29–35.

González Bermejo, Ernesto. "Ahora doscientos años de soledad." *Marcha* (Montevideo), no. 1510 (11 September 1970): 30–31. Reprinted in *García Márquez habla de García Márquez,* edited by Alfonso Rentería Mantilla (q.v.), pp. 49–64. Reprinted and translated as "And Now, Two Hundred Years of Solitude," in *Conversations with Gabriel García Márquez,* edited by Gene H. Bell-Villada (q.v.), pp. 3–30.

Gossaín, Juan. "García Márquez escribe sus memorias." *El Heraldo* (Barranquilla), 21 May 1981.

Guibert, Rita. "Gabriel García Márquez." In *Seven Voices: Seven Latin American Writers Talk to Rita Guibert,* translated by Frances Partridge, with an Introduction by Emir Rodríguez Monegal, pp. 305–37. New York: Random House, 1973. Reprinted in *Conversations with Gabriel García Márquez,* edited by Gene H. Bell-Villada (q.v.), pp. 31–58.

Hamill, Pete. "Love and Solitude." *Vanity Fair,* March 1988, pp. 124–31, 191–92.

Kennedy, William. "The Yellow Trolley Car in Barcelona and Other Visions: A Profile of Gabriel García Márquez." *The Atlantic* 231, no. 1 (January 1973): 50–58. Reprinted in *Conversations with Gabriel García Márquez,* edited by Gene H. Bell-Villada (q.v.), pp. 59–78.

Monsalve, Alfonso. "Una entrevista con García Márquez: La novela, anuncio de grandes transformaciones." *Lecturas Dominicales* in *El Tiempo* (Bogotá), 14 January 1968, p. 4.

Mora, Rosa. "Gabriel García Márquez: He escrito mi libro más duro, y el más triste." *El País* (Madrid) 15 May 1996: 1 and 32.

"Mucho de lo que he contado es la primera vez que lo digo." [No interviewer given.] *América Latina* (Moscow) 25, no. 1 (1980); 79–105.

Norvind, Eva. "Intelectuales interrogan a GGM." *Hombre de Mundo* (Mexico City), 1977. Reprinted in *García Márquez habla de Garcia Márquez,* edited by Alfonso Rentería Mantilla (q.v.), pp. 151–54.

Osorio, Manuel. "Poco café y mucha política." *Cuadernos para el diálogo* (Madrid), 1978. Reprinted in *García Márquez habla de García Márquez,* edited by Alfonso Rentería Mantilla (q.v.), pp. 179–84.

Pereira, Manuel. "La revolución cubana me libró de todos los honores detestables de este mundo." *Bohemia* (Havana), 1979. Reprinted in *García Márquez habla de García Márquez,* edited by Alfonso Rentería Mantilla (q.v.), pp. 201–9.

Pombo, Roberto. "García Márquez habla de su nuevo libro." In *Repertorio crítico sobre Gabriel García Márquez,* edited by Juan Gustavo Cobo Borda (q.v.), pp. 453–60.

Prego, Omar. "Conversación con Gabriel García Márquez." *Cuadernos de Marcha* (Mexico City) 3, no. 15 (September–October 1981): 69–77.

Rentería Mantilla, Alfonso, ed. *García Márquez habla de García Márquez.* Bogotá: Rentería Mantilla Ltda., 1979.

Salgar, José. "¿Hacia Dónde Va Gabo?" *Magazín Dominical* in *El Espectador* (Bogotá), 11 November 1971, pp. 6–7.

Samper Pizano, Daniel. "El novelista García Márquez no volverá a escribir." *Lecturas Dominicales* in *El Tiempo* (Bogotá), 22 December 1968, p. 5. Reprinted as "Gabriel García Márquez se dedicará a la música" in *García Márquez habla de García Márquez,* edited by Alfonso Rentería Mantilla (q.v.), pp. 21–27.

Sarret, Josep. "Estoy tan metido en la política que siento nostalgia de la literatura." *El Viejo Topo* (Barcelona), 1979. Reprinted in *García Márquez habla de García Márquez*, edited by Alfonso Rentería Mantilla (q.v.), pp. 211–18.

Schóo, Ernesto. "La gran novela de América." *Primera Plana* (Buenos Aires), June 1967. Reprinted in *García Márquez habla de García Márquez*, edited by Alfonso Rentería Mantilla (q.v.), pp. 11–16.

Simons, Marlise. "The Best Years of His Life: An Interview with Gabriel García Márquez." *New York Times Book Review*, 11 April 1988, p. 48. Reprinted in *Conversations with Gabriel García Márquez*, edited by Gene H. Bell-Villada (q.v.), pp. 163–67.

———. "García Márquez on Love, Plagues, and Politics."' *New York Times Book Review*, 21 February 1988, pp. 1, 23–25. Reprinted in *Conversations with Gabriel García Márquez*, edited by Gene H. Bell-Villada (q.v.), pp. 154–62.

Stone, Peter H. "Gabriel García Márquez." *The Paris Review* 82 (Winter 1981): 45–73.

Suárez, Luis. "El periodismo me dio conciencia política." *La Calle* (Madrid), 1978. Reprinted in *García Márquez habla de García Márquez*, edited by Alfonso Rentería Mantilla (q.v.), pp. 195–201.

Torres, Miguel. "El novelista que quiso hacer cine." *Revista de Cine Cubano* (Havana), 1969. Reprinted in *García Márquez habla de García Márquez*, edited by Alfonso Rentería Mantilla (q.v.), pp. 45–48.

Urondo, Francisco. "La buena hora de GGM." *Cuadernos Hispanoamericanos*, no. 232 (April 1969): 163–68. Reprinted in *García Márquez habla de García Márquez*, edited by Alfonso Rentería Mantilla (q.v.), pp. 71–74.

Vargas, Raúl. "El nuevo Quijote de la literatura española." *Pueblo* (Madrid), 1968. Reprinted in *García Márquez habla de García Márquez*, edited by Alfonso Rentería Mantilla (q.v.), pp. 17–19.

Vargas Llosa, Mario, and Gabriel García Márquez. *Diálogo: La novela en América Latina*. New York: Ediciones Latinoamericanas, 1972.

"'El viaje a la semilla." [No interviewer given.] *El Manifiesto* (Bogotá), 1977. Reprinted in *García Márquez habla de García Márquez*, edited by Alfonso Rentería Mantilla (q.v.). pp. 159–67. Translated and reprinted as "Journey Back to the Source," in *Conversations with Gabriel García Márquez*, edited by Gene H. Bell-Villada (q.v.), pp. 79–92.

BOOKS AND ARTICLES DEALING WITH GARCÍA MÁRQUEZ

Alemany Bay, Carmen. *"Doce cuentos peregrinos*: Búsqueda fragmentaria de un nuevo modelo narrativo." In *Quinientos años de soledad: Actas del congreso "Gabriel García Márquez,"* edited by Túa Blesa (q.v.), pp. 347–51.

Alfaro, Gustavo. *Constante de la historia de Latinoamérica en García Márquez*. Cali, Colombia: Biblioteca Banco Popular, 1979.

Álvarez, Federico. "Al filo de la soledad." In *Sobre García Márquez*, edited by Pedro Simón Martínez (q.v.), pp. 115–16.

Álvarez-Borland, Isabel. "From Mystery to Parody: (Re)Readings of García Márquez's *Crónica de una muerte anunciada*." *Symposium* 38, no. 4 (Winter 1984–85): 278–86.

———. "The Task of the Historian in *El general en su laberinto*." *Hispania* 76 (September 1993): 439–45.

Anaya, Marta. "Iré de Guayabera Cuando me Entreguen la Presea, Dijo." *Excélsior* (Mexico City), 22 October 1982, pp. 1, 9A, 30.

Aracataca Estocolmo. [No editor.] Reports and recollections by Ana Lucía Mera, Álvaro Castaño Castillo, Germán Vargas, Alfonso Fuenmayor, Guillermo Angulo, and Nereo López. Bogotá: Instituto Colombiano de Cultura, 1983.

Arenas, Reinaldo. "En la ciudad de los espejismos." *Casa de las Américas* (Havana) 7, no. 43 (May–June 1968): 134–38. Reprinted in *Sobre García Márquez*, edited by Pedro Simón Martínez (q.v.), pp. 139–46.

Arnau, Carmen. *El mundo mítico de Gabriel García Márquez*. Barcelona: Ediciones Península, 1971.

A. V. "Un mito que deviene novela." In *Sobre García Márquez*, edited by Pedro Simón Martínez (q.v.), pp. 126–27.

Ávila. Pablo Luis. "Una lectura de *Crónica de una muerte anunciada*." *Casa de las Américas* (Havana) 24, no. 140 (September–October 1983): 28–40.

Bell-Villada, Gene H. "Banana Strike and Military Massacre: *One Hundred Years of Solitude* and What Happened in 1928." In *From Dante to García Márquez: Studies in Romance Literatures and Linguistics Presented to Anson C. Piper*, edited by Gene H. Bell-Villada, Antonio Giménez, and George Pistorius, pp. 391–403. Williamstown: Williams College, 1987. In *Gabriel García Márquez's "One Hundred Years of Solitude": A Casebook*, edited by Gene H. Bell-Villada (q.v.), pp. 127–38.

———. "Journey to Macondo in Search of García Márquez." *Boston Review* 8, no. 2 (March–April 1983): 25–27.

———. "Names and Narrative Pattern in *One Hundred Years of Solitude*." *Latin American Literary Review* 9, no. 18 (1981): 37–46.

———. "Pronoun Shifters, Virginia Woolf, Bela Bartók, Plebeian Forms, Real-Life Tyrants, and the Shaping of García Márquez's *Patriarch*." *Contemporary Literature* 28, no. 4 (Winter 1987–88): 460–82.

———. "What the Apprentice García Márquez Learned from the Master Graham Greene: The Case of 'Un día de éstos.'" *The Comparatist: Journal of the Southern Comparative Literature Association* 24 (2000): 146–56.

———, editor. *Gabriel García Márquez's "One Hundred Years of Solitude: A Casebook"*. New York: Oxford University Press, 2002.

Benedetti, Mario. "García Márquez o la vigilia dentro del sueño." In *Letras del continente mestizo*, pp. 180–89. Montevideo: Arca, 1967.

———, et al. *9 asedios a García Márquez*. Santiago de Chile: Editorial Universitaria S.A., 1971.

Benítez Rojo, Antonio, and Hilda O. Benítez. "Eréndira liberada: La subversión del mito del macho occidental." *Revista Iberoamericana* 50, nos. 128–29 (July–December 1984): 1057–75.

Benson, John. "García Márquez en *Alternativa* (1974–1979): Una bibliografía comentada." *Chasqui* 8, no. 3 (May 1979): 69–31.

———. "García Márquez en *Alternativa* (1978–1980): Una bibliografía comentada." *Chasqui* 10, nos. 2–3 (February–May 1981): 41–46.

Blanco Aguinaga, Carlos. *De mitólogos y novelistas*. Madrid: Ediciones Turner, 1975.

Blesa, Túa, ed. *Quinientos años de soledad: Actas del Congreso "Gabriel García Márquez."* Zaragoza: Anexos de Tropelías, 1992.

Bloom, Harold, ed. *Gabriel García Márquez*. New York: Chelsea House, 1999.

Bost, David. *"Del amor y otros demonios*: García Márquez's Silent Dialogue with the World of *El carnero." South Carolina Modern Language Review* 2, no. 1 (Spring 2003). No pagination. (Electronic publication.)

Boyers, Robert. "The Head of State and the Politics of Eternal Return in Latin America." In *Atrocity and Amnesia: The Political Novel since 1945*, pp. 71–92. New York: Oxford University Press, 1985.

Brotherston, Gordon. "An End to Secular Solitude: Gabriel García Márquez." In *The Emergence of the Latin American Novel*, pp. 122–35. New York: Cambridge University Press, 1977.

Bushnell, David. "¿El primer Nobel historiógrafo?" *Revista de Estudios Colombianos* 7 (1989): 32–35.

Caballero, Antonio. "El amor en los tiempos del Nobel." *Semana* (Bogotá) 187 (3–9 December 1985): 28–35.

Camacho Delgado, José Manuel. "La religión del amor en la última narrativa de Gabriel García Márquez." *Letras de Deusto* 27 no. 74 (January–March 1997): 155–70.

Canfield, Martha. *Gabriel García Márquez*. Bogotá: Procultura, 1991.

———. "El patriarca de García Márquez: Padre, poeta y tirano." *Revista Iberoamericana* 50, nos. 128–29 (July–December 1984): 1017–56.

Cano, Luis C. *"Noticia de un secuestro* de Gabriel García Márquez: Entre el cuento popular y el reportaje." *Revista Iberoamericana* 207 (April–June 2004): 419–30.

Carballo, Emmanuel. "Gabriel García Márquez: Un gran novelista latinoamericano." In *9 asedios a García Márquez*, by Mario Benedetti et al. (q.v.), pp. 22–37.

Carrillo, Germán Darío. *La narrativa de Gabriel García Márquez*. Madrid: Ediciones de Arte y Bibliofilia, 1975.

Carullo, Sylvia Graciela. "The Real Model and the Imagined Model in *Of Love and Other Demons." Readerly/Writerly Texts: Essays in Literature, Literary/Textual Criticism, and Pedagogy* 4, no. 1 (Fall–Winter 1996): 157–64.

Carvalho, Susan. "García Márquez Transcribed: The Genre of the Non-Fiction Novel." *Revista de Estudios Hispánicos* 35, no. 3 (2001): 447–66.

Castaño Restrepo, Germán. *Culture populaire colombienne et production littéraire dans "Los funerales de la Mamá Grande" de Gabriel García Márquez*. Master's thesis, Université de Paris III, 1981.

Castro, Juan Antonio. *"Cien años de soledad* o La crisis de la utopía." In *Homenaje a Gabriel García Márquez: Variaciones interpretativas en torno a su obra*, edited by Helmy Giacoman (q.v.), pp. 267–77.

Cobo Borda, Juan Gustavo. *Para llegar a García Márquez*. Bogotá: Ediciones Temas de Hoy, S.A., 1997.

———, editor. *Repertorio crítico sobre Gabriel García Márquez*. 2 vols. With an introduction by the editor. Bogotá: Instituto Caro y Cuervo, 1995.

Coetzee, J. M. Review of *Memories of My Melancholy Whores*. *The New York Review of Books* 53, no. 3 (23 February 2006): 5–6.

Collazos, Oscar. *García Márquez: La soledad y la gloria. Su vida y su obra*. Barcelona: Plaza y Janés, 1983.

"Colombia saltó de júbilo." *El Tiempo* (Bogotá), 22 October 1982, p. 3D.

Conway, Christopher. *The Cult of Bolívar in Latin American Literature*. Gainesville: University Press of Florida, 1993.

Cowie, Lancelot. "Bolívar: Entre la historia y la ficción." *Cuadernos Americanos* no. 104 (2004): 32–42.

Cussen, John. "García Márquez's *Of Love and Other Demons*." *The Explicator* 55 (22 September 1996): 53–54.

Davis, Mary E. "The Town That Was an Open Wound." *Comparative Literature Studies* 23, no. 1 (Spring 1986): 24–43.

Deaver, William O. "Obsesión, posesión y opresión en *Del amor y otros demonios*." *Afro-Hispanic Review* 19, no. 2 (Fall 2000): 80–85.

Díaz Arenas, Ángel. *Reflexiones en torno a "Noticia de un secuestro" de Gabriel García Márquez: La 'historia' y sus límites*. Kassel: Edition Reichenberger, 1998.

Diego, Gerardo. "Insomnio." In *Primera antología*, p. 158. Buenos Aires: Espasa-Calpe, 1942.

Domínguez, Luis Adolfo. "La conciencia de lo increíble." In *Sobre García Márquez*, edited by Pedro Simón Martínez (q.v.), pp. 135–38.

Dorfman, Ariel "La muerte como acto imaginativo en *Cien años de soledad*." In *Homenaje a Gabriel García Márquez: Variaciones interpretativas en torno a su obra*, edited by Helmy F. Giacoman (q.v.), pp. 107–38.

Earle, Peter, ed. *García Márquez: El escritor y la crítica*. Madrid: Taurus, 1981.

Echavarría, Arturo. "El tiempo recobrado (en Aracataca y Combray): En torno a *Vivir para contarla*." In *Gaborio: Artes de releer a Gabriel García Márquez*, edited by Julio Ortega (q.v.), pp. 253–67.

Esteban, Ángel, and Stéphanie Panichelli. *Gabo y Fidel: El paisaje de una amistad*. Bogotá: Planeta, 2004.

Fajardo Valenzuela, Diógenes. "El mundo africano en *Del amor y otros demonios* de Gabriel García Márquez." *América Negra* 14 (1997): 101–24.

Fau, Margarita Eustella. *Gabriel García Márquez: An Annotated Bibliography, 1947–1979*. Westport, Conn.: Greenwood Press, 1980.

Fau, Margarita Eustella, and Nelly S. De González. *Bibliographic Guide to Gabriel García Márquez, 1979–1985*. Westport, Conn.: Greenwood Press, 1986.

Fernández-Braso, Miguel. *Gabriel García Márquez: Una conversación infinita*. Madrid: Editorial Azur, 1969.

Fiddian, Robin. "A Prospective Post-Script: A Propos of *Love in the Time of Cholera*." In *Gabriel García Márquez: New Readings*, edited Bernard McGuirk and Richard Cardwell (q.v.), pp. 191–205.

Flores Olea, Víctor. "*El amor en los tiempos del cólera*: El libro de una educación sentimental." *Cuadernos Americanos* 264, no. 1 (January–February 1986): 202–8.

Font Castro, José. "Las claves reales de *El amor en los tiempos del cólera*." *El País* (Madrid), 19 January 1986, pp. 14–15.

Franco, Jean. "The Limits of the Liberal Imagination: *One Hundred Years of Solitude* and *Nostromo.*" In *Gabriel García Márquez's "One Hundred Years of Solitude": A Casebook*, edited by Gene H. Bell-Villada (q.v.), pp. 109–26.

———. "Un extraño en el paraíso." In *Sobre García Márquez*, edited by Pedro Simón Martínez (q.v.), pp. 128–30.

"Gabo." *El Tiempo* (Bogotá), 23 October 1982, pp. 1D–4D.

"Gabo, Nobel de Literatura." *El Tiempo* (Bogotá), 22 October 1982, pp. 1A, 9B.

"Gabriel García Márquez, el octavo escritor de habla española que obtiene el Nobel." *Uno Más Uno* (Mexico City), 22 October 1982, p. 211.

Gallagher, D. P. "Gabriel García Márquez." In *Modern Latin American Literature*, pp. 144–63. New York: Oxford University Press, 1973.

Galvis, Silvia. *Los García Márquez*. Bogotá: Arango Editores, 1996.

García, Eligio. *La tercera muerte de Santiago Nasar. Crónica de la crónica*. Madrid: Mondadori, 1987.

García, Julieta. "Amor y erotismo en *Del amor y otros demonios* de Gabriel García Márquez." *Espéculo* 35. www.ucm.es/info/espéculo/numero35/delamor/html

García Conde, Luisa. "*El general en su laberinto*: Un encuentro en la historia de América Latina." In *Quinientos años de soledad: Actas del congreso "Gabriel García Márquez,"* edited by Túa Blesa (q.v.), pp. 511–19.

García Márquez, Eligio. *Tras las claves de Melquíades: Historia de "Cien años de soledad."* Bogotá: Grupo Editorial Norma, 2001.

Giacoman, Helmy F., ed. *Homenaje a Gabriel García Márquez: Variaciones interpretativas en torno a su obra*. Long Island City, N.Y.: Las Américas, 1972.

González, Aníbal. "Viaje a la semilla del amor: *Del amor y otros demonios* y la nueva narrativa sentimental." *Hispanic Review* 73 (Autumn 2005): 389–408.

González, Nelly Sfeir de. *Bibliographic Guide to Gabriel García Márquez, 1986–1992*. Westport, Conn.: Greenwood Press, 1994.

———. *Bibliographic Guide to Gabriel García Márquez, 1992–2002*. Westport, Conn.: Greenwood Press, 2003.

González Echevarría, Roberto. *Myth and Archive: A Theory of Latin American Narrative*. New York: Cambridge University Press, 1990.

Griffin, Clive. "The Humor of *One Hundred Years of Solitude*." In *Gabriel García Márquez's "One Hundred Years of Solitude": A Casebook*, edited by Gene H. Bell-Villada (q.v.), pp. 53–66.

Grossman, Edith. "Truth is Stranger than Fact." *Review* 30 (September–December 1981): 71–73.

Gullón, Ricardo. "García Márquez o el olvidado arte de contar." in *Homenaje a Gabriel García Márquez: Variaciones interpretativas en torno a su obra*, edited by Helmy F. Giacoman (q.v.), pp. 143–69.

Hancock, Joel. "Gabriel García Márquez's 'Eréndira' and the Brothers Grimm." *Studies in Twentieth Century Literature*, no. 1 (1978): 43–52.

Harss, Luis. "Gabriel García Márquez o la cuerda floja." In *Los nuestros*, pp. 381–419. Buenos Aires: Editorial Sudamericana, 1966.

Harss, Luis, and Barbara Dohmann. "Gabriel García Márquez, or the Lost Chord." In *Into the Mainstream: Conversations with Latin American Writers*, pp. 310–41. New York: Harper & Row, 1967.

Henríquez Torres, Guillermo. *El misterio de los Buendía: El verdadero trasfondo histórico de "Cien años de soledad."* Bogotá: Editorial Nueva América, 2003.

Hernández de López, Ana María, ed. *En el punto de mira: Gabriel García Márquez.* Madrid: Editorial Pliegos, 1985.

Ianes, Raúl. "Para leerte mejor: García Márquez y el regreso de la huérfana colonial." *Romance Notes* 39, no. 3 (Spring 1999): 345–56.

Janes, Regina. *Gabriel García Márquez: Revolutions in Wonderland.* Columbia: University of Missouri Press, 1981.

———. *"One Hundred Years of Solitude": Modes of Reading.* Boston, Twayne, 1991.

Jarvis, Barbara M. "El halcón y la presa: Identidades ambiguas en *Crónica de una muerte* anunciada." Translated by Daniel Iglesias. In *En el punto de mira: Gabriel García Márquez,* edited by Ana María Hernández de López (q.v.), pp. 218–29.

Joset, Jacques. "El cobre puro de la cabellera radiante." In Daniel Balderston et al., *Literatura y otras artes en América Latina,* pp. 43–50. Iowa City: University of Iowa Press, 2004.

Kercher, Dona M. "García Márquez's *Crónica de una muerte anunciada*: Notes on Parody and the Artist." *Latin American Literary Review* 13, no. 25 (January–June 1985): 90–103.

Kerk, R. A. "Patterns of Place and Visual-Spatial Imagery in García Márquez's *Del amor y otros demonios*." *Hispania* 79, no. 4 (December 1996): 772–86.

Kline, Carmenza. *Los orígenes del relato: Los lazos de ficción y realidad en la obra de Gabriel García Márquez.* Bogotá: Ceiba Editores, 1992.

Klooster, Wim. "La version garciamarquiana del universo bolivariano: Historia y ficción en *El general en su laberinto*." *Foro Hispánico* 1 (1991): 57–63.

Koenig, Hans-Joachim. "*El general en su laberinto*: ¿Un ataque a la historia patria?" In *Literatura-historia-política: Articulando las relaciones entre Europa y América Latina,* edited by Sonia Steckbauer and Günther Maihold, pp. 43–60. Madrid: Iberoamericana, 2004.

Kulin, Katalin. *Creación mítica en la obra de García Márquez.* Budapest: Editorial de la Academia de Ciencias de Hungría, 1980.

Kutzinski, Vera M. "The Logic of Wings: Gabriel García Marquez and Afro-American Literature." *Latin American Literary Review* 13 (1985): 133–46.

Leante, César. *Gabriel García Márquez: El hechicero.* Madrid: Pliegos, 1996.

Leonard, John. "García Márquez versus Simón Bolívar." In *The Last Innocent White Man in America, and Other Writings,* pp. 233–49. New York: The New Press, 1993.

———. Review of *Of Love and Other Demons. The Nation* 260, no. 3 (12 June 1995): 836–40.

Lerner, Isaías. "A propósito de *Cien años de soledad*." *Cuadernos americanos,* año 28, vol. 162, no. 1 (January–February 1969): 186–200. Reprinted in *Homenaje a Gabriel García Márquez: Variaciones interpretativas en torno a su obra,* edited by Helmy F. Giacoman (q.v.), pp. 251–65.

Levine, Suzanne Jill. *El espejo hablado: Un estudio de "Cien años de soledad."* Caracas: Monte Ávila, 1975.

Llácer Lorca, Eusebio, and Esther Enjuto Castellanos. "Historia novelada o novela histórica: El general Bolívar en el laberinto de García Márquez." *Cuadernos americanos* 16 (May–June 2002): 151–61.

López de Abiada, José M. "La niña, el exorcista y el amor demonizado." *Cuadernos Hispanoamericanos* 548 (February 1996): 150–55.

López de Martínez, Adelaida. "El neorrealismo de Gabriel García Márquez." In *En el punto de mira: Gabriel García Márquez*, edited by Ana María Hernández de López (q.v.), pp. 239–49.

López Michelsen, Alfonso. "López presenta la novela." *El Tiempo* (Bogotá), 6 December 1985, p. 7.

López Morales, Eduardo E. "La dura cáscara de la soledad." In *Sobre García Márquez*, edited by Pedro Simón Martínez (q.v.), pp. 166–77.

López, Nereo. "Testimonio del fotógrafo. Humanas y hermosas anécdotas de la delegación folklórica colombiana en Estocolmo." In *Aracataca Estocolmo* (q.v.), pp. 91–95.

Loveluck, Juan. "Gabriel García Márquez, narrador colombiano." In *9 asedios a García Márquez*, by Mario Benedetti et al. (q.v.), pp. 52–73.

Ludmer, Josefina. *"Cien años de soledad:" Una interpretación*. Buenos Aires: Editorial Tiempo Contemporáneo, 1972.

McGuirk, Bernard, and Richard Cardwell, eds. *Gabriel García Márquez: New Readings*. New York: Cambridge University Press, 1987.

McMurray, George R. *Gabriel García Márquez*. New York: Frederick Ungar, 1977.

———. "García Márquez's *El general en su laberinto*: History and Fiction." *Confluencia: Revista Hispánica de Cultura y Literatura* 5, no. 1 (Fall 1989): 19–23.

Maldonado Denis, Manuel. *La violencia en la obra de García Márquez*. Bogotá: Ediciones Sudamérica, 1977.

March, Kathleen M. *"Crónica de una muerte anunciada*: García Márquez y el género policiaco." *Inti*, nos. 16–17 (Autumn 1982–Spring 1983): 61–70.

Marco, Joaquín. "La antítesis del poder: Dictadura, vejez y soledad: De *El otoño del patriarca* a 'Buen viaje, señor presidente.'" In *Quinientos años de soledad*, edited by Túa Blesa (q.v.), pp. 65–72.

Martin, Gerald. *Gabriel García Márquez: A Life*. Toronto: Viking Canada, 2008.

Martínez, Pedro Simón. *Sobre García Márquez*. Montevideo: Biblioteca de Marcha, 1971.

Martínez, Tomás Eloy. "La imagen ante el espejo." In *Gaborio: Artes de releer a Gabriel García Márquez*, edited by Julio Ortega (q.v.), pp. 197–99. (Review of *Vivir para contarla*.)

Maturo, Graciela. *Claves simbólicas de García Márquez*. 2d ed. Buenos Aires: Fernando García Cambeiro, 1977.

Mejía Duque, Jaime. *Mito y realidad en Gabriel García Márquez*. Valparaíso: Ediciones Universitarias de Valparaíso, n.d.

Méndez, José Luis. "Los peregrinos extraviados." *Torre: Revista general de la Universidad de Puerto Rico* 10, no. 38 (1996): 157–66.

Mendoza, María Luisa. "Las primeras horas como galardonado." *Excélsior* (Mexico City), 22 October 1982, pp. 1, 22.

Mendoza, Plinio Apuleio. *Aquellos tiempos con Gabo*. Barcelona: Plaza y Janés, 2000.

———. "18 años atrás." In *García Márquez habla de García Márquez*, edited by Alfonso Rentería Mantilla (q.v.), pp. 90–92.

Meneses, Carlos. Review of *La increíble y triste historia de la cándida Eréndira y de su abuela desalmada*. *Sin Nombre* (San Juan) 4, no. 1 (July–September 1973): 81–84.

Menton, Seymour. *Latin America's New Historical Novel*. Austin: University of Texas Press, 1993.

———. *La novela colombiana: planetas y satélites*. Bogotá: Plaza y Janés, 1978.

Minta, Stephen. *Gabriel García Márquez: Writer of Colombia*. London: Jonathan Cape, 1987.

Montaner, María Eulalia. *Guía para la lectura de "Cien años de soledad."* Madrid: Castalia, 1987.

Montes Doncel, Rosa Eugenia. "Intertextos líricos renacentistas en la narrativa última de García Márquez." In *Retórica y texto*, edited by Antonio Ruiz Castellanos, Antonia Víñez Sánchez, and Juan Saéz Durán, pp. 394–96. Cádiz: Universidad de Cádiz, 1998.

Morello-Frosch, Marta. "Función de lo fantástico en *La increíble y triste historia de la cándida Eréndira y de su abuela desalmada* de García Márquez." *Symposium* 38, no. 4 (Winter 1984–1985): 321–30.

Moreno Blanco, Juan. "Transculturación amerindia en la narrativa de Gabriel García Márquez." *Estudios de literatura colombiana* 10 (January–June 2002): 41–58.

Muro, Miguel Ángel. "Peculiaridad y dificultad de la novela histórica: *El general en su laberinto*." *Tropelías: Revista de teoría de la literatura y literatura comparada* nos. 7–8 (1996–97): 247–59.

Navascués, Javier de. "Espacio e identidad: *Doce cuentos peregrinos*." In *Quinientos años de soledad: Actas del congreso "Gabriel García Márquez,"* edited by Túa Blesa (q.v.), pp. 459–64.

Nemes, Graciela Palau de. Review of *El otoño del patriarca*. *Hispamérica* 4, nos. 11–12 (1975): 173–83.

Oberhelman, Harley D. *The Presence of Faulkner in the Writings of García Márquez*. Lubbock: Texas Tech Press, 1980.

———. *The Presence of Hemingway in the Short Fiction of Gabriel García Márquez*. Fredericton, N.B.: York Press, 1994.

Olsen, Margaret. "La patología de la africanidad en *Del amor y otros demonios* de García Márquez." *Revista Iberoamericana* 68, no. 201 (October–December 2002): 1067–80.

Ortega, Julio, ed. *Artes de releer a Gabriel García Márquez*. Mexico City: Jórale Editores, 2003.

———. "Cien años de soledad." In *Homenaje a Gabriel García Márquez: Variaciones interpretativas en torno a su obra*, edited by Helmy F. Giacoman (q.v.), pp. 173–83.

———. "Del amor y otras lecturas." *Cuadernos Hispanoamericanos* 539–40 (May–June 1995): 273–80.

———. "Memoria de mis putas tristes." *Cuadernos Hispanoamericanos* 657 (March 2005): 71–78.

———. "The Reader in the Labyrinth." In *Historical Criticism and the Challenge of*

Theory, edited by Janet Levarie Smarr, pp. 81–92. Urbana: University of Illinois Press, 1993.

———, editor, with the assistance of Claudia Elliot. *Gabriel García Márquez and the Powers of Fiction*. Austin: University of Texas Press, 1988.

———, editor. *Gaborío: Artes de releer a Gabriel García Márquez*. Mexico: Jórale Editores, 2003.

Oviedo, José Miguel. "*El amor en los tiempos del cólera* de García Márquez." *Vuelta* 10, no. 114 (May 1986): 33–38.

———. "Gabriel García Márquez: La novela como taumaturgia." In *García Márquez: El escritor y la crítica*, edited by Peter Earle (q.v.), pp. 171–88.

———. "García Márquez en el laberinto de la soledad." In *Quinientos años de soledad: Actas del congreso "Gabriel García Márquez,"* edited by Túa Blesa (q.v.), pp. 73–80.

———. "Macondo: Un territorio mágico y americano." In *9 asedios a García Márquez*, by Mario Benedetti et al. (q.v.), pp. 89–105.

Palencia-Roth, Michael. "*Crónica de una muerte anunciada*: El *Anti-Édipo* de García Márquez." Paper read at the meeting of the Association of American Colombianists, Bogotá, June 1986.

———. "*Del amor y otros demonios*: Tragedia inquisitorial, beatificación africana." In *Apuntes sobre literatura colombiana*, edited by Carmenza Kline, pp. 111–22. Bogotá: Ceiba Editores, 1997.

———. *Gabriel García Márquez: La línea, el círculo y la metamorfosis del mito*. Madrid: Gredos, 1983.

———. "Labyrinths of Love and History." *World Literature Today* 65 (1991): 54–58.

———. "Los peregrinajes de García Márquez o la vocación religiosa de la literatura." In *Quinientos años de soledad: Actas del congreso "Gabriel García Márquez,"* edited by Túa Blesa (q.v.), pp. 81–90.

———. "La primera novela de García Márquez después del Premio Nobel." *Boletín Cultural y Bibliográfico* (Bogotá) 24, no. 12 (1987): 3–17.

———. "Prisms of Consciousness: The 'New Worlds' of Columbus and García Márquez." In *Critical Perspectives on Gabriel García Márquez*, by Bradley A. Shaw and Nora Vera-Goodwin (q.v.), pp. 15–32.

———. Review of *Memoria de mis putas tristes*. *Cuadernos Hispanoamericanos* 657 (March 2005): 71–78.

Patán, Federico. "Una novela de postrimerías." *Revista de Estudios Colombianos* 7 (1989): 47–49.

Peel, Roger M. "The Short Stories of Gabriel García Márquez." *Studies in Short Fiction* 8, no. 1 (Winter 1971): 159–68.

Pelayo, Rubén. *Gabriel García Márquez: A Critical Companion*. Westport, Conn.: Greenwood Press, 2001.

Penuel, Arnold M. "The Sleep of Vital Reason in García Márquez's *Crónica de una muerte anunciada*." *Hispania* 68 (December 1985): 753–66.

———. "Symbolism and the Clash of Cultural Traditions in Colonial Spanish America in García Márquez's *Del amor y otros demonios* 80, no. 1 (March 1997): 38–48.

Pons, María Cristina. *Memorias del olvido: La novela histórica de fines del siglo XX*. Mexico: Siglo XXI, 1996.

Pope, Randolph. "Lectura literaria de *El general en su laberinto.*" *Revista de Estudios Colombianos* 7 (1989): 36–38.

"Premio Nobel a García Márquez." *El Tiempo* (Bogotá), 22 October 1982, pp. 1, 2D–3D.

Prieto, René. "The Body as Political Instrument: Communication in *No One Writes to the Colonel.*" In *Gabriel García Márquez: New Readings*, edited by Bernard McGuirk and Richard Cardwell (q.v.), pp. 33–44.

Rama, Ángel. "García Márquez entre la tragedia y la policial o crónica y pesquisa de la crónica de una muerte anunciada." *Sin Nombre* 13, no. 1 (October–December 1982): 7–27.

———. "Un novelista de la violencia americana." In *Homenaje a Gabriel García Márquez: Variaciones interpretativas en torno a su obra*, edited by Helmy F. Giacoman (q.v.), pp. 57–72.

———. "El patriarca solo dentro de un poema cíclico." In *La novela en América Latina: Panoramas 1920–1980*, pp. 435–54. Bogotá: Instituto Colombiano de Cultura, 1982.

Ramírez, Sergio. "Nada llega a perderse." In *Gaborio: Artes de releer a Gabriel García Márquez*, edited by Julio Ortega (q.v.), pp. 183–86.

Ramos, Juan Antonio. *Hacia el otoño del patriarca: La novela del dictador en Hispanoamérica*. San Juan: Instituto de Cultura Puertorriqueña, 1983.

Rincón, Carlos. "Streams out of Control: The Latin American Plot." In *Gabriel García Márquez's "One Hundred Years of Solitude": A Casebook*, edited by Gene H. Bell-Villada (q.v.), pp. 153–169.

Rodríguez Monegal, Emir. "Novedad y anacronismo de *Cien años de Soledad.*" In *Homenaje a Gabriel García Márquez: Variaciones interpretativas en torno a su obra*, edited by Helmy F. Giacoman (q.v.), pp. 15–42.

Rohter, Larry. "García Márquez Portrays Bolívar's Feet of Clay." *New York Times* 138 no. 47913 (26 June 1989): C13, C15, C19.

Roses, Lorraine. "A Code of Many Colors: *One Hundred Years of Solitude* and Biblical Writ." In *Justina: Homenaje a Justina Ruiz de Conde en su ochenta cumpleaños*, edited by Elena Gascón-Vera and Joy Renjilian-Burgy, pp. 171–78. Erie, Pennsylvania: ALDEEU, 1992.

———. "The Sacred Harlots of *One Hundred Years of Solitude.*" In *Gabriel García Márquez's "One Hundred Years of Solitude": A Casebook*, edited by Gene H. Bell-Villada (q.v.), pp. 67–78.

Ruffinelli, Jorge. "*Crónica de una muerte anunciada*: Historia o ficción." In *En el punto de mira: Gabriel García Márquez*, edited by Ana María Hernández de López (q.v.), pp. 271–83.

Saldívar, Dasso. *García Márquez: El viaje a la semilla: La biografía*. Madrid: Alfaguara, 1997.

Samper, María Elvira. "*The General in His Labyrinth* Is a 'Vengeful' Book." In *Conversations with Gabriel García Márquez*, edited by Gene H. Bell-Villada (q.v.), pp. 168–180.

Santamaría, Germán. "El Nobel de Gabo. Un día para recordar." *El Tiempo* (Bogotá), 24 October 1982, pp. 1A, 4B.

———. "Quiero recibir el Nobel con Vallenatos." *El Tiempo* (Bogotá), 25 October 1982, pp. 1A, 6A.

Shaw, Bradley A., and Nora Vera-Goodwin, eds. *Critical Perspectives on Gabriel García Márquez.* Lincoln, Nebraska: Society of Spanish and Spanish-American Studies, 1986.

Shaw, Donald L. "*Chronicle of a Death Foretold*: Narrative Function and Interpretation." In *Critical Perspectives on Gabriel García Márquez*, edited by Bradley A. Shaw and Nora Vera-Goodwin (q.v.), pp. 91–104.

Silva-Cáceres, Raúl. "La intensificación narrativa en *Cien años de soledad.*" In *Sobre García Márquez*, edited by Pedro Simón Martínez (q.v.), pp. 120–26.

Solotorevsky, Myrna. "*Crónica de una muerte anunciada*: La escritura de un texto irreverente." *Revista Iberoamericana* 50, nos. 128–29 (July–December 1984): 1077–91.

Speratti-Piñero, Emma Susana. "De las fuentes y su utilización en 'El ahogado más hermoso del mundo.'" In *Homenaje a Ana María Barrenechea*, edited by Lía Schwartz Lerner and Isaías Lerner, pp. 549–55. Madrid: Castalia, 1984.

Steenmeijer, Maarten. "Racismo utópico en *Del amor y otros demonios.*" *Espéculo* 27 (July–October 2004): no pages.

Swanson, Philip. *The Cambridge Companion to Gabriel García Márquez.* New York: Cambridge University Press, 2009.

Tedio, Guillermo. "*Del amor y otros demonios* o las erosiones del discurso inquisitorial." *Espéculo* 29 (March–June 2005): no pages.

Thomas, Katherine M. "The Demon of Solitude." *Palara* (Publications of the Afro-Latin/American Research Association) 17 (Fall 2003): 17–25.

El Tiempo (Bogotá), 22–25 October 1982. Extensive coverage and commentary on announcement of García Márquez's Nobel Prize.

Todorov, Tzvetan. "Macondo en París." In *García Márquez: El escritor y la crítica*, edited by Peter Earle (q.v.), pp. 104–13.

Tyler, Anne. Statement on García Márquez in "Writers' Writers." Anonymous questionnaire in *New York Times Book Review*, 4 December 1977, p. 70.

Vargas, Germán. "Un personaje: Aracataca." In *Sobre García Márquez*, edited by Pedro Simón Martínez (q.v.), pp. 131–34.

Vargas, José A. "*El general en su laberinto*: Una subversión del discurso de la proceridad." *Kañina* 18, no. 2 (1994): 71–82.

Vargas Llosa, Mario. "El Amadís en América." In *Sobre García Márquez*, edited by Pedro Simón Martínez (q.v.), pp. 106–11.

———. *García Márquez: Historia de un deicidio.* Barcelona: Barral, 1971.

Vargas V., José Ángel. "Biografía, historia y literatura (a propósito de *El general en su laberinto*)." *Kañina* 18, no. 1 (January–June 1994): 43–50.

Vargas Vargas, José Ángel. "*El general en su laberinto*: Hacia un verosímil latinoamericano." *Sociocriticism* 8.1 (no. 15) (1992): 37–57.

Velasco, Mary-Ann. "Analogías entre la iglesia católica y las religiones africanas en *Del amor y otros demonios.*" In *Narrativa hispanoamericana contemporánea*, edited by Ana María Hernández de López, pp. 257–63. Madrid: Pliegos, 1996.

Vidal Ruales, María Stella. "Presencia de la cosmovisión yoruba en *Del amor y otros demonios.* In *Colombia en el contexto latinoamericano*, edited by Myriam Luque,

Montserrat Ordóñez, and Betty Osorio, pp. 305–16. Bogotá: Universidad de Los Andes, 1997.

Volkening. Ernesto. "Anotado al margen de *Cien años de soledad*." In *Sobre García Márquez*, edited by Pedro Simón Martínez (q.v.), pp. 178–206.

———. "A propósito de *La mala hora*." In *Homenaje a Gabriel García Márquez: Variaciones interpretativas en torno a su obra*, edited by Helmy F. Giacoman (q.v.), pp. 89–95.

———. "Gabriel García Márquez o el trópico desembrujado." In *Homenaje a Gabriel García Márquez: Variaciones interpretativas en torno a su obra*, edited by Helmy F. Giacoman (q.v.), pp. 75–86.

Weldt-Basson, Helene. "The Purpose of Historical Reference in Gabriel García Márquez's *El general en su laberinto*." *Revista Hispánica Moderna* 47 no. 1 (June 1994): 96–108.

Wilkie, James W., Edna Monzón de Wilkie, and María Herrera-Sobek. "Elitelore and Folklore: Theory and a Test Case in *One Hundred Years of Solitude*." *Journal of Latin American Lore* 4 (1978): 183–223.

Williams, Raymond L. *Gabriel García Márquez*. Boston: Twayne Publishers, 1984.

Wood, Michael. *Gabriel García Márquez: "One Hundred Years of Solitude."* New York: Cambridge University Press, 1990.

Zamora, Lois Parkinson. "Ends and Endings in García Márquez's *Crónica de una muerte anunciada*." *Latin American Literary Review* 13, no. 25 (January–June: 1985): 104–16.

Zavala, Iris M. "*Cien años de soledad*: Crónica de indias." In *Homenaje a Gabriel García Márquez: Variaciones interpretativas en torno a su obra*, edited by Helmy F. Giacoman (q.v.), pp. 200–212.

———. "*One Hundred Years of Solitude* as Chronicle of the Indies." Translated by Gene H. Bell-Villada. In *Gabriel García Márquez's "One Hundred Years of Solitude": A Casebook*, edited by Gene H. Bell-Villada (q.v.), 109–26.

Zuluaga Osorio, Conrado. *Puerta abierta a Gabriel García Márquez: Aproximación a la obra del Nobel colombiano*. Barcelona: Editorial Casiopeia, 2001.

GENERAL WORKS

Adorno, T. W., Else Frenkel-Brunswick, Daniel J. Levinson, and R. Nevitt Sanford. *The Authoritarian Personality*. New York: W. W. Norton, 1950.

Arana, Marie. *Cellophane*. New York: Dial Press, 2006.

Asturias, Miguel Ángel. *Eyes of the Interred*. Translated by Gregory Rabassa. New York: Delacorte, 1973.

———. *The Green Pope*. Translated by Gregory Rabassa. New York: Seymour Lawrence/Delacorte, 1971.

———. *El señor Presidente*. Translated by Frances Partridge. New York: Atheneum, 1964.

———. *Strong Wind*. Translated by Gregory Rabassa. New York: Seymour Lawrence/ Delacorte, 1968.

Bakhtin, Mikhail. *Rabelais and His World*. Translated by Hélène Iswolsky. Cambridge: Massachusetts Institute of Technology Press, 1968.

Barnes, John. *Evita, First Lady: A Biography of Eva Perón*. New York: Grove Press, 1978.

Barth, John. "The Literature of Exhaustion." *The Atlantic* 220, no. 2 (August 1967): 29–34.

———. "The Literature of Replenishment." *The Atlantic* 245 no. 1 (January 1980): 65–71. Reprinted in *The Friday Book*, pp. 193–206. New York: Putnam, 1984.

Bascom, Williams. *Sixteen Cowries: Yoruba Divination from Africa to the New World*. Bloomington: Indiana University Press, 1980.

Beauvoir, Simone de. *Old Age*. Translation by Patrick O'Brian. London: André Deutsch, 1972.

Beckett, Samuel. *Stories and Texts for Nothing*. New York: Grove Press, 1967.

———. *Three Novels by Samuel Beckett. Molloy. Malone Dies. The Unnameable*. New York: Grove Press, 1963.

Bell-Villada, Gene H. *Borges and His Fiction: A Guide to His Mind and Art*. Revised edition. Austin: University of Texas Press, 1999.

———. "Criticism and the State (Political and Otherwise) of the Americas." In *Criticism in the University*, edited by Gerald Graff and Reginald Gibbons, pp. 124–44. Evanston: Northwestern University Press, 1985.

Bellow, Saul. *The Adventures of Augie March*. New York: Penguin, 1984.

Bergquist, Charles. *Coffee and Conflict in Colombia, 1866–1910*. Durham: Duke University Press, 1978.

Bowden, Mark. *Killing Pablo: The Hunt for the World's Greatest Outlaw*. New York: Atlantic Monthly Press, 2001.

Bradley, Andrew Cecil. "Hegel's Theory of Tragedy." In *Oxford Lectures on Poetry*. New York: Macmillan, 1911. Reprinted in *Criticism: The Foundations of Modern Literary Judgment*, edited by Mark Schorer, Josephine Miles, and Gordon McKenzie, pp. 55–66. New York: Harcourt, Brace, 1948.

Braun, Herbert. *The Assassination of Gaitán: Public Life and Urban Violence in Colombia*. Madison: University of Wisconsin Press, 1985.

Bruce-Novoa. *Chicano Authors: Inquiry by Interview*. Austin: University of Texas Press, 1980.

Burroughs, Edgar Rice. *Tarzan of the Apes*. 1912. Reprint. New York: Ballantine, 1963.

Camus, Albert. *The Plague*. Translated by Stuart Gilbert. New York: Random House, 1965.

Carpentier, Alejo. *Reasons of State*. Translated by Frances Partridge. New York: Alfred A. Knopf, 1976.

Carrasquilla, Tomás. *Obras completas*. Introduction by Roberto Jaramillo. Medellín: Editorial Bedout, 1955.

Carrera Damas, Germán. *El culto a Bolívar*. Bogotá: Universidad Nacional de Colombia, 1987.

Castrillón, Alberto. *120 días bajo el terror militar*. Bogotá: Ediciones Tupac Amaru, 1974.

Cepeda Samudio, Álvaro. *La casa grande*. Bogotá: Plaza y Janés, 1979.

Chomsky, Aviva. *Linked Labor Histories: New England, Colombia, and the Making of a Global Working Class.* Durham: Duke University Press, 2008.

Columbus, Christopher. *Four Voyages to the New World: Letters and Selected Documents.* Translated and edited by R. H. Major. Introduction by John E. Fagg. New York: Corinth, 1961.

Crassweller, Robert D. *Perón and the Enigmas of Argentina.* New York: W. W. Norton, 1987.

———. *Trujillo: The Life and Times of a Caribbean Dictator.* New York: Macmillan, 1966.

Cunninghame Graham, R. B. *The Conquest of New Granada: Being the Life of Gonzalo Jiménez de Quesada.* Boston: Houghton Mifflin, 1922.

Defoe, Daniel. *A Journal of the Plague Year.* Introduction by Anthony Burgess. Baltimore: Penguin, 1966.

Diederich, Bernard. *Somoza and the Legacy of U.S. Involvement in Central America.* New York: E. P. Dutton, 1981.

Edwards, Gary, and John Mason. *Black Gods: Orisa Studies in the New World.* Brooklyn: Yoruba Theological Archministry, 1985.

Eliade, Mircea. *The Sacred and the Profane: The Nature of Religion.* Translated by Willard Trask. New York: Harcourt, Brace, 1957.

Espenak, Fred. *World Atlas of Solar Eclipse Paths.* http://eclipse.gsfc.nasa.gov/SEatlas/SEatlas.html

Ewell, Judith. *Venezuela: A Century of Change.* Stanford: Stanford University Press, 1981.

Fals Borda, Orlando. "Lo sacro y lo violento, aspectos problemáticos del desarrollo en Colombia." In *Once ensayos sobre la violencia,* by E. J. Hobsbawm et al. (q.v.), pp. 25–52.

Faulkner, William. *Absalom, Absalom!* New York: Random House, 1966.

———. *As I Lay Dying.* New York: Random House, 1964.

———. *The Hamlet.* New York: Random House, 1956.

———. *Light in August.* New York: Random House, 1972.

———. *Sanctuary.* New York: Random House, 1962.

———. *Sartoris.* New York: New American Library, 1953.

Federman, Raymond. *The Twofold Vibration.* Bloomington: Indiana University Press, 1982.

Fischer, Ernst. *The Necessity of Art: A Marxist Approach.* Translated by Anna Bostock. Baltimore: Penguin, 1963.

Flaubert, Gustave. *Sentimental Education.* Translated with an Introduction by Robert Baldick. Baltimore: Penguin, 1964.

Fluharty, Vernon Lee. *Dance of the Millions: Military Rule and the Social Revolution in Colombia 1930–1956.* Pittsburgh: University of Pittsburgh Press, 1957.

Friedemann, Nina S. de. *Carnaval en Barranquilla.* Bogotá: Editorial La Rosa, 1985.

———, and Jaime Arocha. *De sol a sol: Génesis, transformación y presencia de los negros en Colombia.* Bogotá: Planeta, 1986.

———. *La saga del negro: Presencia africana en Colombia.* Bogotá: Instituto de Genética Humana, Pontificia Universidad Javeriana, 1993.

Fuenmayor, Alfonso. *Crónicas sobre el grupo de Barranquilla*. Bogotá: Instituto Colombiano de Cultura, 1978.

Fuentes, Carlos. *La nueva novela hispanoamericana*. Mexico City: Joaquín Mortiz, 1969.

Galíndez Suárez, Jesús de. "Un reportaje sobre Santo Domingo." *Cuadernos Americanos* 80 (March–April 1955): 37–56. Reprinted in English, *Dictatorship in Spanish America*, edited by Hugh M. Hamill, pp. 174–87. New York: Alfred A. Knopf, 1968.

Galsworthy, John. *The Forsyte Saga*. New York: Scribner's, 1934.

Galvis, Silvia, and Alberto Donadi. *Colombia Nazi, 1939–1945*. Bogotá: Planeta, 1986.

Garcilaso de la Vega. *Obras completas*. Edited by Elias B. Rivers. Columbus: Ohio State University Press, 1964.

Garcilaso de la Vega, El Inca. *Royal Commentaries of the Incas*. Translated with an Introduction by Harold V. Livermore. Austin: University of Texas Press, 1966.

Gilard, Jacques. "El grupo de Barranquilla." *Revista Iberoamericana* 50, nos. 128–29 (July–December 1984): 905–35.

Granda, Germán de. *Estudios lingüísticos, hispánicos, afrohispánicos y criollos*. Madrid: Gredos, 1973.

———. "Un afortunado filónimo bantú: *Macondo*." In *Estudios lingüísticos, hispánicos, afrohispánicos y criollos*, (q.v.), pp. 634–44.

———. "Toponimia de origen bantú centro-occidental (Kikongo y Kimbundu) en el área geográfica de Cartagena (Colombia)." In *Estudios lingüísticos, hispánicos, afrohispánicos y criollos* (q.v.), pp. 268–76.

Gutiérrez Cely, Eugenio, and Fabio Puyo Vasco. *Bolívar día a día*. 3 vols. Bogotá: Procultura, S.A., 1983.

Hardwick, Elizabeth. "The Fictions of America." *New York Review of Books*, 25 June 1987, pp. 12–18.

Hemingway, Ernest. *The Short Stories of Ernest Hemingway*. New York: Macmillan, 1987.

Henao, Jesús María, and Gerardo Arrubla. *History of Colombia*. Translated and edited by J. Fred Rippy. Chapel Hill: University of North Carolina Press, 1938.

Henderson, James D. *When Colombia Bled: A History of the Violencia in Tolima*. Tuscaloosa: University of Alabama Press, 1985.

Hobsbawm, E. J. "La anatomía de 'La violencia' en Colombia." In *Once ensayos sobre la violencia*, by E. J. Hobsbawm et al. (q.v.), pp. 11–13.

———, et al. *Once ensayos sobre la violencia*. Bogotá: Centro Gaitán, 1985.

Irby, James East. *La influencia de William Faulkner en cuatro narradores hispanoamericanos*. Mexico City: Universidad Nacional Autónoma de México, 1956.

Isaacs, Jorge. *María*. Edited with an Introduction by Gustavo Mejía. Madrid: Sociedad General Española de Librería S.A., 1983.

Jahn, Janheinz. *Muntu: An Outline of the New African Culture*. Translated by Marjorie Grene. London: Faber and Faber, 1961.

Jimeno, Ramón, and Steven Volk. "Colombia: Whose Country Is This, Anyway?" *NACLA Report on the Americas* 17, no. 3 (May–June 1983): 2–35.

Johnson, John J. *Simón Bolívar and Spanish American Independence, 1783–1830*. New York: Van Nostrand, 1968.

Joyce, James. *Ulysses*. New York: Random House, 1967.

Kafka, Franz. *Selected Short Stories*. Translated by Willa and Edwin Muir. Introduction by Philip Rahv. New York: Random House, 1952.

Kawabata, Yasunaki. *House of the Sleeping Beauties and Other Stories*. Translated by Edward G. Seidensticker. Palo Alto: Kodansha International, 1969.

Kennedy, William. *Ironweed*. New York: Penguin, 1984.

Kepner, Charles David, Jr. *The Banana Empire: A Case Study of Economic Imperialism*. New York: Vanguard Press, 1935.

Kirkpatrick, Ralph. *Domenico Scarlatti*. Princeton: Princeton University Press, 1953.

Kline. Harvey E. *Colombia: Portrait of Unity and Diversity*. Boulder, Colo.: Westview Press, 1983.

Koning, Hans. "They Also Serve . . . ." *Monthly Review* 37, no. 2 (June 1985): 22–24.

Krauss, Rosalind. "Poststructuralism and the 'Paraliterary.'" *October*, no. 13 (1980): 36–40.

Lampedusa, Giuseppe di. *The Leopard*. Translated by Archibald Colquhoun. New York: Pantheon, 1960.

Lernoux, Penny. *Cry of the People: The Struggle for Human Rights in Latin America—the Catholic Church in Conflict with U.S. Policy*. New York: Penguin, 1982.

Lévi-Strauss, Claude. *The Elementary Structures of Kinship*. Revised edition. Translated by James H. Bell, John Richard von Sturmer, and Rodney Needham. Boston: Beacon Press, 1969.

Levy, Kurt L. *Tomás Carrasquilla*. Boston: Twayne, 1980.

Lewis, C. S. *The Allegory of Love: A Study in Medieval Tradition*. New York: Oxford University Press, 1936. (1988 printing.)

Lieuwen, Edwin. *Venezuela*. New York: Oxford University Press, 1965.

Lombardi, John V. *Venezuela: The Search for Order, the Dream of Progress*. New York: Oxford University Press, 1982.

Lüthi, Max. *Once upon a Time: On the Nature of Fairy Tales*. Translated by Lee Chadeayne and Paul Gottwald. New York: Frederick Ungar, 1970.

Lynch, John. *Simón Bolívar: A Life*. New Haven: Yale University Press, 2006.

Madariaga, Salvador de. *Bolívar*. New York: Pellegrini and Cudahy, 1952.

Mailer, Norman. *Barbary Shore*. New York: Universal Library, 1963.

———. *The Naked and the Dead*. New York: Holt, Rinehart, and Winston, 1948.

Malaparte, Curzio. *The Skin*. Translated by David Moore. Boston: Houghton Mifflin, 1952.

Mann, Thomas. *Buddenbrooks*. Translated by H. T. Lowe-Porter. New York: Random House, 1984.

Manzoni, Alessandro. *The Betrothed*. Translated with an Introduction by Bruce Penman. New York: Penguin, 1972.

Masur, Gerhard. *Simón Bolívar*. Albuquerque: University of New Mexico Press, 1948.

Mauss, Marcel. *The Gift: Forms and Functions of Exchange in Archaic Societies*. Translated by Ian Cunnison. New York: W. W. Norton, 1967.

Mellen, Joan. *Magic Realism. Literary Topics, Volume 5*. New York: Gale Group, 2002

1928. La masacre en las bananeras. Bogotá: Ediciones Libres, 1972.

Minter, David. *William Faulkner: His Life and Work*. Baltimore: Johns Hopkins University Press, 1980.

Morrison, Toni. *Song of Solomon*. New York: New American Library, 1978.

Murphy, Joseph. *Working the Spirit: Ceremonies of the African Diaspora*. Boston: Beacon Press, 1994.

Mutis, Álvaro. "El ultimo rostro." In *La muerte del estratega: Narraciones, prosas y ensayos*, pp. 89–103. Mexico City: Fondo de Cultura Económica,1988.

Nabokov, Vladimir. *Ada or Ardor: A Family Chronicle*. New York: McGraw Hill, 1980.

Nichols, John. *The Milagro Beanfield War*. New York: Ballantine, 1976.

O'Connor, Francis V. "The Influence of Diego Rivera on the Art of the United States during the 1930s and After." In *Diego Rivera: A Retrospective*, edited by Detroit Institute of the Arts, pp. 157–83. New York: W. W. Norton, 1986.

http://w3/lac.net/-moonweb/Santeria/Drum/Oddua.html.

Oquist, Paul. *Violence, Conflict, and Politics in Colombia*. New York: Academic Press, 1980.

Pigafetta, Antonio. *Primer viaje en torno del globo*. Translated by Federico Ruiz Morcuende. Madrid: Espasa-Calpe, 1963.

Pocaterra, José Rafael. *Memorias de un venezolano de la decadencia*. Vol. 1. Caracas: Monte Ávila, 1979.

Propp, Vladimir. *Morphology of the Folktale*. Translated by Laurence Scott. Introduction by Svatava Pirkova-Jakobson. 2d ed. Revised and edited with a Preface by Louis A. Wagner. Introduction by Alan Dundes. Austin: University of Texas Press, 1968.

Rabelais, François. *The Histories of Gargantua and Pantagruel*. Translated by J. M. Cohen. Baltimore: Penguin, 1955.

Rama, Ángel. "Los dictadores latinoamericanos en la novela." In *La novela en América Latina: Panoramas 1920–1980*, pp. 361–69. Bogotá: Instituto Colombiano de Cultura, 1982.

Reichel-Dolmatoff, G. *Colombia*. New York: Praeger, 1965.

Rippy, J. Fred. *The Capitalists and Colombia*. New York: Vanguard Press, 1931.

Rivera, José Eustasio. *La vorágine*. Edited with an Introduction by Cristina Barros Stilavet. Mexico City: Porrúa, 1972.

———. *The Vortex*. Translated by Earle K. James. New York: Putnam, 1935.

Robbe-Grillet, Alain. *For a New Novel: Essays on Fiction*. Translated by Richard Howard. New York: Grove Press, 1966.

Rodríguez Freire, Juan. *El carnero: Conquista y descubrimiento del nuevo reino de Granada . . . .* Edited by Miguel Aguilera. Bogotá: Biblioteca de Cultura Colombiana, 1963.

Rodríguez Fresle, Juan. *The Conquest of New Granada*. Translated by W. C. Atkinson. London: Folio Society, 1961.

Rojas Herazo, Héctor. *Respirando el verano*. Bogotá: Ediciones Tercer Mundo, 1962.

Rourke, Thomas. *Gómez: Tyrant of the Andes*. New York: William Morrow, 1936.

———. *Man of Glory: Simón Bolívar*. New York: William Morrow, 1941.

Rulfo, Juan. *El llano en llamas*. Mexico City: Fondo de Cultura Económica, 1953.

———. *Pedro Páramo*. Mexico City: Fondo de Cultura Económica, 1955.

———. *The Burning Plain*. Translated with an Introduction by George Schade. Austin: University of Texas Press, 1967.

———. *Pedro Páramo*. Translated by Margaret Sayers Peden. Foreword by Susan Sontag. New York: Grove Press, 1994.

Sánchez, Gonzalo. "La violencia y sus efectos en el sistema político colombiano." In *Once ensayos sobre la violencia*, by E. J. Hobsbawm et al. (q.v.), pp. 209–57.

Sale, Roger. *Fairy Tales and After: From Snow White to E. B. White*. Cambridge, Mass.: Harvard University Press, 1968.

http://en.Wikipedia.org/Wiki/Shango.

Silva, José Asunción. "Una noche." In *Obra completa*, Foreword by Miguel de Unamuno, and Notes by B. Sanín Cano, pp. 35–37. Medellín: Editorial Bedout, 1970.

Siniavsky, Andrei. *On Socialist Realism*. Translated by George Dennis. New York: Pantheon Books, 1960.

Smith, Earl E. T. *The Fourth Floor: An Account of the Castro Communist Revolution*. New York: Random House, 1962.

Sophocles. *Antigone*. Translated by Elizabeth Wyckoff. In *Sophocles I*, edited by David Grene and Richmond Lattimore, with an Introduction by David Grene, pp. 157–204. Chicago: University of Chicago Press, 1960.

———. *Oedipus the King*. Translated by David Grene. In *Sophocles 1*, edited by David Grene and Richmond Lattimore, with an Introduction by David Grene, pp. 9–76. Chicago: University of Chicago Press, 1960.

Suetonius. *The Twelve Caesars*. Translated by Robert Graves. Revised with an Introduction by Michael Grant. New York: Penguin, 1980.

Theroux, Paul. *The Mosquito Coast*. New York: Avon Books, 1983.

Tyler, Anne. *Dinner at the Homesick Restaurant*. New York: Berkeley Books, 1983.

Up de Graff, F. W. *Head-Hunters of the Amazon: Seven Years of Exploration and Adventure*. Foreword by Kermit Roosevelt. New York: Duffield & Co., 1923.

Updike, John. *The Coup*. New York: Alfred A. Knopf, 1978.

———. *Couples*. New York: Alfred A. Knopf, 1968.

Urrutia, Miguel. *The Development of the Colombian Labor Movement*. New Haven: Yale University Press, 1969.

Valle-Inclán, Ramón del. *Tirano Banderas*. Mexico City: Espasa-Calpe, 1983.

Valverde, Umberto. "La nueva respuesta de la literatura colombiana." *Revista Iberoamericana* 50, nos. 128–29 (July–December 1984): 853–59.

Vespucci, Amerigo. *The Letters of Amerigo Vespucci and Other Documents Illustrative of His Career*. Translated with Notes and an Introduction by Clements R. Markham. London: Hakluyt Society No. 90, 1894.

Walker, Alice. *The Color Purple*. New York: Harcourt Brace Jovanovich, 1982.

Warren, Robert Penn. *All the King's Men*. New York: Harcourt, Brace, 1946.

Werz, Nikolaus. "Reflexiones sobre la imagen de Bolívar y la enseñanza de la historia en Venezuela." In *Enseñanza de la historia, libros de texto y conciencia histórica*, edited by Michael Riekenberg, pp. 103–21. Buenos Aires: Alianza, 1991.

Wilbert, Johannes, and Karin Simoneau, with Michel Perrin, eds. *Folk Literature of* the Guajiro Indians. Vol. 1. Introduction by Michel Perrin. Los Angeles: UCLA Latin American Center Publications, 1986.

Wode, Peter. *Blackness and Race Mixture: The Dynamics of Racial Identity in Colombia.* Baltimore: Johns Hopkins University Press, 1993.

Woolf, Virginia. *"Jacob's Room" and "The Waves": Two Complete Novels.* New York: Harcourt, Brace, 1950.

———. *Mrs. Dalloway.* New York: Harcourt, Brace, 1964.

———. *Orlando.* New York: Harcourt Brace Jovanovich, 1973.

———. *To the Lighthouse.* New York: Harcourt, Brace, 1964.

Zalamea, Jorge. *El gran Burundún Burundá ha muerto.* Havana: Casa de las Américas, 1968.

Zalamea Borda, Eduardo. *Cuatro años a bordo de mí mismo: Diario de los cinco sentidos.* Medellín: Editorial Bedout, n.d.

CPSIA information can be obtained
at www.ICGtesting.com
Printed in the USA
LVHW030636081221
705585LV00006B/679